Underwater and Maritime Archaeology

in

Latin America and the Caribbean

One World Archaeology Series
Sponsored by the World Archaeological Congress
Series Editors: Joan Gero, Mark Leone, and Robin Torrence

One World Archaeology volumes contain carefully edited selections of the exemplary papers presented at the World Archaeology Congress (WAC), held every four years, and intercongress meetings. WAC gives place to considerations of power and politics in framing archaeological questions and results. The organization also gives place and privilege to minorities who have often been silenced or regarded as beyond capable of making main line contributions to the field. All royalties from the series are used to help the wider work of the organization. The series is published by Left Coast Press, Inc. beginning with volume 48.

61 *Coexistence and Cultural Transmission in East Asia, Naoko Matsumoto, Hidetaka Bessho, and Makoto Tomii (eds.)*
60 *Bridging the Divide, Caroline Phillips and Harry Allen (eds.)*
59 *Archaeologies of Placemaking*, Patricia E. Rubertone (ed.)
58 *Managing Archaeological Resources*, Francis P. McManamon, Andrew Stout, and Jodi A. Barnes (eds.)
57 *Landscapes of Clearance*, Angèle Smith and Amy Gazin-Schwartz (eds.)
56 *Underwater and Maritime Archaeology in Latin America and the Caribbean*, Margaret E. Leshikar-Denton and Pilar Luna Erreguerena (eds.)
55 *Archaeologies of Art*, Inés Domingo Sanz, Dánae Fiore, and Sally K. May (eds.)
54 *Archaeology and Capitalism*, Yannis Hamilakis and Philip Duke (eds.)
53 *Living under the Shadow*, John Grattan and Robin Torrence (eds.)
52 *Envisioning Landscapes*, Dan Hicks, Laura McAtackney, and Graham Fairclough (eds.)
51 *Rethinking Agriculture*, Tim Denham, José Iriarte, and Luc Vrydaghs (eds.)
50 *A Fearsome Heritage*, John Schofield and Wayne Cocroft (eds.)
49 *Archaeology to Delight and Instruct*, Heather Burke and Claire Smith (eds.)
48 *African Re-Genesis*, Jay B. Haviser and Kevin C. MacDonald (eds.)

Underwater and Maritime Archaeology in Latin America and the Caribbean

Edited by
Margaret E. Leshikar-Denton
and
Pilar Luna Erreguerena

Routledge
Taylor & Francis Group
LONDON AND NEW YORK

First published 2008 by Left Coast Press, Inc.
First paperback edition 2011.

Published 2016 by Routledge
2 Park Square, Milton Park, Abingdon, Oxon OX14 4RN
711 Third Avenue, New York, NY 10017, USA

Routledge is an imprint of the Taylor & Francis Group, an informa business

Library of Congress Cataloging-in-Publication Data

Underwater and maritime archaeology in Latin America and the Caribbean / Margaret E. Leshikar-Denton, Pilar Luna Erreguerena, editors.
p. cm.—(One world archaeology series ; 56)
Includes bibliographical references and index.
ISBN 978-1-59874-262-6 (hardback : alk. paper)—ISBN 978-1-59874-263-3 (paperback : alk. paper)—ISBN 978-1-59874-747-8 (eISBN)
1. Underwater archaeology—Latin America. 2. Underwater archaeology--Caribbean Area. 3. Latin America—Cultural policy. 4. Caribbean Area—Cultural policy. I. Leshikar-Denton, Margaret E. II. Luna Erreguerena, Pilar.
F1408.3.U49 2008
930.1'02804—dc22
2008021109

ISBN 978-1-59874-262-6 hardcover
ISBN 978-1-59874-263-3 paperback

Contents

List of Illustrations

List of Tables

We dedicate this
book to the
Latin American and
Caribbean countries
that constantly face challenges and
overcome
obstacles in their struggle to
protect and manage their
underwater cultural
heritage

Foreword

Underwater archaeology is a relatively new subdiscipline that is only now passing from a pioneering period that spanned the last half of the 20th century. Underwater archaeology refers to the environment in which the practice of archaeology is undertaken. The field has already made many excellent contributions not only to our understanding of human interaction with inland waters, the sea, and the maritime environment, but also to our basic understanding of our prehistory and history. In addition, anthropologically oriented archaeology of shipwreck sites has developed important interpretations of the human past. The potential of underwater archaeology to augment our understanding of humanity and the past, however, remains largely unfulfilled because of a number of problems. These include unresolved conflicts with treasure hunters, lack of consistent public outreach and hence a lack of public appreciation and support, and the relative youth of the discipline. Issues of access to sites and how to provide effective protection, as well as rapid technological change, are challenges that, when met, could provide significant opportunities and results.

Underwater archaeological sites may consist of the remains of ships (shipwrecks), boats (boat finds), other watercraft or vessels, and aircraft as well as cultural material that was accidentally lost or deliberately deposited into the water. It includes remains of structures that were originally built wholly or partly underwater (such as fish traps, crannogs, bridges, piers, jetties, and wharves). It also includes the remains of human activity that originally took place on dry or marshy land that has subsequently been inundated, either by rising water levels or by marine (or fluvial) erosion, or during catastrophic events such as earthquakes.

The aims of underwater archaeology (including the closely related subfields of marine, maritime, and nautical archaeology) are to integrate archaeological data and interpretation into the broader study of the human past, emphasizing not only materials from submerged sites, but also from a range of maritime activities, arguably one of the more universal of human endeavors. Inasmuch as two-thirds of the Earth is covered by water, many human civilizations have turned to the sea, lakes, rivers, and other water sources for sustenance, transportation, and warfare. To obtain as complete an understanding of the past as possible, archaeological reconstructions of the past, as well as anthropological interpretations of human behavior, need to include information derived from submerged or underwater sites.

Over the next century, archaeologists working in this field will focus on better integration of their data and interpretation with the wider professional community and better dissemination of their research to the public. Archaeologists will continue to combat treasure hunting and commercial salvage of archaeologically significant shipwrecks by adopting the late 20th-century development of new technologies that have unlocked the potential to discover, examine, excavate, or plunder sites at any depth in the ocean.

The Fifth World Archaeology Congress (WAC-5) held in Washington, DC, in 2003 saw an Underwater and Maritime Archaeology Theme for the first time. This included eleven sessions covering such different topics as the UNESCO *Convention on the Protection of the Underwater Cultural Heritage* (2001), public outreach, avocational involvement, management of maritime and underwater sites, and conservation of waterlogged materials. The session on Underwater and Maritime Archaeology in Latin America and the Caribbean was subsequently selected for publication in this volume.

Latin America and the Caribbean have been faced with many of the difficulties associated with the activities of treasure hunting and the destruction of underwater cultural heritage. Fortunately, several countries in the region have established institutions or programs to identify, protect, manage, and interpret their underwater and maritime cultural heritage. The chapters in this volume demonstrate some of the advances that have taken place throughout the region and show how high-quality archaeological investigation and public interpretation can be done, often at relatively low cost.

We hope that underwater and maritime archaeology will continue to be represented at WAC in the future and we thank One World Archaeology for this first encouraging publication on the topic.

Mark Staniforth and Dolores Elkin
Co-convenors of the Underwater and Maritime Archaeology Theme at WAC-5

Acknowledgments

We extend our deepest gratitude to Joan Gero and the organizers of the Fifth World Archaeological Congress, held in 2003 in Washington, DC, and to Mark Staniforth and Dolores Elkin, co-convenors of the Underwater and Maritime Archaeology Theme. We also thank WAC for assisting several of the Latin American and Caribbean participants through waiving registration fees and providing housing, so that they could attend. We are grateful to Left Coast Press for supporting the One World Archaeology series and being the means by which this volume will reach the readers' hands, and to Carole Bernard, our editor at Left Coast Press, for guiding us through the complex editorial process. We make a special acknowledgment for Robin Torrence, General Series Editor for this volume, who patiently read and edited each chapter with a professional and practical approach. Without her encouragement and generous assistance, this book would have never seen the light.

This book would not exist without the valuable participation of all authors, who made an effort not only to participate in the congress but also to revise and deliver their works to us on time. Special thanks to our colleagues and friends Donald H. Keith and Paul F. Johnston for their insights in summarizing the papers at the Underwater and Maritime Archaeology in Latin America and the Caribbean WAC session.

We extend our special recognition and gratitude to Rosamaría Roffiel in Mexico, whose patient and professional work was essential in the creation of this volume.

Margaret E. Leshikar-Denton
Chair, Society for Historical Archaeology UNESCO Committee
Member, ICOMOS International Committee on
Underwater Cultural Heritage

Pilar Luna Erreguerena
Head of Underwater Archaeology in Mexico
National Institute of Anthropology and History
Member, ICOMOS International Committee on
Underwater Cultural Heritage
May 28, 2008

CHAPTER 1

The Foundations of Underwater and Maritime Archaeology in Latin America and the Caribbean

Margaret E. Leshikar-Denton and
Pilar Luna Erreguerena

INTRODUCTION

Remarkable and diverse prehistoric, pre-Columbian, and historical archaeological sites abound throughout Latin America and the Caribbean (LAC). The maritime landscape features coastal settlements, defensive forts, freshwater sources, fishing-related activities, navigational aids, anchorages, harbors, ports, shipbuilding sites, shipwrecks, and survivor camps. Waves of change have been constant over time, reflecting the dominance and servitude of various societies from the earliest indigenous inhabitants and great civilizations of the Olmec, Maya, and Aztec in Mesoamerica and the Incas in Peru—through European explorers and conquerors, settlers, indigenous and African-enslaved laborers, merchants, colonial powers—to diverse modern cultures.

Among the most endangered and troubled archaeological sites in LAC are shipwrecks. In 1537, after Columbus's 1492 encounter with the New World, Spain established a system of armed protection for homeward-bound convoys of treasure-laden merchantmen, many of which were lost to treacherous shoals, storms, or human pursuit. Sadly, these shipwrecks have been valued less for their contribution to heritage than for their economic potential. For those who would plunder, the quest for treasure threatens the finite and nonrenewable cultural remains of all watercraft—indigenous and local craft, ships of exploration and discovery, treasure galleons, slave transports, vessels of pirates and privateers, merchantmen, and warships. Treasure hunting emerges as the greatest threat to their protection and management. Treasure hunters entice governments with promises of sure profits, but the overall result has been destruction of LAC heritage sites and no sign of financial reward for participating countries.

This book addresses the emerging research endeavors of maritime archaeologists in LAC, despite the significant difficulties they often face when undertaking projects. The authors provide insight into the constant but increasingly successful battle fought by regional professionals and their agencies against numerically larger and financially better equipped treasure hunters. Case studies of exciting and cutting-edge research, conservation, site preservation, and interpretation offer inspiration for the future. Discussions about the unique legal circumstances in various countries establish a comparative framework for understanding different histories of archaeological research and practice.

In LAC, the approach is very "real world." Researchers themselves are committed to addressing not only meaningful archaeological research and arguments but also to using creative methods of cultural resource management (CRM) in their fight to establish frameworks of protection for maritime heritage resources. Most contributors to this volume live and work in LAC. They demonstrate the commitment to local control of heritage. By uniting our approaches to both research and heritage management, we hope to gain wider support within and beyond the LAC region.

A UNIFIED APPROACH

Maritime archaeologists in LAC have faced challenges in communication because of political and geographical separation, diverse languages, cultures, and legal traditions. But in today's global world of discourse, nations are uniting to command greater international strength on a range of social, political, cultural, and economic issues. They are also comparing their experiences with commercial salvage operations and *bona fide* archaeology. More and more, governments, institutions, and museums are cooperating with each other and with local and overseas nonprofit organizations, as well as academic institutions, to understand and interpret their underwater and maritime cultural heritage (UCH). Successful archaeological research projects, museum exhibitions, and preservation of sites *in situ* are becoming preferred uses of UCH, empowering countries to gain long-term academic, educational, cultural, and economic profit through protecting and managing their heritage.

Important Themes

At the 2003 Fifth World Archaeology Congress (WAC-5), we organized the session Underwater and Maritime Archaeology in Latin America and the Caribbean, which included nineteen presentations from eight countries; it inspired this book, an important review of underwater and maritime archaeology in the region, constructed primarily around the work of local archaeologists that only began in the last quarter of the 20th century. The emerging nature of this research and associated management strategies in LAC uniquely highlight case studies that will be useful to a global audience, particularly in light of the new UNESCO *Convention on the Protection of the Underwater Cultural Heritage* (2001), on the eve of its coming into effect and being implemented. Even countries that do not ratify this convention will recognize that it sets a formidable international standard. In this book, we focus on the themes of heritage legislation, management, research, meaning to descendant communities, and the future. We support the use of the powerful term "cooperation" as the way forward to achieve success: cooperation in sharing knowledge, technical skills, professional expertise, and protection and management of a common regional and world heritage. By sharing our experiences with a global audience, we aim to assist others, especially those in emerging situations, to incorporate the most productive steps into their quest and, most importantly, to never give up believing that they, too, can protect and manage their UCH, no matter what their conditions and obstacles are.

History of Cooperation

This work builds on a tradition of cooperation among LAC archaeologists, heritage professionals, and governments, assisted at times by foreign individuals and institutions. Professional underwater and maritime archaeology emerged in the region in the late 1970s and focused for several decades on individual survey and excavation projects in a variety of countries (Bequette 1996; Clifford 1991; Cook 1997; Fontánez Aldea 1997; Foster and Beeker 1997; Geddes 1992; Hall 1991, 1993, 1994, 1997a; Hamilton 1991, 1997; Haviser 1997; James and Beeker 1994; Keith 1987, 1988, 1997a, 1997b, 2006; Keith and Simmons 1985; Leshikar 1988, 1992, 1993; Leshikar-Denton 1997c, In press; Leshikar-Denton and Pedley 1994; Luna Erreguerena 1997, 1998; Nagelkerken 1985, 1989, 1998; Neville, Neyland, and Parrent 1992; Smith 1988a, 1988b, 1993, 2000).

In the symposium Problems and Progress in Underwater Cultural Resource Management in the Caribbean, Bermuda, and Mexico, held at the 1997 Society for Historical Archaeology Conference, Corpus Christi, Texas, the foundations of organized communication among professionals from LAC was laid (Conrich 1997; Gray 1997; Hall 1997b; Keith 1997c; Leshikar-Denton 1997b; Luna Erreguerena 1997; Nagelkerken and Ayubi 1997). This symposium broadly defined underwater CRM as "taking action to responsibly protect underwater cultural heritage," and suggested CRM goals for government departments, academic institutions, nonprofit organizations, and individuals (Leshikar-Denton 1997a).

In October 1999, the Mexican National Committee of the International Council on Monuments and Sites (ICOMOS) included a Scientific Committee on Underwater Archaeology as part of its 12th General Assembly ICOMOS Mexico '99 and within the framework of the World Congress on the Conservation of Monumental Heritage. Experts from fourteen countries (Argentina, Colombia, Uruguay, Venezuela, Mexico, the Cayman Islands, Puerto Rico, the United States, Canada, Portugal, Denmark, the Netherlands, Norway, and Australia) shared the progress achieved in their respective nations and discussed common issues such as treasure hunters, the need to create relevant laws, capacity building, funding sources, and the urgency to develop regional and international cooperative agreements and partnerships under the umbrella of the emerging UNESCO Convention (Elkin et al. 2001; Keith 2001; Leshikar-Denton 2001a; Luna Erreguerena 2001a, 2001b). Mexico's Instituto Nacional de Antropología e Historia (National Institute of Anthropology and History, INAH) published the proceedings as *Memorias del Congreso Científico de Arqueología Subacuática ICOMOS* (Luna Erreguerena and Roffiel 2001).

Chapters and articles from LAC have appeared in *Indian Ocean Week 1997 Proceedings*, the *International Handbook of Underwater Archaeology*, and *Patrimonio Cultural Subacuático/Underwater Cultural Heritage*, among other publications: Bermuda (Smith and Harris 2002); Mexico (Luna Erreguerena 1998, 2002, 2004a); Argentina (Elkin 2002, 2004; Valentini 2004); Colombia (García, Del Cairo, and Fuquen 2004); the Bahamas (Pateman 2004); Cuba (Echeverría Cotelo 2004); Jamaica (Hamilton 2004); and the Cayman Islands and the Caribbean (Leshikar-Denton 1996, 1998, 2001b, 2002, 2004). Case studies of threats to sites in Mexico, Argentina, the Dominican Republic, Jamaica, Turks and Caicos, the Cayman Islands, and Panama appear in *Underwater Cultural Heritage at Risk* (Grenier, Nutley, and Cochran 2006).

ICOMOS Charter and UNESCO Convention

LAC have united to support international initiatives that address UCH, especially the *ICOMOS International Charter on the Protection and Management of Underwater Cultural Heritage* (1996) (ICOMOS

Charter), which defines best professional practice and the *UNESCO Convention on the Protection of the Underwater Cultural Heritage* (2001) (UNESCO Convention), which establishes an international legal framework. These two documents and supporting material about their development, ratification, and implementation are available on their respective Internet web sites (ICOMOS 1996; UNESCO 2001).

In 1997, the Forum of Ministers of Culture and Officials Responsible for Cultural Policy of LAC created the Technical Commission on Underwater Cultural Heritage (*Report on the Status* 1998). Participants from Argentina, Barbados, Colombia, Cuba, the Dominican Republic, Ecuador, Haiti, Honduras, Jamaica, Mexico, Panama, Trinidad and Tobago, and Uruguay met in June 1998 in Santo Domingo with a resource person from UNESCO (Leshikar-Denton 2002). The cornerstone document acknowledged by the meeting was the ICOMOS Charter. In addition, the Latin American and Caribbean Group (GRULAC) examined the draft UNESCO Convention and submitted regional recommendations to the first meeting of governmental experts at UNESCO headquarters in Paris in July 1998. The first GRULAC meeting participants had signed the *Santo Domingo Declaration* (1998), agreeing that: Underwater cultural heritage is the property of the state in which it is found and the heritage of humanity; intervention in this heritage must be carried out only by specialists for scientific purposes; countries should cooperate, to mitigate economic and technical limitations for management of this heritage; countries' cultural authorities should begin to subscribe to agreements on this issue; UNESCO and ICOMOS should play a role in the transfer of technical assistance and logistical support so that countries may gain underwater archaeological expertise under the best conditions; the draft UNESCO Convention should be ratified; and countries should modify their current legislation in accordance with the convention.

Members of the technical commission met again in March 1999 to prepare for the second UNESCO experts' meeting, held in Paris in April 1999. A third experts' meeting took place in Paris in July 2000. The fourth and final meeting of governmental experts was held in March/April and July 2001. GRULAC was a formidable group; thirty-three countries were present at this meeting, which resulted in adoption of the convention by the forum. Ultimately, the convention was adopted on November 2, 2001 at the 31st General Conference of UNESCO; there were eighty-seven votes in favor, four against, and fifteen abstentions, which set an international standard for the treatment of UCH worldwide. Contributors to this volume served in delegations at the Paris negotiations (Elkin/Argentina, Gray/Jamaica, Luna Erreguerena/Mexico, and Leshikar-Denton/ICOMOS).

UNESCO has held regional conferences to assist countries in understanding the convention and to encourage its ratification. Conferences have been held in: Kingston, Jamaica (2002); Maputo, Mozambique (2003); St. Lucia (2003); Hong Kong (2003); Dakar, Senegal (2004); Bogotá, Colombia (2004); Rabat, Morocco (2006); Sri Lanka (2007); Quito, Ecuador (2007); and St. Lucia (2008). The LAC meetings resulted in the Kingston Declaration, the St. Lucia Recommendations (Leshikar-Denton 2003; UNESCO 2004:137, 139), the Bogotá Recommendations (UNESCO/ICUCH/Ministry of Culture of Colombia Heritage Direction w/d), and the Quito Meeting on the Protection of the Underwater Cultural Heritage (see www.unesco.org/es/quito).

By the close of May 2008, seventeen nations had completed all steps for ratification or acceptance: Panama (5/20/2003), Bulgaria (10/6/2003), Croatia (12/1/2004), Spain (6/6/2005), the Libyan Arab Jamahiriya (6/23/2005), Nigeria (10/21/2005), Lithuania (6/12/2006), Mexico (7/5/2006), Paraguay (9/7/06), Portugal (9/21/2006), Ecuador (12/1/2006), Ukraine (12/27/2006), Lebanon (1/8/2007), St. Lucia (2/1/2007), Romania (7/31/07), Cambodia (11/24/07), and Cuba (5/26/08). About one-third of these ratifications have been made by LAC countries. The convention comes into effect when twenty countries ratify, and those countries will have the advantage of appointing the Scientific Technical Commission on Underwater Cultural Heritage.

Having participated in the development of the ICOMOS Charter and UNESCO Convention, we see their practical usefulness for the global community. These powerful instruments can be used as tools to stem the tide of destruction to UCH in LAC and the world, irrespective of a country's affluence and global influence. With a little good fortune, other countries will emulate the leadership roles taken by LAC in recognizing the value of their finite and nonrenewable UCH and take affirmative action to identify, protect, and manage it.

LEGISLATION TO PROTECT SHIPWRECKS

We have pointed out that treasure hunting is the greatest threat to protection and management of underwater cultural heritage in our region. Governments are constantly approached and tempted into entering nonbeneficial agreements with persuasive applicants, commonly from more affluent countries. Among nations whose case studies are highlighted in this volume, Mexico, Argentina, and the Cayman Islands are exemplary in not having granted permits to salvors in the past quarter-century; of these, only Argentina has achieved specific national legislation to protect UCH. A review of the situation in Cuba, Haiti, the Dominican

Republic, Puerto Rico, Anguilla, Martinique, Guadeloupe, Barbados, and Trinidad and Tobago is presented in Leshikar-Denton (2002).

Pilar Luna's account (Chapter 2) addresses Mexico's struggle with treasure hunters, especially from the United States, who have repeatedly sought permits to exploit shipwrecks in Mexican waters (Luna Erreguerena 2004b). U.S. legislation grants privileges to salvors and allows commercialization of finds in some states; this is not only a threat to North American UCH, but a negative example for all countries (Lenihan 2001). In the absence of specific national legislation to protect UCH, INAH has used the existing Federal Law on Archaeological, Artistic and Historical Monuments and Zones (1977) and its Regulations for Archaeological Research in Mexico (1972) to prevent permits to treasure hunters. Chapter 2 reveals the process in Mexico that led to the country's bold step to ratify the UNESCO Convention on July 5, 2006, becoming the eighth country to do so.

Dolores Elkin (Chapter 9) relates that the first legal protection of UCH in Argentina began in 1983, after the discovery of the 18th-century British sloop of war HMS *Swift*; it was declared provincial historical heritage, and a museum was created to house the archaeological collection. Ever since, there has been no case of treasure hunting or commercial exploitation of UCH, other than the occasional souvenir collecting by divers. Today, at a national level, law number 25743, passed in 2003, provides blanket protection for all terrestrial and underwater archaeological remains that are at least 100 years old; it applies to all territories under national jurisdiction. Several provinces, including those along the Patagonian coast, have passed compatible regulations in the last decade. But despite having voted in 2001 to adopt the UNESCO Convention, Argentina has yet to ratify it.

Uruguay does not have specific legislation to protect UCH and did not adopt the UNESCO Convention in 2001. It does not specifically authorize private enterprises directed by "treasure hunters," but has granted them access to underwater sites. However, this has started to change (Chapter 10; E. Martínez, personal communication; A. Lezama, personal communication). In the last twenty years, the Comisión del Patrimonio Cultural de la Nación (National Commission for the Cultural Heritage) has struggled to change the government's attitude regarding UCH. Since the 1990s, the commission has worked toward public awareness, invited international experts to assist in training students, and promoted principles of the UNESCO Convention. In September 2006, the government approved Decree 306/06, through which the executive power will not accept applications submitted by private enterprises to search for historical shipwrecks, will cancel those in progress, will respect those that have a contract for a certain time-period, and will not grant new permits. Only applications for scientific projects will be accepted. The commission is advocating for specific legislation and for Uruguay to ratify the UNESCO Convention; meanwhile, the country is facing legal suits from private enterprises.

Leshikar-Denton and Scott-Ireton (Chapter 14) note that the Cayman Islands government enacted the Abandoned Wreck Law in 1966, whereby all historical shipwrecks that have been on the seabed for more than fifty years are vested in the British Crown. This provision has been used to protect sites, but the law does not recognize shipwrecks as cultural property. It was enacted to ensure that the government receives a percentage of the value of shipwrecks; once the government enters an agreement with a prospector, it must return at least one half of the value of the wreck to the prospector. If the government retains salvaged artifacts, it must pay the prospector a percentage of their appraised value, effectively giving up rights to more than 50% of a shipwreck and paying the salvor to buy it back. But the Cayman Islands have denied all applications from treasure hunters. Prosecutions for violations in 2002, resulting in imprisonment and fines, are on record. In the 1990s, the Ministry of Culture appointed a Marine Archaeology Committee to review the Abandoned Wreck Law. The committee concluded that the law was inadequate and that new legislation should be drafted. As the new legislation is still in development, it can take into account the standards set in the ICOMOS Charter and the UNESCO Convention.

Surprisingly, in Bermuda, the Turks and Caicos Islands, and Jamaica, where significant professional archaeological excavations have achieved success, governments have also granted salvage permits. Bermuda, however, has recently achieved an astounding victory in national legislation. In Chapter 12, Edward Harris navigates through the plight of Bermuda, which over the past half century has experienced the destruction of much of its UCH, particularly shipwrecks at the hands of treasure hunters. The Wreck and Salvage Act (1959) proved ineffective, so Harris and his supporters tirelessly worked to establish a new law, which reached fruition with the passing of the Bermuda Historic Wrecks Act (2001). Bermuda's actions are internationally important and compare favorably to the most current and professionally acceptable models anywhere.

The Turks and Caicos Islands enacted the Historic Wrecks Ordinance (1974), a law based on the U.K.'s Protection of Wrecks Act (1973) (Leshikar-Denton 2002). Though British law requires that sites be designated for protection, the Turks and Caicos ordinance provides that all vessels on the seabed for at least fifty years are vested in the Crown; persons who commit offenses can be fined or imprisoned. The governor can make regulations that prescribe the forms or procedures for granting licenses. The private Turks and Caicos Islands National Museum has assisted the government in developing a process for permit applications, including specific forms designed to exclude all but professional work (Keith 1997c), but periodically the government still issues permits for nonarchaeological operations. In Chapter 13, Sadler demonstrates how the museum's *Trouvadore* research program can benefit the local population on multiple levels. He maintains that licenses should not be issued to those who sell what they find, but only to qualified researchers. Although a law is in place, he would like to see appropriate interpretation of the regulations and the monitoring of licenses so that *Trouvadore* and other important sites are not lost.

Gray (Chapter 15) describes how Jamaica established the Institute of Jamaica in 1879 and enacted the Jamaica National Trust Commission Act in 1958 and the Jamaica National Heritage Trust Act in 1985. In the 1980s and 1990s, Jamaica invited cooperative professional archaeological projects with the Institute of Nautical Archaeology (INA) and Texas A&M University (TAMU), as discussed by Hamilton (Chapter 16) and Smith (Chapter 17), and did not entertain treasure-hunting applications. It was therefore doubly surprising when Jamaica issued a permit to a U.S.-based commercial firm in 1999 and renewed the permit in 2002, while simultaneously hosting a regional UNESCO meeting in support of the UNESCO Convention (2001). Jamaica National Heritage Trust (JNHT) archaeologists, by upholding professionalism in their permit requirements, blocked progress for the permittee. Recently, Jamaica appeared to be returning to a preservation-oriented path, but Gray (Chapter 15) argues that in 2007 there is still a lack of clarity.

Jamaican heritage managers have little time to develop site inventories and coordinate professional research projects; instead, they are on guard to keep heritage management decisions that are contrary to international ethics, as outlined in the ICOMOS Charter (1996) and UNESCO Convention (2001), at bay. They spend time enforcing permit requirements for commercial firms that have been granted conditional permits by the government. The result is a mixed message from the government that places Jamaica's public heritage managers in difficult situations. Commercial firms also experience unfulfilled expectations. Nobody wins.

The Netherlands Antilles includes the islands of Curaçao (Chapter 18) and Bonaire (Chapter 19), located near the coast of Venezuela, and St. Maarten, St. Eustatius, and Saba, located east of Puerto Rico. Nagelkerken and Ayubi (1997) point out that in the Netherlands Antilles, existing legislation is being amended to come into agreement with the 1992 Treaty of Malta, which applies not only to the European archaeological heritage but also to that in the Netherlands Antilles.

HERITAGE MANAGEMENT

If underwater archaeology is a young discipline in LAC, its heritage management is younger. Political, economic, and social factors have meant that the situation is far from ideal. Still, countries are taking various actions to responsibly protect UCH through traditional and other more creative means. In some locations, government departments, institutions, and museums lead the way; in others, leadership originates in private organizations and museums that seek to influence the behavior of governments. Without a doubt, committed individuals can greatly enhance opportunities for success.

In addition to creating effective legislation, chapters in this volume propose the following: Mitigate impacts to endangered sites; disallow treasure hunting; create site inventories; protect and interpret sites *in situ* if possible; excavate only when there are scientific objectives, adequate funding, professional staff, and provisions for documentation, conservation, curation, and reporting; involve the public; and share results of research with the public through museum exhibitions, the media, and publications (Leshikar-Denton 1997a). In LAC, combining protection and management of UCH with sustainable economic and tourism objectives is a powerful driving force. By recognizing this key issue, it is possible to advocate that even the least economically advantaged countries should invest their resources in protection, management, and interpretation of their maritime heritage.

Luna Erreguerena (Chapter 2) chronicles the recent but intense development of underwater archaeology in Mexico. By 2003, INAH created a project entitled Special Programs of the Subdirección de Arqueología Subacuática (Vice-Directorate of Underwater Archaeology), through which a team of researchers in Campeche are searching offshore for remains of the 1630–1631 New Spain fleet, surveying sites in coastal waters, and advocating public awareness and stewardship of the vast UCH in that region. Fishermen have become allies in identifying and protecting sites, turning in artifacts collected in the past, and participating in fieldwork, while a permanent archaeologist post has been created in Campeche to interface with authorities and institutions. Plans are underway to create underwater museums at several appropriate coastal maritime heritage sites, where an official guide will accompany and inform visitors and provide informational brochures. The local community will be strategically involved to increase interest in UCH and understanding of its cultural, educational, and economic value through sustainable tourism. Finally, Mexico is compiling an inventory of shipwrecks on Banco Chinchorro, Quintana Roo, a biosphere reserve nominated nationally in 2004 for consideration by UNESCO to become a World Heritage Site on the basis of natural and cultural criteria (Luna Erreguerena and Carrillo Márquez 2005).

Maritime heritage management is addressed in Argentina in several ways. At the government level, the Underwater Archaeology Program (PROAS) of the National Institute of Anthropology is conducting projects along the Patagonian coast, raising public awareness, increasing the dissemination of information, and stimulating a greater public involvement in the protection of this heritage (Chapter 9, and Elkin, personal communication).

The Department of Archaeology at the Universidad de la República Oriental del Uruguay (University of the Oriental Republic of Uruguay) created an Underwater Archaeology Program (PAS) in 2000, to promote research and to train specialists (Chapter 11). PAS considers that heritage has a value based on the use that society gives it, rather than an inherent value. To generate management strategies, it is essential to understand the local culture and to establish dialog between the research group and the local population. So, PAS trains heritage preservation and tourism professionals by involving them in research projects and conferences and giving them written reports (Lezama, personal communication). However, there is concern that in spite of government's positive attitude change regarding appropriate management of UCH, Uruguay's serious socioeconomic situation could foster the idea that commercial exploitation of UCH is a way to obtain financial resources. Thus, there is an urgent need to demonstrate that scientific treatment of this legacy is feasible and to provide a cultural product before the issue emerges again in the political arena (Martínez, personal communication).

Chapter 12 introduces Bermuda's foundations of heritage management in 1974 with the establishment of the Bermuda Maritime Museum. Serving not only as a cultural and educational venue with exhibitions celebrating the island's maritime history, the museum developed as a professional institution adhering to international ethics on archaeology and conservation. From 1980 forward, Director Edward Harris promoted the preservation of shipwreck heritage and established cooperative research and field-school programs with qualified overseas institutions, such as East Carolina University (Greenville, North Carolina) and Brown University (Providence, Rhode Island). This approach has enabled Bermuda to make considerable progress in documenting the island's shipwrecks and, since 1989, publishing results of that work in the annual *Bermuda Journal of Archaeology and Maritime History*. By educating the public and lobbying for professional ethics, Bermuda achieved its exemplary heritage law in 2001.

The Turks and Caicos Islands have granted permits to treasure hunters that allowed salvage of shipwrecks in their waters (Keith 1997c, 2006), but in 1980, when an early 16th-century wreck was discovered on Molasses Reef, inaccurately proclaimed to be Columbus's *Pinta*, the governor called in experts for their assistance. The foundations of heritage management were laid down when Donald Keith (1987, 1988, 1997b, 1997c, 2001, 2006) excavated the "Molasses Reef wreck" between 1982 and 1985 and subsequently undertook its conservation. At the end of the 1980s, the Turks and Caicos National Museum, a publicly funded nonprofit trust sanctioned by the government, was created; it opened to the public in 1991, with the Molasses Reef wreck as the central exhibition.

Since that date, a museum support facility comprising an exhibition workshop, conservation labs, a curatorial facility, a lecture room, and a combination office/library have been established. The museum continues at the forefront of heritage management initiatives in the Turks and Caicos by organizing archaeological fieldwork; establishing a review process for proposals to conduct excavations; undertaking archival research in overseas repositories; locating and recording artifact collections taken from the islands and arranging for their repatriation; recording oral histories; identifying and registering historical structures in the islands; and facilitating collection, conservation, and rebinding of national archives. Sadler (Chapter 13) describes the most recent work of the museum and the nonprofit organization, Ships of Discovery in the search for the wreck of the slave-ship *Trouvadore*, a ship that carried ancestors of many current island residents not only to the island's shores, but to freedom from slavery. In spite of these profoundly positive advances, the government still considers proposals for shipwreck salvage, putting this very heritage at risk.

Leshikar-Denton and Scott-Ireton (Chapter 14) introduce a chronology of steps taken in maritime heritage management in the Cayman Islands: a 1979–1980 INA survey resulting in an inventory of seventy-seven sites; a 1979 law creating the National Museum, which opened to the public in 1990; research on the "Wreck of the Ten Sail," resulting in a museum exhibition, a National Archive publication, a Postal Service stamp issue, and a Currency Board commemorative coin for its 1994 bicentenary; hiring an archaeologist; enlarging the shipwreck inventory to 140 sites and recording terrestrial sites; and advocating for new legislation.

The museum, archive, National Trust, and Department of Environment had a tradition of cooperation, but in 2002 they established a formal Maritime Heritage Partnership, combining heritage, education, and recreational tourism through a three-tiered approach—to protect, manage, and interpret the islands' maritime heritage sites. By 2003, they launched an interactive land-based Maritime Heritage Trail that encourages public visits to thirty-six sites throughout the three islands; these are marked by signs and interpreted with a poster/guide. A managed and interpreted shipwreck preserve system for divers and snorkelers is envisioned for robust sites like the Norwegian-registered *Glamis* wrecked in 1913. Attention is directed to rare and sensitive sites including HMS *Jamaica* (1715), *San Miguel* (1730), and HMS *Convert* (1794), which require special protection and may reveal unique histories available nowhere else in the world. This layered approach to presenting sites should advance the concepts of understanding, inspiring an appreciation for history and the desire to protect heritage. It also should have long-term benefits for tourism. A dedicated Cayman Islands maritime archaeology program has been proposed and favorably received by the government.

Jamaica has a history of heritage management initiatives dating back to the late 19th century; heritage institutions have attempted to research, preserve, and manage their UCH in the past half century (Leshikar-Denton 2002). Port Royal, a thriving English colonial city (Chapters 16 and 17) subsided into Kingston Harbour in a catastrophic earthquake in 1692. In 1969, Jamaicans were first involved in Philip Mayes's terrestrial archaeological excavations at Port Royal, and the Jamaican Archaeological Research Centre was founded in the Old Naval Hospital. Since 1981, when Donny Hamilton led the TAMU/INA excavation of the underwater city in collaboration with the JNHT, Jamaican archaeologists including Dorrick Gray (Chapter 15) have been trained in this specialty. Gray also received overseas academic training and is a JNHT public archaeologist today.

Conservation of the TAMU/INA/JNHT artifacts has been undertaken at TAMU, while Jamaica established Museums at Port Royal. Now activities affecting the site must be approved by the JNHT, with enforcement facilitated by its proximity to the Jamaica Defence Force base. Management of UCH is more challenging in coastal areas where sites, including Columbus's caravels *Capitana* and *Santiago de Palos*, were run aground in 1503 and numerous Jamaican merchantmen were lost or abandoned over the centuries. Management is exceedingly difficult in the geographically distant and treacherous Pedro Banks, where shipwrecks of many nationalities and time periods have wrecked. Research and enforcement there requires expensive logistical support; thus, little legitimate work has been accomplished and looting is prevalent.

Sites also require designation to be fully protected (Gray 1997). Gray advocates that Jamaica ratify the UNESCO Convention; develop appropriate national legislation; enforce permits for research in accord with the UNESCO Convention; initiate an inventory of UCH; increase training; seek assistance from divers, fishermen, volunteers, and the public to identify sites; and educate stakeholders about appropriate action to take when sites are found. Jamaica's early history is one of preservation, yet in the past decade decisions have been made that jeopardize the future of Jamaica's UCH.

Netherlands Antilles legislation is being amended to comply with the Treaty of Malta. Archaeological projects have been conducted on St. Eustatius, St. Maarten, Curaçao, and Bonaire. On St. Eustatius, the historical anchorage at Orange Bay has been investigated by the Archaeological-Anthropological Institute of the Netherlands Antilles (AAINA), in cooperation with the College of William and Mary (Williamsburg, Virginia) (Nagelkerken 1985; Nagelkerken and Ayubi, 1997). On St. Maarten, HMS *Proselyte*, a captured Dutch frigate that wrecked in 1801, has been mapped by archaeologists under the auspices of the St. Maarten National Heritage Foundation, the Ministry of Culture, the Department of Planning and Environment, and Maritime Archaeology and Research (Bequette 1996); plans are underway to develop a management plan to protect it from further looting, and Bequette recommends that any artifacts recovered from the site should be preserved and displayed at the St. Maarten Museum.

Nagelkerken and Hayes (Chapter 19) describe archaeological work in the historical anchorage at Kralendijk, Bonaire. In Curaçao, at least three projects have been undertaken. AAINA investigated the Dutch frigate *Alphen* that exploded and sank in 1778; it is the only underwater site on the Curaçao monuments list. AAINA also conducted a survey and surface collection prior to construction by the Port Authority on the quay wall of the main commercial wharf at the entrance to Santa Anna Bay (Haviser 1997; Nagelkerken 1989, 1998). In alignment with new worldwide interpretive strategies for shipwrecks, Nagelkerken et al. (Chapter 18) offer a plan to use the SS *Mediator*, lost in 1884 in the Willemstad harbor, as a model for public education about maritime history, underwater archaeology, and research diving. The site, to be preserved *in situ*, has been cleared of overburden and mapped and protected from damage caused by ship traffic in the harbor entrance. It is being prepared for local and tourist diving in conjunction with museum displays at the Curaçao Maritime Museum, with maritime archaeology education coordinated by the Maritime Archaeological and Historical Society (MAHS), submerged cultural resource management by the STIMANA Foundation, and promotional activities by the UNIEK CURAÇAO Foundation.

RESEARCH

Underwater and maritime archaeological research in LAC is enriching not only the collective region but also a worldwide audience, including countries that once conquered and colonized LAC. Since the inception of INAH's underwater archaeology area in 1979, multidisciplinary research projects have been undertaken in Mexican waters, assisted by national and overseas institutions and colleagues (Chapter 2; Luna Erreguerena 2006). Luna's team has developed parallel projects to optimize human and financial resources and time (e.g., three simultaneous projects in Campeche: the 1630–1631 New Spain Fleet Project, the Inventory of UCH in the Gulf of Mexico, and Special Programs of the Subdirección de Arqueología Subacuática).

Meehan and Trejo (Chapter 3) and Rojas (Chapter 4) describe the archival and archaeological search for *Nuestra Señora del Juncal*, one of two flagships of the New Spain fleet that sailed from Veracruz and was lost in a storm in 1631 in the Gulf of Mexico. Analysis of hundreds of manuscripts found in Mexico, Spain, and Cuba and their comparison with ancient and modern cartography have resulted in target search areas in the Sound of Campeche. Factors such as the ship's building specifications, construction modifications, and wrecking process as well as the behavior of the crew and passengers during the tragedy are discussed.

The search for *Nuestra Señora del Juncal* has led to the discovery of more than 100 sites that now comprise an inventory, integrated through GIS, that can be used to identify sites that deserve more extensive study. Moya (Chapter 5) introduces the "Pilar site," located in 1998, and perhaps the only 16th-century shipwreck found in America that has not been compromised by treasure hunters or souvenir collectors. Galindo (Chapter 6) examines the probable 18th-century "Don Pancho site," discovered in 1997, where civil pattern British artillery, three anchors, and forty lead ingots were found.

In Yucatan and Quintana Roo, Mexico, thousands of cenotes (sinkholes) and inundated caves are reported to contain archaeological material dating from prehistoric, pre-Columbian, and colonial times; an atlas of these sites is being compiled with a view to their study and protection. González et al. (Chapter 7) discuss the discovery of extinct animal bones, prehistoric human skeletons, ashes from bonfires lit when caves were dry (over 10,000 years ago), and hundreds of Mayan skulls. Rojas et al. (Chapter 8) review the evidence that cenotes were used as mortuary depositories and not only as offering places; research seeks to determine if the remains are ancestors in a final resting place, or victims of sacrifice, war, or diseases.

Undoubtedly, research on the HMS *Swift* in Puerto Deseado, extensively covered by Elkin (Chapter 9) and Bastida, Grosso, and Elkin (Chapter 10), is the most important current project in Argentina. PROAS, created in 1995 to study, preserve, and manage the nation's UCH, is also studying shipwrecks in Patagonia, southern Argentina (Elkin, personal communication). The Valdés Project began in 2004 to assess, conduct nonintrusive surveys, and provide tourism management guidelines for the shipwrecks of a UNESCO World Heritage site, the Valdés Peninsula, and the adjacent coastal city of Puerto Madryn, in the Province of Chubut. Six of about thirty shipwrecks located within the study area have been preliminarily surveyed and assessed for their historical and/or tourism value. The nonintrusive fieldwork survey of seven underwater and intertidal sites, places the date of the oldest at the mid-19th century. In all cases, site plans were made and wood and/or metal samples taken to assess their cultural and chronological affiliation prior to developing management guidelines. Additionally, a NAS Introduction and Part I course was run for the diving schools and diving operators of Puerto Madryn to raise local awareness. The main sources of financing have been the National Ministry of Culture and the Municipality of Puerto Madryn.

Monte León is a new national park in Argentina, with 40 km of ocean coastline; in 2006, the PROAS team conducted a baseline assessment of its maritime heritage as part of the park's general management plan. One of the ships of Magellan-El Cano's voyage of 1519–1522, the *nao Santiago*, was lost in Patagonia, possibly within what is now Monte Leon National Park. Although no evidence of the *Santiago* was found during extensive fieldwork in 2006–2007—and may never be found—scattered shipwreck remains were located and documented. Wood and metal samples await analysis but suggest dates between the second half of the 19th century and the mid-20th century. The primary funding has come from the Argentinean National Parks Administration and the municipality of Puerto Santa Cruz. Finally, PROAS is also coordinating the *Hoorn* Project, searching for a Dutch ship sunk in 1615.

During the past six years in Uruguay, PAS has developed several projects, some with financial support from the Dirección Nacional de Investigación Científica y Tecnológica (National Direction of Scientific and Technological Research) and academic support from the Comisión Sectorial de Investigación Científica (Sector Commission for Scientific Research) (Lezama, personal communication). Lezama (Chapter 11) presents a rich analysis of navigation in the river of La Plata, one of the most promising areas for underwater archaeological research in Uruguay, where hundreds of shipwrecks wait to be discovered and studied.

In addition, the Comisión del Patrimonio Cultural de la Nación, has sponsored an initial investigation with the Maritime Archaeology Centre of the University of Southampton, United Kingdom, aimed toward developing the Programme of Maritime Archaeology and Inventory of the Submerged Cultural Heritage in Uruguay. The commission also handles reports of archaeological findings around the country, with local community support. Finally, private enterprises must now include underwater cultural resources impact assessments of their proposed work at the port of Montevideo (Martínez, personal communication).

Harris (Chapter 12) notes that scientific projects have been undertaken since the establishment of the Bermuda Maritime Museum in 1974. Archaeological work on the *Sea Venture*, wrecked in 1609 on its way to James Fort Virginia, was carried out by the museum and later by Jon Adams of the Sea Venture Trust (Harris 1997; Leshikar-Denton 1998). In 1981, the museum began working with East Carolina University, headed by William Still and Gordon Watts, whose field schools assisted in survey, recording, excavating, and conserving shipwrecks and resulted in journal articles. Among vessels investigated is the supposed *Santa Lucia* of the 1580s. Smith and Harris (2002) provide additional summaries of research on Bermuda shipwrecks. MAHS has also assisted in underwater research.

Considering land-based archaeology, Harris and Norman Barka uncovered a defensive ditch and pre-1650 artifacts at King's Castle. In 1991, Harris and Richard Gould of Brown University found camouflaging to the fort and seven massive guns of the 1870s at Fort Cunningham. Research at the early English city of St. George's was conducted by the Bermuda National Trust, in cooperation with Marley Brown and the Colonial Williamsburg Foundation. The Bermuda Museum itself is located inside the Keep at the old Royal Naval Dockyard, the largest fort in Bermuda, built when the United States gained independence from Britain.

In the Turks and Caicos Islands, the 16th-century "Molasses Reef wreck" was completely excavated and artifacts conserved in the 1980s under the direction of Donald Keith (1987, 1988, 1997b, 1997c, 2001, 2006). The research provided a wealth of answers to mysteries surrounding the caravel ship-type. Because only 2% of the hull survived, the archaeologists investigated the remains of two similar 16th-century ships to fill in gaps in the analysis. Although the "Highborn Cay wreck" in the Bahamas had lost most of its artifacts to salvors, archaeologists located and test excavated a well-preserved portion of the hull, including the main mast step carved out of the keelson (Keith 1988, 1997a; Smith 1993). The "Bahía Mujeres wreck," located off Mexico's Yucatan Peninsula and surveyed in cooperation with INAH, provided further details (Keith 1988; Luna Erreguerena 1997, 1998; Smith 1993).

In an alternative approach to investigation, the National Museum and Ships of Discovery are searching for the site of the *Trouvadore*, a Spanish ship lost off East Caicos in March 1841. It carried a human cargo of 193 people intended for slavery in Cuba, but who found freedom instead when the ship wrecked on the shores of the Turks and Caicos Islands (Chapter

13). Discovery of a letter in the American Museum of Natural History in New York led the museum to search for further archival information in ten countries on three continents. Field projects have been undertaken to locate the remains of the *Trouvadore*, with one site worthy of further investigation. The importance of this site lies in its potential to illuminate many social, political, and economic issues at the time of its sinking.

Between 1979 and 1980, INA recorded seventy-seven archaeological sites in the Cayman Islands (Chapter 14; Leshikar-Denton 1997b, 2002; Smith 1981, 2000). The team, under Roger Smith's direction, test excavated the "Turtle Bone wreck" in Little Cayman, probably burned in 1669 by Spanish privateers in retaliation for Henry Morgan's sacking of Porto Bello, and the "Duck Pond Careenage" in Grand Cayman. The 1794 "Wreck of the Ten Sail" (HMS *Convert* and nine merchantmen) was investigated by Leshikar-Denton (In press; Leshikar 1993) in the 1990s, with support from TAMU, INA, and the National Museum; during the East End search, thirty shipwrecks and eight terrestrial sites were surveyed, with exposed remains of the *Convert* mapped. The museum facilitated surveys for prehistoric sites by University College London and the Florida Museum of Natural History (Gainesville) in the 1990s, with negative results, suggesting an untouched natural history as late as the 1500s.

Today, Cayman's shipwreck inventory has been built to include more than 140 sites, spanning five centuries from fifteen countries; among them are HMS *Jamaica*, a mid-1700s Spanish wreck, and a couple of 16th–17th-century sites of undetermined nationality. This inventory is a valuable tool for considering protection, management, research and interpretive strategies. The museum also test excavated a turtle-fishing encampment dating to about 1700 on the north coast of Grand Cayman, and has started a terrestrial-site inventory. Research strategies for early and fragile UCH sites are being explored. Shipwrecks embedded in the pristine reefs and sounds of Little Cayman need thorough evaluation in line with a possible World Heritage Site nomination.

Although today Port Royal, Jamaica, is a small isolated fishing village, beneath the ground and the adjacent water of Kingston Harbour lies the only sunken city in the New World, a city that played a pivotal role in Caribbean politics and economics (Chapter 16). Founded in 1655 after the English seized Jamaica from the Spanish, Port Royal went through a spectacular rise involving affluent merchants, pirates, privateers, and planters. Its influence ended catastrophically in 1692 during an earthquake; Port Royal studies fit within an emerging body of "disaster archaeology literature" (Grattan and Torrence 2002). Hamilton suggests in Chapter 16 that those who undertake excavations at what may be the best-preserved 17th-century English site in the world carry great responsibility for proper excavating, recording, conserving, and publishing. Early underwater work in Port Royal was conducted by Edwin Link (1950s) and Robert Marx (1960s); Philip Mayes undertook terrestrial excavations in 1969. Scientific underwater archaeology was conducted on eight buildings and a shipwreck that rammed through one of them under the direction of Hamilton in the 1981–1990 TAMU/INA/JNHT field school excavations at Port Royal.

Hamilton emphasizes the many postexcavation difficulties associated with conserving, maintaining, properly housing, displaying, and interpreting the recovered artifacts, publishing the results, and preserving the site—most of which remains to be excavated. Caring for this vast, unique archaeological site of major historical importance is a daunting responsibility for the Jamaican government. Gray (Chapter 15), addresses management issues for Port Royal and other UCH sites; Leshikar-Denton (2002) summarizes additional underwater fieldwork.

In the 1980s and 1990s, INA unsuccessfully searched for Columbus's two caravels *Capitana* and *Santiago de Palos*, lost in 1503. Six 18th-century merchantmen, however, were discovered; the "Reader's Point wreck" was investigated by JNHT/INA archaeologists, under Greg Cook's direction. The sloop was likely scuttled around the time of the American Revolutionary War after a merchant-trading career. INA also participated with Jamaica in survey work on the Pedro Banks for significant early shipwrecks, although distance, logistics, and funding have precluded major scientific work there. In 1983, the Institute of Jamaica sponsored Leshikar-Denton to document construction of a traditional dugout canoe, made with hand tools in six weeks (Leshikar 1985). A variety of terrestrial projects have been undertaken in Jamaica on colonial sites, sites of enslaved populations, and at prehistoric sites of the Tainos (Chapter 15).

Smith's sole contribution on conservation (Chapter 17) underscores the need for more emphasis, globally, on this aspect of underwater archaeology. Smith assesses glass as an organic artifact category rather than an inorganic one. Donald Keith, discussant for the Latin American and Caribbean session at WAC-5, observed that the underwater environment often preserves things that do not survive in terrestrial settings, but these artifacts often require more conservation; he recommends increasing the number of competent artifact conservators on shipwreck excavation projects. Smith points out that mandates for the display and curation of organic material culture and advances in archaeologically based material science studies create the demand for preservation of organic artifacts. He provides a guide to his cutting-edge research to develop and implement organic polymer preservation techniques to meet the changing needs of museums and educational institutions. Keith observed that the new conservation treatment on Port Royal artifacts will have a far-reaching international application.

AAINA and the College of William and Mary worked in the 1980s in the historical anchorage at Orange Bay, St. Eustatius, Netherlands Antilles used by 17th- and 18th-century European seafarers (Nagelkerken 1985; Nagelkerken and Ayubi 1997); they delineated the size of the anchorage by the dispersion of Dutch, French, and English ceramics, glass, bricks, tiles, and beads. From 1994–1995, St. Maarten institutions and government departments collaborated on research into HMS *Proselyte* (Bequette 1996); archaeologists mapped and delineated the site to develop a proposed management plan.

Surveys of the historical anchorage adjacent to Fort Orange and Kralendijk, at Bonaire, the island's population center, investigated the site's maritime historical landscape and culture, based on the distribution, classification, and production source of artifacts exposed on the seabed (Chapter 19). The 600 artifacts recovered comprise glass bottles, creamware, pearlware, whiteware, and delft ceramics from Holland (65%), England (22%), France (13%), and Germany (1%), with peak use of the anchorage between 1775 and 1850, although artifacts ranged from the 16th century to the 20th. The Dutch warship *Sirene*, lost on June 24, 1831, was found within the anchorage.

The 18th-century Dutch frigate *Alphen*, lost in Santa Anna Bay, was surveyed in the 1980s (Nagelkerken 1989); excavations followed between 1994 and 1998. In 1993, AAINA conducted a survey and limited surface collection, in response to dredging during repair of a quay wall of the Handelskade (commercial wharf) at the entrance to Santa Anna Bay; it revealed 17th–19th-century artifacts (Nagelkerken 1998). Chapter 18 focuses on the wreck of the SS *Mediator*, a ship belonging to the J & R Harrison Line, Ltd., of Liverpool, England, a major commercial trader in trans-Atlantic traffic to the Caribbean during the late 19th century. The steamship collided with another ship in the harbor entrance to Willemstad on July 5, 1884, sinking rapidly with over 750 tons of "fine goods"; the remains were discovered in 1986. Investigation and proposed interpretive plans were addressed above under heritage management.

MEANING TO DESCENDANT COMMUNITIES

An important theme arising from the volume is the meaning of UCH to descendant communities. This is clearly evident in Chapter 13, which provides a fascinating case study of a descendant African community whose ancestors escaped intended slavery in Cuba, through wrecking in the Spanish ship *Trouvadore*. Although this event increased the population of the Turks and Caicos Islands by around 7% with first-generation Africans and surely affected the cultural identity of descendant communities, it had essentially been forgotten until researchers discovered and pursued the truth. Significantly, folklore in the island community of Bambarra yields vestiges of a tale that it was settled by freed people wrecked in a slave ship on the Caicos Bank; suddenly, local people are interested in the *Trouvadore* story and the National Museum, and this otherwise nondescript and not particularly ancient shipwreck is important to an entire nation.

Chapters 2 and 14 underscore the benefits of instilling a sense of participation and ownership of cultural heritage by descendant communities whose involvement has the potential to foster a sense of stewardship though this grass-roots approach to protection and management. Chapter 2 illuminates the range of possibilities from descendants of Mayan communities to European conquerors in Mexico. Maritime heritage interpretation initiatives in Chapter 14 evoke a range of themes that could be relevant to descent communities in the Cayman Islands, empowered by knowledge of their history and achievements: early explorers, origin of maritime place names, historic anchorages, shipwrecks, wrecking practices, lighthouses, seaside forts, shipbuilding, turtle-fishing, and hurricanes.

THE FUTURE

Despite limited resources, many LAC countries have taken steps to address their UCH in creative targeted and focused ways. Still, there is a long road ahead to protect and manage the region's UCH; some countries have yet to begin. As we ponder the past, we should identify the issues raised by these contributions about what will create a better future for UCH both in our area and elsewhere.

Legislation

The landmark decisions made by the LAC countries of Mexico, Panama, Paraguay, Ecuador, St. Lucia, and Cuba to ratify the UNESCO Convention (2001) should be emulated, thereby creating a regional and international domino effect toward its rapid implementation. Although GRULAC created this type of momentum in Paris, which contributed to the official adoption of the UNESCO Convention, it is now time for GRULAC to line up and support its ratification.

It would also be wise for countries to follow the lead of Bermuda and Argentina, which have achieved good national legislation specifically for the protection and management of UCH; ideally, emerging national legislation will mirror internationally developed concepts reflected in the UNESCO Convention (2001) and ICOMOS Charter (1996). Commercial exploitation of UCH should be eliminated once and for all. Government officials in countries who allow it, with knowledge of the widely available international information and opinion to the contrary, not only wear blinkers but also carry the burden of poor government by gambling away the countries' UCH.

In the meantime, existing legislation should be used creatively by heritage managers to the best effect, as is the case in most countries included in this volume. A solid foundation of ethical practices regarding UCH is of utmost importance in launching effective long-range goals.

Heritage Management

Throughout LAC, problems and progress in heritage management emerge side by side. But problems are overcome, and progress is being made. In addition to the traditional concept of management through legislation that governments must agree on, support, and establish, institutions and individuals in LAC are tapping other creative ways to protect and manage their UCH.

Who are the heritage managers? A key to heritage management lies in the human resources dedicated to it. We believe that all countries should seek to establish competent authorities and provide training for people to gain skills in identification, protection, management, research, conservation, and interpretation of UCH. Training is often received overseas or imparted by experts conducting field schools and courses in LAC, such as INA in Jamaica. Mexico has held several multidisciplinary seminars with overseas and local specialists teaching Mexican students and other specialists, and Lezama reports that Uruguay has established the first formal school in LAC dedicated to training in underwater archaeology. The contributions illuminate a trend in this direction with programs emerging within governmental and nongovernmental institutions, departments, and museums. Flexibility in different situations and countries is important, but once established, the key for the pioneers is to institutionalize the progress made by working to achieve good succession planning. Challenges in fiscal and human resources may be faced, but continuity is essential to the long-term success of UCH management and research programs.

PAS in Uruguay observes that UCH takes on the value that society places on it. So, as professionals we must reach out and involve governments and the public in understanding LAC UCH. The Cayman Islands' concept of a three-tiered approach to maritime heritage sites—protect, manage, and interpret—seeks to do just that, through a successive layering of information—the land-based trail for everyone, the shipwreck preserves on robust sites for the adventurous diving public, and the recognition that rare and sensitive sites deserve special treatment. The astonishing Mexican experience in Campeche, where a regional department has been established and fishermen have become great allies in site location and protection, shows that success can be achieved through awareness, respect, and involvement of stakeholders. We should also share results of research with the public through museum exhibitions, the media, and publications, as has been done in Mexico, Argentina, Uruguay, Bermuda, the Turks and Caicos Islands, the Cayman Islands, Jamaica, and the Netherlands Antilles.

The Cayman Islands and Bermuda emerge as perhaps the first LAC countries to begin the creation of inventories of UCH sites in the late 1970s. Larger countries with extensive territorial waters and thus more challenging logistics are making great strides in this area now, especially Mexico and Argentina. All countries should work to achieve inventories of physical archaeological sites, but should not forget to compile files of all primary and secondary references that may lead to discovery or identification of UCH sites. This is the fundamental management tool that a country needs to evaluate what UCH resources are present and to make decisions about its treatment.

The concept of protecting and interpreting sites *in situ* if possible comes across loud and clear with interpretive strategies planned for the SS *Mediator* in Curaçao, the *Glamis* in the Cayman Islands, shipwrecks in Patagonia, Argentina, and UCH in the Bay of Campeche, Mexico. We believe that appropriate access to robust UCH sites is sustainable and benefits local communities through interactive and enjoyable learning, while at the same time providing jobs and tourism opportunities.

Impacts to endangered sites should be mitigated. Basic mitigation measures were taken on historic anchorages and shipwrecks in the Netherlands Antilles, specifically in Bonaire, Curaçao, and St. Maarten. Uruguay has achieved a more formal position, now requiring underwater cultural resources impact assessments for certain areas. All countries should work to establish requirements for impact assessments for projects and mitigation measures for affected UCH sites.

Excavation for research purposes is acceptable when there are scientific objectives, adequate funding, professional staff, and provisions for documentation, conservation, curation, and reporting. We recommend a multidisciplinary and multi-institutional approach to projects. It is here, especially, that we can cooperate regionally and internationally, to teach each other, and to provide technical assistance and expertise for the greatest understanding and outcome. To a limited extent, the sharing of field equipment and personnel to assist in fieldwork has already occurred. This could be expanded to include sharing conservation facilities or perhaps even cooperating to create one or more regional conservation laboratories to share.

Research and Excavation

There are a handful of shipwrecks with abundant cultural material in excellent condition that have been excavated, conserved, and interpreted in museums worldwide. Among them are the *Wasa* (Sweden), *Mary Rose* (England), "Roskilde Ships" (Denmark), *Batavia* (Australia), "Ulu Burun wreck" (Turkey), and *La Belle* (Texas). The Turks and Caicos Islands lead LAC in full excavation of an important shipwreck, the "Molasses Reef wreck." Argentina is committed to serious long-term research and excavation of HMS *Swift*. Mexico is undertaking a complex research project in the search for the *Nuestra Señora del Juncal* and aspires to create a museum to tell the history of five centuries of navigation in Mexican waters. Each site has the role or potential to provide a window into a moment in world history and to provide clues to the social, political, cultural, and economic climate of the time. By reflecting on UCH inventories, once established, countries can learn to recognize and target significant UCH sites that have the greatest potential to widen understanding and knowledge of that nation's heritage as well as that of LAC and the world.

The Challenge

In the past sixty years, the world's UCH has become widely accessible through diving and is an easy target for exploitation. Yet in the past thirty years, profound advances in underwater and maritime archaeological research have proved that UCH has cultural, educational, and economic value. There are indeed alternatives to casting it away to profiteers. We can all do more to find ties between our maritime research interests and present populations; our work will be richer all around if it empowers living communities with knowledge of their cultural, historical, and geopolitical past.

The challenge is great for those who have committed themselves to defending UCH and who aspire to fulfill the principles and the spirit of the ICOMOS Charter (1996) and UNESCO Convention (2001), but we can succeed. The magic term is "cooperation" among stakeholders. Countries, governments, professionals, and the public must communicate and help each other through local, regional, and international agreements and through sharing technical resources and professional expertise. The UNESCO Convention has been an inspiration for those who have made the preservation of UCH a personal cause and a life passion. Obstacles are many and diverse, but creativity, perseverance, and cooperation ensure that progress will continue.

REFERENCES

Bequette, K. E. 1996. The HMS *Proselyte* project: Survey of an eighteenth-century British frigate in Great Bay, Saint Maarten. In *Underwater Archaeology*, S. R. James, Jr. and C. Stanley, eds., 73–75. Corpus Christi, TX: Society for Historical Archaeology.

Clifford, S. A. 1991. A preliminary report on a possible 17th-century shipwreck at Port Royal, Jamaica. In *Underwater Archaeology Proceedings from the Society for Historical Archaeology Conference*, J. D. Broadwater, ed., 80–83. Richmond: Society for Historical Archaeology.

Conrich, B. 1997. Neocolonialism in Anguilla. In *Underwater Archaeology*, D. C. Lakey, ed., 44–49. Corpus Christi, TX: Society for Historical Archaeology.

Cook, G. D. 1997. Reader's Point Wreck. In *Encyclopaedia of Underwater and Maritime Archaeology*, J. P. Delgado, ed., 334. London: British Museum Press.

Echeverría Cotelo, J. 2004. Cuba: The protection of underwater cultural heritage. In *Patrimonio Cultural Subacuático/Underwater Cultural Heritage*, V. Marín, ed., 118–21. Havana: UNESCO.

Elkin, D. 2002. Water: A new field in Argentinean archaeology. In *International Handbook of Underwater Archaeology*, C. Ruppe and J. Barstad, eds., 313–29. New York: Kluwer Academic/Plenum Press.

Elkin, D. 2004. Underwater archaeology in Argentina. In *Patrimonio Cultural Subacuático/ Underwater Cultural Heritage*, V. Marín, ed., 94–101. Havana: UNESCO.

Elkin, D., D. Vainstub, A. Argüeso, and V. Dellino. 2001. Proyecto arqueológico HMS *Swift*, Santa Cruz, Argentina. In *Memorias del Congreso Científico de Arqueología Subacuática ICOMOS*, P. Luna Erreguerena and R. M. Roffiel, coords., 143–62. Mexico City: Instituto Nacional de Antropología e Historia.

Fontánez Aldea, R. 1997. Puerto Rico. In *Encyclopaedia of Underwater and Maritime Archaeology*, J. P. Delgado, ed., 330. London: British Museum Press.

Foster, J. W., and C. H. D. Beeker. 1997. The conquest of a sinkhole: Initial archaeological investigations at El Manantial de la Aleta, East National Park, Dominican Republic. In *Underwater Archaeology*, D. C. Lakey, ed., 27–32. Corpus Christi, TX: Society for Historical Archaeology.

García, M. C., C. Del Cairo, and C. Fuquen. 2004. Fundación underwater cultural heritage in Colombia. In *Patrimonio Cultural Subacuático/Underwater Cultural Heritage*, V. Marín, ed., 115–17. Havana: UNESCO.

Geddes, III, D. G. 1992. Archival research: The search for the Columbus caravels at St. Ann's Bay, Jamaica. In *Underwater Archaeology Proceedings from the Society for Historical Archaeology Conference*, D. H. Keith and T. L. Carrell, eds., 148–51. Kingston, Jamaica: Society for Historical Archaeology.

Grattan, J., and R. Torrence, eds. 2002. *Natural Disasters, Catastrophism and Cultural Change*. London: Routledge.

Gray, D. E. 1997. Managing underwater archaeological resources: The Jamaican experience. Unpublished paper presented at the 30th annual Society for Historical Archaeology Conference, January 8–12, Corpus Christi, Texas.

Grenier, R., D. Nutley, and I. Cochran, eds. 2006. *Underwater Cultural Heritage at Risk: Managing Natural and Human Impacts*. Paris: ICOMOS.

Hall, J. L. 1991. The 17th-century merchant vessel at Monte Cristi Bay, Dominican Republic. In *Underwater Archaeology Proceedings from the Society for Historical Archaeology Conference*, J. H. Broadwater, ed., 84–87. Richmond: Society for Historical Archaeology.

Hall, J. L. 1993. The 17th-century merchant shipwreck in Monte Cristi Bay, Dominican Republic: The second excavation season interim report. In *Underwater Archaeology Proceedings from the Society for Historical Archaeology Conference*, S. O. Smith, ed., 95–101. Kansas City, MO: Society for Historical Archaeology.

Hall, J. L. 1994. Spanish coins, Dutch clay pipes, and an English ship: The 1993 Monte Cristi shipwreck project interim report. In *Underwater Archaeology Proceedings from the Society for Historical Archaeology Conference*, R. P. Woodward and C. D. Moore, eds., 32–29. Vancouver, BC: Society for Historical Archaeology.

Hall, J. L. 1997a. Monte Cristi wreck. In *Encyclopaedia of Underwater and Maritime Archaeology*, J. P. Delgado, ed., 283–84. London: British Museum Press.

Hall, J. L. 1997b. Puerto Rico: Island of enchantment? Paper presented at the 30th annual Society for Historical Archaeology Conference, January 8–12, Corpus Christi, Texas.

Hamilton, D. L. 1991. A decade of excavations at Port Royal, Jamaica. In *Underwater Archaeology Proceedings from the Society for Historical Archaeology Conference*, J. H. Broadwater, ed., 90–94. Richmond: Society for Historical Archaeology.

Hamilton, D. L. 1997. Port Royal. In *Encyclopaedia of Underwater and Maritime Archaeology*, J. P. Delgado, ed., 316–18. London: British Museum Press.

Hamilton, D. L. 2004. Port Royal: A buried treasure. In *Patrimonio Cultural Subacuatico/ Underwater Cultural Heritage*, V. Marín, ed., 102–03. Havana: UNESCO.

Harris, E. 1997. Underwater cultural resource management in Bermuda since World War II: The decline of Bermuda's underwater cultural resources. Unpublished paper presented at the 30th annual Society for Historical Archaeology Conference, January 8–12, Corpus Christi, Texas.

Haviser, J. B. 1997. Curaçao. In *Encyclopaedia of Underwater and Maritime Archaeology*, J. P. Delgado, ed., 121. London: British Museum Press.

ICOMOS International Charter on the Protection and Management of Underwater Cultural Heritage. 1996. Paris: ICOMOS. Available online at www.international.icomos.org/charters/underwater_e.htm (accessed May 23, 2008).

James, S. R., and C. Beeker. 1994. The fifteenth-century shipwrecks of La Isabela: Current investigations. In *Underwater Archaeology Proceedings from the Society for Historical Archaeology Conference*, R. P. Woodward and C. D. Moore, eds., 3–7. Vancouver, BC: Society for Historical Archaeology.

Keith, D. H. 1987. *The Molasses Reef Wreck*. Ph.D. dissertation, Texas A&M University, College Station; University Microfilms, Ann Arbor, Michigan.

Keith, D. H. 1988. Shipwrecks of the explorers. In *Ships and Shipwrecks of the Americas*, G. F. Bass, ed., 45–68. London: Thames and Hudson.

Keith, D. H. 1997a. Highborn Cay wreck. In *Encyclopaedia of Underwater and Maritime Archaeology*, J. P. Delgado, ed., 192–93. London: British Museum Press.

Keith, D. H. 1997b. Molasses Reef wreck. In *Encyclopaedia of Underwater and Maritime Archaeology*, J. P. Delgado, ed., 279–81. London: British Museum Press.

Keith, D. H. 1997c. Problems and progress in underwater archaeology in the Turks and Caicos Islands. In *Underwater Archaeology*, D. C. Lakey, ed., 38–43. Corpus Christi, TX: Society for Historical Archaeology.

Keith, D. H. 2001. The Molasses Reef wreck and the Turks & Caicos National Museum: More than just another site. In *Memorias del Congreso Científico de Arqueología*

Subacuática ICOMOS, P. Luna Erreguerena and R. M. Roffiel, coords., 200–12. Mexico City: Instituto Nacional de Antropología e Historia.

Keith, D. H. 2006. The Molasses Reef wreck. In *Underwater Cultural Heritage at Risk: Managing Natural and Human Impacts*, R. Grenier, D. Nutley, and I. Cochran, eds., 82–84. Paris: ICOMOS.

Keith, D. H., and J. Simmons. 1985. Analysis of hull remains, ballast and artifact distribution of a 16th century shipwreck, Molasses reef, British West Indies. *Journal of Field Archaeology* 12(4):411–24.

Lenihan, D. 2001. The National Park Service and the underwater cultural heritage. In *Memorias del Congreso Científico de Arqueología Subacuática ICOMOS*, P. Luna Erreguerena and R. M. Roffiel, coords., 74–80. Mexico City: Instituto Nacional de Antropología e Historia.

Leshikar, M. E. 1985. Construction of a dugout canoe in the parish of St. Ann, Jamaica. In *Proceedings of the Sixteenth Conference on Underwater Archaeology*, P. F. Johnston, ed., 48–51. Corpus Christi, TX: Society for Historical Archaeology.

Leshikar, M. E. 1988. The earliest watercraft: From rafts to Viking ships. In *Ships and Shipwrecks of the Americas*, G. F. Bass, ed., 13–32. London: Thames and Hudson.

Leshikar, M. E. 1992. Investigation of the Wreck of the Ten Sail, Cayman Islands, British West Indies. In *Underwater Archaeology Proceedings from the Society for Historical Archaeology Conference*, D. H. Keith and T. L. Carrell, eds., 30–34. Kingston, Jamaica: Society for Historical Archaeology.

Leshikar, M. E. 1993. *The 1794 Wreck of the Ten Sail: A historical study and archaeological survey*. Ph.D. dissertation, Texas A&M University, College Station; University Microfilms, Ann Arbor, Michigan.

Leshikar-Denton, M. E. 1996. Underwater cultural resource management in Mexico and the Caribbean. In *Underwater Archaeology*, S. R. James, Jr. and C. Stanley, eds., 57–60. Corpus Christi, TX: Society for Historical Archaeology.

Leshikar-Denton, M. E. 1997a. Problems and progress in underwater cultural resource management in the Caribbean, Bermuda and Mexico. Abstracts, 30th annual Conference on Historical and Underwater Archaeology, January 8–12, Corpus Christi, Texas.

Leshikar-Denton, M. E. 1997b. Underwater cultural resource management: A new concept in the Cayman Islands. In *Underwater Archaeology*, D. C. Lakey, ed., 33–37. Corpus Christi, TX: Society for Historical Archaeology.

Leshikar-Denton, M. E. 1997c. Caribbean, Cayman Islands, Wreck of the Ten Sail. In *Encyclopaedia of Underwater and Maritime Archaeology*, J. P. Delgado, ed., 86–89. London: British Museum Press.

Leshikar-Denton, M. E. 1998. Maritime archaeology in the Caribbean. In *Indian Ocean Week 1997 Proceedings*, G. Henderson, ed., 62–72. Perth: Western Australian Museum.

Leshikar-Denton, M. E. 2001a. Caribbean underwater cultural heritage at Y2K. In *Memorias del Congreso Científico de Arqueología Subacuática ICOMOS*, P. Luna Erreguerena and R. M. Roffiel, coords., 70–73 and addendum. Mexico City: Instituto Nacional de Antropologia e Historia.

Leshikar-Denton, M. E. 2001b. Caribbean underwater cultural heritage in the Year 2001. *Foundation Magazine* 1:1 (Cayman Islands: Cayman National Cultural Foundation).

Leshikar-Denton, M. E. 2002. Problems and progress in the Caribbean. In *International Handbook of Underwater Archaeology*, C. Ruppe and J. Barstad, eds., 279–98. New York: Kluwer Academic/Plenum Press.

Leshikar-Denton, M. E. 2003. Report on the UNESCO regional conference for Latin American and Caribbean States, Kingston, Jamaica, June 17–20, 2002. Unpublished report presented at the Fifth World Archaeological Congress, Washington, DC, June 21–26.

Leshikar-Denton, M. E. 2004. The situation in the Caribbean. In *Patrimonio Cultural Subacuático/Underwater Cultural Heritage*, V. Marín, ed., 80–85. Havana: UNESCO.

Leshikar-Denton, M. E. In press. *The Wreck of the Ten Sail*. Gainesville: University Press of Florida.

Leshikar-Denton, M. E., and P. E. Pedley, eds. 1994. *The Wreck of the Ten Sails*. Our Islands' Past, vol. 2. Grand Cayman: Cayman Islands National Archive and Cayman Free Press.

Luna Erreguerena, P. 1997. Stepping stones of Mexican underwater archaeology. In *Underwater Archaeology*, D. C. Lakey, ed., 50–53. Corpus Christi, TX: Society for Historical Archaeology.

Luna Erreguerena, P. 1998. Aspects of Mexican underwater archaeology. In *Indian Ocean Week 1997 Proceedings*, G. Henderson, ed., 36–41. Perth: Western Australian Museum.

Luna Erreguerena, P. 2001a. Introducción. In *Memorias del Congreso Científico de Arqueología Subacuática ICOMOS*, P. Luna Erreguerena and R. M. Roffiel, coords., 11–13. Mexico City: Instituto Nacional de Antropología e Historia.

Luna Erreguerena, P. 2001b. Pasado, presente y futuro de la arqueología subacuática en México. In *Memorias del Congreso Científico de Arqueología Subacuática ICOMOS*, P. Luna Erreguerena and R. M. Roffiel, coords., 39–49. Mexico City: Instituto Nacional de Antropología e Historia.

Luna Erreguerena, P. 2002. Mexico: A country with a rich underwater legacy. In *International Handbook of Underwater Archaeology*, C. Ruppe and J. Barstad, eds., 269–78. New York: Kluwer Academic/Plenum Press.

Luna Erreguerena, P. 2004a. Underwater archaeology in Mexico. In *Patrimonio Cultural Subacuático/Underwater Cultural Heritage*, V. Marín, ed., 86–93. Havana: UNESCO.

Luna Erreguerena, P. 2004b. La protección del patrimonio cultural subacuático. In *Homenaje a Jaime Litvak*, A. Benavides, L. Manzanilla, and L. Mirambel, coords., 111–25. Mexico City: Instituto Nacional de Antropología e Historia.

Luna Erreguerena, P. 2006. Arqueología subacuática y biología marina. *Revista Ciencia y Desarrollo* 32(197):45–49.

Luna Erreguerena, P., and L. Carrillo Márquez. 2005. Banco Chinchorro. Retos en torno a la conservación, manejo y disfrute del patrimonio mixto (natural y cultural). *Hereditas* 11(1):26–39.

Luna Erreguerena, P., and R. M. Roffiel, eds. 2001. *Memorias del Congreso Científico de Arqueología Subacuática ICOMOS*. Mexico City: Instituto Nacional de Antropología e Historia.

Nagelkerken, W. 1985. Preliminary report on the determination of the location of the historical anchorage at Orange Bay, St. Eustatius, Netherlands Antilles. In *Proceedings of the Sixteenth Conference on Underwater Archaeology*, P. F. Johnston, ed., 60–76. Corpus Christi, TX: Society for Historical Archaeology.

Nagelkerken, W. 1989. Survey of the Dutch frigate *Alphen*, which exploded and sank in 1778 in the harbour of Curaçao. In *Proceedings of the Thirteenth International Congress for Caribbean Archaeology*, E. Ayubi and J. Haviser, eds., 771–92. Willemstad, Curaçao: Archaeological-Anthropological Institute of the Netherlands Antilles.

Nagelkerken, W. 1998. Nineteenth-century Dutch Pearlware recovered in the harbor of Curaçao, Netherlands Antilles. In *Underwater Archaeology*, L. E. Babits, C. Fach, and R. Harris, eds., 104–10. Corpus Christi, TX: Society for Historical Archaeology.

Nagelkerken, W., and E. Ayubi. 1997. Underwater cultural resource management in the Netherlands Antilles. Paper presented at the 30th annual Society for Historical Archaeology Conference, January 8–12, Corpus Christi, Texas.

Neville, J. C., R. S. Neyland, and J. M. Parrent. 1992. The search for Columbus's last ships: the 1991 field season. In *Underwater Archaeology Proceedings from the Society for Historical Archaeology Conference*, D. H. Keith and T. L. Carrell, eds., 148–51. Kingston, Jamaica: Society for Historical Archaeology.

Pateman, M. 2004. The evolution of the protection of underwater cultural heritage in the Bahamas. In *Patrimonio Cultural Subacuático/Underwater Cultural Heritage*, V. Marín, ed., 46–47. Havana: UNESCO.

Report on the Status of the Convention for Safeguarding Underwater Cultural Heritage. 1998. Tenth Meeting of the Forum of Ministers of Culture and Officials Responsible for Cultural Policy of Latin America and the Caribbean, December 4–5, Bridgetown, Barbados.

Santo Domingo Declaration. 1998. Forum of ministers of culture and officials responsible for cultural policy of Latin America and the Caribbean: First meeting of the technical commission on underwater cultural heritage, June 16.

Smith, Jr., C. E., and E. C. Harris. 2002. Underwater cultural heritage in Bermuda. In *International Handbook of Underwater Archaeology*, C. Ruppe and J. Barstad, eds., 299–312. New York: Kluwer Academic/Plenum Press.

Smith, R. C. 1981. The Maritime Heritage of the Cayman Islands: Contributions in Nautical Archaeology. Unpublished MA thesis, Texas A&M University, College Station.

Smith, R. C. 1988a. The voyages of Columbus: The search for his ships. In *Ships and Shipwrecks of the Americas*, G. F. Bass, ed., 33–44. London: Thames and Hudson.

Smith, R. C. 1988b. Treasure ships of the Spanish Main: The Iberian-American maritime empires. In *Ships and Shipwrecks of the Americas*, G. F. Bass, ed., 85–106. London: Thames and Hudson.

Smith, R. C. 1993. *Vanguard of Empire*. Oxford: Oxford University Press.

Smith, R. C. 2000. *The Maritime Heritage of the Cayman Islands*. Gainesville: University Press of Florida.

UNESCO Convention on the Protection of the Underwater Cultural Heritage. 2001. Paris: UNESCO. Available online at http://portal.unesco.org/en/ev.php-URL_ID=13520&URL_DO=DO_TOPIC&URL_SECTION=201.html (accessed May 23, 2008).

UNESCO. 2004. *Patrimonio Cultural Subacuático. América Latina y el Caribe/Underwater Cultural Heritage*. Havana: UNESCO.

UNESCO/ICUCH/Ministry of Culture of Colombia Heritage Direction (w/d) Memoirs. Regional workshop seminar of Latin American and the Caribbean community about UNESCO's Convention on the Protection of the Underwater Cultural Heritage. Bogota: UNESCO.

Valentini, M. P. 2004. Reflections from under the water. In *Patrimonio Cultural Subacuático/Underwater Cultural Heritage*, V. Marín, ed., 104–11. Havana: UNESCO.

CHAPTER 2

The Submerged Cultural Heritage in Mexico

Pilar Luna Erreguerena

INTRODUCTION

Mexico's experience with managing terrestrial cultural heritage began more than 200 years ago, when the so-called Aztec calendar was found in downtown Mexico City. Since then, official and social awareness regarding the existence and value of this cultural legacy and the importance of protecting it have been built in a gradual but strong way. Mexican cultural patrimony is under the care of the Instituto Nacional de Antropología e Historia (National Institute of Anthropology and History, INAH), created in 1939 as an official agency to protect, study, and conserve cultural remains throughout the nation. One of INAH's first tasks was to start an inventory of cultural heritage sites, a project that has continued until the present. By 2000, there were more than 30,000 land sites registered across the country, ranging from hunters' seasonal camps to pre-Columbian ceremonial sites and cities. However, the register represents only 15% of the estimated 200,000 sites (Martínez Muriel 2000:16–17).

Since its creation, INAH, which has centers in all the states, has undertaken many archaeological projects throughout Mexico and has founded two schools to train anthropologists, archaeologists, linguistics, ethnohistorians, and curators: the Escuela Nacional de Antropología e Historia (National School of Anthropology and History, ENAH) and the Escuela Nacional de Conservación, Restauración y Museografía Manuel del Castillo Negrete (National School of Conservation, Restoration and Museography Manuel del Castillo Negrete). Among INAH's main goals is dissemination of knowledge concerning national patrimony through exhibits, publications, lectures, videos, web sites, etc. It runs 108 museums throughout the country: five national, thirty regional, and seventy-three local and on-site. INAH is also involved in supporting a national program to create community museums, of which there are now 180 (Fernández and Montemayor 2000:70–87).

In contrast, the submerged cultural heritage found in marine and continental waters, which comprises prehistoric, pre-Columbian, and colonial vestiges, has been almost ignored. For many years, only treasure hunters and divers benefited from the extensive underwater remains, although it is as rich and vast as Mexico's terrestrial cultural heritage. Fortunately, the situation changed radically in February 1980 when INAH created the Departamento de Arqueología Subacuática (Underwater Archaeology Department), which was promoted to a vice-directorate in 1995. The department's aims are to protect, preserve, research, and disseminate Mexico's submerged legacy.

INAH PROJECTS

The first Mexican underwater archaeologists were self-taught and had to work almost "by ear." The guidance and assistance of North American colleagues from the Institute of Nautical Archaeology and from Ships of Discovery, both based in Texas, were of major importance. From 1980 to 1990, several projects in marine and inner waters were completed with only five archaeologists. By 1993, only two were still in the field and it was obvious that something had to be done to avoid the extinction of Mexican underwater archaeology. It was urgent to find young archaeologists with a passion to defend and study the underwater heritage.

To solve the problem, the first underwater archaeology Master's-level course was offered in Mexico City during 1994, including a field season in the Caribbean. This marked the beginning of a new stage in national underwater archaeology. Thirty professors from Mexico, the United States, and Canada shared their knowledge and experience with twenty undergraduate students of archaeology and conservation. All students graduated and most have collaborated in INAH's underwater archaeological work (Luna Erreguerena 2000). Another important change was that INAH's Subdirección de Arqueología Subacuática (Underwater Archaeology Vice-Directorate) increased its participation in international forums such as the Advisory Council on Underwater Archaeology (ACUA), the International Committee on the Underwater Cultural Heritage (ICUCH) from ICOMOS and UNESCO.

The third important change was that major research projects were initiated: (1) the 1630–1631 New Spain fleet research project; (2) the Inventory and diagnosis of submerged cultural resources in the Gulf of Mexico; and (3) the Underwater Archaeological Atlas for recording, studying, and protecting cenotes (sinkholes) in the Yucatan Peninsula. A more recent project entitled Special programs of the Subdirección de Arqueología Subacuática includes five programs: (1) attention to reports of cultural material findings, (2) dissemination, (3) training, (4) conservation of archaeological material recovered from submerged sites, and (5) agreements for national and international collaboration.

Fleet and Inventory Projects

The New Spain fleet Project began in 1995 with intensive archival research in Mexico, Spain, and Cuba. Its main goals are the location, research, recovery, and preservation of the remains of the New Spain 1630–1631 fleet; the historic reconstruction of the events that took place before, during, and after the wreck; and the analysis of the trans-Atlantic navigation processes related to 17th-century maritime accidents. Several of the ships were wrecked in 1631 in the Gulf of Mexico, en route to Spain with one of the most important cargoes of that time fifteen months after they sailed from Cádiz.

The fleet's flagships were *Nuestra Señora del Juncal* and *Santa Teresa*, which were carrying a significant part of the cargo. Although the project is aimed at studying the fleet as a whole, we have given more attention to *Nuestra Señora del Juncal*, because we have survivors' testimonies regarding the approximate area where the sinking occurred. Since the 1970s, the existence of such information has attracted numerous groups of treasure hunters, mainly foreigners, who have tried by all means to obtain permits to exploit shipwrecks in Mexican waters. All of these have been stopped by INAH.

In six field seasons (1997–2006), specialists have participated from national and international institutions, as well as students, specialized divers, and local fishermen. We have worked with a remote sensing system called ESPADAS (Equipments and Systems of the Platform for the Acquisition of Archaeological Submerged Data), designed with the assistance of the Submerged Cultural Resources Unit from the U.S. National Park Service and based on their ADAP (Archaeological Data Acquisition Platform) system. So far, 203 magnetic anomalies have been located and recorded. Of these, eighty-two contain cultural material visible on the seabed and date from the 16th century to the present. None of these belong to the fleet, but they have enriched our project, Inventory and diagnosis of submerged cultural resources in the Gulf of Mexico, which was initiated in 1997 at the same time as the first field season of the fleet project.

Cenotes and Inundated Caves in the Yucatan Peninsula

The third INAH project is the Underwater Archaeological Atlas for recording, studying, and protecting cenotes (sinkholes) in the Yucatan

Peninsula, the aim of which is to record, study, and protect cenotes in the Yucatan Peninsula. It was initiated in 1999 after reports made by cave divers regarding findings of prehistoric, pre-Hispanic, and colonial material in the states of Yucatan and Quintana Roo, where there are thousands of cenotes and inundated caves. As a result of four field seasons, important material has been recovered, including bones of Pleistocene fauna, human remains dating from more than 10,000 years ago, Mayan skulls, skeletons and ceramics, and remains of bonfires lit thousand of years ago when the cave was dry.

To optimize time and resources, a bevy of multidisciplinary specialists study the materials in a field laboratory. Besides underwater archaeologists, there are physical anthropologists, palaeontologists, curators, biologists, hydrologists, and others. Preservation *in situ* is always the first choice. However, elements that need further study or are in danger of looting or destruction are recovered and taken to Mexico City's laboratories for more intensive treatment and analysis. Some of the material is also under study in Mexican, North American, and British laboratories.

Among the most important findings to date are the presence of early inhabitants in some of the submerged caves in Quintana Roo (González et al., Chapter 7) and the conclusion that it is possible that Mayan people used these bodies of water not only for offerings to their gods but also as mortuary deposits (Rojas et al., Chapter 8). Another significant accomplishment is that the Instituto de Investigaciones Antropológicas (Institute of Anthropological Research) at the Universidad Nacional Autónoma de México (National Autonomous University of Mexico, UNAM) made the first facial reconstruction of a Mayan individual with intentional cranial deformation using a Mayan skull from the cenote San Antonio in Yucatan, which probably dates from about A.D. 600. This study was showcased in a documentary entitled "Mysteries of Yucatan," made and transmitted repeatedly since July 2002 by the Discovery Channel and by a local cultural TV channel.

Five Special Programs

Although the project Special programs of the Subdirección de Arqueología Subacuática only began in 2003, it has already achieved important goals. Its five programs have been applied in several parts of the country but have been developed most extensively in the state of Campeche, in the Mayan Peninsula, where many sites have been detected and recorded in coastal waters with the support of local fishermen and guides. Dissemination of information about cultural heritage is made through lectures, power-point presentations, exhibits, and interviews in the local press, radio, and television. Annual training by specialists from Mexico, Canada, and the United States has been given not only to members of INAH's Subdirección de Arqueología Subacuática, but also to diving instructors, fishermen, and other local community members who collaborate in our projects. Treatment of material recovered in these waters is under way at the main laboratory of the local university. Finally, there has been collaboration with public and private institutions as well as other sectors of local community.

PROTECTING CULTURAL HERITAGE

Mexico has signed and ratified several international treaties, such as the United Nations Convention Law of the Sea (UNCLOS), approved in December 1982 and ratified in 1983, but has not created a specific law regarding underwater cultural heritage. However, INAH has operated through the Ley Federal sobre Monumentos y Zonas Arqueológicos, Artísticos e Históricos (Federal Law on Archaeological, Artistic, and Historical Monuments and Zones) (INAH 1972) and its Disposiciones Reglamentarias para la Investigación Arqueológica en México (Regulations for Archaeological Research in Mexico) (INAH 1977) to control archaeological investigation and to avoid looting and damage to the national patrimony.

Although the federal law refers to the cultural heritage in general, the submerged cultural heritage has been specifically taken into consideration within the regulations. In the case of Spanish shipwrecks dating from colonial times, a principle called "reversion" is applied, meaning that all Spanish properties in Mexico that were not negotiated became national property from the moment Spain recognized Mexico's Independence (Luna Erreguerena 1996).

INAH has a Council of Archaeology, which is the national body authorized to receive, evaluate, and approve or reject any archaeological project in Mexican territory, land or water, according to the Reglamento del Consejo de Arqueología (Norms of the Council of Archaeology) (INAH 1978) and the above-mentioned federal law and regulations. It can also stop any authorized project that is not fulfilling the stated requirements. The council has played an important role in our on-going struggle against treasure hunters.

According to the cited federal law, INAH is responsible for the protection, research, and conservation of all cultural heritage dating up to the end of the 19th century and includes underwater cultural patrimony. However, there have been cases in which, despite the Consejo de Arqueología decision to deny a permit, treasure hunters have ignored INAH's refusal and have taken their proposals to different government agencies, including the Supreme Court of Justice. Their argument is that the federal law is not clear enough. The Supreme Court's verdict categorically stated that, according to Article 2 of the Ley General de Bienes Nacionales (General Law of National Properties) (2004), cultural material found in national waters is considered public property belonging to the nation and, therefore, no one can dispose of it (www.camaradediputados.gob.mx).

Another important law is the Ley de Navegación (Law of Navigation) (2004). Article 130 states that maritime derelicts located in national waters and containing archaeological, historical, or cultural material, according to the Ley Federal sobre Monumentos y Zonas Arqueológicos, Artísticos e Históricos, are property of the nation. Additionally, whoever makes the finding is obliged to immediately inform the maritime authorities and officially declare the findings to the cited authority within twenty-four hours after arrival in port (www.camaradediputados.gob.mx). Although the federal law and its regulations have been applied successfully so far, UNESCO's Convention on the Protection of Underwater Cultural Heritage (discussed below) will be an important tool to reinforce these legal instruments that Mexico has in this matter.

Before underwater archaeology was recognized as a special area within the INAH, some recoveries had been made by assorted groups of divers who collected colonial material from shipwrecks in the Gulf of Mexico and the Mexican Caribbean and pre-Columbian objects from continental waters such as the Cenote Sagrado (Sacred Sinkhole) of Chichén-Itzá in Yucatan, the Manantial de la Media Luna (Half Moon Spring) in the state of San Luis Potosí, and the two lagoons formed in the crater of a volcano known as the Nevado de Toluca or Xinantécatl. Most of that material remained as personal trophies or souvenirs, either in Mexico or overseas. Because they were never conserved, some objects have totally disintegrated or show an advanced state of deterioration (Luna Erreguerena 2002).

Although INAH's Council of Archaeology has been able to stop major treasure hunters, minor looting continues. There have been a few cases in which this minor looting has been detected. For instance, in 1999 some divers went into a cenote in Cozumel and took out some pieces. INAH's Center in Quintana Roo was informed; individuals there notified the local police; and the divers were sent to jail. This probably would not have happened earlier, before the profession of underwater archaeology had successfully raised people's consciousness about defending their cultural heritage.

MEXICO AND THE UNESCO CONVENTION

In 1986, Mexican historian Luis Villoro wrote in the book *UNESCO at the XXI Century's Threshold*: "The presence of Mexico at UNESCO has always been an important one. Mexico has participated in an active way in most of UNESCO programs and has a wide prestige in all its bodies. Mexico's position toward this Organisation has always been a supportive one and has been manifested in moments of crisis" (53–54). Twenty years ago, nobody could imagine that UNESCO would cross the threshold of the 21st century with the adoption of such an important document as the Convention on the Protection of Underwater Cultural Heritage.

In 2003, the same year as the Fifth World Archaeological Congress in Washington, DC, the theme of the World's Day of Monuments and Sites, originally declared by UNESCO on April 18, 1982, was The Underwater Cultural Heritage—Stories under the Sea. This allowed people all over the world to learn more about the existence and value of this legacy and supported our efforts in our own countries regarding the convention's ratification. As a member of the Mexican delegation, I had the privilege of participating in several of the meetings that took place at UNESCO's headquarters and was able to express my country's position about such important issues as warships, jurisdiction, and public access to sites. The exchange of ideas, knowledge, and experience with other experts, especially from those at ICUCH ICOMOS, ACUA, and the Society for Historical Archaeology's UNESCO Committee was certainly an enriching experience.

At the end of the fourth meeting of experts, Mexico voted in favor of the text of the convention. In November 2001, at the 31st General Conference, UNESCO adopted the document. Before approving ratification, INAH named a commission to evaluate the convention from a technical and academic perspective. The final report asserted that there was no obstacle for the ratification (INAH 2003). Further, the legal implications were carefully weighed by other proper authorities. Official commissions verified that none of the convention's articles would be against or contradictory with national laws or interfere with national sovereignty. This was important because, once ratified and adopted, the convention would occupy a significant place in the Mexican arena and would be superior to other national laws.

Finally, on April 25, 2006, the National Congress approved the ratification of the convention. The notification was published in the government's Diario Oficial de la Federación (2006:15) (Federation's Official Publication) on June 2, 2006 and on July 4, Ambassador Pablo Latapí Sarre delivered Mexico's ratification to UNESCO's General Director M. Matsuura. Thus, Mexico became the eighth country to ratify this important document and will be part of the group that, according to the convention,

> may establish a Scientific and Technical Advisory Body composed of experts nominated by the States Parties with due regard to the principle

of equitable geographical distribution and the desirability of a gender balance ... that shall appropriately assist the Meeting of States Parties in questions of a scientific or technical nature regarding the implementation of the Rules (UNESCO 2006).

Ratifying the convention is only one part of the equation. The other and equally vital aspect will be the ways in which managers and underwater archaeologists, supported by authorities, will apply the principles stated in this historic document. INAH's underwater archaeology area has a great responsibility to spread information about the importance of UNESCO's Convention and Mexico's position regarding specific items or articles that have a more direct effect on our underwater cultural heritage among government ministries, federal and state agencies, national organizations, institutions, and individuals. A power-point presentation was made to support the process of ratification. Lectures about UNESCO's Convention have been and will be given to professionals, diving groups, fishermen communities, and the general public, especially in those places where underwater archaeology projects are occurring now, such as the states of Campeche, Yucatan, and Quintana Roo, in the Yucatan Peninsula, Veracruz in the Gulf of Mexico, and Baja California on the Pacific Ocean. Copies of the Spanish version of the convention have been distributed.

Since 1980, when INAH created its underwater archaeological area, projects in marine and continental waters have followed many of the principles stated in UNESCO's Convention (e.g., a multidisciplinary, inter-institutional, and international approach and creation of a bridge of cooperation between institutions and individuals from countries such as Argentina, Colombia, Honduras, Uruguay, Canada, and the United States, including Puerto Rico). This has allowed better training of young archaeologists and curators as well as the transfer of advanced technology. Also, a continuing effort has been made to raise consciousness regarding the value of this patrimony and the need to protect it against damage and commercial exploitation. Cooperation among local divers, fishermen, and authorities has been achieved in some cases. Other aspects of Mexican underwater archaeology that meet the UNESCO Convention's rules are as follows: nonintrusive work, *in situ* preservation as the first option, special protection of natural environment in cases where this may be affected by the archaeological work, and long-term preservation of recovered objects.

INAH is convinced that the convention is an international instrument that will provide a uniform ruling criterion for those countries that ratify it. Also, it will benefit those nations without or limited legislation about their underwater cultural heritage. Given the world's many problems at this time, underwater cultural heritage could become as menaced and damaged as other cultural legacies. We must be aware that its preservation will require international cooperation and responsible work to consolidate what has been gained until now and to move on to the next step. In this sense, UNESCO's Convention will play an important role. Its implementation will certainly be one of the major challenges and benefits in the 21st century.

OBSTACLES AND ACHIEVEMENTS

Among the main obstacles we have faced have been insufficient funds, lack of qualified archaeologists, and high costs of a proper vessel for offshore research. From mid-1995 to mid-1998, we received important economic support from the Fideicomiso para el Rescate de Pecios (Trust for the Recovery of Shipwrecks), but from 1998 aid was significantly reduced and finally canceled in 2002. Since then, we have knocked on many doors seeking funds. However, it has been the financial support from INAH that has kept Mexican underwater archaeologists in the water. Sometimes we have received support from state governments, ministries, private associations, companies, and even individuals.

Although we have focused on training underwater archaeologists and curators, most of the people who took the 1994 course are gone and there is still a lack of qualified personnel. New people have come and training goes on, but it is not enough if we consider the magnitude and complexity of the projects we are involved in. Besides the need for good archaeologists with high ethical standards, divers must be highly trained, be able to use mixed gases, and have multiple credentials (i.e., deep diving, cavern diving, and full cave diving).

Another major problem has been obtaining appropriate vessels for our field seasons. In 1997, for the first campaign of the New Spain fleet and the inventory projects, we hired the ship *Oceatec*. Later, ironically, this ship was sold to North American treasure hunters who applied to work in Mexican waters but were rejected by INAH. Because of the support of the national university, we were able to use the oceanographic research vessel *Justo Sierra* for the 1998 field season, but the rent is quite high. Our 1999 field season at the Sound of Campeche had to be cancelled at the last minute for lack of a proper vessel. There was only a partial field season in Veracruz, using a ship borrowed from the Ministry of Communications and Transport. In this case, as there was no room on board for the researchers and their equipment, a base station had to be installed in a local hotel. In spite of these limitations and with the help of colleagues from the USA/NPS Submerged Cultural Resources Unit, we located and recorded seven magnetic anomalies, of which cultural material was visible in just two cases. One of these corresponds to the

US *Somers*, a North American warship sunk in 1846 during the War of Intervention (known in the United States as the Mexican-American War). The first digital image of this vessel was obtained in that field season through side scan sonar.

Fighting treasure hunters has been another obstacle because of the high investment of time and energy this constant threat requires. Despite these and other challenges, Mexican underwater archaeology has matured and it is important to note some of our achievements:

- development of Mexican underwater archaeology and contribution to the knowledge of national past;
- raising awareness regarding the existence and the importance of a cultural heritage that few people previously valued;
- location and record of ninety-five sites containing cultural material in marine waters;
- design and application of new methodologies, especially with work in inundated caves;
- location of three sites dating from the 16th century;
- recovery of the oldest (16th-century) bronze cannon found in American waters;
- biological, sediment, and physic-chemical parameter studies in the most important sites;
- correction in modern maps of the locations of keys and reefs in the Gulf of Mexico;
- initiation of an underwater archaeological atlas of the Yucatan Peninsula;
- compilation of important archival material and the creation of a library specializing in underwater archaeology and related topics as well as navigation in the 17th century; and
- dissemination of Mexican underwater archaeology in national and international academic forums and mass media, including the preparation of three videos and comparative catalogs of pre-Columbian and colonial artifacts as well as the publication of an extended article about the cenotes project published in 2003 by the *National Geographic* magazine (Vesilind 2003:72–92).

As we all know, life is made up of cycles. This has been very true regarding the history of Mexican underwater archaeology. It is always a sowing time, with good but difficult harvests. We need to continue to be creative to keep moving ahead. Plans exist. Besides our own commitment, our colleagues' and friends' support will, as usual, be a valuable inspiration and a source of strength in helping us fulfill this task. Only through a joint effort of governments, specialists, and diverse sectors of society will the survival of the world's cultural heritage, either on land or underwater, be guaranteed.

REFERENCES

Diario Oficial de la Federación. 2006. *Órgano del Gobierno Constitucional de los Estados Unidos Mexicanos*, vol. 633, no. 2, June 2 (1st section), p. 15. Mexico City.

Fernández, M. A., and E. Montemayor. 2000. *Memorial. Patrimonio de Todos*, vol. 2, Los espacios de la memoria. 70–87. Mexico City: Consejo Nacional para la Cultura y las Artes/Instituto Nacional de Antropología e Historia/Editorial Espejo de Obsidiana.

Instituto Nacional de Antropología e Historia (INAH). 1972. *Ley Federal sobre Monumentos y Zonas Arqueológicos, Artísticos e Históricos*. Mexico City: Instituto Nacional de Antropología e Historia.

Instituto Nacional de Antropología e Historia (INAH). 1977. *Disposiciones Legales del Patrimonio Cultural*. Mexico City: Instituto Nacional de Antropología e Historia.

Instituto Nacional de Antropología e Historia (INAH). 1978. *Reglamento del Consejo de Arqueología y Disposiciones Reglamentarias para la Investigación Arqueológica en México*. Mexico City: Instituto Nacional de Antropología e Historia.

Instituto Nacional de Antropología e Historia (INAH). 2003. Internal documents regarding the feasibility of ratifying the UNESCO Convention from an academic, technical, and legal point of view. Mexico City.

Ley General de Bienes Nacionales. 2004. Available online at www.camaradediputados.gob.mx (accessed March 7, 2008).

Ley de Navegación. 2004. Available online at www.camaradediputados.gob.mx (accessed March 7, 2008).

Luna Erreguerena, P. 1996. Preservación del patrimonio cultural sumergido. Unpublished paper presented at the Cámara de Diputados del H. Congreso de la Unión, February 8, Mexico City.

Luna Erreguerena, P. 2000. La importancia del patrimonio cultural sumergido. In *Memorial. Patrimonio de Todos*, vol. 8, A. Martínez, D. Ortega and C. Vader, eds., 233–45. Mexico City: Consejo Nacional para la Cultura y las Artes/Instituto Nacional de Antropología e Historia/Editorial Espejo de Obsidiana.

Luna Erreguerena, P. 2002. Mexico. A country with a rich underwater legacy. In *International Handbook of Underwater Archaeology*, C. Ruppe and J. Barstad, eds., 269–78. New York: Kluwer Academic/Plenum Press.

Martínez Muriel, A. 2000. La arqueología en México. In *Memorial. Patrimonio de Todos*, vol. 8, A. Martínez, D. Ortega and C. Vader, eds., 13–17. Mexico City: Consejo Nacional para la Cultura y las Artes/Instituto Nacional de Antropología e Historia/Editorial Espejo de Obsidiana.

UNESCO. 2006. Available online at http://portal.unesco.org (accessed March 7, 2008).

Vesilind, P. J. 2003. Las tumbas acuáticas de los mayas. *National Geographic en Español*, October, 72–92. Mexico City: Editoral Televisa.

Villoro, L. 1986. La UNESCO, crisis y perspectivas. In *México en la UNESCO en el Umbral del Siglo XXI*, 53–54. Mexico City: Cuadernos SEP/CONALMEX.

CHAPTER 3

Nuestra Señora del Juncal: Her Story and Her Shipwreck

Patricia Meehan H. and Flor Trejo Rivera

INTRODUCTION

Nuestra Señora del Juncal was the designated *capitana* (flagship) of a fleet that sailed to New Spain in 1630 under General Miguel de Echazarreta. When the general died only a few days before departing San Juan de Ulúa, Veracruz, for the voyage home, Admiral Manuel de Serrano assumed command of the fleet. His ship, *Santa Teresa*, then took over as *capitana*, and *Nuestra Señora del Juncal* became the *almiranta* (vice-admiral's ship).

The fleet departed on October 14, 1631. By then, it was north winds season and every sailor knew that it was not a good time to navigate safely. One of the survivors of the shipwreck, a Jesuit clergyman, testified that the ship had been badly loaded and was leaking even before they left (Real Academia de la Historia 1632).

On the fourth day of sailing, the fleet was hit by a northern windstorm, causing it to take on water. Three or four days later, it was hit by yet another north wind. At this time, the stem broke and the stern side was damaged. As a result, the ship began taking on even more water. Crewmen and passengers alike made great efforts to seal the gaps and prevent flooding, but the water level continued to rise to two *palmos* (418 mm/1.369 ft) above the hold deck beams.

After a few days, the situation became critical and the main mast had to be cut to keep the ship stable and lighten her. Next, the artillery, merchandise chests, old rigging, galley, and spare sails were jettisoned, but to no avail. The vessel was so damaged that it "spit bolts." The crew attempted to fasten the sides with lead slabs and wooden sheets, but the flooding continued. As *Nuestra Señora del Juncal* could no longer be handled, she came across. Hitting the water resulted in even more damage, and "all the wood from the inside and outside was shaking" (AGI, México 360 1631a).

After rolling on her starboard side, *Nuestra Señora del Juncal*'s stern rose as she plunged to the depths. At the last moment, the small lifeboat, which had become stuck while trying to rescue the principal passengers, was cut loose. The constable was able to sever the cable that tied it to the portside and the water hitting *Nuestra Señora del Juncal*'s stern-castle pushed it away from the sinking ship. The lifeboat managed to escape the whirlpool made by the stern, the last portion of the ship to sink. It was All Saints Eve (October 31), and thirty-nine people reached the lifeboat and were saved (AGI, México 360 1631a).

Historical research has made it possible to partially reconstruct the shipwreck and to delve deeper into the historical context surrounding it. This research has made it evident that since the construction of *Nuestra Señora del Juncal*, throughout its useful life and up to its loss, social, political, and economic factors played important roles. This chapter goes beyond the shipwreck as an event and interprets the life of the ship within the context of situations surrounding her and Spain's policies regarding the West Indies trade, its control, and protection. It examines the fleet system and how it was functioning when *Nuestra Señora del Juncal* was built and in use.

An important consideration for this research is the building of the ship. *Nuestra Señora del Juncal* was built when the Spanish Crown was attempting to control the shipbuilding industry to meet its needs and expectations. Therefore, to understand the ship's building specifications such as typology, size, and shape, historical documents were analyzed. Archival research has also shed some light on several aspects of the ship's life and the modifications applied to its structure. This research suggests reasons why the ship wrecked. Once the shipwreck is located and archaeological research is carried out, it may help us understand the information obtained from the material remains and from the analysis of the deposition and postdeposition processes of the shipwreck site.

AN EMPIRE IN CRISIS

The 1630 New Spain fleet was under the command of General Miguel de Echazarreta and Admiral Manuel Serrano. The convoy was comprised of thirteen ships loaded with precious metals, money to pay and maintain the military personnel in Havana and Puerto Rico, dyes, textiles, leather, fine woods, chocolate, and medicinal herbs (AGI, México 31 1631b). The cargo carried by the fleet on its return voyage was needed to fill the empire's coffers. Three long years had gone by since the last shipment of precious metals and merchandise had been received from New Spain.

The fleet had been anchored at the fortress of San Juan de Ulúa in Veracruz since October 1630. The preparations for departure involved various tasks and logistics that complicated the process. Furthermore, every movement had to be authorized by the king through permits emitted by the Casa de la Contratación (House of Trade), both of which were located on the other side of the Atlantic.

Previous tragic events influenced the preventive measures taken before the 1630 fleet's departure. The 1628 New Spain fleet, under the command of Juan de Benavides, was attacked by thirty-two Dutch pirate ships off the Cuban coast on its return voyage. It was the first time an entire fleet had fallen into enemy hands (Phillips 1991:19–25). This event inspired the Dutch pirates to be even bolder and more daring in American waters, and the Spanish sailors seriously questioned their ability to defend themselves.

The repercussions of these events were evident in the precautions taken before the departure of the fleet in October 1631. At the beginning of that year, Felipe IV received news that the Dutch were arming several warships. The king suspected that they were planning to attack the fleet that was about to set sail from Veracruz and this all but paralyzed the preparations. In several letters, the king warned the Marquis of Cerralbo, viceroy of New Spain, and Miguel de Echazarreta, the fleet's general, to take all necessary precautions, not only in the Gulf of Mexico, but also in Cuban waters. He ordered General Tomás de Larraspuru, a captain with an excellent military record, to secure the Veracruz-Havana route. He was to advise General Echazarreta when to depart and when and where to rendezvous with the ships that would escort them safely to the Cuban coast (AGI, México 3 1632; AGN 1631).

In January 1631, rumors of enemy ships reached Spain, and two months later news arrived from Havana that Dutch pirates were in the Caribbean. The paperwork required for departure was given top priority, but word from General Larraspuru did not arrive. The merchants began to load the cargo in March, but by July there still had been no news, so they ceased their preparations. On September 13, General Echazarreta's long-awaited permission to weigh anchor finally arrived. He was told to meet Larraspuru on the 28th of that same month at "the capes" (probably Cape San Antonio and Cape Corrientes off the southern point of the island of Cuba), where he would be waiting to safeguard their route to Havana (AGI, México 3:1632). At the end of September, the fleet continued on to San Juan de Ulúa. General Echazarreta was doing everything possible to speed things up but was faced with interminable procedures and paperwork.

General Echazarreta, who had been ill since leaving Spain, died in Veracruz on October 12, 1631. Admiral Manuel Serrano, the fleet's pilot and General Martín de Vallecilla, who had just arrived from Spain with his convoy, decided to depart in spite of the difficulties and the threat of bad weather (AGI, Santo Domingo 133 1631). The convoy headed for Castile was loaded with tax money collected over the two years that no fleet had sailed. Even the insignia ships carried a considerable amount of precious metals and articles from the West Indies that were highly valued in Europe.

Nuestra Señora del Juncal was not the storm's only victim. Four others—the *capitana Santa Teresa*, two merchantmen, and one frigate—also wrecked. Around eight ships, some badly damaged, were able to reach the safety of different ports.

CONSTRUCTION OF *NUESTRA SEÑORA DEL JUNCAL*

During the 16th and 17th centuries, most of the fleets bound for the West Indies were manufactured on the Cantabrian coast in northern Spain. The majority were built in Biscay and Guipuzcoa Provinces where the shipbuilding tradition went at least as far back as the 12th century (Odriozola Oyarbide 1993:37–38).

Nuestra Señora del Juncal was built in Guipuzcoa, Basque country, from 1622 to 1623 by Antonio de Ubilla. The hull was built in the Fuenterrabía shipyard (AGI, Contratación 4896 1629a; AGI, Contratación 819 1629–1630) and at the end of 1622 it was sent to the Bordalaborda shipyard in the Pasajes Strait to be finished and outfitted (Archivo Histórico de Protocolos de Gipúzkoa [AHPG] 3–451 1622).

At this time, the Spanish Crown protected the Basque shipbuilding industry. Further, government decrees encouraged the construction of armada ships to be placed in the Crown's service. In 1622, the year in which *Nuestra Señora del Juncal* was built, Felipe IV ordered the construction of the Guipuzcoa Naval Squadron and offered loans to shipwrights for the manufacture and outfitting of the ships (Archivo General de Guipúzcoa 1646).

It is possible that Antonio de Ubilla took advantage of this shipbuilding momentum and the availability of materials to build his ship, but he never signed a formal contract with the Crown. Even though he held several public offices during the first decades of the 17th century and (AGS, Guerra y Marina 1011 1630) had family ties in the Indies, Cádiz, Seville, and Madrid, there is no record he had naval or shipbuilding experience. In 1625, he owned a small 38-ton frigate (AHPG, 3–451 1625), but there is no evidence that he or his wife, María de Izaguirre, had previously owned or built any other vessel. Nevertheless, they decided to invest their inheritances in *Nuestra Señora del Juncal*. As soon as the construction and outfitting were completed, they moved her to Cádiz already loaded with a cargo of iron ore and other Basque merchandise (AGI, Contratación 4896 1629a; AGI, Contratación 819 1629–1630).

Soon after arrival in Cádiz, Antonio de Ubilla and his wife gave Juan de Casanova and Domingo de Atallomendia, residents of Cádiz and Seville respectively, power of attorney to sell the ship (AGI, Contratación 819 1624:13v–15v). The vessel was not sold, but became part of a merchant marine fleet commanded by General Gabriel de Chávez that set sail for the West Indies the following year (AGI, Contratación 2899 1605–1626).

17TH-CENTURY SHIPBUILDING

The first part of the 17th century was an important time in shipbuilding history. Until then, the Crown's influence on shipbuilding has been limited to fomenting trade and protection regulations. Designs and methods were not standardized but were based on those of individual craftsmen and shipbuilding guilds that had evolved over centuries of experience in the trade. Different types of vessels were used indiscriminately for all activities. However, the creation of the West Indies Trade Route Guard resulted in the need for specialized vessels and gave rise to a series of discussions as to their ideal features. The Crown realized how important it was to own a complete navy, even though it only owned a few ships and did not have the means to build more. As a result, it had to rely on private vessels that were contracted or confiscated for service.

King Felipe III formulated a series of shipbuilding ordinances to regulate and unify naval construction. The first was published in 1607 and then renewed in 1613 and 1618 (Odriozola Oyarbide 1998:97; Phillips 1991:55). In the opinion of Carla Rahn Phillips (1991:54), the main purpose was to impose more control over the industry and make private shipbuilders toe the line and satisfy the government's needs. The ordinances were intended to regulate the type of ships built, their size and proportions, the origin of the raw materials, and the work force employed. Obviously, the ordinances were not well received by either shipbuilders or seamen. This gave rise to a huge debate in shipbuilding that lasted several years among men with years of experience in navigation and was encouraged by the government. In spite of corrections made on two occasions, the 1618 ordinances also failed—the Basques and northern shipwrights refused to abide by them because of technical and economic considerations. Even the authorities were very cautious about trying to enforce them.

Despite attempts to unify shipbuilding, which certainly occurred to some extent, construction of vessels for the Carrera de Indias (West

Indies trade route) was still highly influenced by the experience and craftsmanship of the shipwrights. *Nuestra Señora del Juncal* was built under the 1618 ordinances, but it is difficult to know her exact building specifications because there are no drawings or plans that give us more detailed descriptions. The ordinances theoretically regulated the construction of the Carrera de Indias vessels, as well as the squadrons guarding the coasts of Spain, but they did not specify a term or typology for the resultant vessels. Although this is not evident in the ordinances, the historical documents show that at that time, there was a difference between a number of different types of ships.

1. Merchantmen that were *naos* or merchant galleons—typology given by Olesa Muñido (1981:23, 142) and Moya Blanco (1981:156)—were built and owned by private shipbuilders. They had a bigger hold for cargo so the main deck was built higher. They should be seaworthy for the trans-Atlantic voyage and be built with special materials and techniques to protect the hulls against deterioration in the warm waters of the Americas.
2. Galleons of the Armada del Mar Océano (squadron of the Royal Navy) were built by the Crown in the royal shipyards or by private shipwrights under contract to the king. The monarch would grant loans, which would have to be paid back during the following four years. During this time, the ships were required to serve in the armada in exchange for a kind of rent. These galleons had a longer keel, shorter draft, and thinner planking.
3. Galleons of the Armada de la Guarda de la Carrera de Indias (West Indies Armada) were also built by the Crown or private shipwrights under contract. The designs of the West Indies galleons were based on three needs. First, they needed strength to stand up in battle, to carry the necessary artillery, and to employ it efficiently and effectively. Second, they needed to transport precious metals. Not to be overlooked was that the crew usually took advantage of the trip to carry other commercial items (Serrano Mangas 1989:30). Third, the galleons needed to navigate in shallow waters, such as the sandbar of Sanlúcar de Barrameda. This was an unavoidable passage on the way to the port of Seville by way of the Guadalquivir River, where many ships had sunk, cargo and all (Serrano Mangas 1989:20–27). Therefore, tonnage and draft became two main issues. Within this category, distinctions were

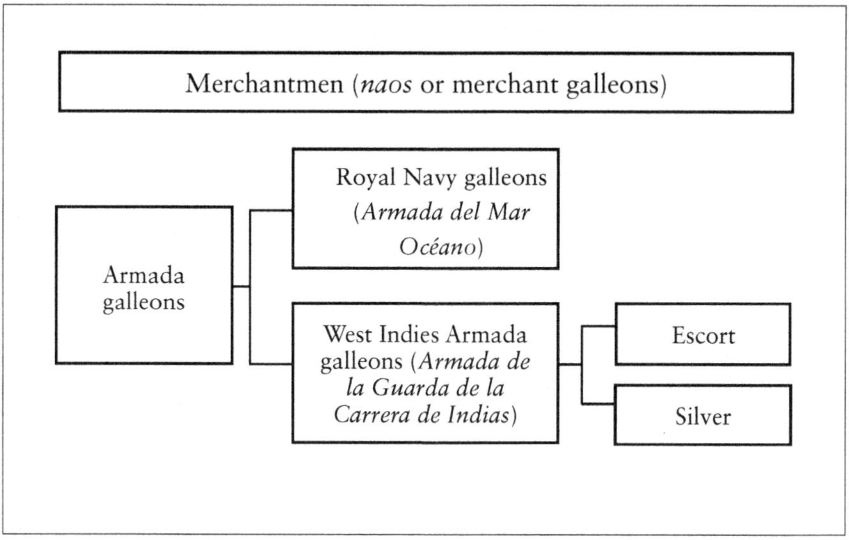

Figure 3.1 High-board ships prevailing in the first third of the 17th century in Spain.

also made between "escort galleons" and "silver galleons," which were better built and stronger that the others because they had to be even more suitable for battle and capable of protecting the precious metal (see Figure 3.1) (Serrano Mangas 1989:20).

According to the study carried out by Serrano Mangas (1989:22) when the *Nuestra Señora del Juncal* was built, the shipbuilding industry reached a kind of fork in the road. The differences between the galleons built for the Armada del Mar Océano squadrons and those destined for the Carrera de Indias increased. Nevertheless, the dissimilarity between the Carrera de Indias galleons and the merchant *naos* is not so clear. They coexisted during the 16th century, maintaining differences in cargo capacity and structure; by the 17th century, however, both had increased their tonnage and assumed similar features (Phillips 1991:73–79). It is difficult to differentiate these as they were used indiscriminately in a wide range of uses.

One of the peculiarities attributed to the galleon was its specialization as a warship. In 1540, Álvaro de Bazán built galleons for the armadas. Although his designs were ultimately not successful, he contributed a great deal to an increased military application. This meant that ships were to be built stronger and reinforced on the inside and to have improved artillery placement. Because of these and other

Table 3.1a Life of *Nuestra Señora del Juncal.*

Date	Events
1622	Antonio de Ubilla built the hull in the Fuenterrabía shipyard.
October 1622	The hull was moved to the Bordalaborda shipyard in the Pasajes Strait.
1623	The construction was completed and she was outfitted.
September 1623	She was sent to Cádiz to be sold or to participate in the West Indies fleets as a merchantman. She was loaded with a cargo of iron ore and other merchandise.
March 1624	Antonio de Ubilla gave Power of Attorney to his son. Antonio de Ubilla, Juan de Casanova, and Domingo de Atallomendia to administrate and/or sell the ship.
July 14, 1624	She traveled as a merchantman in the fleet to New Spain, under the command of General Gabriel de Chávez.
1625	New Spain (port of Veracruz). She was sheathed and received other repairs and modifications.
July 17, 1625	She departed from Veracruz to Havana, Cuba, with the fleet.
1625–1630	She remained in Cádiz, in the Carraca inlet.
October 1626	She received careening (superficial).
December 15, 1626	She was inspected by the officials who were looking for ships to name as flagships and vice-admirals' ships for the New Spain fleet of 1627. She was not selected; nevertheless, the officials recommended some modifications. They were probably not carried out.
August 2–September 30, 1628	Complete careening. She was so deteriorated that she was sinking in the port.
End of 1628	She received an inspection visit to be merchantman in the fleet that would depart for New Spain in 1629.
January 1629	Both fleets destined for New Spain and to South America in 1629 were canceled.
March 9–April 28, 1629	She received an inspection visit to be merchantman in the fleet that would depart for New Spain in 1629.
May 4, 1629	She was confiscated for service as flagship in the fleet destined for New Spain commanded by General Carlos de Ibarra, later substituted by General Miguel de Echazarreta.

Table 3.1a (*continued*)

Date	Events
May–August 1629	Repairs were done on the ship; the masts and the planks of the main deck were replaced.
May 30–end of June 1629	She received another careen, this one ordered by General Carlos de Ibarra.
December 1629	King Felipe IV confirmed the naming of *Nuestra Señora del Juncal* as flagship of the 1630 New Spain fleet.
April 21, 1630	The careening and modifications were concluded. The careening and repairs, as started in the *Avería* contract, were carried out to make her stronger and more seaworthy. The modifications were basically meant to make the ship capable of carrying and using artillery, carrying *azogue* (mercury) on the trip to New Spain and silver on the return trip.
April 30, 1630	The rigging and loading of the cargo began.
July 28, 1630	She departed from Cádiz as flagship of the feet destined for New Spain under the command of General Miguel de Echazarreta.
October 5, 1630	The fleet arrives in the port of Veracruz in New Spain.
First half of 1631	She probably received careening, although this is not confirmed by historic documents.
October 12, 1631	General Miguel de Echazarreta died of illness. Admiral Manuel Serrano took command of the fleet and his ship, the *Santa Teresa,* took over as flagship. *Nuestra Señora del Juncal* became the vice-admiral's ship, commanded by Andres de Aristizaval.
October 14, 1631	The fleet departed from the port of Veracraz toward Havana, where it would meet with the West Indies Armada and the *Tierra Firme* fleet.
October 17, 1631	The fleet was hit by the first north wind. *Nuestra Señora del Juncal* began to take on water.
October 20, 1631	The fleet was hit by another north wind. More flooding occurred. The stern broke and a side of the stern was damaged. Passengers and crew tried to keep water out by scaling the gaps, pumping the bilges, and boiling water with olive jars. They also jettisoned merchandise chests, old cables, and all the spare sails. By night fall, the fleet had dispersed.

Table 3.1b Life of *Nuestra Señora del Juncal*.

October 21, 1631	The flagship signaled to turn toward the coast of Tabasco, but it was impossible. The ship did not respond and took on even more water.
October 22, 1631	The vice-admiral decided to head for the coast of Campeche, instead of attempting to reach Havana.
October 25, 1631	The main mast was cut and jettisoned, as were cannons (six bronze and one iron) from the stern castle and the bow, an anchor, more merchandise chests, and other items.
Around October 27, 1631	More attempts were made to stop water from entering: caulking from the inside and nailing lead sheets on the outside of the hull. But this was not successful; water kept coming in and the hull began spitting bolts.
October 31, 1631	In the morning, the pilot announced there was no possibility of saving the ship. Everyone became unruly and stopped bailing water, so it reached a level of 2 *palmos* (or 408 mm) over the deck-beams. The vice-admiral ordered the sailors to put the lifeboat in the water to save the important passengers and commanders. But this was unsuccessful because they needed the main mast to lift it out. At night, the ship rolled to its starboard side but managed to straighten again. She rolled a second time, but remained on her starboard side. Then she pitched from the bow and started sinking very suddenly, raising her stern. The lifeboat was cut away from the ship and kept afloat. *Nuestra Señora del Juncal* sank, creating a huge in its wake. Only thirty-nine people found their way to the lifeboat and were saved; 311 drowned.

innovations, the Spanish galleon began to evolve but by the end of the first decades of the 17th century, it was still not a true warship (Phillips 1991:76–77). The hull had been fortified and the ship was completely armed. Also, it carried a much larger crew than needed just to sail it but it was also used for transporting commercial cargo (Phillips 1991:79).

At the beginning of the 17th century, merchant *naos* were smaller than the galleons, although there was little difference in the type of structure and rigging. A merchant *nao* could have less fortification and armaments than a galleon of a similar size, but more frames, cannons, and gun ports were often added if necessary (Phillips 1991:79).

To type *Nuestra Señora del Juncal* more accurately, it might be helpful to consider the following points:

1. From the outset, a ship was designed and built in accordance with the function she would be required to carry out. Some of the specific features that were included at the time of construction could not be totally changed, but they could be modified to some extent.
2. Also of importance was who built them: a private shipwright, a private shipwright under contract with the Royal Administration, or the Crown directly.
3. Finally, ships were at times modified to carry out different functions, possibly even changing their typology.

From the information obtained to date, it seems clear that *Nuestra Señora del Juncal* was not built as a warship for the king's armadas. Antonio de Ubilla could have signed a contract with the Crown, because the cost of building a galleon was considerably higher than that of a merchant *nao*, but he clearly built the ship with his own resources hoping to sell her for a profit or to use her as a trade vessel in the merchant marine (see Tables 3.1 and 3.2).

We therefore conclude that *Nuestra Señora del Juncal* was conceived and built as a merchant *nao*. Nevertheless, when she was named *capitana* of the New Spain fleet in 1629, some structural modifications were made to enable her to carry out the new military functions. In this case, it could be said that she became an "escort galleon" for the Armada de la Guarda de la Carrera de Indias. She could never have become a silver galleon because, as Serrano Mangas (1989:22) states, these were designated from the time the keel was mounted in the shipyard and it was impossible to modify them later to make them suitable for carrying silver.

Table 3.2 *Nuestra Señora del Juncal*'s main features.

	***Nuestra Señora del Juncal*'s measurements in codos**	***Nuestra Señora del Juncal*'s measurements in metric system**
Breadth (*manga*)	19 *codos*	10.92 m
Bottom floor (*plan*)	9 *codos*	5.17 m
Draft (*puntal*)	9½ *codos*	5.46 m
Length (*eslora*)	60⅓ *codos*	34.67 m
Keel (*quilla*)	48 *codos*	27.58 m
Space between main and upper deck	3½ *codos*	2.01 m
Tonnage	669 tons	

	Number	**Type**
Decks	3	2 *cubieratas*, 1 *puente corrida*

Masts	4	Main mast, foremast, mizzen, and bowsprit
Sailing rig	2 sets (one in use and one as a spare set)	Main mast: square main mast, square main topmast, possibly square topgallant Foremast: square foremast sail, square top foremast sail Mizzen: lateen mizzen Bowsprit: square spritsail, possibly a spritsail topsail
Cannons	Uncertain between 24 and 30 (twenty-three bronze at least one iron ordinance)	8 demicannon: 16 lb bronze, between 31 and 33 quintales (1,426.31 and 1,518.33 kg) 10 third-cannons: 10 lb bronze, between 21 and 23 *quintales* (966.21 and 1058.23 kg) 5 demiculverins: 10 lb bronze, between 32 and 33 *quintales* (1472.32 and 1.518.33 kg) (AGI, Contratacíon 3868, 1630:1–2), plus other iron artillery.
People on board	350 (thirty-nine survivors; 311 drowned in the shipwreck)	

1 *codo*= 0.5747 m (Caballero 1997:152); 1 *quintal* = 100 Castilian pounds = 46.01 kg (Phillips 1991:338)

AS *CAPITANA* OF THE 1630 FLEET

Since the trans-Atlantic commercial trade route between Spain and the New World was established in the 16th century, the Spanish Crown participated in its regulation. The stakes were high and there was a decided interest in maintaining strict control over trade as well as assuring the safety of the cargos and crews. The fleets not only faced unfavorable weather conditions but continuously risked attack by Dutch, English, and French pirates. These assaults occurred both on the high seas and in the ports of the New World.

Shortly after the first pirate attacks in 1521, each merchant marine fleet was required to add two armed ships for protection, the *capitana* and the *almiranta*. To arm and man these, a special tax called *avería* (average) was levied on merchandise that arrived from the West Indies and other ports. By the 17th century, a squadron called the Armada de la Guarda de la Carrera de Indias had been formally created to escort the merchantmen and transport silver, especially on the return voyages (Caballero Juárez 1997:57–59). The squadron was made up of eight galleons and two or three tenders. In addition, a *capitana*, an *almiranta*, and two tenders accompanied each fleet sailing to New Spain.

Nuestra Señora del Juncal was chosen to serve as *capitana* of the fleet scheduled to set sail in 1629. The loss of the 1628 fleet, together with the news that pirates continued to ambush ships along the trade routes and ports of the West Indies, raised fears about safety. Other complications also made it necessary to postpone the departure date of the *Nuestra Señora del Juncal*'s fleet until the following year.

In theory, the administration of the *avería* designated the flagships and vice-admirals' ships at the beginning of each year once the generals had been named and the allowed tonnage published. The selection process included a previous visit to gauge the ships, as well as assess their condition. The changes or additions needed, such as artillery, supplies, sailors, and military personnel, were duly noted (AGI, Indiferente General 433 1627:fol. 49v).

Theoretically, between 1629 and 1630 the Armada de la Guarda de la Carrera de Indias galleons could not be built abroad and had to comply with the 1618 ordinances. Previously built ships were only selected if their specifications were similar to those mentioned in the latest ordinances (Real Academia de la Historia [1681] 1987:vol. 8, book IV, pp. 31–32). Other recommended requirements of the ships were that "They could not be too old, preferably only one previous voyage. They should be strong and well structured, with good sails and steering, seaworthy and well outfitted with masts, sails, rigging and rudders" (Fernández de Navarrete 1971:vol. 22, doc. 18, fol. 54). Furthermore, they should be capable of carrying cargo and have two gun decks, which were considered sufficient defense in time of need.

The administrators of the Casa de la Contratación were authorized to purchase, order the manufacture of ships, or confiscate them with or without the owner's consent (AGI, Indiferente General 433 1627:fols. 49v–50). Preferably, the ships selected were the property of the royal navies or of shipwrights who had constructed them under contract with the king. But in reality, it was usually necessary to confiscate private merchant vessels because there were not enough warships with the required capacity and characteristics.

One of the main problems faced by the *avería* administrators in 1630 was the scarcity of armada ships and of private ships suitable for use as silver or escort galleons. The armada or the Tierra Firme fleet (destined for South America) that had set sail in April of that year had already taken the few available. To make matters worse, the ships that made the trip the previous year had been forced to winter over in the West Indies. By the end of the 16th century, the shortage of ships had become a problem, but the situation grew worse in the 1620s and 1630s. This was partly because the confiscated vessels were not receiving their rent from the Crown. The shipwrights had to spend so much on outfitting and sailing their ships that they were left without sufficient funds to continue building new ones, even had they been so inclined. This forced the authorities to use ships that did not fulfill the required specifications. It became necessary to use merchantmen as *capitanas* and *almirantas*, even though they were not strong enough. Alterations were improvised to turn them into warships, but they could not really substitute the vessels specifically built for that purpose. Such was the case of *Nuestra Señora del Juncal.*

ADDITIONS AND MODIFICATIONS

Repairs and modifications were carried out continuously throughout a ship's life for different reasons, such as structural repair of damaged parts, modifications to adapt a ship to carry out specific functions, or correction of defects in the original construction. One of the basic repair procedures was careening. Its main objective was to guarantee that the ship was perfectly watertight. It included a strict assessment of all the nails and bolts together with a thorough caulking. There were many types of careening depending on the extensiveness of the procedures. A complete careen required exposing the keel by heaving the ship down on one side; a partial one was limited to the sides of the hull down as far as the waterline (Serrano Mangas 1995:38–39).

After *Nuestra Señora del Juncal* returned from the New Spain in 1625, she remained docked in Cádiz (*Estero de la Carraca*) until she sailed again as part of the 1630 fleet. During this period, she received several careens. The first occurred in October 1626, when repairs were made because of its poor and damaged condition (Archivo Histórico Provincial de Cádiz [AHPC] 5504; 1630a:fols. 53–54v). The next careen we know of occurred from August to September 1628. The ship was in very poor condition; she had taken on so much water that she was about to go under. On this occasion, it was necessary to carry out a full careen (AHPC 5504 1630c:fols. 56–57). This was probably done before she was chosen as *capitana*. Throughout 1629, two more careens were carried out, one during March and April, and the second one throughout the month of June. The Casa de la Contratación and *avería* administrators required this last one after she was designated *capitana* (AHPC 5504 1630b:fols. 55–56).

As the fleet did not set sail in 1629, it is possible that even another careen was required before sailing in 1630. Notice was sent to the *avería* administrators on April 23, 1630, informing them that carpentry and careening was concluded and that loading could begin (AGI, Contratación 4896 1630:fol. 249). Finally, when *Nuestra Señora del Juncal* was in the port of Veracruz in 1631, it should have received a careen, as was stipulated in the *capitana* contract, although no written proof of this has yet been found. It may not have been carried out because the records state that she was taking on water before she left on her final voyage (Real Academia de la Historia 1632:fol. 646).

Nuestra Señora del Juncal also received structural modifications. During her first voyage, while anchored in the port of San Juan de Ulúa waiting to return to Spain, she was sheathed and other "necessary and precise beneficial measures" were done (AGI, Contratación 5117 1629b). Unfortunately, these were not named or described.

Sheathing was often done to reinforce an older ship's internal structure. Serrano Mangas explains that the process of sheathing consisted of lining the hull with planks of wood and reinforcing the structure with a thick wooden belt that ran along the widest wale as well as half way through the total length of the vessel (O'Scanlan 1974:233; Serrano Mangas 1989:34–35). The Diccionario Marítimo Español (Spanish Maritime Dictionary) (O'Scanlan 1974:233) defines *embonar* or sheathe as to add wooden planks or nail slabs on top of the ship's planking from the main wale to the keel to increase the breadth and therefore make it more stable.

Sheathing was also sometimes carried out on Spanish ships that had been built under the 1618 ordinances to compensate for their lack of breadth and to increase the ships' stability. At that time, too, it was customary to raise the breadth as a fraudulent measure to increase the capacity of the holds by reducing the space between decks. This was accomplished by lifting up the main deck, which caused the draft to increase more than advisable and made the sides more convex. These modifications affected the proportions of the vessel. As the keel and frames were neither reinforced nor lengthened, this weakened the frame in comparison to the body it supported. The ship lost strength, speed, and offensive capability. To compensate for this, sheathing was used to increase its beam, displacement and buoyancy, which stabilized the vessel (Serrano Mangas 1985:73–78, 1989:35; Donald Keith, personal communication).

According to the report filed in 1629 by the Conde de Puebla (Count of Puebla), Casa de la Contratación president, *Nuestra Señora del Juncal* had been sheathed in the West Indies, although the reasons for this were not given (AGI, Contratación 5117 1629b). Why was *Nuestra Señora del Juncal*, a ship less than two years old, sheathed and altered? Was it to increase cargo capacity or correct construction defects? We cannot answer these questions with the available information. Basque and Cantabrian shipwrights did not strictly adhere to the ordinances, so it is not certain if her beam was too narrow (Serrano Mangas 1989:35). There is no written evidence that the ship was modified for the purpose of increasing cargo space. Thus, it is certainly worth noting that after her first trans-Atlantic voyage, it was necessary to make alterations, for whatever reason, and it was done in spite of the regulations in effect at that time. The 1618 ordinances prohibited sheathing because it was overused and fraudulent. In fact, they state that ships with sheathing could not be chosen to sail the Carrera de Indias (Real Academia de la Historia [1681] 1987:vol. 8, book IV, pp. 31–32). Nevertheless, this practice continued. Because of the shortage of ships at that time, in 1628 the king published a decree allowing sheathing in those vessels that so required it "because of proportions, adjustments or reinforcements." This decree excluded those ships that had raised the decks (Veitia y Linaje 1981:book II, chapter XIV, para. 10).

When a ship was chosen to serve as *capitana* or *almiranta* for the Armada de la Guarda de la Carrera de Indias, instructions were given regarding its modifications and repairs. The contract with the *avería* administration naming *Nuestra Señora del Juncal* as a *capitana* stated that the owner had to outfit the ship. This included providing the necessary cables, anchors, rigging, sets of nails, pitch, and ballast. The owner was also responsible for the carpentry work on the hull, decks, masts, and spars that had been indicated during the inspection. Finally, the owner had to see that the ship was careened for the voyage.

Some of the work done on the ship was stipulated in the contract. It proposed general modifications to strengthen the vessel, such as fortifying the decks and sides, as well as other necessary repairs (AGI, Contratación

4896 1629a:fols. 221v–222). All kinds of accessories were to be installed for the use of the artillery. Gun ports had to be opened and storerooms made to order for the biscuits and powder (Museo Naval de Madrid 1631). Other precise and specific alterations were required as a result of the inspection visit that was part of the *capitana*'s selection process.

It is not known exactly what modifications were ordered and carried out on *Nuestra Señora del Juncal.* It has not been possible to locate the records of the 1628–1629 inspection. When the ship was visited in 1627, orders were given to review the condition of the masts, yards or spars, and topmasts; to carry out many important repairs aimed to make her more seaworthy; and to give the hull enough strength to support the artillery. These included adding: (1) eight orlop beams, (2) twelve ridders on each side from the keelson to the hold deck spaced from the bow to the stern, (3) thick stuff wherever necessary, and (4) four knees fixed where the ledges of the hold deck begin (AGI, Contratación 4845 1627). It is possible that this was not actually done, because the vessel was not chosen to form part of the armada. Nevertheless, similar alterations aimed at strengthening the vessel must have been carried out to prepare her to serve as an escort galleon in 1630.

ADDITIONAL FEATURES

Capacity or Tonnage

Records of *Nuestra Señora del Juncal*'s tonnage vary from 650 to 800. The *capitana* contract mentions a capacity of 650 tons "more or less" (AGI, Contratación 4896 1629a:fols. 221–226). Perhaps the most reliable source is the gauge certificate prepared by Francisco García de Veas during his visit in 1627. It includes the ship's measurements and states the capacity as 669 tons (AGI, Contratación, 5173 1627). The gauging method was that proposed by Cristóbal de Barros in 1590, and reestablished in the 1618 ordinances (Caballero Juárez 1997:163).

The 1618 ordinances established a limit on the tonnage of ships sailing the Carrera de Indias for safety reasons. They stated that the vessels sailing the Carrera de Indias, including those built under contract to the king and private merchantmen, could not have a breadth wider than 18 *codos* (10.34 m). Therefore, the tonnage could not surpass 624 tons—lower than *Nuestra Señora del Juncal*'s—because of the damage caused as a result of size. Large vessels unrig more easily. During bad weather, the ships lose parts, such as masts, spars, or rudders and, on not finding replacements, are abandoned. And on entering and departing the sandbars, they are in danger because they take on water. The fleets sail in the summer, and larger ships need much more wind than small or medium-sized vessels. So the others have to wait for them, and this delays the arrival of the fleets. When meeting the enemy, the smaller ships can be turned windward more easily and are more manageable (Real Academia de la Historia [1681] 1987:vol. 8, book IV, pp. 31–32).

Also, from 1628 to 1633, the *avería* contract dictated that ships chosen to serve in the armada or as flagships or vice-admiral's ships could not exceed 600 tons (AGI, Indiferente General 433 1627:fol. 51v). On the other hand, Fernando Serrano Mangas (1989:25) points out that the ideal tonnage for galleons was between 450 and 600.

Is *Nuestra Señora del Juncal*'s tonnage relevant to its performance as a *capitana*? Between 1625 and 1630, *Nuestra Señora del Juncal* remained docked in Cádiz waiting her turn to set sail again. In spite of the shortage of ships, she was not considered suitable to form part of the Armada de la Guarda de la Carrera de Indias. In 1627, Casa de la Contratación ministers turned her down to serve both as a merchantman for the West Indies fleets and for service in the armada, partly on the basis that she was too large (AGI, Contratación 5173 1627).

Tumble-Home/Flare

As stated in Chapter 22 of the 1618 ordinances: "For the ship to be seaworthy and buoyant, with enough tumble-home, not too straight-sided, nor wobbly, it is preferable to close the upper deck the same amount as the beam is opened, that would be three and one half *codos* below the deck" (Real Academia de la Historia [1681] 1987:vol. 8, book IV, p. 26).

Tumble-home is described as "the amount by which the two sides of a ship are brought in towards the centreline after reaching their maximum beam. It is the opposite of flare in which the sides curved outwards" (Kemp 1988:896). Tumble-home, then, refers to the practice of making the sides of a vessel curve inward as they go up, so the widest part of a ship is well below the gunwale. This made the ships steadier when they began to carry numerous cannons mounted in the gunwales. It put the guns on the upper deck closer to the centerline. Too much flare or insufficient tumble-home caused ships with heavy artillery to roll from side to side, which made it more difficult to aim the guns accurately (Donald Keith, personal communication).

According to the previously mentioned report filed in 1629 by the Casa de la Contratación president, the ship had not been previously considered apt for war or service in the armada "because she had insufficient tumble-home and moved too much with the artillery" (AGI, Contratación 5117 1629b).

We cannot be sure if *Nuestra Señora del Juncal* had been turned down because her flare made it more difficult to aim the artillery or because it made her unstable and less manageable. Most probably it was both. Nevertheless, in spite of the previous decisions, in 1629 *Nuestra Señora del Juncal* was chosen as *capitana* and heavily armed. Could this have made her unstable and unable to ride out the heavy storm? It is likely that the rolling may have weakened her hull and caused her to take on more water. The survivors' testimonies indicate that the ship's crew jettisoned many items, including seven cannons—one of iron and six of *bronzeá*—and one anchor (AGI, México 360:fol. 14). This is significant because at that time good artillery was very expensive and hard to come by (Serrano Mangas 1989:115); it would not have been thrown overboard except in a dire emergency. The reports do not specify if the crew resorted to sacrificing the ordinance just to lighten the ship or because they thought the cannons, in particular, were endangering her stability.

FINAL CONSIDERATIONS

By the time *Nuestra Señora del Juncal* plunged into the water and was deposited on the seabed, a great number and variety of objects and structures had already been thrown into the sea (old sails and rigging, merchandise chests, the galley, seven cannons, one anchor, and the main mast). Commercial items and equipment must have floated around and shifted during the storm or were moved about intentionally to carry out maneuvers to save the ship. Containers such as olive jars were used to bail out the water; they had to have been taken out of their original storage location and were broken and scattered around the ship. The structure's coherence was most probably very weak as the stem broke; nails and bolts popped out and the wood shook during the storm. Survivors of the shipwreck managed to cut the lifeboat loose and save thirty-nine people as well as a small quantity of gold and silver.

This information is important for understanding the deposition and postdeposition processes the ship underwent. Nevertheless, archives have also shed light on more information that may broaden our understanding of the social, political, economical, and technological context in which *Nuestra Señora del Juncal* was built, sailed, and lost. In other words, it offers more possibilities of historical and archaeological interpretations regarding the role of ships in the complex historical context of the early 17th-century Spanish Empire.

Nuestra Señora del Juncal formed part of the system organized by the Spanish Crown to maintain communication with its overseas lands, its trade, and transport of tributes and taxes, which was important income. This complex system was conditioned by diverse political and economic factors that compromised its efficiency. The growing crisis of the Spanish Empire and the risk of losing it to northern European rivals forced the

Spanish to adopt defensive policies that were costly, both in money and efforts of public officials. This situation is directly reflected in all aspects of *Nuestra Señora del Juncal*'s life, her construction, her role in the West Indies trade route, and wreckage.

Nuestra Señora del Juncal was built in Guipuzcoa, where there was a long history of expertise in shipbuilding. The Crown fomented the naval industry of this region to satisfy the Indies trade requirements. The ship was built at a time in which the demand for ships (both for royal service and for private commercial operations) surpassed production possibilities. In response to this, the Crown's intentions were to build its own navy. But, as this was not possible, it proceeded to promote the private construction of ships that could serve official interests. The Crown began regulating shipbuilding to homogenize it and imposed specific technological features to ensure that the ships built would be suitable for the functions required. This marked an important moment in Spanish shipbuilding, which had previously been based on traditional methods and shipwrights' expertise. Thus, these regulations were not always followed down to the letter, and the shipwright's experience still prevailed. Historic sources only give us a general idea of the construction features. Therefore, we hope to discover traces in the material remains that will help us comprehend this fusion of craftsmanship and regulations.

A great variety of archival documents and current research shows that there was not only one type of high-board ship participating on the Carrera de Indias. There were structural differences between merchant vessels or *naos* and armada galleons for the Armada del Mar Océano and Armada de la Guarda de la Carrera de Indias. There was even a distinction between escort and silver galleons. Nevertheless, these sources do not facilitate a total understanding of these differences. Typology is also complicated by the fact that all the different types were used indiscriminately as needed.

Regardless of these overlaps, it is possible to hypothesize about her type based on information found in documents. A public officer of Fuenterrabía, using his scarce, inherited resources, built *Nuestra Señora del Juncal*. He took advantage of the modest facilities of this port to build the hull. He did not have a contract with the Crown to build it, so fewer regulations were probably applied. Antonio de Ubilla built the ship as a merchant *nao* in hopes of receiving the economic rewards such vessels had earned in the past. When it was commissioned as *capitana* for the 1629 (later 1630) fleet, it had only traveled once to New Spain and had then remained docked and deteriorating in the Bay of Cádiz. During this time, she was never considered worthy of serving as *capitana*, in spite of the overwhelming scarcity of ships at the time. Some of the reasons given by officials for this rejection include her large size and insufficient tumble-home and the fact that she had been sheathed during her maiden voyage.

Finally, during her life, *Nuestra Señora del Juncal* received many repairs and structural modifications for military functions. It is not certain that any of these modifications played a role in the ship's lack of seaworthiness or stability, but they were either political or technical aspects that officials found worth mentioning in their reports . . . and they will make an imprint on the archaeological record.

ACKNOWLEDGMENTS

Our thanks to Socorro Prous, Lourdes Odriozola, Cruz Apestegui, Fernando Serrano Mangas, and Pablo Emilio Pérez Mallaina for their help in the research in the historic archives in Spain. We are also grateful to Diane Hermanson for the English translation and proofreading; Roberto Galindo, Octavio González, and Edgar Merino for the illustration; and Pilar Luna, Robert Parthesius, and Donald Keith for their support, encouragement, and valuable observations and recommendations.

REFERENCES

Archivo General de Guipúzcoa. 1646. Memorial dado por la Villa de San Sebastián, en la Junta particular, de las razones que se le ofrecen sobre las fábricas, que Su Majestad manda se hagan en Guipúzcoa. JD-MI-2-12-321, Guipúzcoa, Spain.

Archivo General de Indias (AGI), Contratación 2899. 1605–1626. Libro de registros de naos que se despachan para las Indias 1605–1626. Fol. 185v. Seville, Spain.

Archivo General de Indias (AGI), Contratación 5173. 1627a. En Manos de Don Fernando Ruiz de Contreras sobre la elección de las naos para la flota de Nueva España. 2 de marzo de 1627. Book 2, fols. 242v–245. Seville, Spain.

Archivo General de Indias (AGI), Contratación 4845. 1627b. Visita, reconocimiento y arqueamiento de las que han de servir de Capitanas y Almirantas que este año de 1627 han de ir a las Provincias de Nueva España y Honduras. Seville, Spain.

Archivo General de Indias (AGI), Contratación 4896. 1629a. Asiento de la nao nombrada Nuestra Señora del Juncal de la flota de Nueva España dueño contador Antonio de Ubilla que otorgó por Juan Martínez de Aldavé en virtud de su poder. Fols. 221–226. Seville, Spain.

Archivo General de Indias (AGI), Contratación 5117. 1629b. Carta del Conde de la Puebla 4 de mayo 1629. Inclusa carta del mismo de 17 de marzo del mismo año. Seville, Spain.

Archivo General de Indias (AGI), Contratación 819, No. 1. 1629–1630. Martin de Yturain y consortes vecinos de Cádiz y dueños de nao con el contador Antonio de Ubilla vecino de Fuenterrabía y dueño que fue de ella sobre el modo de hacer el asiento que se había de tomar con la avería. Fol. 3. Seville, Spain.

Archivo General de Indias (AGI), Contratación 4896. 1630. Petición hecha por Juan Martínez de Aldavé. 21 de abril de 1630. Fols. 248–249v. Seville, Spain.

Archivo General de Indias (AGI), Indiferente General 433. 1627. Asiento y certificación que los señores Presidente, y del Consejo Real de las Indias tomaron con Adriano de Legaso, sobre el despacho de las Armadas y flotas de las Indias por el tiempo de seis años, de 1628 a 1633. 27 de septiembre de 1627. Book 4, fols. 39–82v. Seville, Spain.

Archivo General de Indias (AGI), México 360. 1631a. Autos hechos por el gobernador de Mérida, Yucatán, 24 de enero de 1631. No. 1, fols. 14–16. Seville, Spain.

Archivo General de Indias (AGI), México 31. 1631b. Relación de la plata, reales, grana, añil, seda, cueros, brazilete y otros géneros que van registrados en la flota del general Miguel de Echazarreta. 14 octubre 1631. No. 1, fol. 19. Seville, Spain.

Archivo General de Indias (AGI), México 3. 1632. Duplicado de lo que fue en la flota del general Miguel de Echazarreta que se perdió y en los dos avisos que han salido de este reino en 1632. 9 de enero 1632. Doc. 215. Seville, Spain.

Archivo General de Indias (AGI), Santo Domingo 133. 1631. Declaración de Josefe de Siguereda, sobre las noticias de la flota del puerto de Veracruz para el de La Habana a cargo del Almirante Manuel Serrano. Veracruz, 6 diciembre 1631. No. 2, doc. 23. Seville, Spain.

Archivo General de Indias (AGI), Contratación 819. 1624:fols.13–15v. Poder otorgado a Juan de Casanova por el Contador Antonio de Ubilla 12 de marzo de 1624. Seville, Spain.

Archivo General de la Nación (AGN) (México). 1631. Al marqués de Cerralvo, virrey de la Nueva España, para que remita al gobernador de La Habana los bastimentos y municiones que solicita para la defensa de la isla de Cuba. La Habana 14 enero 1631. Reales cédulas originales, vol. 1, exp. 65, fols. 115–117.

Archivo General de Simancas (AGS), Guerra y Marina 1011. 1630. De parte. En 8 de octubre 1630. El Consejo de Guerra sobre la pretensión que Antonio de Ubilla tiene de que Vuestra Majestad le haga merced de titulo de su secretario. Simancas, Spain.

Archivo Histórico de Protocolos de Gipúzkoa (AHPG), 3–451, Protocolos Notariales del Partido Judicial de San Sebastián. 1622. Obligación que el Capitán Miguel Saenz de Benessa y Esquibel y el Contador Antonio de Ubilla otorgan a favor del Capitán Antonio Luz de Cando por unos basos que les da para el bote de sus galeones al Pasaje. En 30 de octubre 1622. Registros de escrituras 1609–1625, Escribano: Zuloaga, Escribanía de Fuenterrabía, fols. 111–112.

Archivo Histórico de Protocolos de Gipúzkoa (AHPG), 3–451, Protocolos Notariales del Partido Judicial de San Sebastián. 1625. Poder de Martín Saenz de Alchacoa y Gracia de Descarga para Juanes de Belzo Ybañez de Alchacoa para que puedan vender una pinaza suya y navegar con ella. En 16 de junio 1625. Registros de escrituras 1609–1625, Escribano: Zuloaga, Escribanía de Fuenterrabía, fols. 227–228v.

Archivo Histórico Provincial de Cádiz (AHPC) 5504. 1630a. Certificación de Carta de Pago. 9 de enero de 1630. Escribano: Sebastián García Moreno, fols. 53–54v.

Archivo Histórico Provincial de Cádiz 5504. 1630b. Certificación de Carta de Pago. 9 de enero de 1630. Escribano: Sebastián García Moreno, fols. 55–56.

Archivo Histórico Provincial de Cádiz 5504. 1630c. Certificación de Carta de Pago. 10 de enero de 1630. Escribano: Sebastián García Moreno, fols. 56–57.

Caballero Juárez, J. A. 1997. *El Régimen Jurídico de las Indias Siglos XVI y XVII.* Mexico City: Universidad Nacional Autónoma de México/Instituto de Investigaciones Jurídicas.

Fernández de Navarrete, M. 1971. Instrucción de los Veedores de las Armadas de Nueva España y Tierra Firme. Madrid 3 de marzo de 1573. In Colección de documentos y manuscritos compilados por Fernández de Navarrete, vol. 22, doc. 18, fol. 54, facsimile. Madrid: Museo Naval.

Kemp, P., ed. 1988. *The Oxford Companion to Ships and the Sea*. Oxford: Oxford University Press.

Moya Blanco, C. 1981. La arquitectura naval de los Austrias. In *El buque en la Armada Española*, 79–112. Madrid: Sílex.

Museo Naval de Madrid. 1631. Instrucciones para el viaje de la Armada de la Guarda de las Indias dadas por Thomás de Larraspuru, Junio 1631. Colección Vargas Ponce, vol. 1, doc. 211, fol. 474.

Odriozola Oyarbide, L. 1993. La familia Olazabal. Ilustres constructores navales del siglo XVII. *OARSO 93* Errentería Segunda Época, 28:37–38.

Odriozola Oyarbide, L.1988. La construcción naval en Gipuzkoa. Siglos XVI–XVIII. *Itsas Memoria. Revista de Estudios Marítimos del País Vasco* (Magazine of Maritime Studies of the Basque Country) 2:93–146.

Olesa Muñido, F. F. 1981. La Marina Oceánica de los Austrias. In *El buque en la Armada Española*, 114–45. Madrid: Sílex.

O'Scanlan, T. 1974. *Diccionario Marítimo Español*, 233. Madrid: Museo Naval.

Phillips, C. R. 1991. *Seis Galeones para el Rey de España. La Defensa Imperial a Principios del Siglo XVII*. Madrid: Alianza Editorial.

Real Academia de la Historia. 1632. Relación verdadera de lo que sucedió en la capitana del General Miguel de Echazarreta hecha por un religioso de la Orden de Juan de Dios a petición del padre comisario Fray Alonso de los Reyes. Papeles varios de Jesuitas, Ms 9/3687, doc. 114, fol. 646.

Real Academia de la Historia. 1987. *Recopilación de Leyes de Los Reinos de Las Indias*, 1681, Primera edición facsímile, Tomo 4, Edición Conmemorativa del V Centenario del Descubrimiento de América en el LXXV Aniversario de la Escuela Libre de Derecho. Mexico City: Escuela Libre de Derecho, Miguel Ángel Porrúa.

Serrano Mangas, F. 1985. *Los Galeones de la Carrera de Indias, 1650–1700*. Seville, Spain: Escuela de Estudios Hispanoamericanos de Sevilla, Consejo Superior de Investigaciones Científicas.

Serrano Mangas, F. 1989. *Armadas y Flotas de la Plata (1620–1648)*. Spain: Banco de España.

Serrano Mangas, F. 1995. *Tratado de la Galafatería y Carena de las Naos y en la Forma en que se Debe Hacer de Unos Documentos Náuticos Titulados Tratados Varios Manuscritos y aquí Hechos Encuadernar por Juan Antonio Rico de la Mata el Año de 1689*. Barcelona: Llagut.

Veitia y Linaje, J. 1981. *Norte de la Contratación de las Indias Occidentales*. Madrid: Ministerio de Hacienda.

CHAPTER 4

Nautical Charts and Measurement Systems of the 17th Century

Carmen Rojas Sandoval

If appropriate methods are used, nautical charts contain a great deal of useful information for identifying potential survey areas for locating 17th-century shipwrecks. Advances in nautical charts of the 17th and 18th centuries, such as the use of longitude and the transition from the *portulano*[1] tradition to the Mercator projection, make it possible to make detailed analyses of the charts. The nautical charts created in this period to navigate in American waters contain an extraordinary amount of valuable information. Arguments about their poor precision or their classification as artistic rather than scientific documents are ill founded and unnecessarily restrictive, as I show in this chapter.

THE DISASTER

At sunset on November 1, 1631, the ship *Nuestra Señora del Juncal* was unable to endure the relentless northerly winds and started to sink. The ship stayed afloat for just a few minutes, and only thirty-nine passengers managed to swim to a life craft. They were rescued by another ship belonging to the same fleet that had been dispersed by the wind and were taken to the port of Villa de San Francisco de Campeche. Testimonies about the incident were provided by the survivors, who included the boatswain and a priest, and the correspondence between the captains of the fleets based in Veracruz and Havana as well as the viceroy himself. The references mentioned in the accounts, interrogations, and letters refer to latitude and different distances in leagues, and to an island in the Campeche Bay and at the coast.

INTERPRETING THE TESTIMONIES

Relevant methods are required to interpret the distances and locations provided in the testimonies. These can then be used to propose areas

Table 4.1 League.

League	Year	Author	Observations	Value	Result of one league in m
Columbus league	1492	Comellas 1991	Calculated with Italian mile (1,477.3 m)	4 Italian miles	5,909.2
Columbus league	1492	Comellas 1991	Calculated with Roman mile (1,480 m)	4 Italian miles	5,920
League	1587	García de Palacio 1993		3 miles or 30,00 steps or 15,000 feet	5,553
English, French, and other leagues	1734	González Cabrera 1970	Calculated with Humboldt's nautical mile	3 miles	6,478
Spanish and Portuguese leagues	1734	González Cabrera 1970		3 ½ miles	6,478
Dutch and Flemish leagues	1734	González Cabrera 1970		4 miles	7,404
League	1784–1817	Florescano 1973		5,572.7 meters	5,572.7
Post-league	1808	Humboldt 1991		3,894 meters	3,894

Marine or "20 to one degree" league	1808	Humboldt 1991	5,555.55 meters	5,555.55
League	1808	Humboldt 1991	5,572.7 meters	5,572.7
League	1831	O'Scanlan, Timoteo 1974	6,650 Castillian varas (1 Castillian vara = 0.8359 meters)	5,558.735
League	1908	Robelo 1995	4,190 meters or 5,000 varas	4,190
League		Stampa 1949	4,190 meters or 5,000 varas or 2.6 miles	4,190
Land league		Hamiliton 1934	4,400 meters or 3 Roman miles	4,400
Nautical league	16th–17th C	Jarmy 1980	4 Roman miles or 3.7 land miles or 3.2 nautical miles or 5.9 km	5,900
League		Martínez 1997	5,500 meters	5,500
Spanish League		Herrera 1997	6,342 meters	6,342
Spanish League		Apestergui 1998	6,276 meters	6,276
Dutch League		Apestergui 1998	7,811.95 meters	7,811.95

for surveying for the shipwreck site. The first method required in this analysis is to translate the measurements used by the persons describing the disaster into modern values. Because the fleet belonged to the Spanish Crown and because it was forbidden to have foreigner sailors on their fleets, the official unit was the league. To find out the exact length of the league referred to in the testimonies, accounts written by different authors, officials of the *arte de marear* (art of sailing), 19th-century travelers such as Alexander Von Humboldt (Humboldt 1991), and modern historians were compiled and analyzed.

The league was an approximate measure used for distance or itinerary. Its magnitude varied from one country to another and even from one period to another. The word comes from the Latin *baxo*. The 1726 *Diccionario de Autoridades* (Real Academia Española 1989) states that a league is equivalent to the distance a man can walk in one hour. The nautical league was commonly used during the age of European maritime exploration. According to the *Diccionario Marítimo Español* (O'Scanlan 1974:334), the league "was used as the type" for the "estimated count," in other words in calculating distances traveled by sea (see Table 4.1). By "type," we mean that it could be converted into other linear measurements such as the mile or stadium.

From an early age, the value of the league was related to a degree on land; the league is a linear measurement and the degree an angular measurement that could take any linear value depending on the size of the sphere. For this reason, naval treatises from the 15th to 18th centuries used this equivalence to tell how many leagues there were at any degree of the Earth. Up to the 18th century, the only figure available for calculating distance by coordinates was latitude, as longitude was impossible to calculate at that time. Latitude was obtained by observing the degree to which the pole star was above the horizon, or by measuring the height of the sun and consulting the declination charts prepared for this purpose.

Navigation treatises have always calculated the value of a "long degree" to be 17½ leagues. A long degree is obtained from the maximum circumferences of the Earth, such as the equator and the meridians ("maximum circle"), whereas parallels are "smaller circles" because their linear distance decreases the closer they are to the poles.

As there seems to be no clear reason behind the preference for one value or another (Falero 1989:112), the degree does not have an absolute linear equivalent. In ancient times, a consensus regarding the extension of the Earth's circumference did not exist, whereas mathematical geographical solutions could not be applied until several centuries later.

Eratosthenes (276–195 B.C.) was the first geographer we know about who calculated the Earth's circumference and the linear value of the degree.

He concluded that 1° consisted of 700 stadia, which means, according to the interpretations of Wolfgang Torge (1980), that Eratosthenes' Earth had a perimeter of 39,375 km, whereas, according to José Luis Comellas (1991:111–15), the result is 36,000 km. Unlike Eratosthenes, Ptolemy (130 B.C.), who based his calculations on Posidonius, believed 1° on Earth was equivalent to 500 stadia (Comellas 1991:111–15). Nevertheless, it seems that Ptolemy and Posidonius' 500 stadia were equivalent to Eratosthenes' 700, as they referred to Alexandrian stadia, which were longer than those used by Eratosthenes (Comellas 1991:111–15).

The 9th-century caliph Al-Ma'mum ordered that his cosmographers walk 1° of latitude to measure the extension of 1° of the Earth (Laguarda 1987:31–34). The results were registered by Ibn Yunus, Abul-Fida, Al-Jwarizmi, and Al-Fraganus, who reported values amounting to 56 miles, 56.25 miles, and 56.66 miles. Al-Fragano was studied by Toscanelli, who was, in turn, read by Christopher Columbus, who believed that 1° on Earth was 56.66 miles (Comellas 1991:114, 183). It is believed that Columbus reached the conclusion that the Earth was smaller than his European contemporaries thought because he used a Latin mile, which is shorter than an Arab mile (Comellas 1991:111–15).

It is not known if after Columbus's time navigators obtained the actual measurement of the Earth or confirmed Eratosthenes' figure—which is closer to the actual measurement than the one produced by Ptolemy or his interpretations. Navigation treatises do not discuss the matter and merely provide the different measurements of the Earth's circumference according to whether they used one or another kind of league. This resulted in a redundancy that was practical at the time, but that was impossible to escape from.

The Treaty of Tordesillas in 1494 between Spain and Portugal, which established the line dividing their dominions, set at 370 miles to the west of the Cabo Verde and the Azores islands by (Prieto 1971), did not reach a consensus to establish the equivalence of the 370 miles. Proportions between the league and the mile also varied according to different countries or navigators (Comellas 1991; González Cabrera 1970; Jarmy 1988).

After consulting an extensive group of nautical authors dating from the 16th to the 18th centuries as well as several modern authors, it is clear that relating the value of a league to the measurement of the Earth is not possible. The other measurement that could help us is the mile, but we have no absolute value for it either.

At present, the nautical mile, or simply the mile, is equivalent to one minute's arc of the Earth's latitude; however, international agreements have given the mile the conventional value of 1,852 m (6,075 ft). We therefore find that the mile currently used is considerably longer than the ancient mile. Values presented give us the following equivalencies in leagues and meters: Value 1 = 4,170 m (13,677 ft); Value 2 = 5,553 m (18,214 ft); Value 3 = 6,478 m (21,253 ft).

The equivalences of leagues in meters that seem most appropriate for the year 1631 are derived from both proportions (1:3 and 1:3½), using Humboldt's nautical miles. However, the figure we get by using a short mile (1,000 steps or 5,000 ft) mentioned by the nautical authors of the age should be considered. Considering the proportion between leagues and miles, the ratio that seems most accurate is 1:3. It is highly likely that the pilots and captains of the 1630–1631 fleet and the vice-admiral's ship were aware of the work of García de Palacio written in 1587, which mentions the 1:3 equivalence, but not of the work of González Cabrera written in 1734, which differentiates the Spanish league of 1:3½ from the English one of 1:3, although it does not rule out the existence of the 1:3½ ratio in 1631. One observation arising from the aforementioned scale is that the Spanish nautical league in the past may have been shorter than it was in the 18th and 19th centuries.

It is possible that the testimony of the boatswain from the *Nuestra Señora del Juncal* wreck may have referred to a kind of short league that was the custom. This could explain why he mentioned "so many *land* leagues from the coast of Campeche," which could be a simple redundancy to specify "towards the land of the coast of Campeche," or might be the key to identifying that the league he used was equivalent to the land league or "post-league" which measured 3,894 m (12,772 ft) according to Humboldt. This does not mean that the experienced sailor used land leagues, merely that the different nautical leagues included one whose value was similar to the land league.

PROJECTION OF TESTIMONIES ONTO NAUTICAL CHARTS

The second step of the methodology was to look for maps of the time so that the testimonies could be projected on them using the elements of the maps themselves (scales, league rules, degree divisions). Most of the 17th-century nautical maps of New Spain that we know of were published by Italian, Dutch, French, or English cartographers who recorded a large part of what had been revealed by explorations on their maps, although the Spanish tried to stop them from having access to reliable information. It is possible to conduct serious studies of 17th-century cartography from these reproductions, even if they are not originals or are ornate reproductions, if those that were decorative objects with no real scientific content can be distinguished from maps for which the decoration is a complement that does not affect the cartographic value. Even if a chart is decorated, there is no reason to doubt—without a serious analysis—that the information is not similar to that of maps in daily use. Maps that contained the entire Earth were called "universal maps," whereas those that represented just one part, whether it be large or small, were particular or "quarter maps"; these maps include nautical charts or maritime charts. As today, pilots who crossed from one continent to another used different quarter maps that covered variable extensions.

In the 17th century, navigation between America and Spain combined routes on the open sea with the old method called *cabotaje*, which consisted of sailing close to the coast using the land mass as guide. In nautical maps from New Spain, we can see the *portulano* tradition as well as "flat charts." *Portulano* maps are so-called because they indicate the routes used to sail from one port to another and are based on observing the coast directly with a compass (Martín-Merás n.d.). A characteristic element of these maps is that they have a system of sixteen or thirty-two lines that radiated from one or several points to indicate the directions. They also included a graphic scale that could be used for approximate calculations of the distances but did not feature a graduation to indicate the latitude.

As the use of latitudes acquired a great deal of importance in navigation on the open sea, flat charts started to include meridians and parallels as well as direction lines as in *portulano* maps (Comellas 1991). Flat charts are a halfway point between *portulano* maps and the Mercator projection, as they have equidistant meridians, but the linear value of degrees in latitudes other than the equator is lower than the value shown to be uniform.

To correct the error generated by the unequal linear value of the degree, nautical authors used several truncated or "pitipie" (graduated) league scales relevant to the different latitudes. For the charts used to navigate the route between Veracruz and Havana in the 17th century, only a league scale was used. In the Mercator projection, the meridians do not converge, which means the distance between the parallels is enlarged to stop the poles from becoming too distorted. This relation is named "growing latitudes." Charts drawn up with the Mercator projection probably corresponded to the so-called reduced or grown-degree charts, which had unequal or increased north south degrees. Another kind of chart was the "dual-graduation chart," which presented a small auxiliary graduation of latitudes, some 3° shorter than the general graduation. This was one of the solutions for the problem of the difference between estimated latitudes and those obtained from astronomical observation, especially in the long routes to the Indies and when sighting land in Terranova (Arroyo 1989).

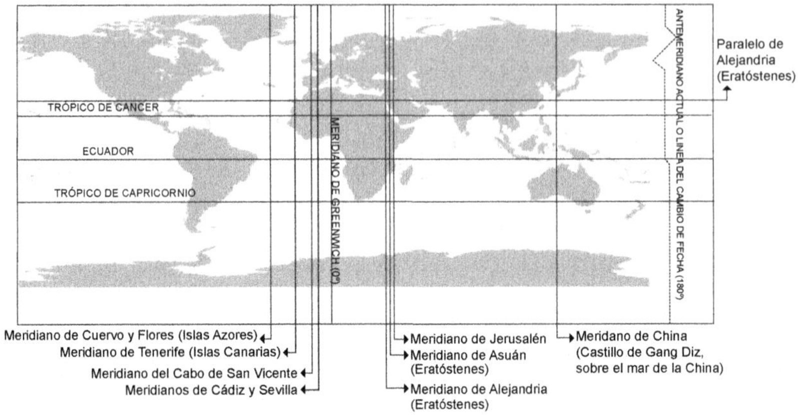

Figure 4.1. Meridians used as origin in the 16th–18th centuries.

To determine coordinates in the 17th century, the equator was used to locate astronomical observations of latitude, but there was still no consensus regarding which meridian was to be used to begin the counting. In addition to this practice, the technology required to determine longitude in a practical way did not exist. According to 18th-century author José González Cabrera (1970), Seville and Portuguese charts showed the first meridian to be the line passing through the Cuervo, Flores, or San Miguel islands in the Azores; Dutch and French charts showed it on Tenerife, one of the Canary Islands. Other meridians used as the first meridian at that time included the Cabo Verde Islands and San Vicente Cape in Portugal (Figure 4.1).

The historical explanation about charts and navigation helps us understand why Pedro de Medina (1964) wrote that in 1563 that a maritime chart should contain the following characteristics:

- layout of the land's coasts on the same path, distance, and height to be found by the navigation;
- specifics to be found during the navigation such as islands, islets, banks or bars, sandbanks, and reefs;
- lines showing the thirty-two winds;
- graduation; and
- truncated leagues.

As we have seen, the maps we can use to locate the 1631 wreck of *Nuestra Señora del Juncal* in the Bay of Campeche should be largely similar to a maritime chart and should contain all these elements. In this study, over

100 old maps were reviewed and eight were selected because they had the relevant criteria. The chosen maps were enlarged and the area of interest was copied as were any necessary elements. Next, the references provided by the survivors of *Nuestra Señora del Juncal* were traced on the maps using the latitude graduation and scale of each map.

Two examples demonstrate the procedures. The first is the *Insulae Americanae in Oceano Septentrionali cum Terris Adiacentibus*, printed in 1634 by Nicolas Sanson d'Abbeville and published by Guillermo Blaeu (taken from Antochiw 1994) (Figure 4.2). This map came from Amsterdam not Spain, although it may have been copied from a Spanish map as it includes all the elements contained in a maritime chart. The second is the *Mapa Marítimo del Golfo de México e Islas de la América* from 1755, signed by Tomás López and Juan de la Cruz (taken from Antochiw 1994) (Figure 4.3). This map is a "reduced point quarter map," or a flat chart of Spanish origin and has a certifying text which says: "for the use of sailors in this part of the world," which means it must be an original maritime chart or a true copy of one.

If we project onto both maps the geographical references to the wreck that were mentioned in the testimonies, such as latitude and distance in

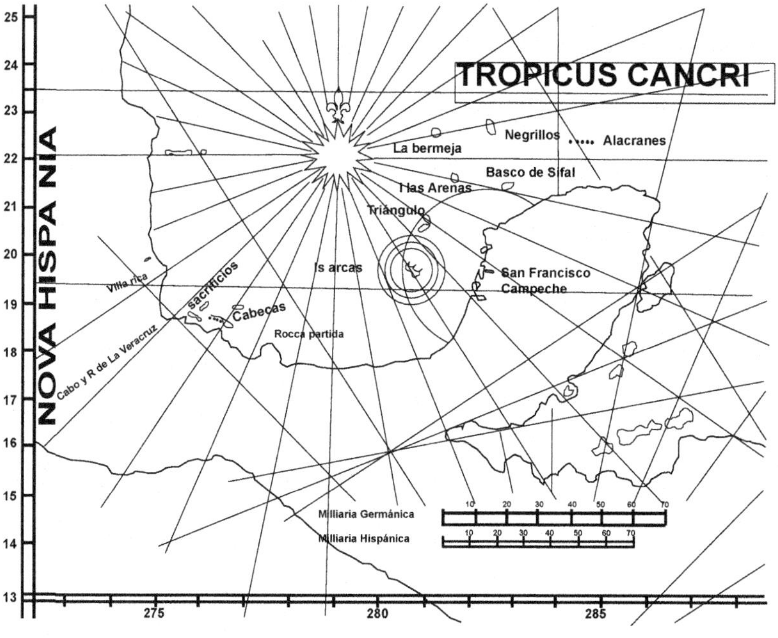

Figure 4.2. *Insulae Americanae in Oceano Septentrionali cum Terris Adiacentibus*, 1634, Nicolas Sanson d'Abbeville.

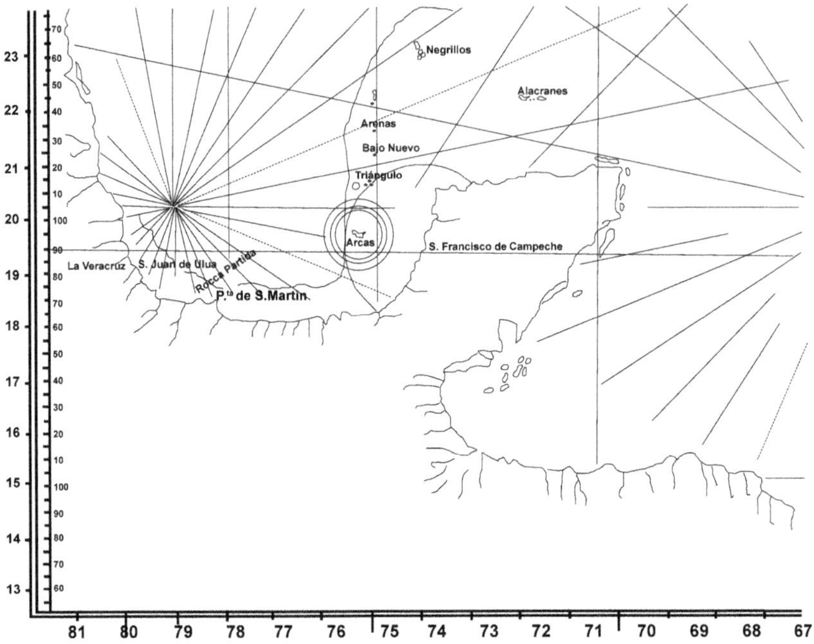

Figure 4.3. Maritime map of the Gulf of Mexico and islands from the Americas, 1755, Tomás López and Juan de la Cruz.

leagues to the coast and to an island, the information coincides. Note, however, that if we project these references directly onto a modern map, the latitude does not coincide with the references in leagues, which is the result of not considering the cartographical context of the time, as it is shown here. Only after we study the references to obtain the values closest to those used by the persons themselves and project them onto the maritime maps of the time using their elements is it possible to see that the testimonies are coherent. The references in leagues, converted into kilometers, were then projected onto a modern maritime map, bearing in mind that the latitude would not coincide. Cruz Apestegui (1998) notes that the magnetic pole variation since the 17th century and the consequent rotation of the parallels and meridians was of the order of 3.5 grades to the west. The calculated coordinates projected on a corrected grid then coincide with the testimonies in different points.

FINAL COMMENTS

The latitude and distances in leagues coinciding in the ancient maps that were studied are highly important for identifying areas to search for the wreck of *Nuestra Señora del Juncal*. In prior calculations made by other investigators, latitude had not been considered as crucial information because it was believed to be the result of cartographic imprecisions of the time. Considering the variation of the magnetic pole since the 17th century, however, the projection of the coordinate with a corrected grid, the result demonstrates that the rest of the testimonies coincide. The point is that it is necessary that the testimonies be evaluated with the tools of the age in question.

For the study discussed here, the latitude mentioned by the boatswain coincides with the distance from the island mentioned, if it is projected in a map with the characteristics of the nautical charts of the time. With the different league values obtained, thanks to ancient navigation manuals (called itineraries), it was possible to project the potential search areas onto a modern map and give preference to those within the quadrant of the latitude mentioned.

The new interpretations also consider a wider series of values for the league and include the possibility that one of the references may have been calculated using the short league similar to a land post-league. Including these new figures increases the number of positions for the proposed survey areas. This study offers useful tools for cartographic interpretation that could be used widely in maritime archaeological investigations.

NOTE

1. Type of chart to navigate from port to port; used from the 13th to the 16th centuries.

REFERENCES

Antochiw, M. 1994. *Historia de la Cartografía de la Nueva España*. Mexico City: Gobierno del Estado de Campeche.

Apestegui, C. 1998. Nota relativa al la localización del galeón *Nuestra Señora del Juncal*. Proyecto de Investigación de la Flota de la Nueva España de 1630–31. Unpublished report, Instituto Nacional de Antropología e Historia, Mexico City.

Arroyo, R. 1989. Estudio del tratado del esphera y del arte de marear 1535. In *Tratado del Esphera y del Arte de Marear 1535*, F. Falero, ed., 14–15. Castellón, Spain: Ministerio de Defensa y Ministerio de Agricultura, Pesca y Alimentación.

Comellas, J. L. 1991. *El Cielo de Colón. Técnicas Navales y Astronómicas en el Viaje del Descubrimiento*. Madrid: Tabapres.

Cortés, M. 1990. *Breve Compendio de la Esfera y del Arte de Navegar 1551*. Madrid: Estudio de Mariano Cuesta Domínguez/Editorial Naval/Museo Naval.

Falero, F. 1989. *Tratado del Esphera y del Arte de Marear 1535*. Castellon, Spain: Estudio de Ricardo Arroyo Ruiz Zorrilla. Ministerio de Defensa y Ministerio de Agricultura, Pesca y Alimentación.

Florescano, E., and I. Gil, eds. 1973. *Descripciones Económicas Generales de Nueva España 1784–1817*. Mexico City: Instituto Nacional de Antropología e Historia.

González Cabrera, J. 1970. *Navegación Especulativa y Práctica 1734*. Madrid: Universidad de San Francisco/Ediciones José Porrúa Turanzas.

Herrera, J. M. 1997. Desarrollo metodológico de la selección de áreas de búsqueda de acuerdo a la investigación archivística. Proyecto de Investigación Flota de la Nueva España de 1630–31. Unpublished report, Instituto Nacional de Antropología e Historia, Mexico City.

Humboldt, A. 1991. *Ensayo Político sobre el Reino de la Nueva España 1822*. Mexico City: Editorial Porrúa.

Jarmy, M. 1988. *La Expansión Española Hacia América y el Océano Pacífico*. Mexico City: Fontamara 31.

Laguarda, R. A. 1987. Fundamentación histórica del descubrimiento de América. Montevideo.

Martín-Merás, M. L. n.d. *Cartografía Marítima Hispana. La Imagen de América*. Madrid: Lunwerg Editores S. A.

Medina, P. de. 1964. *Regimiento de Navegación 1563*. Madrid: Edición facsímil, Instituto de España.

O'Scanlan, T. 1974. *Diccionario Marítimo Español 1831*. P. 334. Madrid: Museo Naval de Madrid.

Prieto, C. 1971. *El Océano Pacífico: Navegantes Españoles del Siglo XVI*. Mexico City: Alianza Editorial.

Real Academia Española. 1989. *Diccionario de Autoridades 1726*. Madrid: Edición facsímil, Editorial Gredos.

Robelo, C. A. 1995. *Diccionario de Pesas y Medidas Mexicanas Antiguas y Modernas y de su Conversión. Para Uso de los Comerciantes y de las Familias*. Mexico City: Imprenta Cuauhnahuac.

Stampa, M. 1949. The evolution of weights and measures in New Spain. *Hispanic American Historical Review* 29(29):1.

Torge, W. 1980. *Geodesia*. Mexico City: Editorial Diana.

CHAPTER 5

Riddles in the Dark: Human Behaviors in the Interpretation of a 16th-Century Wreck

Vera Moya Sordo

Since its discovery in Mexican waters approximately seven years ago, the Pilar site has been considered an important find for the project on the Inventory and diagnosis of submerged cultural resources in the Gulf of Mexico being carried out by the Subdirección de Arqueología Subacuática (Underwater Archaeology Vice-Directorate) of the Instituto Nacional de Antropología e Historia (National Institute of Anthropology and History, INAH).[1] The site is particularly important because it dates to the 16th century and has not been seriously disturbed by treasure hunters or sport divers. It is also significant that the remains were detected while surveying with remote sensing that included cesium magnetometer, digital side-scan sonar, and echo-sounder techniques.

Pilar is important not only because it is one of the earliest naval archaeological sites detected in the Gulf of Mexico but also because the site is a potential source of knowledge that will help us understand the maritime way of life of the time and the possible causes and consequences of events, especially those related to naval accidents. Although the site has not been excavated, the remains lying on the sea bottom have been thoroughly studied to investigate how the wreck occurred and the functions of the artifacts found there. Even more importantly, efforts have been made to understand cultural aspects such as attitudes and behaviors that the sea has hidden in this remote wreck. (Preliminary studies on this site can be found in Luna Erreguerena 1999, Herrera 2001, and Moya 2003.) Although we are aware that the archaeological record is an incomplete representation of the past society we are trying to understand, we also know that an independent item can be used to infer human activities by following the traces using interpretative theory (Delgado 1998:386) and behavioral archaeology (Schiffer 1976).

Clearly, the site is there because of a maritime accident. But to understand the complexity of this phenomenon, we need to go beyond the rigorous archaeological analysis of material remains and use other sources of knowledge such as historical data and literature. These can enable us to explore new ways of understanding the processes that could have been involved in the wrecking of a 16th-century ship and permit us to examine and reflect on some of the attitudes and behaviors of the people who experienced such events. Because navigation is a complex phenomenon made up of components from industry, trade, politics, art, history, science, and technology, a multidisciplinary approach using the methods and sources of archaeology, history, and the arts is required to provide a full and rich reconstruction of past events such as the shipwreck at the Pilar site.

ARCHAEOLOGY OF THE SHIPWRECK

The material remains of the Pilar site were found lying 2–3 m deep on the south face of the bar formed by the South and East Triángulos Keys, an area of abundant coral heads and strong currents in the Sound of Campeche, Gulf of Mexico (Figure 5.1). Five anchors, six wrought-iron ordnance pieces (two *bombarda* and four *verso* type cannons), seven breech chambers, and other materials like shot and anchor fragments compose the site. No other archaeological evidence, such as ballast, hull remains, or any other type of material that could be part of the cargo or that could have been related to the site, was detected. Furthermore, there is still no indication of the ship's nationality or its point of departure. However, the study of the material remains and their position in this archaeological context has allowed us to examine a hypothesis for the probable causes of the disaster, how it could have occurred, and some possible final consequences.

The artifacts from the Pilar have diagnostic attributes of the early 16th century. The anchors have a spindly tiller and are longer than the breadth of the palms. Also, the orientation of the stock nuts is parallel to the plane of the palms. It is important to mention that the ring of one of these five anchors is crushed and three have broken tillers and incomplete flukes. In addition, two were found with their fragments nearby. The fact that the palms of most of the anchors are very worn down and even broken may indicate that they were forced beyond their endurance. (Luna Erreguerena 1999:125–126; Herrera 2001:215). The artillery is represented by breech-loading pieces. Two of these are heavy *bombardas,* a type that appeared at the end of the 14th century (Manucy 1985:3). Four are revolving cannons called *verso* that appeared at the beginning of the 16th century (in Boti 1998:189) (Figure 5.2). The spatial association of elements, as well as the damage patterns on many of the

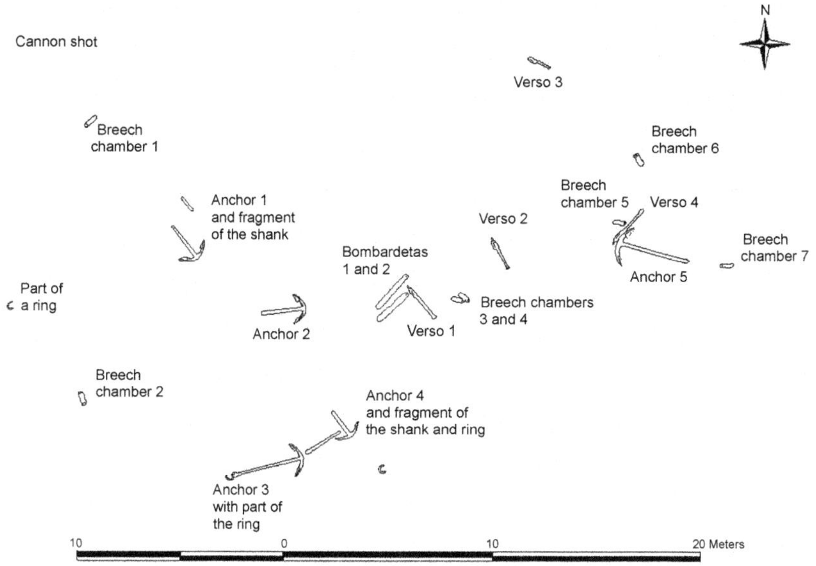

Figure 5.1 Pilar site map (drawn by Donald H. Keith, Félix Frías, and Jorge M. Herrera/Subdirección de Arqueología Subacuática/Instituto Nacional de Antropología e Historia).

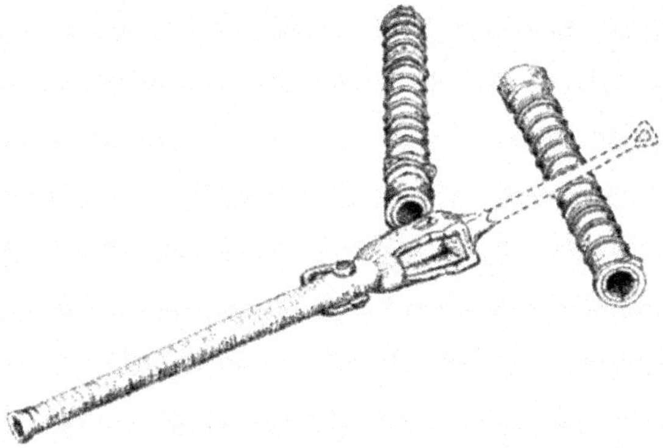

Figure 5.2 Hypothetical reconstruction of the Pilar site *bombardas* and *verso* (Herrera 2001:207).

artifacts, reveals patterns of human behavior that have been observed in other archaeological contexts from naval accidents in other parts of the world that took place in a similar landscape setting. These examples have helped us comprehend the particular wrecking process represented in our site. What events occurred during the wreck? What behavioral patterns can be reconstructed from it?

Following Muckelroy and Gibbs's model of human behavior during different stages of a shipwreck (preimpact threat, preimpact warning, impact; postimpact, and rescue and postdisaster phases) (Gibbs 2006:4–19; Muckelroy 1978:158), we developed a series of hypotheses. Beginning with the first two phases, preimpact threat and warning, we propose that the ship, pulled by strong currents, was driven into the keys. A state of alert was sounded. The crew began running out some of the anchors to stop the ship from being thrown toward the keys. Possibly the anchors broke as a result of the stress produced by the ship and the current pulling in opposite directions.

The distribution of artifacts at the site indicates that the eastern anchor could have been the first thrown over in an attempt to prevent the ship from being trapped or while trying to stop it. The four anchors located at the western part seem to have been the last to be thrown overboard and they appear to lie along the same line, as if the ship was steadily drawn along a course headed toward the inside of the reef, precisely where the currents hit. It is possible that some moments before, the sailors tried to throw some load overboard to lighten the ship and make it easier to control, as was frequently done in such cases. The ordnance could have been jettisoned in an attempt to stop the ship from running aground in the lows (coral heads), but it is also possible that it could have fallen into the sea because of the ship's violent movements.

There are two possibilities for the final result: The ship could have gone down or it could have escaped its fate after a long struggle. In terms of the third phase—the impact—the more reasonable hypothesis is that the ship was crushed against the reef and went down, as it was almost impossible for a ship that has been dragged onto or run into the reef to navigate against the currents and strong winds and get free. Remains lying in shallow waters, where strong currents constantly hit the keys, could substantiate our conclusion. Additional support for this hypothesis is that on the magnetic map obtained from the site's geophysical survey, the final line of the last transect seems to continue precisely inside the keys, where most of the absent material (like the ballast) could perhaps be found (Herrera 2001:220–221) (Figure 5.3). Unfortunately, it was impossible to continue the survey because of the difficult conditions for navigation, but this is an important task for future research.

It therefore seems most likely that the ship crashed into the reef, breaking up into pieces over the ridges. Remains such as metal, stone (for example, the ballast), ceramics, and glass should remain inside the keys. This seems to be indicated both by the anchors' orientation and the last

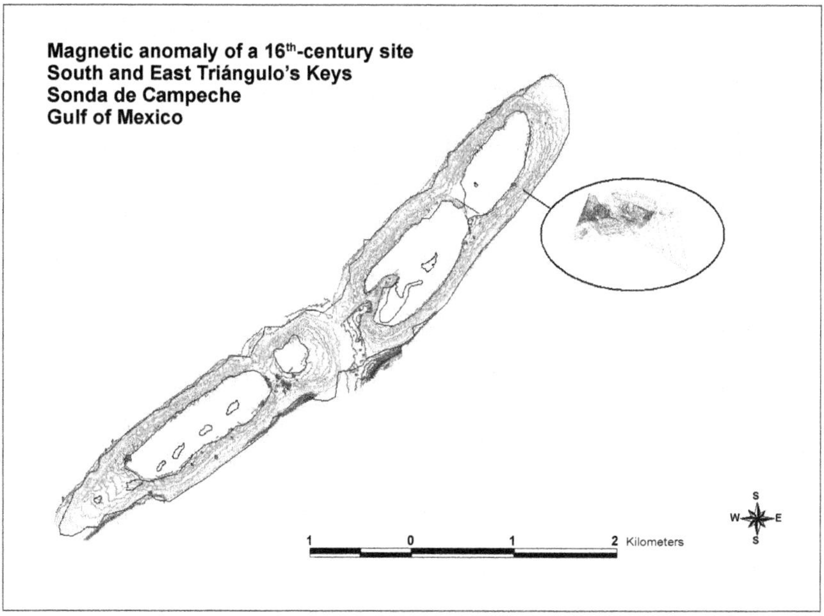

Figure 5.3 Location of Pilar site anomaly on the south face of the barrier formed by the South and East Triángulo's Keys (drawn by Donald H. Keith, Félix Frías, and Jorge M. Herrera/Subdirección de Arqueología Subacuática/Instituto Nacional de Antropología e Historia).

magnetic transect. When the ship crashed, most of the timbers must have broken into pieces and floated away or disintegrated. If any of the hull's structure or other remains survived, they are most probably completely covered by the reef itself, or by the hardpan. Paradoxically, this could very well have served as a protective shield. It is also conceivable that survivors or other people interested in recovering these materials could have rescued some objects at the time of the wreck (postimpact phase). It is also possible that there could have been more recent salvage attempts (rescue and postdisaster phases), but there is no evidence of recent disturbances at the site.

Beyond archaeological remains, there are a number of questions to be answered about the wreck of the ship at the Pilar site. For example, how did the crew or passengers on board experience the incident? What resulting reactions or behaviors can be distinguished? Besides the traces that remain in the archaeological site, where could we find references that would help explain how these accidents occur and how people react in such situations? Another useful avenue of research is the written word, either in historical documents or the beauty of a literary text. These sources show other ways of understanding and listening to the voices from the past and tell us about the attitudes and feelings of the people who suffered such an event. In the next section, I explain how this information has been used to interpret this 16th-century archaeological site and enrich knowledge about human activities involved in the disaster around the time of the wreck.

COMPARING ARCHAEOLOGICAL REMAINS AND TEXTS

Shipwrecks have darkened people's visions since ships began to sail the world's seas. In fact, the main connotations of the word "shipwreck" are loss and misfortune. Perhaps that explains why Álvar Núñez Cabeza de Vaca (1992) called his 1555 chronicle *Naufragios y Comentarios* (Shipwrecks and Commentaries). This text describes the arduous eight-year-long explorations undertaken by a group of soldiers (Martínez 1997:127), although no ship was wrecked during the expedition.

Once the discovery voyages to the New World began, the number of shipwrecks increased significantly. Sometimes the accidents occurred far from land, and no survivors could tell of the crew and passengers' final destinies. Fortunately, the incidents were not always such absolute mysteries. On occasion, shipwreck survivors succeeded in reaching land. Then "all the details of the shipwreck, besides the penalties suffered afterwards, were known" (Cabeza de Vaca 1992). The story of the event became the news of the day. It was not only documented in the official written reports of the survivors, but spread by oral transmission. Little by little, these stories found their way into the literary genre known as shipwreck testimonies, which, in the opinion of many, were "rarely written with style" (in Martínez 1997:11).

Nevertheless, news about shipwrecks was not limited to this kind of text. Shipwrecks have been more than incidents resulting in terrible consequences and losses for everyone involved. They have constituted not only the main theme of many documents and chronicles, but also that of myths, legends, and stories reflected in many songs, novels, tales, and poems from all times and cultures that have embraced maritime customs. Perhaps that is why the bravery of sailors and the suffering of survivors are described not only in newspaper stories, chronicles, and official records, but in epic stories like *The Odyssey* that narrates the untiring struggle by humans against the forces of nature. In most cases, nature and people's attitude toward it directly determine the causes of shipwrecks. It is in this constant and continuous interplay between humans and the forces of nature that certain behavior patterns are repeated over and over again. Fortunately, besides being evident in archaeological contexts, they have been included in a variety of chronicles and literary texts. In these, certain parallels can be perceived between shipwreck causes and processes. The fears and anguish that sailors and passengers have felt throughout the ages can also be discerned.

Consequently, these approaches can be used to supplement the archaeological and geographical information used to develop our wreck hypothesis. For example, an anecdote of an accident that occurred near Alacranes reef in the Sound of Campeche, Gulf of Mexico, narrated by the chronicler Gonzalo Fernández de Oviedo in his *Historia General y Natural de las Indias* (General and Natural History of the Indies) (1992, originally published in 1535) is also an important aid. This well-known event occurred in 1524, and the details were compiled by Oviedo based on the story that one of the survivors, Alonso Zuazo, told him personally. This incident is interesting not only because it happened during the 16th century and involved a military ship, but also because the ship went down after crashing into the Alacranes reef. It is worth mentioning that Oviedo (1992) dedicates his fifth book of his *Historia General* (1492–1548) to the "Unfortunates and Wrecks." The first of his stories refers to the dangers he personally experienced and confronted at sea; that is why he is not considered as a "saloon" chronicler but a real adventurer.

The events entailing Zuazo's ship have allowed us to answer one of the main questions arising from our site context analysis: What circumstances could have made a ship sail so near the keys, considering the danger of this action? One possibility is that it was because of the recklessness of the pilot who, although knowing the key's presence (which was surely used as a geographical reference during navigation), as well as the proximity of the shoals, was overconfident about his navigational skills. Then the currents trapped the ship and dragged it down. Another possibility is that the ship was driven by strong winds or hit by an unexpected powerful storm that pushed it directly to the keys. That is just what happened to Zuazo's caravel as Oviedo describes:

> and being gulfing and having experienced adverse times, after navigating for a long time, one day, at midnight, that counted twenty of the month of January at the year 1524, such a severe storm came, that in many times they see themselves covered by the waves of the sea, such for being a big storm as for being such a little caravel that it hardly reached forty five tones . . . and without knowing where they were, nor being able to steer the ship, nor of taking advantage of the needle or the quadrant, nor any other thing that could bring them self-confidence or any kind of welfare . . . and at quarter of dawn, of the next day they laid at wild and very rough rocks, shores, and reefs, where the ship broke up in a

> lot of pieces, and they lost what they carried (Fernández de Oviedo 1992:324).

In such a situation, how do the ship's crew and passengers react? Quite possibly with desperation. It is probable that when that precise and unfortunate moment in time arrived, those in the throes of death may have prayed with tears in their eyes or seen their dreams and nightmares as part of reality. It seems that this happened to crew and passengers of Zuazo's caravel, when in the middle of the confusion, they saw a "big light guiding them" and "a lot of dolphins like fathering pigs that seemed to fly across the air around the ship, along with other horrible and frightening signs, without any hope of life and without knowing where they were or even being able to control the ship" (Fernández de Oviedo 1992:324).

Such manifestations form a fundamental part of seamen's beliefs and were used to explain the causes of maritime disasters. In those times, the meteorological reasons, combined with human error or negligence, were not considered to be the only causes. On a number of occasions, these kinds of accidents were associated with moral issues, like men's sins, or attributed to fantastic or diabolic creatures' interference. These ideas were the result of superstitious notions inherent to the maritime culture that continued until the 19th century (in Pérez-Mallaína 1996:78). Such thoughts and beliefs could easily have been held by any 16th-century crew at those last moments of despair while they were trying to stop the ship from crashing onto dangerous reefs.

Fernández de Oviedo's written testimony of a shipwreck helps explain how the accident that generated the archaeological context could have happened and how people might have reacted. Besides Oviedo's story, contemporary literature like Shakespeare's *The Tempest* or Lope de Vega´s *Dragontea* can help us understand the range of human behavior displayed when people face drowning at sea. One could envision, for example, that at the final moment of our ship, when the last goodbyes were pronounced and tears shed, the laments of the men may have been like those exclaimed by those in *The Tempest*:

Some voice:	Mercy on us! . . . We split, we split! Farewell, my wife and children! Farewell, brother! We split, we split, we split!
Antonio:	Let's all sink with the king!
Sebastián:	Let's take leave of him!
Gonzalo:	Now would I give a thousand furlongs of sea for an acre of barren ground; long heath, brown furze,

> anything. The wills above be done! But I would fain die a dry death. (Shakespeare, *The Tempest*, Act I, Scene I [Hume and Sherman 2003])

Finally, although there is no information about the fate of the crew of the ship located at the Pilar site, perhaps some survived as happened in Zuazo's wreck, where a few "escaped all rising or mounting over the rocks" (Fernández de Oviedo 1992:325). Nevertheless, it would be risky to conjecture about what happened to the crew of our wrecked ship. Their fate cannot be ignored, but for now it can only be left to our imagination.

LEARNING FROM THE PILAR

The Pilar site's maritime disaster is only one example of the many naval disasters that occurred in the Triángulos Keys area through the centuries. These accidents can help us understand how these happened and to solve important unknowns in interpreting regional maritime activities such as: What made ships navigate near the dangerous reefs? What circumstances could have forced ships to get close to the reefs? The fact that many of the wrecks took place in the proximity of keys suggests two possibilities. People might have had previous knowledge of the keys, which were shown in the 16th-century cartography, and actually used them as landmarks for navigation. In the absence of technology like radar or lighthouses, natural geographical sites such as islands and keys were important for marking routes and determining distances. In some cases, however, the ships may have been navigating along unknown or little-known routes for which there was only a cursory knowledge of the direction of the strongest currents and winds or the location of shoals and reefs.

Historical and literary sources have given us new understanding of the complexity of some of the social aspects of shipwrecks. Fortunately, in the case of the five-century-old archaeological remains found at the Pilar shipwreck site, we also have the opportunity to study relevant historical and literary sources. Combing the records from archaeology, history, and literature gives us an opportunity to gain a fuller and richer reconstruction of past shipwreck events.

NOTE

1. The contents of this chapter are the result of many hours of research, and a great deal of effort and multidisciplinary team work, resulting in an important body of data, including site record forms, maps, field notes, images and reports (Luna Erreguerena 1998, 1999) that are filed in the Technical Archives of INAH's Underwater Archaeology

Vice Directorate. In the previous edition of this book it was not mentioned that some of the initial hypotheses about the site were developed by researchers that participated in the 1998 field work, including Donald H. Keith and Jorge M. Herrera, whose ideas can be found in Herrera's thesis El navegante complejo. Antropología, complejidad, sensoramiento remoto y SIG en la Arqueología Marítima (2001). Herrera 2001 appeared in the references section of this chapter in the earlier publication, and is specifically cited in the text of this edition.

REFERENCES

Boti, L., coord. 1998. *Naufragio en Inés de Soto. Un Hallazgo de Cuatro Siglos.* Havana: Corporación Cimex SA/Carisub SA.

Delgado, J. P., ed. 1998. *Encyclopaedia of Underwater and Maritime Archaeology.* Pp. 386–88. New Haven, CT: British Museum Press.

Fernández de Oviedo, G. 1992. *Historia General y Natural de las Indias.* Madrid: J. A. de los Ríos.

Gibbs, M. 2006. Cultural site formation processes in maritime archaeology: Disaster response, salvage and Muckelroy 30 years on. *International Journal of Nautical Archaeology* 35(1):4–19.

Herrera, J. M. 2001. El navegante complejo: Antropología, complejidad, sensoramiento remoto y SIG en la arqueología marítima. Unpublished thesis, Escuela Nacional de Antropología e Historia, Mexico City.

Luna Erreguerena, P. 1998. Proyecto de Investigación Flota de la Nueva España 1630–1631, Informe de actividades (Marzo 1997 a Febrero 1998). Unpublished report, Instituto Nacional de Antropología e Historia, Mexico City.

Luna Erreguerena, P. 1999. Proyecto de Investigación Flota de la Nueva España 1630–1631, Informe de actividades (Marzo 1998 a Febrero 1999). Unpublished report, Instituto Nacional de Antropología e Historia, Mexico City.

Manucy, A. 1985. *Artillery through the Ages. A Short Illustrated History of Cannon, Emphasizing Types Used in America.* Washington, DC: Division of Publications/ National Park Service/US Department of the Interior.

Martínez, J. 1997. *Pasajeros de Indias. Viajes Trasatlánticos en el Siglo XVI.* Madrid: Alianza Universidad.

Moya Sordo, V. 2003. Arqueología de un accidente marítimo: procesos sociales y fenómenos naturales en un naufragio de la época de exploración y reconocimiento trasatlánticos en el Golfo de México. Unpublished thesis. Escuela Nacional de Antropología e Historia, Mexico City.

Muckelroy, K. 1978. *Maritime Archaeology.* Cambridge: Cambridge University Press.

Núñez Cabeza de Vaca, A. 1992. *Los Naufragios.* Madrid: Castalia.

Pérez-Mallaína, P. 1996. *El Hombre frente al Mar. Naufragios en la Carrera de Indias durante los Siglos XVI y XVII.* Seville, Spain: Universidad de Sevilla.

Schiffer, M. B. 1976. *Behavioural Archaeology: First Principles.* New York: Kluwer Academic/Plenum Press.

Shakespeare, William. 2003. Hume P. and Sherman, W., eds. *The Tempest.* York, England: Norton Critical Editions.

CHAPTER 6

An 18th-Century British Shipwreck in the Gulf of Mexico

Roberto Enrique Galindo Domínguez

INTRODUCTION

In this chapter I discuss the cultural affiliations and approximate chronology of an 18th-century site found in the Gulf of Mexico through analysis of the artifacts registered *in situ* and their distribution. The diverse material remains include civil-pattern British artillery from the second half of the 18th century and an impressive collection of lead ingots very similar to the "small pig" style. The analyses presented below lead to a hypothesis that the shipwreck is British in origin.

DESCRIPTION

The site was discovered through a towing prospection survey during the 1997 field season. It was named Don Pancho in honor of the local guide who took us there (Figure 6.1). The survey was conducted as part of the research project of the 1630–1631 New Spain fleet and the Inventory and diagnosis of submerged cultural resources in the Gulf of Mexico, carried out by the Subdirección de Arqueología Subacuática (Underwater Archaeology Vice-Directorate) of the Instituto Nacional de Antropología e Historia (National Institute of Anthropology and History, INAH).[1]

The site is in the Sound of Campeche, Gulf of Mexico, southwest of the Triángulos Sur Key. It occupies an area of approximately 1,000 m^2 (10,764 ft^2) and rests within coral formations in sandy areas at a depth between 2.20 m (7.2 ft) and 4.30 m (14 ft). During the 1997 field season, three anchors, two cannons, and assorted lead elements were registered *in situ*. Some were made of ballast stones, metal, glass, and rigging fragments. Twenty lead ingots were recorded by

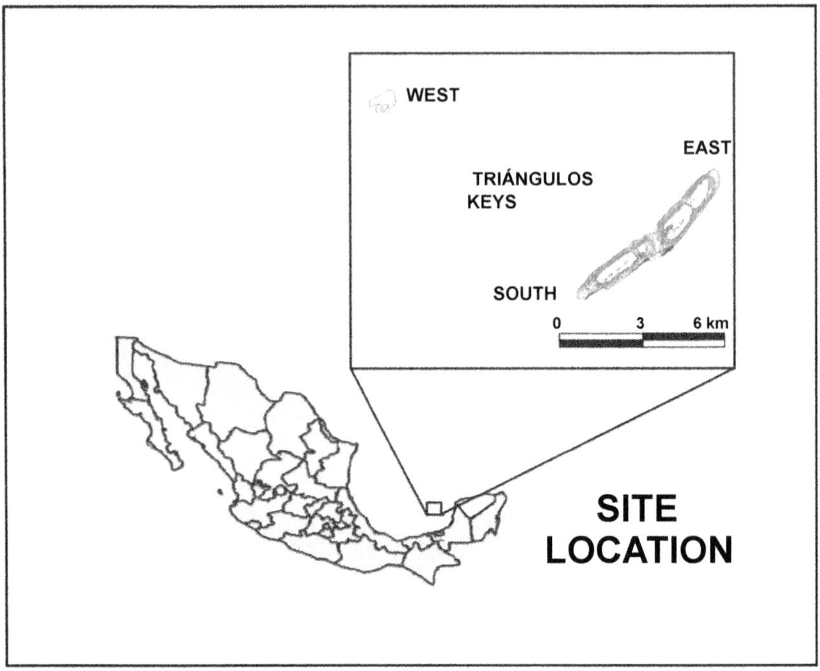

Figure 6.1 Site location (drawn by Jorge Manuel Herrera and Roberto Galindo/Subdirección de Arqueología Subacuática/Instituto Nacional de Antropología e Historia).

drawings, photography, and video, and one ingot was collected as a representative sample.

In 1998, the site was relocated by INAH using a remote sensing system called ESPADAS (Equipments and Systems of the Platform for the Acquisition of Archaeological Submerged Data), developed after the ADAP (Acquisition Data Archaeological Platform) created by the Submerged Resources Centre of the United States National Park Service. A magnetometer survey in the area identified two rudder gudgeons, another anchor, and some iron shot. Because one of the ingots identified during the 1997 season was missing, we decided to recover them all, which resulted in our finding another twenty buried in the sand. A sounding lead, twenty-two lead bullets, two lead fragments, and iron shot were also extracted, as we believed they were at risk of being looted. These objects belonged to a ship that, according to the analyses of artifact distributions at the wreck site reported below, wrecked rather than ran aground as we had previously suspected (Luna Erreguerena 1998, 1999).

CULTURAL AFFILIATION

The marks observed on one of the cannons suggest that the ship is British in origin. The guns are similar in size and appearance. On one of the pieces, various marks were identified that provide a great deal of information about the date and cultural affiliation of the shipwreck. With the help of Dr. Donald H. Keith, founder and president of Ships of Discovery based in Texas, the detailed drawings of the gun were sent to Rudi Roth in Switzerland, a well-known expert on artillery. His opinion and comments have been very useful.

The gun was identified as a British 6-pounder with a civil pattern of 4' 6". This type of gun would not correspond to the common pieces from a British Navy ship but was more likely to be derived from a merchant vessel. The length of the gun from trunnions to muzzle is too short to reach the gun port of a British warship. Furthermore, the gun's walls are not thick enough to resist the normal powder load of a navy ship and would not suit the common British practice of loading guns with additional round shot or grape shot, which consisted on a box-like container or package full of lead bullets (Roth 1998). The marks found on the piece confirm the hypothesis of its British origin.

The gun's first reinforcement has weight marks corresponding to the English style of the time. It shows the numbers 11-2-12, which from left to right stand for hundred weight (cwt), fourth of a cwt, and simple pounds. This mark can be explained as follows: "c" stands for hundred, according to the Roman numerals, and "wt" is the abbreviation for weight. This contraction refers to "hundred weight" or 100 lbs of 1.12 modern pounds each. One cwt therefore equals 112 modern pounds. The fourth of cwt is a quarter of a "hundred weight," that is to say 28 lbs. A simple pound equals 1.12 modern pounds. Based on this information it is possible to calculate the gun's weight: 11-2-12 means 11 (112 lbs) + 2 (28 lbs) + 12 (1 lb) = 1,300 modern pounds.

Another important inscription on the first reinforcement is a crowned letter "P" (Figure 6.2). This refers to the term "Crown Proof," which has to do with both merchant and civil tests performed on each gun tube. These exercises were held during the second half of the 18th century in Woolwich, where all artillery pieces were sent. If the guns passed the test, they were marked with a broad arrow if destined for the official service and with a Crown Proof if they were to be used for civilian purposes. There is not much information available regarding pieces for the civil services; nevertheless, it is known that gun smelters tried to reproduce the naval patterns of the time. When this specific gun was smelted, the pattern used was the Armstrong-Frederick. Another inscription—the number 8—was located on the

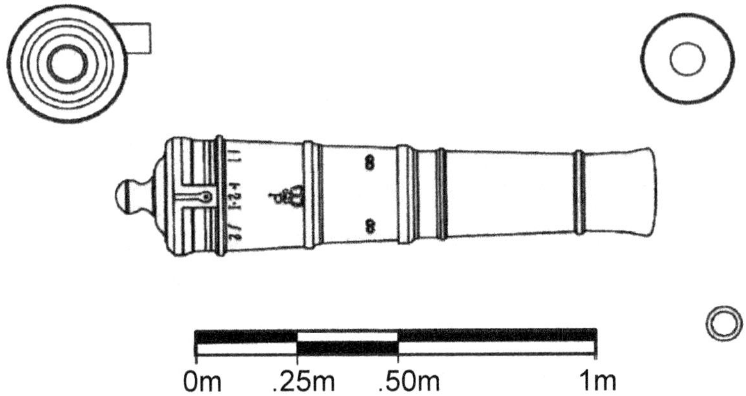

Figure 6.2. Cannon with P crowned (drawn by Donald H. Keith/ Subdirección de Arqueología Subacuática/Instituto Nacional de Antropología e Historia).

second reinforcement. During the 18th century, this number would possibly refer to a station, a battery, or a ship mark (Roth 1998).

Even if the gun can be identified as British, the ship carrying it might not have been British. Artillery trafficking was a common practice, both for commercial reasons or in order to recycle pieces from a captured enemy ship. There are many reasons why vessels carried armament from different countries. For instance, the Dutch East India Company vessel *Mauritius*, wrecked in 1609, transported armament from Holland, England, and Portugal (Brown 1997; Roth 1995). Between the 17th and 18th centuries, England and Sweden were the only European countries capable of producing enough iron guns to export in large quantities. For this reason, the guns do not necessarily indicate the ship's nationality (Brown 1997:104).

Because the specific guns found on the wreck were used for merchant vessels and not Royal Navy ships, the ship might have belonged to the East India Company (Roth 1995). Another indicator of the ship's nationality is that since the 17th century, the form of lead ingots differed depending on their origin. English ingots normally had a boat-like structure, whereas Spanish ingots were rectangular and French examples had a "salmon shape." Most of the ingots found in the Don Pancho site are flat fronted and convex sided, very similar in shape to the English ones.

In 17th-century England, it was common to manufacture ingots called "big pigs," which had a weight of around 308 lbs, and "small pigs" or "pieces" that were used during the second half of the 18th century and weighted approximately 154 lbs (Price, Muckelroy, and Willies 1980:25). The ingots found in the Don Pancho site weigh 142.5 lbs on average. In addition, two pieces have a "broad arrow" on their flat side; this mark was used by the British government on some of its property (Brown 1997:108). This contradicts our first hypothesis supported by the cannon characteristics, that the ship has a civil origin. However, the fact that the cannon and some English-type ingots were found in the site does not necessarily mean that the vessel came from England.

The lead ingots may have had a double function. Because of their weight and form, which was usually the same, they might have been used as ballast in the ship's hold. In this case, the lead was not only transported as cargo but was also used for an important task. In this way, it cost little to transport it and saved valuable cargo space.

The trade in lead among European countries and their possessions in other continents can be confirmed by the collection of ingots from shipwrecks from different nationalities exhibited in the British Museum. Most of the lead comes from British mines, regardless of the ship's port of origin. They could be English vessels or from the Dutch East India Company or *Verenigde Oostindische Compaign* (VOC). Such is the case of the ingots found in a VOC ship that wrecked in Needle, near the Wight Islands in 1627, and the *Hollandia* lost in 1743 on the Sicilian coast. In both cases, the transported lead came from the Derbyshire islands, which, along with the mines of South Yorkshire, dominated international lead production during the first half of the 18th century (Craddock and Hook 1997:145–46). Despite the fact that the pieces found in the Don Pancho site might have been transported by a ship of another nationality, no other elements have been identified that may suggest another origin. Consequently, all the evidence leads to the conclusion that the wreck at the Don Pancho site is, in fact, an English vessel.

INFERENCES FROM ARTIFACT DISTRIBUTIONS

The spatial distribution of the ingots within an area of approximately 6 x 7 m (19.5 x 23 ft) and the fact that most of them were found lying one on top of each other on their flat side suggests that the pieces remained in the same position in which they were placed onboard the ship. The question is why they were placed in this specific position. If the pieces had been placed on their convex side, they would not have been as stable inside the ship's hold. The position of the pieces on their flat side contradicts the hypothesis that convex-shaped ingots were easier to handle, as was suggested about the ingots found in the *Kennemerland* vessel, a Dutch East Indiaman wrecked in 1664 off the coast of Stoura Stack, Scotia. The *Kennemerland* ingots present a form similar to the ones found in the Don Pancho site, which presumably allows better handling as it is possible to stick hands underneath the sides to lift them from the ground without difficulty (Price, Muckelroy, and Willies 1980:7–10). A more important priority, however, was to maintain the stability of the pieces once they were placed inside the ship. These ingots weighed more than 29 lbs, which could have posed a risk of movement during a storm or rough seas. If the ingots were to move, they could destroy the transported cargo or even affect the structure of the vessel.

Another fact that led us to think that the distribution of the ingots on the seabed might be the same as that in the ship came to light thanks to one of the divers who was at the bottom while the ingots were being extracted. When some of the divers reached the surface, one of the pieces detached from the net and instead of sinking in a vertical line, it slid diagonally approximately 3 m (10 ft) before reaching the bottom. The diver on the bottom watched the ingot's trajectory and noted how the convex side hit the seabed. If the pieces discovered had been thrown from the ship, they would not have been found on top of one another but would made been scattered along the bottom and some of them would made landed flat side up.

There was a central group of approximately 3 x 2 m (10 x 6.5 ft), which consisted of more than half of the pieces occupied an area. A second group of seven pieces located 1.50 m (5 ft) to the southeast from the main group covered an area of 1 x 1.50 m (3.3 x 5 ft). A third group of six pieces was located within an area of 1 x 1 m (3.3 x 3.3 ft) to the south of the main group and at a distance of 1 m (3.3 ft). Finally, there were two isolated pieces. One was 2 m (6.5 ft) away from the group of six pieces toward the southwest, and the other was located 1.5 m (5 ft) away from the main group in a northerly direction.

Based on the spatial distribution of the artifacts, we reached two possible interpretations of the wreckage:

1. When hitting the reef, the lower part of the ship's hull broke and became detached from the rest of the ship. This allowed the group of ingots to hit the bottom directly, thus avoiding the diagonal sliding of the central pieces. This suggests that those ingots placed

on the edges may have moved in other directions forming the minor groups and the isolated ingots described above.

2. There is a possibility that the ship wrecked and sank intact together with its ballast load inside the hold. If we apply this hypothesis, we can explain why the ingots were found in a position very similar to the one in which they were loaded, if we allow for a small displacement of the ingots at the moment the hull hit the seabed.

Our shipwreck theory is reinforced by the presence of the two rudder gudgeons that were attached to the sternpost (Figure 6.3). The only way they could have been detached from the ship would be if the sternpost had broken with the rudder still attached. This, apart from causing the loss of the rudder, would also have led to the destruction of the stern and

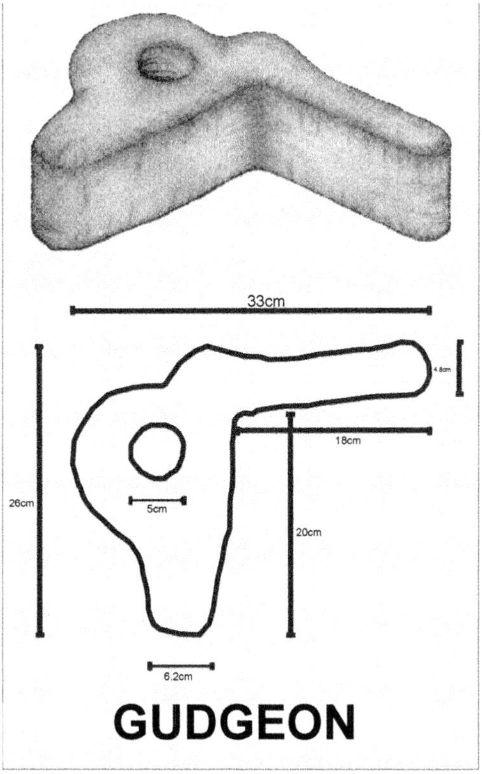

Figure 6.3 Gudgeon (drawn by Damián Vainstub and Roberto E. Galindo/Subdirección de Arqueología Subacuática/Instituto Nacional de Antropología e Historia).

the unavoidable shipwreck. The fact that we have not found any pintles indicates that they could have remained attached to the rudder and were lost if the rudder had completely detached from the ship's sternpost and was swept away with the stream. This suggestion needs further study, as the pintles could lie under the sediment (Galindo and Herrera 2002).

To date, only the material detected on the surface of the site has been studied. To better understand the wrecking process through analysis of how ship parts and contents were distributed across the site, it would be ideal to include buried items. At this stage, however, it is still possible to reveal aspects of the events by studying the orientation of the wreckage. The location of objects inside a ship is closely related to the final distribution of the elements within the archaeological context of a maritime accident (Martin 1997:2). In the case of the Don Pancho site, some artifacts from the stern were found to the northwest, followed by some heavy elements like guns and ingots, which apparently were stored somewhere in the middle of the ship; three of the anchors were located around these elements (Figure 6.4). As seen in Figure 6.4, rudder gudgeons and a sounding lead, which might have been in hands of the pilot or some other officer, were found in the stern area. Usually, sailing instruments and other special devices were reserved for the officer's use, and their storage place was in an officer's cabinet in the ship's stern.

Turning now to the anchors, one was 15 m (49 ft) north of the group of ingots, whereas the second was found to the east 8 m (26 ft) away from the group. The third lay 15 m (49 ft) south from the lead pieces. One isolated anchor, very similar to the others, was found 117 m (384 ft) to the west of the main concentration. Its shank pointed directly to the concentration of ballast at the Don Pancho site. This circumstantial evidence seems to indicate that the anchor is associated with the site. A similar incident occurred with an isolated anchor in the Molasses Reef wreck, in the Turks and Caicos Islands. In this case, the piece was 50 m (164 ft) east to the site, and its shank was pointing to the ballast mound, enabling Keith (1987:161) to relate the anchor with the wreck event.

It is possible that the distribution of the anchors in relation to the rest of the materials has to do with the way they were handled in an attempt to avoid the loss of the ship or to mitigate the effects of the disaster (Gibbs 2006:10). Following this line of argument, it is possible that the isolated anchor represents an attempt to avoid the impact with the reef. When this operation was not successful, the ship probably went straight toward the coral heads. It was then that the crew probably tried to use the other three anchors to orient the ship into another direction. However, the wreck shows that this strategy also failed. This hypothesis is supported by the fact that the anchors' shanks were found facing the

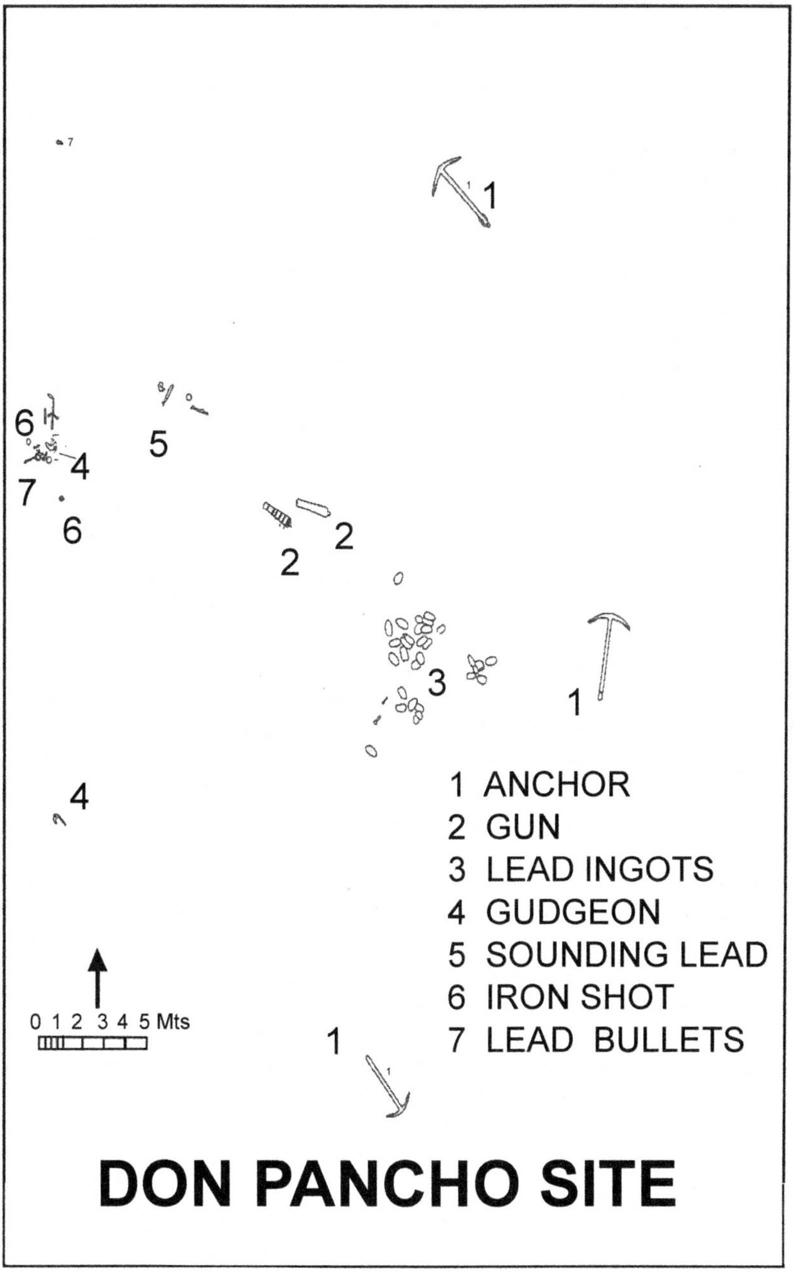

Figure 6.4 Site plan (drawn by Octavio del Río and Santiago Analco/ Subdirección de Arqueología Subacuática/Instituto Nacional de Antropología e Historia).

central area where the ship finally wrecked. The disposition of all the materials indicates that the crew must have been alert because the time the ship was at least 200 m (656 ft) from the key and acted rapidly in the face of the imminent wreck (Gibbs 2006:11) because the main concentration of materials is approximately 100 m (328 ft) from the part of the key that is not submerged.

To more precisely associate the location of these remains to the ship's structure, it would be necessary to conduct test excavations and to expand the intrasite magnetic survey using a systematic metal detector survey. A similar approach was used in 1970 when trying to determine the orientation of the *Dartmouth* wreckage, a second-rate ship that wrecked in 1690 in the United Kingdom. In that case, the vessel's orientation was determined using spatial analysis of the different categories of the artifacts found (Colin 1997:2).

THE LEAD INGOTS

After finishing *in situ* recording to construct a site map, we proceeded with the extraction of the ingots. Once an ingot was selected, a diver would place a net beside it, holding it while two other divers lifted the ingot and placed it inside the net with its convex side facing down. They would then close the net and hook it to a lifting balloon. When the ingot was in the net and the balloon was inflated, the divers would lead it to the surface and place the ingot in the boat. Another lifting method consisted of grabbing the ingot, turning it up so the net would stay underneath it, and continuing with the recovery procedure.

All the recovered ingots had concretions on their surfaces. The ingots were treated and cleaned through chemical and mechanical processes using materials such as hydrochloric acid and disodic salt, both of which were diluted in water. In some ingots, concretions were intentionally left as an example of their original condition; these can still be seen on the convex side of the pieces.

A photographic record and detailed drawings were made before and after the cleaning processes. This procedure facilitated the comparative analysis because the handling of 107.8- to 173.8 lbs pieces is not an easy job. Of the forty pieces, thirty-two had marks made by incision, and of these fifteen also contain holes. The marks and the holes are located on the upper and flat sides of the ingots; the depth of the markings varies and some are poorly visible. These variations may be explained in several ways: (1) some ingots were immediately marked after manufacture; (2) the marks were made when the ingot had cooled and was almost solid; (3) the marks were made long after they were finished; (4) the marks were not printed with the same device or the same strength.

Most of the ingots are oval shaped, but rectangular, semi-triangular, and irregular forms are also present. On the sides of some are striations that occurred during the cooling process and are not a result of different liquid lead pouring times (Price, Muckelroy, and Willies 1980:17). Using the detailed drawings and the photographic records, it is possible to compare the forms, marks, weights, and dimensions of the ingots to study possible relationships and the variability in their characteristics. We have experimented with combinations such as form-weight, form-marks, form-dimensions, dimension-marks, dimension-weight, and marks-weight, but so far we have not been able to establish any relationship through those comparisons.

We also tried to find out if the marks followed a sequence but we have not been successful yet. For instance, some of the pieces show the same mark with similar weight, form, and dimensions, but there are also other ingots that share similar marks but are quite different from each other. Finally, the idea of the marks being related to weight and dimension has been totally eliminated. All the analyses have led us to infer that the Don Pancho site collection most likely consists of ingots manufactured at different times and by different smelters. As mentioned above, we identified the "broad arrow" in two ingots, a fact that reinforces the hypothesis of the British origin of the ship.

Through the superposition of the detailed drawings, we were able to compare and differentiate some of the pieces according to their manufacturing process. It is possible that some of them were made in the same cast; nevertheless, even among the most similar ingots, there are differences regarding dimension, form, and weight. This may be because of the quantity of metal that was poured into the cast.

Two possible manufacturing procedures have previously been considered. The pieces may have been manufactured with prefabricated casts made of a material more resistant than lead or the melted lead was poured into holes in sand beds. If this is the case, is it possible that more than one ingot could be manufactured in the same sand mould? If this turns out to be correct, then the deformation of the sand holes, caused by subsequent liquid lead pouring, could explain why some ingots are similar but still differ in profile, form, and dimension.

In terms of this specific ingot collection, characteristics representative of both manufacturing procedures have been observed. Some of the oval-shaped ingots that share mark similarities also show holes generally located at the end of the piece. This indicates they might have been made in prefabricated casts and the holes were made to pull them out with a metal bar. In contrast, irregular pieces do not have holes and were likely to have been manufactured in sand beds. If this is the case, their extraction would have been simpler and again reinforces the hypothesis that the ingots were manufactured by different smelters.

Although the marks on the artillery are associated with commercial shipping and those on the ingots with the British Navy and we did not find any artifacts that could indicate another source, the wreck seems likely to have had an English origin. We cannot establish, however, whether the ship that of a commercial company, the navy, or a privateer. Finally, it is important to mention that the site has not been excavated. Obviously, the materials and artifacts found and recorded *in situ* are only part of the shipwreck and there must be other cultural elements under the sediment. For this reason, the hypothesis of British origin represents only the first major step toward understanding the archaeological context of the Don Pancho site.

NOTE

1. The contents of this chapter are the result of many hours of research, and a great deal of effort and multidisciplinary team work, resulting in an important body of data, including site record forms, maps, field notes, images and reports (Luna Erreguerena 1998, 1999) that are filed in the Technical Archives of INAH's Underwater Archaeology Vice Directorate. In the previous edition of this book it was not mentioned that some of the initial hypotheses about the site were developed by researchers that participated in the 1998 field work, including Donald H. Keith and Jorge M. Herrera, whose ideas can be found in Herrera´s thesis El navegante complejo. Antropología, complejidad, sensoramiento remoto y SIG en la Arqueología Marítima (2001). Herrera 2001 appeared in the references section of this chapter in the earlier publication, and is specifically cited in the text of this edition.

ACKNOWLEDGMENTS

My deep gratitude to the Instituto Nacional de Antropología e Historia, especially to the Subdirección de Arqueología Subacuática for supporting my participation at the 2003 Fifth World Archaeology Congress in Washington, DC. I also thank everyone who made this publication possible.

REFERENCES

Brown, R. 1997. Arms and armour from wrecks: An introduction. In *Artifacts from Wrecks. Dated Assemblages from the Late Middle Ages to the Industrial Revolution*, M. Redknap, ed., 101–09. Exeter, UK: Oxbow Books.

Martin, Colin J. M. 1997. Ships as integrated artifacts: The archaeological potential. In *Artifacts from Wrecks. Dated Assemblages from the Late Middle Ages to the Industrial Revolution*, M. Redknap, ed., 1–13. Exeter, UK: Oxbow Books.

Craddock, P., and D. Hook. 1997. The British Museum collection of metal ingots from dated wrecks. In *Artifacts from Wrecks. Dated Assemblages from the Late Middle*

Ages to the Industrial Revolution, M. Redknap, ed., 143–54. Exeter, UK: Oxbow Books.

Galindo, R., and J. M. Herrera. 2002. Don Pancho site: Evidence of an eighteenth century British maritime casualty. Unpublished paper presented at the 35th Conference on Historical and Underwater Archaeology of the Society for Historical Archaeology, January 11, Mobile, Alabama.

Gibbs, M. 2006. Cultural site formation processes in maritime archaeology: Disaster response, salvage and Muckelroy 30 years on. *The International Journal of Nautical Archaeology* 35(1):4–19.

Keith, D. 1987. "The Molasses Reef wreck," INA, Exploration and Discovery Research Team. Manuscript, College Station, TX.

Herrera, J.M. 2001a. Desnaufragando Historias: Antropología y Arqueología en Tres Accidentes Navales en la Sonda de Campeche. In *Amerística, la Ciencia del Nuevo Mundo*, Año 4. No. 7, 67–129.

Herrera, J.M. 2001b. El navegante complejo. Antropología, complejidad, sensoramiento remoto y SIG en la Arqueología Marítima. Unpublished thesis, Escuela Nacional de Antropología e Historia, Mexico City.

Luna Erreguerena, P. 1998. Proyecto de Investigación Flota de la Nueva España 1630–1631, Informes de actividades (Marzo 1997 a Febrero 1998). Unpublished report, Instituto Nacional de Antropología e Historia, Mexico City.

Luna Erreguerena, P. 1999. Proyecto de Investigación Flota de la Nueva España 1630–1631, Informe de actividades (Marzo 1998 a Febrero 1999) y Propuesta de Investigación (Marzo-Diciembre 1999). Unpublished report, Instituto Nacional de Antropología e Historia, Mexico City.

Price, R., K. Muckelroy, and L. Willies. 1980. The Kennemerland site. A report on the lead ingots. *The International Journal of Nautical Archaeology and Underwater Exploration* 9(1):7–25.

Roth, R. 1995. The reporting of ordnance: The guns of the Mauritius, a casebook study. In *The Archaeology of Ships of War*, International Maritime Archaeology Series, vol. 1, M. Bound, ed., 120–29. Oxford: Oxford University Press.

Roth, R. 1998. Report on the cannons from a Shipwreck at Bahía de Campeche. Manuscript on file at the Subdirección de Arqueología Subacuática/Instituto Nacional de Antropología e Historia, Mexico City.

CHAPTER 7

Evidence of Early Inhabitants in Submerged Caves in Yucatan, Mexico

Arturo H. González González, Carmen Rojas Sandoval, Eugenio Acevez Núñez, Jerónimo Avilés Olguín, Santiago Analco Ramírez (†), Octavio del Río Lara, Pilar Luna Erreguerena, Adriana Velázquez Morlet, Wolfgang Stinnesbeck, Alejandro Terrazas Mata, and Martha Benavente Sanvicente

INTRODUCTION

The Yucatan Peninsula is generally considered poor in terms of preservation of paleontological or archaeological remains. This is essentially the result of geochemical and geomorphologic conditions in the region such as the absence of soils covering the limestone bedrock and the ubiquitous presence of jungle vegetation (e.g., humin acids). These conditions explain the general absence of fossil remains older than about 2,000 years B.P. Recent discoveries of late Pleistocene fossils in cenotes (sinkholes) and submerged caves, however, markedly alter this view. For example, remains of Pleistocene horse (*Equus conversidens*), lama-like camelids (*Hemiauchenia* sp.), elephants (*Gomphotherium floridanum*), and the skull of a bat (*Desmodus* sp.) were recently described as coming from a submerged cave at Papakal in the state of Yucatan (Polaco, Rojas, and González 2002).

In 2001, the project Underwater Archaeological Atlas for recording, studying, and protecting cenotes (sinkholes) in the Yucatan Peninsula was approved by the Consejo de Arqueología (Council of Archaeology) of the Instituto Nacional de Antropología e Historia (National Institute of Anthropology and History, INAH). Over the past five years, our multidisciplinary team has recorded numerous prehistoric sites within the system of submerged cenotes and caves of the Yucatan Peninsula, mostly located near Tulum in the Mexican state of Quintana Roo. Our findings include ashes from human fireplaces as well as diverse and abundant remains of Pleistocene vertebrates, mainly mammals. In addition, three human skeletons provide evidence for late Pleistocene settlement of the Yucatan Peninsula, southeastern Mexico.

GEOLOGY AND CLIMATE

The geology of the Yucatan Peninsula is homogeneous and relatively simple. A sequence of shallow water limestone up to 3,000 m (9,840 ft) thick dating from between late Cretaceous and sub-recent age overlies a metamorphic basement detected in the subsurface (López Ramos 1975; Ward, Weidie, and Back 1985; Ward et al. 1995). In the study area (between Tulum and Akumal in the state of Quintana Roo), the bedrock consists of white massive limestone that caps the cave system and forms the substrate of the jungle. Limestone below this layer is brown to yellow and appears to be less resistant, forming concave overhangs. Its stratigraphic age appears to be from Oligocene to basal Miocene, as indicated by the characteristic absence of Paleocene–Eocene large benthic foraminifera and the abundance of Peneroplidae. This early Neogene age concurs with the geological map of Yucatan that indicates lower Neogene sediments for the area north of Tulum.

At 13,000 years B.P., sea level in the Yucatan Peninsula was 65 m (213 ft) lower than today (Blanchon and Shaw 1995) as a result of the enormous amount of ice covering the Northern Hemisphere. Consequently, groundwater levels near the coast of Yucatan were also much deeper than today and at least the upper floors of the vast cave system of Yucatan must have been dry to depths of 50 m (164 ft) and more.

Climatic changes at the end of the Pleistocene led to deglaciation and an increase of the global sea level. Along the northern and western coasts of the Yucatan Peninsula (states of Campeche and Yucatan), wide extensions of land were flooded; along the eastern coast (state of Quintana Roo), the continental platform is narrow and the geographic changes in the coast line are less explicit. However, in this area, Pleistocene cliff lines were leveled out and disappeared. In consequence, most of Quintana Roo is elevated only a few meters above recent sea level.

The increase in sea level during early Holocene deglaciation appears to have occurred within short periods of time, or even within "catastrophic events." This interpretation is based on the presence of *Acropora palmata*, a dominant component in reefs throughout the Caribbean. *A. palmata* forms monospecific colonies in 0–5 m (0–16 ft) water depth and is restricted to a maximum depth of 10 m (33 ft). Fossil reefs with

A. palmata are therefore used to determine fossil water levels and coast lines, and their unaltered aragonitic skeletons are used to obtain precise radiometric assignations of the ages of these reefs.

The existence of dry caves allowed humans to occupy these sites at least temporarily. There is evidence that caves were used as shelters, including fireplaces where animals were cooked as well as funeral sites. In the deep parts of the cave system, people likely searched for sweet water, which must have been extremely rare on the karstic surface of the Yucatan Peninsula. Global increase of water levels at the end of the Pleistocene led to the gradual flooding of caves, thus sealing and preserving the evidence for this presence of preceramic man in the area.

Diverse and abundant archaeological and paleoanthropological evidence in the deep and isolated inner parts of the Yucatan system of caves and cenotes contrasts with the absence near entrances and openings, even though human activities must have concentrated here. However, the subsequent collapse of cave roofs and deposition of coarse-grained sediment (limeclast breccias) in these places, as well as recent jungle vegetation and soil, likely buried any human evidence under a thick layer of debris, thus impeding systematic scientific research activities.

PALEOANTHROPOLOGY

How and when the first groups of humans arrived at the American continent is one of today's most contentious scientific questions. Models to explain the origin and the number of migrations are based on archaeological, anthropophysical, genetic, and linguistic evidence. The majority of these models suggest a high degree of difference in biological variability before and after the first migration, which requires a time period of 20 ky or more. Other proposals suggest numerous long-distance migrations and a recent arrival, approximately 12 ky B.P. The possible source areas of these migrations include Siberia, Mongolia, Southeast Asia, and the South Pacific.

Different routes have been suggested, but the most traditional view sustains that Mongoloid populations from northeast Asia crossed the Strait of Bering via a land bridge that formed near the end of the last glaciation, some 12 ky ago. At their arrival on the North American continent, they created the Clovis tradition, supposedly the oldest archaeological culture on the continent. A second alternative suggests that a non-Mongoloid population from southeast Asia, using boats and following the Pacific coast line along the Strait of Bering and south along the coast of Canada and the United States. These groups could have arrived about 15 ky ago and would thus be older than the Clovis culture.

A third scenario suggests migration via the Pacific Ocean, coming from Oceania and Polynesia, with the arrival of the first settlers in Central and South America. However, this latter model is no longer in favor because of evidence indicating a late settlement of the Easter Island in Chile. Finally, a Solutrean population from Europe could have followed a route through the North Atlantic, following the southern front of the ice cap (González and Destefano Farías 2002). This model remains speculative because of the distances, the temporal hiatus between the Solutrean and the Clovis cultures and the lack of evidence in Greenland and Canada. Regardless of the scenario proposed, the Yucatan Peninsula plays a key role in understanding the early settlement of tropical Americas (Bate and Terrazas 2002).

The earliest published evidence for human presence on the Yucatan Peninsula documents a small hunting campsite at Los Tapiales in the western highlands of Guatemala, which has an associated charcoal ^{14}C age of 10,710±170 (Tx-1631) B.P. (García-Bárcena 1982). Subsequently, flaked stone tools were excavated at the Loltun cave in the state of Yucatan, from nonceramic levels; they were reportedly found in association with extinct faunal elements. At Aktun Ha, a submerged cave close to Tulum in Quintana Roo, anthropogenic charcoal recently returned a date of 9155±75 B.P. (INAH-2011).

METHODOLOGY FOR UNDERWATER STUDY OF PREHISTORIC CAVES

Cave diving is dangerous; many experienced divers have lost their lives in submerged caves. According to the statistics, the highest number of accidents results from disorientation, leaving the base line, very deep diving (the recommended maximum depth is 39 m) (128 ft), lack of air because of not reserving two-thirds for the way back, and not using three lights (NSS-CDS 1992). These are challenges even for the most advanced divers; ongoing training and fitness are vital. Guidelines state that divers should always have a partner who can give assistance in a difficult situation; duplicate tanks, extra masks, and three lamps are obligatory. The base line should have arrowheads indicating the direction and distance toward the next exit, and the dive must be discussed in detail beforehand.

These instructions and regulations make any underwater archaeology project a difficult and logistically complex task. Because of limited air supply and required cautionary measures, the time researchers can remain in the site is extremely restricted. It varies greatly according to the distance to the cave entrance and depth of the immersion. For instance, in deep sites (e.g., below 25 m water depth) (82 ft), the amount of time at the archaeological site is frequently reduced to a few minutes and most of the time is used subsequently for decompression.

For this project, we use methods that allow us to improve the structure of dives and increase the amount of time on location. Protocols are established individually for each site. These procedures lead to a higher output of archaeological evidence recovered in less time as well as better scientific documentation of our work. Further, they improve researchers' security.

Base Lines

Archaeological evidence is often located hundreds of meters from the closest entrance, in complicated underground mazes tens of meters below the surface. To find the way out of this labyrinth, the diver follows enrolled lines, or strings, which connect the entrance/exit with the archaeological sites. These "base lines," or "lines of life," were placed by the first explorers who entered the cave. The lines initiate at a geographic point with GPS reading and its coordinates are located in a map.

Along its course, the lifeline is fastened to projecting rocks, or stalagmites. These intermittent fixed points, located at an approximate distance of 10 m (33 ft) or less between each other, are used as references to measure distances from the cave walls, ceiling, or floor and provide the means for constructing a three-dimensional map of the system and the route to an archaeological or paleontological site.

Recording and Collection in Low Visibility

Visibility is rapidly lost in caves because of the volatility of fine-grained silt and clay sediment, which can easily be stirred up even by a light touch of a fin or by water movement. Zero visibility is one of the most important sources of danger in cave diving and has led to many lethal accidents. As excavation of the archaeological evidence at our site is necessary and thus removal of sediment is called for, only divers with experience in zero visibility are allowed in the excavation.

In the Yucatan caves that have been explored, the sediment layer is thin and only partially covers the cultural material. Particles are extremely fine grained, clay to silt-sized. For excavation, sediment is gently stirred up by injecting water with a pipette or forming small water currents by moving the hands. This maneuver obstructs visibility and recording and is therefore always scheduled for the end of the dive. Sometimes it takes hours, days, or even weeks for the sediment to settle, especially when water currents are low. Long periods of time are therefore necessary between immersions to allow sediment to settle and to have enough visibility for diver security.

Using this procedure, evidence covered by a fine layer of sediment can be detected, but excavation can be extremely time consuming. For instance, the excavation of preceramic human skeletons preserved in the Yucatan caves required multiple visits. The recovery of the Naharon skeleton (discussed below) required more than forty immersions by a team of four scientists and divers over a period of more than a year. In these specific cases, however, our methodologies have been shown to be of great value. Our detailed and cautious procedure allowed us to recover almost complete skeletons (up to 90% of the bones present) and to make a taphonomic study. For instance, our data indicate that skeletization was *in situ*, even suggesting a funeral, and that it occurred at a time when caves were dry.

SITES AND PREHISTORIC EVIDENCE

Naharon I Human Skeleton

The Naharon or Cristal cenote, Quintana Roo, is located approximately 6 km (3.72 miles) inland (west) from the present northeastern Yucatan coastal shoreline, approximately 128 km (79.5 miles) southwest of Cancun. This cenote is the entrance to an extensive underwater cave system named Naranjal. Bones comprising the Naharon I skeleton were recorded and collected in a series of dives conducted over a twelve-month period from about a 3 m^2 (32 ft^2) area, 368 m (1,207 ft) northwest of the cenote entrance and 22.6 m (74 ft) deep (Figure 7.1).

The material consists of seventy-one identified specimens that correspond to forty-five bones of a single individual, which is approximately 80% of the complete human skeleton. Only the vertebral bones were found in their articulated position. Naharon I was determined to be a female based on the angle of the great sciatic notch. The age of the individual at the time of death is estimated at twenty-five–thirty years old, based on the morphology of the auricular surface of the left ileum (Lovejoy et al. 1985), the complete fusion of the epiphyses of the long bones, and the partial obliteration of the sutures of the skull (Meindl and Lovejoy 1985). A complete fusion of the second and third cervical vertebrate may be a congenital condition. The third lumbar vertebra shows an osteophytic rim, the product of work stress (Aufderheide and Rodríguez-Martín 1998). In the skull, the region of lambda shows porotic hyperostosis, and the roof of the orbits has little marked *criba orbitalia*. In the frontal bone, there is evidence of a trauma that was completely healed at the time of death. The cranial index was calculated

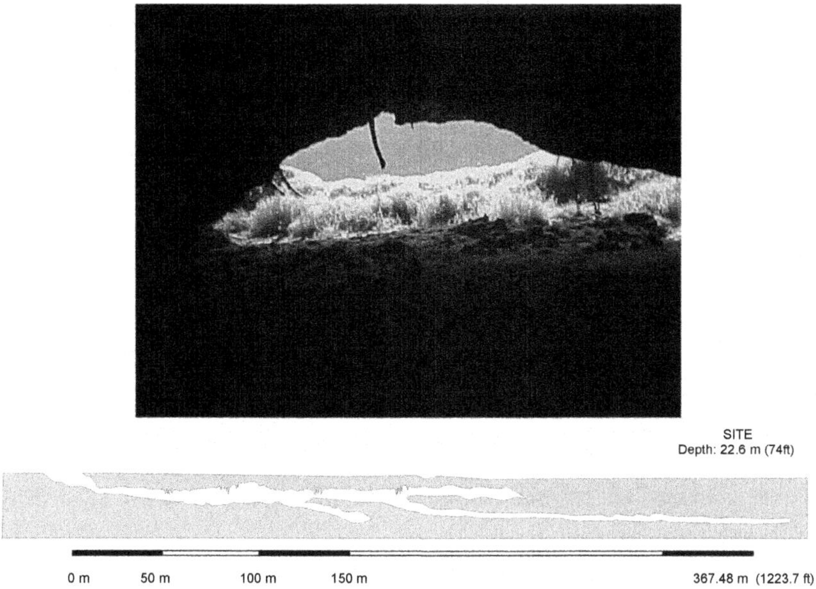

Figure 7.1 The human skeleton at Naharon was found 368 m northwest of the cenote entrance at a depth of 22.6 m (photograph by Arturo H. González; drawn by Carmen Rojas/Subdirección de Arqueología Subacuática/Instituto Nacional de Antropología e Historia).

at 76.96, a value that corresponds to a mesocranium pattern. This feature is extremely uncommon in humans discovered on the American continent before 8,000 B.P. (Powell and Neves 1999).

Las Palmas I

A second skeleton was discovered in the Naranjal cave system 369 m (1, 210.6 ft) west of the Las Palmas cenote, at a depth of 22.6 m (74.15 ft). Excellently preserved with a light brown color, this skeleton is >90% complete. The individual is mostly articulated, with only minor disintegration because of gravity. It was found in a lying position, bent to the left, with the legs and arms flexed and drawn toward the body. This situation strongly suggests that the original position of the body was upright and seated, possibly wrapped in a sack (Figure 7.2). If this interpretation is correct, it would indicate an intentional funerary deposit. Morphometric measurements suggest that the Las Palmas woman was 152 cm (5 ft) tall, with an estimated weight of 58 kg (127.6 lbs), and between forty-four and fifty years old at the time of her death.

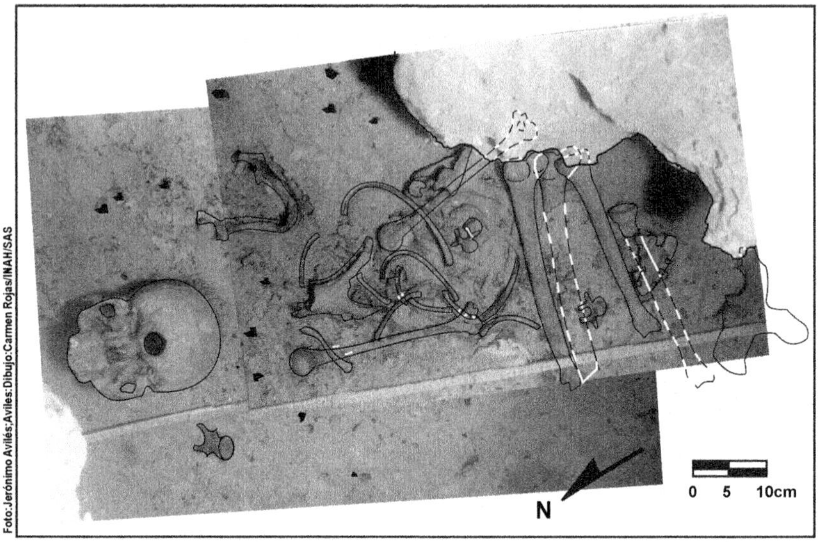

Figure 7.2 Skeleton of an adult female discovered at Las Palmas. Note that the body is mostly articulated, with only minor disintegration because of gravity. The skeleton is in a lying position, bent to the left, with the legs angled and drawn toward the body. About 90% of the skeleton has been recovered (photograph by Eugenio Acevez and Jerónimo Avilés/Subdirección de Arqueología Subacuática/Instituto Nacional de Antropología e Historia).

At 25 m (82 ft) west of the Las Palmas skeleton, charcoal is abundant, forming a large cluster on the cave floor. The charcoal strongly indicates the presence of an ancient fireplace. Two charcoal samples were radiometrically dated by the INAH laboratory in Mexico City: 8941±39 B.P. (INAH-2123) and 7740±39 B.P. (INAH-2119). The charcoal thus points to repeated human occupation of the cave. The articulated remains of a small mammal *Urocyon cinereoargenteus* (fox) were found 15 m (49 ft) from the human skeleton.

El Templo I

Eighteen kilometers (11.2 miles) north of Tulum and 1.5 km (0.93 miles) from the village of Chemuyil, in Quintana Roo, a third human skeleton was discovered in the El Templo cave. The entrance to this extended system is through a low cavern, with only the floor flooded by a few centimeters of water (cat walk). A permanent base line is fixed at the top of the cavern, above the entrance to the submerged cave. Navigation in the cave is relatively simple, following the white and nodded base line without noticing two possible jumps at 20 seconds to the right and at two minutes to the left. Distance to the skeleton is approximately 160 m (525 ft) through a nearly horizontal tunnel of 2 x 2.5 m (6.5 x 8 ft) in diameter, with maximum depths of 17 and an average depth of 14 m (46 ft). The halocline is at a depth of approximately 11 m (36 ft).

The El Templo individual was a male, twenty-five–thirty years old at the time of death (Terrazas and Benavente 2006). The skeleton is mostly articulated. The remains are poorly preserved, because of salt water erosion under the halocline (Figure 7.3). As a result of this decay, the bones are very light. They have fragmented *in situ* and superficially dissolved, so almost the entire organic material has been lost. Nevertheless, approximately 70% of the skeleton has been recovered.

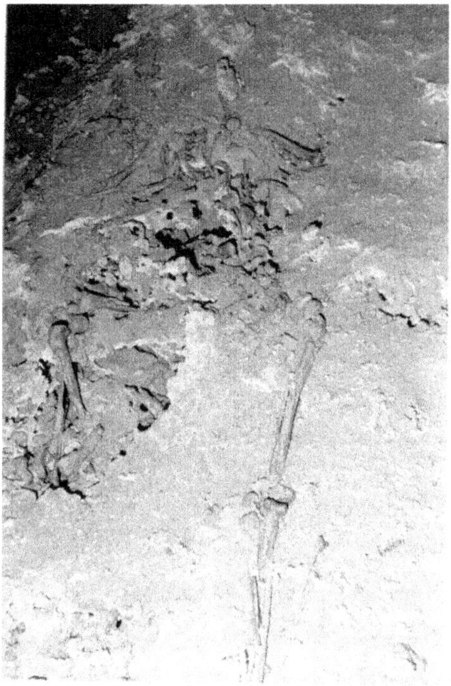

Figure 7.3 Skeleton of an adult male discovered at El Templo, with a dorsal decubit position of the body. Preservation of the bones is poor as a result of salt water dissolution, but about 70% of the skeleton has been recovered (photograph by Eugenio Acevez and Jerónimo Avilés/Subdirección de Arqueología Subacuática/Instituto Nacional de Antropología e Historia).

PALEONTOLOGICAL EVIDENCE

Nai Tucha

The entrance to the Nai Tucha cave system is located in a circular depression 20–30 m (65.5–98 ft) in cross-section, which was formed by the collapse of overlying limestone. A cone-shaped mount of debris is in the center of the sinkhole.

Bones of Pleistocene fossils have been discovered at Nai Tucha, *ca.* 680–700 m (2,230–2,296 ft) from the cave entrance. Preservation of vertebrate bones is excellent. The cave sediment consists entirely of autigenic aragonite and dolomite framboids. No siliciclastic matter or bioclasts have been recognized, indicating there were no water currents that would have brought detrital matter into the cave.

Several fossils have been identified so far.

- Nonarticulated bones of *Gomphotherium* (Figure 7.4). We identified a mandible containing a molar that corresponds to a juvenile individual as well as an isolated tooth of an adult specimen
- A complete and apparently articulated individual of an extinct tapir. Charcoal is abundant in the proximity of the fossil bones, but an ancient fireplace could not be reconstructed.

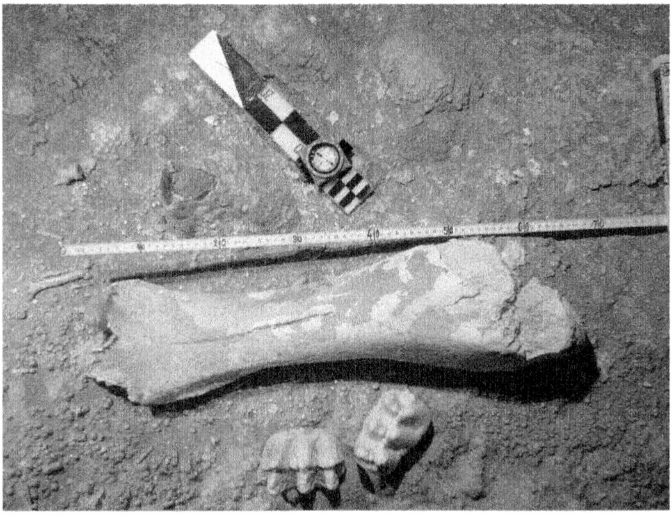

Figure 7.4 Molar and large bone of a proboscid, likely a gomphothere, discovered at Nai Tucha (photograph by Eugenio Acevez/Subdirección de Arqueología Subacuática/Instituto Nacional de Antropología e Historia).

ARRIVAL OF HUMANS ON THE YUCATAN PENINSULA

When was the Yucatan Peninsula settled? Before this research was carried out, the oldest artifacts and human remains known from the region were assigned to ages of between 2,000 and 4,000 years B.P.; they belonged to Mayan or pre-Mayan civilizations. Nevertheless, a much earlier settlement during the so-called first migration, about 11,000 B.P., was theoretically thought possible (Hammond 1982). Now we know that evidence for this hypothesis is preserved in the submerged caves of Quintana Roo. With the new results at hand, it is evident that humans arrived in the Yucatan Peninsula early, during the late Pleistocene or earliest Holocene. Several lines of evidence support this interpretation.

Decoration of the Subterraneous Chambers

The submerged caves and cenotes of Quintana Roo are fully decorated by stalactites and stalagmites, from near surface levels down to at least 40 m (131 ft). The presence of speleothemes indicates that caves must have been dry for many thousands of years. From the geological situation, it is clear that the cave system formed during periods of low sea level, during the Pleistocene. The system was subsequently drowned during the early Holocene sea level rise between 13,000 and 7,600 B.P., as described previously. The presence of gomphothere bones with stalagmitic overgrowth (e.g., Nai Tucha) clearly suggests that these fossils date from the dry phase of the cave, with a minimum age of 7,600 B.P.

Fossil Assemblages

A late Pleistocene age is clearly indicated for the assemblage of fossil mammals found in the cave system in the states of Quintana Roo and Yucatan. We identified the American horse (*Equus conversidens*), camelids (*Hemiauchenia* sp.), giant armadillo (*Glyptotherium* cf. *G. floridanum*), tapir (*Tapirus bairdii*; at Nai Tucha), and proboscidians (*Gomphoterium* sp.; at Nai Tucha). These animals disappeared from the American continent 13,300–12,900 B.P. (Fiedel and Hayes 2004; Hayes 2006) during a massive extinction event near the end of the Pleistocene.

Although a direct correlation with coeval human occupation of the caves is difficult to establish at present, occasional evidence exists. For instance, at the cenote La Chimenea, 15 km (9.32 miles) north of the city of Tulum, charcoal is concentrated in a depth of 23 m (75.5 ft), suggesting an ancient fireplace. The charcoal is associated with molars and bones of the camelid *Hemiauchenia macrocephala*. According to our initial research, the fossil bones are partially burned, indicating that the animal was cooked and consumed by humans. Consequently, a direct correlation exists in the Yucatan Peninsula cenotes between the presence of humans and *Hemiauchenia macrocephala*, a species that disappeared at the end of the Pleistocene.

The assemblage of fossil mammals identified during our research also suggests that the surface of the Yucatan Peninsula was considerably dryer during the late Pleistocene. Horses (*Equus conversidens*), camelids (*Hemiauchenia* sp.), giant armadillos (*Glyptotherium* cf. *G. floridanum*), and proboscideans (*Gomphoterium* sp.) are widely known from coeval strata of the American continent and are regularly associated with open grassland or shrub vegetation, visibly unlike the low jungle of today.

Taphonomy

The human skeletons of El Templo, Las Palmas, and Naharon are found in depths of 15–30 m (49–98 ft) in the cave system, levels that were flooded during early stages of the Holocene sea level rise. They were found at distances of 160 m (525 ft) to almost 400 m (1,312 ft) from the closest entrance.

Is it possible that dead bodies floated to their present locations during the sea transgression or later? This scenario appears impossible to us. It would mean that individuals floated for several hundred meters through a cave system of tunnels and open galleries decorated with speleothemes and were subsequently deposited almost in their entirety, without major loss or disintegration of bones. For example, the Las Palmas skeleton is almost fully articulated, even with the anatomical connections of hand carpals and feet tarsals in their corresponding positions. These bones are the first to disintegrate and fall off a body floating in the water for a longer period of time. This situation clearly indicates *in situ* skeletization of the bodies, which could only have happened in a dry cave. The situation of the Naharon skeleton is similar. Although the position of some bones has been changed by the activity of recreational cave divers, tarsals and phalanges remain in their corresponding position of feet and hands.

In contrast, cenotes in Quintana Roo and Yucatan also contain abundant Mayan skeletons. These individuals have been thrown into the water where they floated for some time, until corpses finally sank to the ground and were deposited. These bodies are always disintegrated, and heads, foot, and finger bones are usually dispersed over a large area (González, Rojas, and del Río 2001).

The flexed position of the Las Palmas woman even suggests an intentional situation, perhaps a funeral, in which the corpse was likely wrapped in a sack. This is suggested by the flexed position of legs and arms, which are drawn to the body, and the originally upward position. A funeral would clearly require a place that was dry at the time when the bodies were placed. In the deep parts of the Yucatan cave system (below 20 m depth) (65.5 ft), these conditions existed for the last time during early stages of the early Holocene sea-level transgression.

Cranial Morphology

According to preliminary morphometric analyses, cranial morphologies of the three Yucatan skeletons (especially Las Palmas) differ considerably from those of pre- and post-Hispanic Mayas, and from typical Paleoindian material known from the United States and Mexico. The cranial morphometry resembles older (late Pleistocene–early Holocene) rather than recent Paleoamerican skulls from North and South America. Interestingly, the closest similarities are with individuals recovered from Tehuacán, Puebla, Mexico (specimen Tc50 E.5), and in China (Specimen 3 of the Upper Cave). These findings suggest that the individuals from Naharon, Las Palmas, and El Templo do not correspond to Mayan populations. In contrast, they suggest that the three individuals discovered in the caves of Quintana Roo lived in the area thousands of years earlier.

CONCLUSIONS

Submerged caves near Tulum in the state of Quintana Roo are rich in fossil and prehistoric evidence that throw light on the early settlement of the Yucatan Peninsula. We discovered an abundant and diverse Pleistocene fossil assemblage previously unknown for the region, consisting of the American horse (*Equus conversidens)*, camelids (*Hemiauchenia* sp.), giant armadillo (*Glyptotherium* cf. *G. floridanum*), tapir (*Tapirus bairdii)*, and proboscideans (*Gomphoterium* sp.), among others. The extinction of these mammals is known to be abrupt in other parts of the North American continent and dated to a short period of time between 13,300 and 12,900 B.P. (Fiedel and Hayes 2004; Hayes 2006). In some cases, a direct correlation was established between the presence of these animals and human occupation of the cave system. At La Chimenea, for example, fossil bones of the camelid *Hemiauchenia macrocephala* are partially burned, as a result of cooking in an ancient fireplace.

A late Pleistocene to early Holocene settlement of Yucatan Peninsula is also indicated by the presence of other charcoal concentrations interpreted as fireplaces, as discussed previously for Las Palmas. At the cave of Aktun Ha, a small cavity was used in an isolated rock, about 60 cm (2 ft) above the cave ground (Figure 7.5). Charcoal samples from this niche were dated to 9.154±74 C14 years B.P. [INAH-2011] and 9.180±60 C14 years B.P. (Beta-166199). Associated with this fireplace, the same chamber also contained possible lithic tools.

Our most important discoveries are three nearly complete articulated human skeletons, which we propose date to the latest Pleistocene–early Holocene period. The taphonomic circumstances suggest that at least two (Las Palmas and El Templo) represent intentional burial. Cranial morphology indicates similarities with "old" (late Pleistocene–early Holocene) Paleoamerican skulls (Archeolithic) from North and South America, but they differ considerably from morphologies of pre- and post-Hispanic Mayas, or other Paleoindian crania. The possible funeral of El Templo and Las Palmas individuals and *in situ* skeletization of the three bodies must have occurred in a dry cave during the late Pleistocene sea level low or during early stages of the early Holocene transgression. Present-day levels were reached at about 7,600 B.P., but the three corpses were found in deeper levels of the cave system, between 20 and 30 m

Figure 7.5 Niche cavity in the "chamber of ancestors" at Aktun Ha. Note that charcoal was placed in this niche, which is located about 60 cm above the cave ground in a large tear-shaped rock. The cavity is approximately 40 cm wide, 40 cm high, and 35 cm deep (photograph by Eugenio Acevez/Subdirección de Arqueología Subacuática/Instituto Nacional de Antropología e Historia).

(65.5 and 98 ft) in depth. Drowning of these levels must have occurred hundreds or even thousands of years earlier.

Our new set of data suggests that humans reached and settled the Yucatan Peninsula during an early wave of migration of the American continent, prior to the end of the Pleistocene, as early as 13,000 B.P. It is interesting to note that they consumed big mammals such as camels and elephants, even though the coast line was only few kilometers away. On the other side, we found no evidence for the use of seafood (e.g., shells).

The paleoanthropological and paleontological potential of the Yucatan cave and cenote system appears to be enormous. After only six years of research, we have discovered more than twenty-five sites with prehistoric evidence, in addition to dozens of sites with Mayan human remains and artifacts. However, this growing scientific importance contrasts with the ongoing and increasing tourist development of the Riviera Maya, accompanied by rapid and ubiquitous construction and uncontrolled use of the fragile groundwater system. In the near future, these activities may harm if not destroy the cave system and its thus far unpolluted aquifers, and with them many prehistoric sites not even known to us now.

ACKNOWLEDGMENTS

The location and recording of prehistoric submerged caves and water bodies with cultural evidence were achieved thanks to the great support from cave divers and colleagues working in Quintana Roo and Yucatan. Without their valuable collaboration and information, we would not have been able to obtain this information. We thank James Cook, William Phillips, Robert Schmittner, Samuel Meachan, Roberto Chávez, Roberto Hashimoto, Luis F. Martínez, Sebastian Genijovich, Marco Rotzinger, Germán Yáñez, Andreas Mattens, Scott Carnahan, Sergio Granuchi, Karin Boucher, Fernando Rosado, Enrique Soberánes, Raúl González, Guillermo Acosta, Joaquín García-Bárcena, Joaquín Arroyo, Oscar Polaco, Paul Blanchon, Luis Marín, Elva Escobar, Magdalena de los Ríos, Erv Taylor, Alistair Pike, Thomas Highman, Silvia González, José C. Jiménez, Mónica López Portillo, Carlos Serrano, Fernando Sánchez, Sergio Grosejan, Felipe Bate, Ximena Chávez, Fidencio Rojas, Aldo Castro, Rodrigo González, Susana Xelhuatzin, and Paolo Testelli.

REFERENCES

Aufderheide, A. C., and Rodríguez-Martín, C. 1998. *The Cambridge Encyclopedia of Human Paleopathology.* Pp. 93, 96. Cambridge: Cambridge University Press.

Bate, L. F., and A. Terrazas. 2002. Arqueología, genética y lingüística: Sugerencias en torno al tema del poblamiento americano. *Boletín de Antropología Americana* 38.

Blanchon, P., and J. Shaw. 1995. Reef drowning during the last deglaciation: Evidence for catastrophic sea-level rise and ice-sheet collapse. *Geology* 23:4–8.

Fiedel, S. J., and G. Hayes. 2004. A premature burial: Comments on Grayson and Meltzer's "Requiem for Overkill." *Journal for Archaeological Science* 31(1):121–31.

García-Bárcena, J. 1982. El precerámico de Aguacatenango, Chiapas, México. *Prehistoria* 110:68.

González, A. H., and A. Destefano Farías, eds. 2002. *Fosiles de México: Coahuila una ventana a través del tiempo*. Mexico City: Gobierno del Estado de Coahuila.

González, A. H., C. Rojas, and O. del Río. 2001. Informe del registro arqueológico realizado en los cenotes Angelita, Sistema La Quebrada y Aktun Ha, en Quintana Roo, y San Antonio, Papakal y Tac Che, en Yucatán. Subdirección de Arqueología Subacuática. Instituto Nacional de Antropología e Historia, Mexico City. On file.

Hammond, N. 1982. *Ancient Maya Civilization*. New Brunswick, NJ: Rutgers University Press.

Hayes, G. 2006. First contact megafaunal extinctions in the Americas at the end of the Pleistocene. In *2nd Simposio Internacional del Hombre Temprano en América*, J. C. Jiménez-López, O. J. Polaco, G. Martínez Sosa, and R. Hernández Flores, eds., 91–116. Mexico City: Instituto Nacional de Antropología e Historia.

López Ramos, E. 1975. Geological summary of the Yucatan Peninsula. In *The Ocean Basins and Margins, the Gulf of Mexico and the Caribbean*, vol. 3, A. E. M. Narin and F. G. Stehli, eds., 257–82. New York: Kluwer Academic/ Plenum Press.

Lovejoy, O., R. S. Meindl, R. P. Mensforth, and T. J. Barton. 1985. Multifactorial determination of skeletal age at death: A method and blind tests of its accuracy. *American Journal of Physical Anthropology* 68:1–14.

Meindl, R. S., and O. Lovejoy. 1985. Ectocranial suture closure: A revised method for the determination of skeletal age at death based on the lateral-anterior sutures. *American Journal of Physical Anthropology* 68:57–66.

National Speleological Society-Cave Diving Section (NSS-CDS). 1992. In *Cave Diving Manual: An Overview*, J. Prosser and G. V. Grey, eds., 377. Branford, FL: The Cave Diving Section of the National Speleological Society, Inc.

Polaco, O. J., C. Rojas, and A. H. González. 2002. Una nueva fauna pleistocénica de la Península de Yucatán, México. *Proceedings of the VIII Congreso Nacional de Paleontología*, November 13–15, Guadalajara, Mexico.

Powell, J. F., and W. A. Neves. 1999. Craniofacial morphology of the first Americans: Pattern and process in the peopling of the New World. *Yearbook of Physical Anthropology 1999* 42:153–58.

Terrazas, A., and M. Benavente. 2006. Informe técnico del análisis osteológico correspondiente al periodo junio 2003–julio 2005. In *Informe técnico parcial. Atlas arqueológico subacuático para el registro, estudio y protección de los cenotes en la Península de Yucatán. Agosto del 2003 a agosto del 2006*, A. H. González and C. Rojas, co-directors, 1–36. Archivo Técnico de Arqueología, Instituto Nacional de Antropología e Historia, Mexico City.

Ward, W. C., A. E. Weidie, and W. Back. 1985. Geology and hydrogeology of the Yucatan and quaternary geology of northeastern Yucatan Peninsula. In *New Orleans Geological Society*, 160 pp. New Orleans: NOGS Publications.

Ward, W. C., G. Keller, W. Stinnesbeck, and T. Adatte. 1995. Yucatan subsurface stratigraphy: Implications and constraints for the Chicxulub impact. *Geology* 23:873–76.

CHAPTER 8

Mayan Mortuary Deposits in the Cenotes of Yucatan and Quintana Roo, Mexico

Carmen Rojas Sandoval, Arturo H. González González, Alejandro Terrazas Mata, and Martha Benavente Sanvicente

The Yucatan Peninsula contains a great number of submerged caves and collapsed *dolinas* (sinkholes) of sedimentary limestone origin, locally known as cenotes. The name is derived from the Mayan word *dz'onot.*

After arriving in Yucatan in the 16th century, the Spaniards learned that the Maya made human sacrifices in which bodies were thrown into cenotes. This practice, which continued after the conquest, but which the Spanish suppressed, was reported by 16th-century chroniclers, and later gave rise to the myth of virgin sacrifices. The first skeletons recovered from the Sacred Cenote of Chichén Itzá—at the beginning of the 20th century by Edward Thompson, first consul of the United States in Yucatan—revealed that the Maya did, in fact, make human sacrifices and offerings in sinkholes (Fagan 1984:283; Olivé 1991:126). However, that sample, as well as another obtained in the 1960s by Roman Piña Chán, proved that the Mayas had sacrificed males as well as females, some of whom were children (Hooton 1977; Tiesler 2005).

In 1999, the Subdirección de Arqueología Subacuática (Underwater Archaeology Vice-Directorate) of the Instituto Nacional de Antropología e Historia (National Institute of Anthropology and History, INAH) started a systematic study in some of the cenotes and inundated caves in the Yucatan Peninsula that contained cultural and paleontological material. Because of the chemical characteristics of the water, the lack of light, and the fine and mineralized sediments, these spaces have favored preservation of paleontological and archaeological vestiges.

A variety of archaeological remains have been found in some cenotes, but the ones discussed here stand out because of their significant concentrations of humans remains. Archaeological research is being carried out to determine if the osteological deposits were the results of sacrifices, wars, or massive mortality because of diseases, or if the cenotes with this kind of evidence were selected by the Maya for funerary deposits (i.e., the cenotes were used as aquatic cemeteries). In funerary situations, postmortem treatments were dedicated to the individuals. Sacrificed individuals might also receive postmortem treatments, but the individuals themselves were considered part of the offering. Our recovery techniques were focused on distinguishing between these various types of osteological deposits.

We had two main goals:

1. to identify if the dates of the deposits correspond to pre-Hispanic, colonial, or modern times; and
2. to identify whether the cause of death was natural, sacrificial, war, or disease. It is important to consider whether death from sacrifice or war can be related to violence not detected in the bones. For example, the individuals might have been killed by throwing them into the water, which in these cenotes are around 15 m below the surface. Because of the bottle shape of these cenotes, one cannot climb their walls without a rope or a ladder.

We recorded the deposits to analyze all the osteological groups *in situ*; underwater video and photography were very important for this. Maps were prepared in the field through a geographic information system. Until then, just a small portion of the evidence had been removed for study in field laboratories; after the analyses were completed, the material was returned to the cenotes (Figure 8.1). Some samples were removed permanently for specialized studies in different laboratories.

KARSTIC SYSTEMS AND THE MAYAN INFRAWORLD

The importance of caves and cenotes for the Mayas was documented in the 16th century by Fray Diego de Landa (1994, orig. 1566) and other chroniclers, but the interest in exploring them began in the 19th and early 20th centuries, with travelers like John L. Stephens and Frederick Catherwood (Stephens 1986) and institutions like the Carnegie Institution of Washington (Pearse, Creaser, and Hall 1936). The most famous early recovery of archaeological materials from a cenote is probably the exploration of the Sacred Cenote of Chichén Itzá, carried out by Thompson between 1904 and 1909 (Fagan 1984:283; Hooton

Figure 8.1 Human skull removed from cenote Las Calaveras, Quintana Roo (photograph by Eugenio Acevez/Subdirección de Arqueología Subacuática/Instituto Nacional de Antropología e Historia).

1977:272; Olivé 1991:126), and later by the archaeologist Piña Chán between 1960 and 1961, and 1967 and 1968 (Piña Chán 1960). Isolated explorations of other cenotes were carried out during the 1950s and the 1960s in the cenotes of X-Coton at Mayapán (Smith 1953), Xlacah at Dzibilchaltún, and Agua Azul in Chinkultic (Andrews and Corletta 1995; Luna Erreguerena 1982).

One of the most popular rituals related to the cenotes consisted of tossing victims into the water, a practice called *Chen Ku* by the Maya. Archaeologist Alberto Ruz (1968:151) developed the technical terms "ritual immersion of the sacrificed in the cenotes" for this type of ostuary deposit. This practice was described in the *Relación de las Cosas de Yucatán* by Fray Diego de Landa in the 16th century (1994) and in the *Relación de la Villa de Valladolid* (Garza 1983, vol. 2:5–25). Cenotes were not only appropriate spaces for sacrifices and offerings. Being entrances to the infraworld, as were the caves, they can be considered natural funeral chambers (Manzanilla 1996:30). The use of dry caves as funerary spaces has been documented through archaeological contexts in the states of Chiapas (Blom 1954:123–36) and Quintana Roo (Márquez, Benavides, and Schmidt 1982).

The sacred attribution given to caves and water fountains or sinkholes by the Mayas was related to fertility and the world of the dead, called *Xibalba*, since those places constituted access points to the infraworld as well as symbolic steps between the world on Earth and the underground world (Recinos 1995). Moreover, the Maya considered the caves and the cenotes as places for the birth of life, containers of virgin water called *suhuy ha* (Thompson 1975), the point of origin for some groups of lineages (Carmack and Mandloch 1983:181–82), and suitable spaces to practice various activities and rituals, as in the Mexican caves of Loltun in the state of Yucatan (González 1980; Velázquez 1980), Xtacumbilxunaan in the state of Campeche (Zapata et al. 1990), and various caves near the coast of Quintana Roo (Martos 2002; Rissolo 2003).

The Mayan infraworld, identified in the karstic systems, was associated with different mythological beings and fantastic animals such as the *moan* bird, as it was named by Eduard Seler, and which was a manifestation of the god of death (Garza 1995:89). Some representations of the *moan* bird show a combination of a bird and a dog because both animals are often associated with fantastic beings of night characters (Garza 1995:89). The dog is the one that leads the souls of the dead to the *Xibalba*. Its relationship with humans allows it to substitute humans as the victim of the sacrifice. Fray Diego de Landa reported that in the ceremony of the month of *moan*, the Mayas used to sacrifice a dog with cocoa-colored spots (Landa 1994).

MAYAN MORTUARY DEPOSITS IN THE CENOTES

The cenotes with a significant concentration of human remains that we studied include Las Calaveras in the state of Quintana Roo, and San Antonio and Canún in the state of Yucatan (González and Rojas 2002; González, Rojas, and Del Río 2001, 2003; Terrazas et al. 2002). Another deposit was found in the cenote San José, outside the walls of the Mayapán city in the state of Yucatan (González Uc 1999; Tiesler 2005) (Figure 8.2).

Las Calaveras is located inside the pre-Hispanic city of Punta Laguna, 15 km north of the city of Cobá. In this cenote we registered the remains of 118 individuals; there were no other archaeological remains on the surface of the bottom (Figure 8.3). Previous surveys suggested that Punta Laguna was first occupied during the pre- and post-Classic periods (Benavides and Zapata 1991). It seems that during the Classic Period, when the city of Cobá was thriving, there were no important settlements at the site of Punta Laguna. However, it is possible that Las Calaveras was used during the Classic, as occurred with some caves after the abandonment of their related cities (Rissolo 2003).

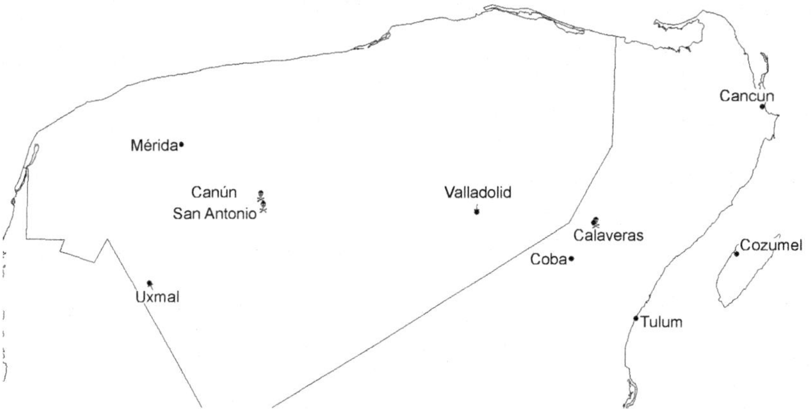

Figure 8.2 Location of cenotes discussed in the chapter (drawn by Carmen Rojas/Subdirección de Arqueología Subacuática/Instituto Nacional de Antropología e Historia).

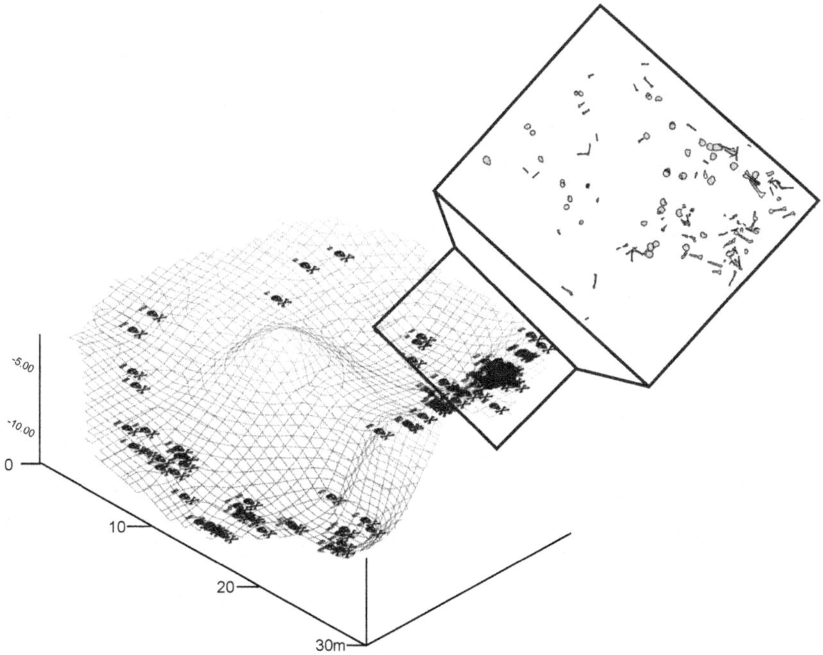

Figure 8.3 Three-dimensional map with the distribution of the human bones found in cenote Las Calaveras, Quintana Roo (drawn by Lisseth Pedroza/Subdirección de Arqueología Subacuática/Instituto Nacional de Antropología e Historia).

Cenotes San Antonio and Canún are south of the city of Mérida, in the municipality of Homún. In San Antonio, twenty-eight individuals, one *metate* or grounding stone, four colonial ceramic vessels, and sixteen groups of animal bones were found. In Canún, the remains of at least fourteen individuals, twenty pre-Columbian ceramic vessels from Late pre-Classic to Early Classic periods, and eight groups of animal bones were recorded by our team. This last cenote includes one osteological group with one complete skeleton of an adult and a few bones of a child, found in a small niche 3 m below the surface, in association with bird and dog bones and pre-Classic ceramic vessels. Another interesting discovery in Canún was the deposit of a female skull with cut marks of defleshing.

The remains of the pre-Hispanic settlements next to the San Antonio and Canún cenotes include house platforms that correspond to the dispersed settlement pattern of the region. These cenotes were also related to two former haciendas, private properties for the exploitation of agave, whose fibers were used until the present to produce ropes, baskets, and similar products.

The proximity of the cenotes to pre-Hispanic Mayan settlements, the generalized presence in the cenotes of individuals with cranial deformation—practiced on babies by the Maya before their fifth year and forbidden (but not totally suppressed) by the Spaniards in the 16th century—and the presence of pre-Hispanic pottery from Late pre-Classic to Early Classic period, in direct association with at least one of the skeletons, support the hypothesis that these deposits were laid down in pre-Hispanic times. The *in situ* study of the skeletal remains, as well as the laboratory analysis that is designed to identify the cause of death and depositional processes, enabled us to detect the existence of different kind of deposits.

METHODOLOGY

To identify the Mayan mortuary practices in cenotes, we favored using taphonomic analysis because this can distinguish if the deposits were the result of human sacrifice or not. In addition, the studies attempt to identify whether there are different social groups in the cenote or whether it was exclusively for certain people. We now review the basic concepts and approaches used in the study.

Cemeteries

Cemeteries are particularly appropriate places in which to dispose of numerous individuals through funerary practices. The osteological deposits can be formed over a long period by the continuous use of the cemetery, or a short period, for example, as the result of mortalities because of natural catastrophes. Once the place is chosen to be a cemetery, it gains significance through the use of funerary ceremonies. The same would have been the case for cenotes but even more so, as they had symbolic meaning for the Maya because subterraneous and aquatic places were associated with the world of the dead, or *Xibalba*. However, when selected for the deposit of certain personages, cenotes became places for a special cult. Usually the term "cemetery" is not used for pre-Hispanic times, even if there are numerous burials. Such a place is usually called a necropolis.

The reconstruction of activities that took place in the cenotes to test a range of hypotheses is based on the following analysis:

I. Observation categories (evidence):
   a. Articulated remains (anatomical connection)
   b. Nonarticulated remains

II. Dispositions of the human body:
   a. Articulated remains
      i. Bodies that remained intact after they had been tossed in, possibly because they were tied up into a bundle or ballasted. The bodies could also have remained articulated because of particular chemical and physical conditions of the water (e.g., temperature, salinity, and depth).
      ii. Bodies carefully deposited in accessible and selected places inside the cenotes, along with ceramic and animal offerings (Figure 8.4).
   b. Nonarticulated remains
      i. Bodies tossed in. It is believed that by floating, bodies went to the edges. In the course of disarticulating, body segments fell to the bottom or were deposited in the natural shelves of the walls.
      ii. Body segments tossed in, such as skulls, extremities, etc. (may retain traces of cutting).
      iii. Dry bones tossed in.

Mortuary Practices: Funerary and Sacrificial Practices

We now turn to a discussion of the possible factors that could have formed the deposits recovered from the cenotes. In general, all the activities that

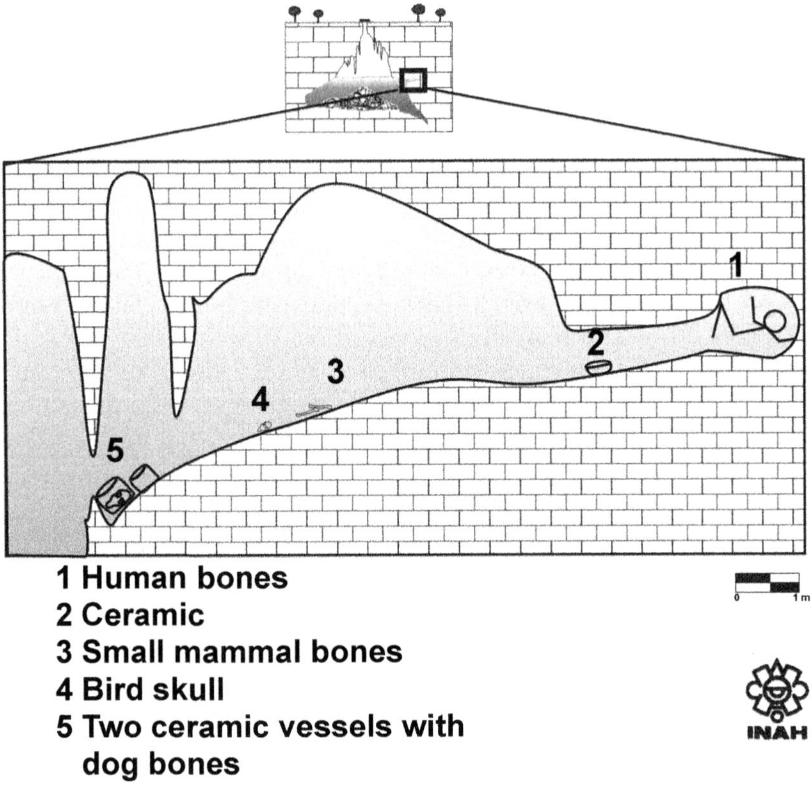

Figure 8.4 A complete human skeleton and a few remains of a child, along with Late pre-Classic vessels and animal bones, were found in a shallow cave in cenote Canún, Yucatan (drawn by Carmen Rojas/Subdirección de Arqueología Subacuática/Instituto Nacional de Antropología e Historia).

involve human remains, either as a cadaver or a skeleton, are considered mortuary practices, which can be considered funerary, sacrificial, or punitive-legal. Funerary practices are the actions and rituals dedicated to an individual, or because of him or her. Through funerary practices, living people commemorate the deceased person, even years after death. By commemorating certain persons, the relatives also show who their ancestors are. In this way, funerary practices are what Patricia McAnany (1995) calls "creation of the ancestors."

In sacrificial practices, the human body is part of the ritual offerings dedicated to some deity, natural phenomena, or an ancestor. In this category, we include the "ritual immersion of the sacrificed" or *Chen Ku*, as in the Sacred Cenote of Chichén Itzá (Ruz 1968). Therefore, human sacrifices are not considered as funerary practices, although the bodies receive mortuary treatments.

Other mortuary practices that could be represented in the cenotes are the punitive-legal ones. Punitive mortuary practices are the acts of collective violence that a dominant group applies to a subordinates to punish them. This would be the case if the skeletons on the cenotes were victims of war. Legal mortuary practices are the punishment of single individuals who disobey the law. Punishment could include mutilation of the body or violent death.

CONCLUSIONS

Different types of deposits have been found in the studied cenotes. Carefully deposited bodies, along with pre-Hispanic ceramics and animal offerings found in shallow areas that were likely dry at certain times, such as the one found in the cenote Canún, support the hypothesis that not all the individuals deposited in the cenotes were sacrificed. The presence of adult males as well as female remains imply that the deposits do not represent victims of war massacres, although this assumes that war victims should be predominantly male. Ongoing refinements to the recording and recovering techniques described above, together with further analyses, will focus on testing these and other alternate hypotheses.

The spatial association of cenotes with pre-Hispanic settlements, the presence of culturally deformed skulls, and the presence of Late pre-Classic to Early Classic pottery, in one case directly associated with one osteological group, supports the hypothesis that the deposits have remained *in situ* since early pre-Hispanic times. The different types of deposits found in the studied cenotes and the presence of carefully deposited bodies along with pre-Columbian ceramics and animal offerings in shallow areas indicate that not all the individuals deposited in the cenotes were sacrificed; some were purposefully laid out within the context of a mortuary ritual. Also, the presence of adult male and female bones does not support the hypothesis that the deposits were caused by conflict.

Following our preliminary analyses of the cenotes, the hypothesis that these sinkholes were selected as places for mortuary and/or funerary deposits (i.e., aquatic cemeteries) seems to be the most plausible explanation for the data we have recovered.

REFERENCES

Andrews, A. P., and C. Corletta. 1995. A brief history of underwater archaeology in the Maya area. *Ancient Mesoamerica* 6(2):101–17.

Benavides, A., and R. L. Zapata. 1991. Punta Laguna: Un sitio prehispánico de Quintana Roo. *Estudios de Cultura Maya* 18:23–66.

Blom, F. 1954. Ossuaries, cremation and secondary burials among the Maya of Chiapas. *Journal de la Société des Américanistes* 9(43):123–36.

Carmack, R., and J. Mandloch, eds. 1983. *Título de Totonicapán*. Mexico City: Universidad Nacional Autónoma de México.

Fagan, B. 1984. *Precursores de la Arqueología en América*. Mexico City: Fondo de Cultura Económica.

Garza, M. de la. 1983. *Relaciones Histórico-Geográficas de la Gobernación de Yucatán (Mérida, Valladolid y Tabasco)*. Mexico City: Universidad Nacional Autónoma de México.

Garza, M. de la. 1995. *Aves Sagradas de los Mayas*. Mexico City: Universidad Nacional Autónoma de México.

González A., and C. Rojas. 2002. Project to register and investigate submerged archaeological remains in Mexican continental waters. Unpublished paper presented at the 35th Conference on Historical and Underwater Archaeology, Society for Historical Archaeology, January 8–13, Mobile, Alabama.

González, A., C. Rojas, and O. Del Río. 2001. Informe del registro arqueológico realizado en los cenotes Angelita, Sistema La Quebrada y Aktun Ha, en Quintana Roo, y San Antonio, Papakal y Tac Che, en Yucatán. Unpublished report, Instituto Nacional de Antropología e Historia, Mexico City.

González, A., C. Rojas, and O. Del Río. 2003. Informe técnico parcial del proyecto Atlas arqueológico subacuático para el registro, estudio y protección de los cenotes en la Península de Yucatán. Noviembre de 2001 a julio de 2003. Unpublished report, Instituto Nacional de Antropología e Historia, Mexico City.

González, E. 1980. Análisis de los materiales arqueológicos de la gruta de Loltún, Yucatán, México. Unpublished Bachelors thesis, Escuela Nacional de Antropología e Historia, Mexico City.

González Uc, E. 1999. Informe del registro de evidencias culturales prehispánicas en cenotes de la amurallada Mayapán. In Trabajos de mantenimiento y conservación arquitectónica en Mayapán, Yucatán, Informe de la segunda temporada, 1997, edited by C. Peraza. Unpublished report, Instituto Nacional de Antropología e Historia, Mexico City.

Hooton, E. 1977. Skeletons from the cenote of sacrifice at Chichén Itzá. In *The Maya and Their Neighbors. Essays on Middle American Anthropology and Archaeology*, 2nd ed., L. C. Hay, ed., 272. New York: Dover Publications.

Landa, D. de. 1994 [1566]. Relación de las cosas de Yucatán. In *Estudio Preliminar y Revisión de Texto*, M. C. León Cázares, ed., 11–79. Mexico City: CONACULTA.

Luna Erreguerena, P. 1982. La arqueología subacuática. Unpublished Master thesis, Universidad Nacional Autónoma de México/Instituto Nacional de Antropología e Historia, Mexico City.

Manzanilla, L. 1996. El concepto del inframundo en Teotihucán. *Cuicuilco* 2(6):29–50.

Márquez, L., A. Benavides, and P. Schmidt. 1982. *Exploración en la Gruta de Xcan, Yucatán*. Mexico City: Instituto Nacional de Antropología e Historia.

Martos, L. A. 2002. *Por las Tierras Mayas de Oriente. Arqueología en el área de CALICA, Quintana Roo*. Mexico City: Instituto Nacional de Antropología e Historia/CALICA.

McAnany, P. 1995. *Living with the Ancestors. Kinship and Kingship in the Ancient Maya Society*. Austin: University of Texas Press.

Olivé, J. C. 1991. Para la historia de la arqueología mexicana. El caso Thompson. *Arqueología* 5:119–27.

Pearse, A. S., E. P. Creaser, and F. G. Hall. 1936. *The Cenotes of Yucatan. A Zoological and Hydrographic Survey*. Washington, DC: Carnegie Institution.

Piña Chán, R. 1960. Cenote Sagrado, 1960. Exploraciones efectuadas por el INAH con la colaboración del CEDAM y Geographic Society. Unpublished report, Instituto Nacional de Antropología e Historia, Mexico City.

Recinos, A., trans. 1995. Popol Vuh. *Las Antiguas Historias del Quiché*. Mexico City: Fondo de Cultura Económica.

Rissolo, D. A. 2003. *Ancient Maya Cave Use in the Yalahau Region, Northern Quintana Roo, Mexico*. Quintana Roo, Mexico: Association for Mexican Cave Studies.

Ruz, A. 1968. *Costumbres Funerarias de los Antiguos Mayas. Seminario de Cultura Maya*. Mexico City: Universidad Nacional Autónoma de México.

Smith, R. 1953. Cenote X–Coton at Mayapán. Unpublished report, Carnegie Institution of Washington, DC.

Stephens, J. L. 1986. *Viajes a Yucatán*. Mexico City: Consejo Editorial de Yucatán, A. C.

Terrazas, A., E. Gaytán, M. Benavente, E. Reynoso, C. Rojas, and A. González. 2002. Diversidad de prácticas mortuorias en el cenote Canún, municipio de Homun en la Península de Yucatán. Unpublished paper presented at the VII Congreso Internacional de la Asociación Latinoamericana de Antropología Biológica. Mexico City.

Thompson, J. E. S. 1975. *The Hil–Caves of Yucatan*, reprint edition by Mercer HC, United States. Norman: University of Oklahoma Press.

Tiesler, V. 2005. What can the bones really tell us? The study of human skeletal remains from cenotes. In *Stone Houses and Earth Lords. Maya Religion in the Cave Context*, K. M. Prufer and J. E. Brady, 341–64. Boulder: University Press of Colorado.

Velázquez, R. 1980. Proyecto Loltun. Informe de los trabajos de campo realizados en las excavaciones de la gruta de Loltun, Yucatán, durante el periodo de junio a diciembre de 1978. Unpublished report, Instituto Nacional de Antropología e Historia, Mexico City.

Zapata, P., R. Lorelei, A. Benavides, and A. Peña. 1990. *La Gruta de Xtacumbilxunaan, Campeche*. Mexico City: Instituto Nacional de Antropología e Historia.

CHAPTER 9

Maritime Archaeology in Argentina at the Instituto Nacional de Antropología

Dolores Elkin

INTRODUCTION

The Underwater Archaeology Program of the Instituto Nacional de Antropología y Pensamiento Latinoamericano (National Institute of Anthropology and Latin American Thought, INAPL) was created in 1995. Its mission was to conduct scientific research about, preserve, and create public awareness concerning the underwater cultural heritage of Argentina. At that time, underwater archaeology was a totally new field within the academic and scientific spheres. Consequently, the program needed to start with the basics, such as training archaeologists in scuba diving and bringing together specialists from related fields to form an interdisciplinary team that could begin dealing with the underwater cultural heritage in the best possible way.

The program has already achieved significant results in a range of activities considered important for the underwater cultural heritage of Argentina (Table 9.1). Perhaps the greatest progress has occurred in the field of legislation. For the first time, Argentina has a national law that protects the submerged cultural heritage. In addition to this general framework, individual provinces are increasingly encouraging and developing legal protection of submerged sites located within their jurisdictional waters.

Scientific research is another important area of our program. At present, there are three archaeological projects, all of them in Patagonia, southern Argentina. This chapter focuses on the first project based on the wreck site of the 18th-century British vessel HMS *Swift*, because we believe it best represents the progress of our underwater archaeology program. A second project is focused on a Dutch ship, the *Hoorn*, which caught fire on the Patagonian coast in 1615, very close to where the HMS *Swift* would sink more than a century later. The third project comprises

Table 9.1 Main activities and accomplishments of the National Institute of Anthropology regarding underwater cultural heritage since its creation in 1995.

INTERNATIONAL LEGISLATION	Technical advice for UNESCO Convention (Argentina voted in favor of the convention)
NATIONAL LEGISLATION	Provision of technical advice and encouragement for a national law, including the protection of underwater cultural heritage (UCH) (passed June 2003)
ARCHAEOLOGICAL RESEARCH	HMS *Swift* Project, Valdés Project, *Hoorn* Project
EDUCATION / DISSEMINATION FOR GENERAL PUBLIC	Teaching courses similar to those of the Nautical Archaeology Society (NAS)
	Teaching NAS courses
	Talks and lectures
	Publications
	Mass media
	Exhibitions

DISSEMINATION IN SCIENTIFIC / ACADEMIC SPHERES	Participation in and organization of conferences (national and international)
	Academic publications
FORMAL ACADEMIC EDUCATION: UNIVERSITY COURSES	Seminar on Underwater Archaeology (one semester) at the University of Buenos Aires, Dept. of Anthropology
FORMAL ACADEMIC EDUCATION: UNIVERSITY-LEVEL THESES	*Licenciatura*, M.A., and Doctoral theses (some completed and some ongoing)
UCH MANAGEMENT	Shipwreck database
	HMS *Swift* Project, Valdés Project, *Hoorn* Project
PARTICIPATION IN FIELDWORK IN OTHER COUNTRIES	Participation in fieldwork in Mexico, Brazil, Chile, Uruguay, England, Portugal, France, and Sri Lanka

the nonintrusive survey of more than twenty shipwrecks ranging from the 18th to the 20th centuries, located in the Puerto Madryn and Peninsula Valdés area, Province of Chubut.

THE HMS *SWIFT* PROJECT

The HMS *Swift* was a British sloop of war that sank in March 1770 in Puerto Deseado, Patagonia (Figure 9.1). The accident took place when the ship hit an uncharted submerged rock during an exploration voyage in the South Atlantic when it was commissioned to defend the British military base of Port Egmont in Malvinas/Falkland islands. The *Swift* was a wooden vessel 28 m (92 ft) long and 8 m (26 ft) wide, armed with fourteen six-pounder iron cannons and twelve swivel guns of smaller caliber (Elkin et al. 2000; Murray 1993, Murray, Elkin,

Figure 9.1 Location of Puerto Deseado, where the HMS *Swift* sank in 1770.

and Vainstub 2003). When sunk, the ship was under the command of Captain George Farmer.

This site is remarkably preserved, which occurred because of a combination of key factors such as a significant degree of burial, fine sediment, cold water, absence of salvage operations, and very little damage to the ship during the accident that caused the sinking. The hull still has a major portion of its visible structure assembled. The artifacts recovered since the wreck was found include a great variety of elements made of ceramic, metal, glass, stone, wood, leather, and wicker. In this section, I summarize the main research results obtained to date.

The wreck was found twenty years ago by local divers of Puerto Deseado and there have been several investigations since then. The first was the nonsystematic recovery of artifacts by local divers. The divers deserve credit for not obtaining commercial benefit from the artifacts and for having encouraged the creation of a museum for the archaeological material. The second investigation was by a team of architects from ICOMOS Argentina. This was intended to be more systematic but it still lacked some archaeological standards and the presence of archaeologists. Finally, in 1997, the governmental authorities of the Province of Santa Cruz, aware of the existence of our recently created underwater archaeology program, asked that our team take charge of the scientific research aspects of the *Swift* project, while the local museum of Puerto Deseado would remain in charge of the conservation of the collection. Most of the management aspects of the project would also be in charge of the local museum; others would be discussed and implemented jointly between both institutions.

RESEARCH GOALS

One of our primary research goals is to use the archaeological record to enhance what can be found from study of the historical documents. Because some historians believe that "(historical) archaeology is just an expensive way of telling us what we already know" (Hutchinson 1995:25), archaeologists should make an effort to go beyond the historical data. Furthermore, it is clear that there is usually some sort of bias in any written statement. This bias can be unintentional—sometimes just related to the social, political, historical, or personal context—or intentional, as is the case when somebody lies or deliberately provides only partial information. Although several authors have shown how archaeology and history can be independent avenues for the knowledge of past human life (Borrero 1991; Little 1994; Orser 1996; South 1977; Zarankin and Senatore 1996), archaeologists often end up falling into a tautological way of working in relation to the historical record: (1) They look for material evidence that can support what is stated in the historical documents; (2) they seem to rely more on the archaeological evidence that is "supported" by historical documents; and (3) they even force the material record to fit into the historical information (Elkin et al. 2001). Given these problems and limitations documents, we still believe they are useful to generate hypotheses to be tested against the archaeological record.

We have obtained several primary sources relating to the *Swift*, such as the ship's plans (both the sheer and profile plan—NMM 3606A—and the deck plan—NMM 3642) as well as a diary written by one of the ship's officers, Lieutenant Erasmus Gower and published in London several years after the accident (Gower 1803). Other relevant documents obtained so far include the court martial (ADM 1/5304), the *Swift*'s Pay Book (ADM 33/458), several documents from the Victualling Board (ADM 110/24; ADM 111/65; ADM 30/44), letters from Captain Farmer (ADM 1-1789), and logbooks and other data concerning previous journeys and commanders of the *Swift* (ADM 51/964; ADM 51/4540; ADM 1/2388; ADM 52/1463). The ship's plans show what the ship could have been like; the diary written by Gower indicates what could have happened during and after the wreck; and so on.

The archaeological research also considers a range of further issues, such as formation processes that involve other disciplines such as marine biology and geology. In the frame of the theoretical approach outlined above, there are several topics currently being considered in the archaeological study of the *Swift*.

By studying the ship's hull and structural components, we address the topics of ship construction and site formation process related to them. By typological, technological, and functional analyses of artifacts, we address issues of the relationship between material culture and social differences as well as the use or function of artifacts on board including food and drink. The study of ecofacts that are interpreted to have been food items complements the study of diet and feeding habits on board. And through biological and sedimentological studies, we address the topic of site formation processes. Needless to say, many of these topics interrelate with each other. These are just the topics we have begun studying on the *Swift* site based on the human, economic, and technological resources available within the project; we intend to expand the research in the future.

RECORDING AND EXCAVATION

In terms of excavation and recording, our goals are to record the position and characteristics of the hull structure and its main components (leaving them *in situ* for the time being), to excavate the site, and to pay special attention to the faunal and botanical communities, as well as the sediment matrix, that are associated with the site. We began by doing a general 3D survey of the site by the standard procedure of laying a baseline and recording elements such as frames and cannons by triangulation. We thus developed a site plan of the visible structural remains and conspicuous elements such as cannons, plus a great number of artifacts scattered over the surface of the sediment (level 0). All of these artifacts were collected.

The excavation uses stratified sampling with the strata identified as sections in the stern, the midship area and the bow. At present we are excavating 8 m^2 (86 ft^2) at the stern area, and we plan to excavate similar portions in the other two areas. The resulting surface of 24 m^2 (258 ft^2) is a statistically significant sample of the whole site. It is worth mentioning that the hull at the excavation area (close to the remains of the mizzen-mast) has a list of 58° to port.

SHIP CONSTRUCTION

Besides the fact that many aspects of the design and construction of small men-of-war like the *Swift* are less documented and studied than those of larger vessels, we also wish to evaluate potential differences between the historical documents, such as the original plans, and the actual structural remains. To date, around 40% of the visible hull remains have been recorded in detail, covering an area between the mainmast and the stern post; the remaining 60% has been drawn more schematically. The starboard side, represented by a wooden wall that rises several meters above sediment level, is the part of the wreck that can be most easily recognized. The frames, external planking, and internal planking are clearly identifiable. Because of the list, only the upper structure of the port side is not buried. The main deck is well preserved from the port side up to close to the centerline. Even caulking remains can still be seen between the planks of the deck.

Toward the stern, we have identified the remains of the mizzen-mast, broken at the main deck partners. Archaeological confirmation of the existence of the mizzen-mast sheds light on some contradictory aspects of the historical documents because the sheer and profile plan shows this element, but the deck plan only has the mainmast and foremast. A similar situation happens in relation to the main deck: On both plans mentioned, it appears with a step where the captain's cabin begins, whereas what we see in the archaeological site is a continuous deck up to the stern.

Besides the sheer and profile plan, another reference to the mizzen-mast of the *Swift* was found in a log of the ship when it was under the command of Captain Raynor in 1769 (ADM/L/S/594). If the *Swift* did not already have three masts at the time it was built (1762), 1769 is when some refitting or modifications seem to have taken place, as that date appears in a bilge pump found at the site. Further archival research, specifically focused on ship's refit history, will be useful in evaluating these types of apparent inconsistencies between documentary and archaeological evidence.

In any event, aside from the case of the mizzen-mast and the continuous main deck, the essence of the ship's design is consistent with what is shown in the original plans. For instance, so far the curvatures of the frames that have been recorded archaeologically are similar to those drawn in the original plan (Murray, Elkin, and Vainstub 2003). The main types of wood identified at the site are oak (*Quercus* sp.) and pine (*Pinus* sp.) (Castro, personal communication), two classic types of wood used for Royal Navy ships of this period (Laird Clowes 1898).

TECHNOLOGY

The construction of the *Swift* involves some technological considerations in terms of its sailing qualities. The *Swift* was copied from the *Epreuve*, a captured French ship with a hull of fine water lines. Basically, because of this shape we can infer that the *Swift* could have been a ship of greater speed and seaworthiness, somewhat more stable and with a greater transportation capacity than the average British sloop. These qualities could have had an influence on the decision to commission her twice—under the command of two different captains—to the rough waters of the South Atlantic. On the other hand, she had an excessive depth in the hold in comparison to the average sloops of the time, and this was surely a disadvantage for performing coastal exploration and surveys (see Murray, Elkin, and Vainstub [2003] for a lengthy discussion on these topics).

In terms of artifacts, technological studies conducted so far have focused on the glass (Figure 9.2). The finds include over twenty so-called wine bottles, defined as dark green bottles with a relatively long neck and cylindrical body, and the similar but shorter "beer style bottles" (Jones and Sullivan 1985). Many of them have the typical irregular or asymmetrical shape of free-blown bottles, and all of them have deep push-ups and a greater amount of glass accumulated at the base of the body. Another type of bottle found at the *Swift* site are those known as "case bottles" (Jones and Sullivan 1985) or "gin bottles" (Moreno 1997). These are usually made of dark green glass; they always have a short neck and a square cross-section in the body; and, as opposed to the free-blown "wine bottles," they were made by blowing glass inside a

Figure 9.2 Sample of glass containers recovered from the HMS *Swift* site (photograph by Museo Mario Brozoski/Instituto Nacional de Antropología y Pensamiento Latinoamericano).

mold. Their cross-section increases in size from the base to the shoulder, to facilitate the extraction of the artifact from the mold. Because of their shape, they fit easily into compartmented boxes or cases, apparently the reason for such a design (Jones and Sullivan 1985:72). Some of these gin or case bottles, of which over a dozen were recovered from the *Swift* site, were found inside a compartmented wooden case, with the cork still in place.

Other glass artifacts recovered from the site include a few jars (*sensu*; Jones and Sullivan 1985:71) very coarsely made of light green glass and that, together with the bottles, form the majority of the glass containers. Most of the rest of the glass assemblage consists of colorless tumblers and stemware, without any decoration or special treatment, ampoulettes (still associated with other components of sand glasses), and several glass panes. The latter are also colorless but translucent instead of fully transparent. Many of them were found complete and stacked. Their shape and size indicate that they were probably in storage for replacing broken window panes at the stern of the ship. Some are engraved with the broad arrow of the British Royal Navy.

Chemical analyses were performed on eight glass elements comprising bottles, jars, a demijohn, and the glass panes just mentioned (Muñiz 1999, 2001; Soncini 2002). The main conclusion is that all the archaeological artifacts contained manganese, an element that is always absent in comparative modern glass samples. Manganese is one of the elements capable of modifying the color of glass (Jones and Sullivan 1985), and this could have been the reason for its use in the manufacture of the *Swift* glass artifacts.

FOOD AND DRINK

What did the people on board the *Swift* eat and drink? During the age of the Georgian Royal Navy, the food items supplied by the Victualling Board normally included bread, beer, beef, pork, peas, butter, cheese, flour, suet, raisins, oatmeal, stockfish, oil, and vinegar. Most of these items are specifically mentioned as supplies for the *Swift* at different times (ADM 110/24; ADM 111/65; ADM 1-1789; ADM 30/44; ADM 52/1463). There was no official issue of spirits in the navy, but significant quantities of spirits such as gin, rum, different types of wine, arrack (a generic term for spirituous liqueurs distilled in the colonies), beer, and brandy were frequently on board (Rodger 1986). The historical documents consulted indicate that most of them were present at some point on the *Swift* (ADM 110/24; ADM 111/65; ADM 1-1789; ADM 30/44; ADM 52/1463).

Turning to the archaeological evidence of food for the crew, the organic remains found to date include an eggshell of what is probably Emperor penguin (*Aptenodytes forteri*) (Frere, personal communication), broken at one of its ends and placed inside a glass tumbler, which held it firmly. This penguin egg, which was found in the cabin that is interpreted as Captain Farmer's, provides very interesting evidence in terms of the use of local resources of the region—the distribution of this species includes the Malvinas/Falkland islands—to complement the provisions supplied by the Admiralty's Victualling Board.

Spices make up another important source of archaeological data. White mustard (*Brassica aff. alba*) and two species of pepper (*Piper nigrum* and *Pimenta officinalis*) have been identified for this site (Museo Argentino de Ciencias Naturales 1983; Rodríguez 2002). These seeds and grains were found inside different types of glass containers, ranging from bottles (of the "wine" and "beer" type) to tumblers and stemware (Figure 9.3). The finding of these condiments is particularly interesting as none of the documents we have consulted mentions them as supplied by the navy. Moreover, one of the sources states that Captain George Farmer, apparently still at Deptford in October 1769, desires "to be supplied with (...) a quantity of mustard seed for a foreign voyage." The Victualling Board decided to deny his request on the basis that "none of the ships which have gone to Falkland Islands (to which place the *Swift* is going) have been supplied with any mustard seed and we have none in

Figure 9.3 Glass bottle containing mustard seeds (photograph by Museo Mario Brozoski/Instituto Nacional de Antropología y Pensamiento Latinoamericano).

store" (ADM 111/65). However, the archaeological record shows that, one way or another, significant quantities of mustard ended up on board the *Swift*.

The last piece of archaeological evidence related to food on board is a type of what was preliminarily identified as animal fat, which was found inside a stoneware jar. This jar was collected among other artifacts at the bow section of the ship, an area that could well correspond to the kitchen. The samples of this material still await chemical analyses, but our hypothesis is that it is the suet so frequently mentioned in the documents from the Victualling Board and related literature (Rodger 1986).

Concerning drink on board, it is risky to make straightforward associations between certain types of bottles and their respective contents, even though, as noted, some bottles acquired popular names on the basis of what they usually contained. Taking advantage of the fact that some bottles (of different types) were found with corks in place and with the aim of providing an independent source of information for the function of bottles as containers of alcoholic beverages, some chemical analyses of the content were performed. The first chemical analysis of the content of one of the cylindrical bottles was conducted by the Mario Brozoski Museum of Puerto Deseado in the 1980s during the early stages of investigations at the *Swift* site. The results indicated that it was a type of sweet, white wine (Dirección Nacional de Química 1982). Even though the provenience of this bottle within the site was not recorded, the result of this analysis is certainly useful in terms of knowing what could have been actually consumed by the *Swift*'s crew.

The gin bottles with the cork in place and inside the wooden case were found more recently by our team of the Instituto Nacional de Antropología. The results of Anion Ion Chromatography performed on five samples unfortunately indicated that the content at the time of recovery was mostly seawater. Additionally, gas liquid chromatography revealed that very little of the original ethanol remained in the samples (UDV Laboratory 2001). Consequently, the archaeological evidence does not yet clarify the contents of these bottles.

ARTIFACT FUNCTION

The functional interpretation of artifacts is a standard procedure in most archaeological research. For instance, even though the main or primary function of the bottles found in the *Swift* would have originally been as containers of alcoholic beverages, our research revealed what could be called a "secondary function" as more generic containers. The same happened with tumblers and stemware. At least in some cases, these artifacts were undoubtedly used to store significant quantities of mustard and pepper.

Artifacts used for secondary or more generalized purposes were probably a recurrent situation on board vessels, where space and materials must be optimized. On historic land sites, artifacts are more likely to have been used for their normal or original purpose. This should be taken into account when making functional interpretations of artifacts from wrecks, particularly as regards the relationship between form and function. One should be particularly cautious about using analogies with land archaeological assemblages of similar chronological or cultural contexts.

SOCIAL STATUS

To evaluate how the archaeological assemblage reflects social and military differences among the people on board, one needs to consider variables such as the investment of energy and skills in the manufacture of the artifacts, how common or rare they are, or how expensive or difficult it was to obtain the respective raw material. Our hypothesis is that there were differences in status, not only between the categories of officers versus ordinary seamen but also within the group of officers and these are in turn reflected in the technological and typological characteristics of some artifacts. The first results are from the excavation at the stern, occupied by the officers. Here we have recovered tableware pieces of very high quality, particularly Chinese export porcelain and different styles of English Creamware and Saltglaze plates and platters (Figure 9.4). No pieces like these were found in other parts of the ship. The case bottles mentioned in previous sections, all of which were also found at the stern, are of better quality than other glass containers found in other parts of the site. Some of these were quite coarsely made.

Other artifacts that might indicate social status are buckles and chamberpots. The only silver buckle found to date comes from the stern; all the rest (mostly made from copper alloys) come from different parts of the ship. Shoe buckles made of silver were used by the gentry of the time (Hume 1982:86). Finally, chamberpots may reflect status differences

Figure 9.4 Sample of Chinese bowls and saucers recovered from the HMS *Swift* site (photograph by Museo Mario Brozoski/Instituto Nacional de Antropología y Pensamiento Latinoamericano).

within the single general category of officers. Though the three found in the *Swift* have no record of provenience, these were items that were not used by ordinary seamen on board so they must have belonged to the officers. There are clear differences in manufacturing quality of the three chamberpots.

SITE FORMATION PROCESSES

The study of site formation processes at the *Swift* site is an important component of our research project. We are searching for recurrent patterns in the associations between archaeological structures and artifacts as well as evaluating the effects natural agents have on archaeological materials. Such an understanding is crucial for an adequate contextual interpretation of the site and for strategies relating to research, survey, excavation, and conservation (Bastida et al. 2004: chap. 10). To monitor the behavior and characteristics of the botanical and faunal communities present at the site, we are conducting an experimental study by using small panels placed in the site that can be subject to the action of biofouling and of marine borers (Bastida et al. 2004:chap. 10).

One of the most conspicuous communities already identified in the panels are tunicates of the group Asidia. These tunicates are quite abundant on exposed frames and beams of the ship, where large algae of the species *Macrocystis pyrifera* can also be found. We intend to evaluate what mechanical effects this algae can have on the ship's structure in combination with the strong currents of the site (Bastida et al. 2004). Our long-term goal of these biological studies, combined with research focused on the physical and chemical characteristics of the water and bottom sediments, is to develop predictive models applicable to the dynamics and evolution of comparable underwater archaeological sites in other parts of the world.

FINAL COMMENTS

In this chapter, I have presented an overview of current research being done by the Underwater Archaeology Program of Argentina's Instituto Nacional de Antropología, with a special focus on the HMS *Swift* research project. I believe the program has made significant achievements, given it started from scratch eight years ago and has an average funding of around $10,000 USC per year for all purposes (including salaries or contracts and fieldwork expenses). I emphasize the results because I hope that our experience in Argentina encourages other Latin American and Caribbean countries that face similar economic constraints not to give up and to find alternative and creative ways to study and manage their underwater cultural heritage. There is no need to sacrifice our underwater cultural heritage to treasure hunters to achieve meaningful results.

It is useful to note key components in the way we work that have proved successful: seeking inter-institutional and international cooperation; devoting considerable time and energy to the dissemination of activities and to raising public awareness; and approaching potential sponsors from both the governmental and the private sectors so that they complement each other. In spite of the looting and damage already inflicted on many of our shipwrecks, Latin American and Caribbean maritime archaeology still has a great deal of potential. Strengthening the bonds among us and between us and other nations of the world will surely place us in a good position for the future.

ACKNOWLEDGMENTS

I thank the main institutions that have sponsored our underwater archaeology program: Fundación Antorchas, Secretaría de Cultura de la Nación, and Consejo Nacional de Investigaciones Científicas y Técnicas, all from Argentina. Also, my deepest gratitude to Amaru Argüeso, Ricardo Bastida, Virginia Dellino, Mónica Grosso, Cristian Murray, and Damián Vainstub.

REFERENCES

ADM 1/5304. Court martial to the HMS *Swift* crew, September 29, 1770. London: Public Record Office.

ADM 33/458. HMS *Swift* pay book. London: Public Record Office.

ADM 51/4540. HMS *Swift*. Daily log of the voyaging conditions from Saturday July 9th, 1763 to Wednesday July 13th, 1763.

ADM/L/S/594. Journal of the proceedings of His Majesty's Sloop Swift. John Raynor Log Commander commencing July 9th 1766 and ending June 1st 1769 kept by Lieutenant Joseph Harris.

ADM 110/24. Victualling. Out-letters (1768–1771).

ADM 111/65. Victualling Board and Comittees (1769).

ADM 1–1789. Captain Farmer's letters. Letter given in hand on Board His Majesty's Frigate Tamar in Port Egmont this 19th February 1770 From Anthony Hunt, To Captain George Farmer Commander His Majesty's Sloop Swift.

ADM 30/44. Victualling office precedent book.

ADM 52/1463. Master's Log Swift (1763 Nov.–1769 June).

ADM 1/2388. Letters from Captain John Raynor to the Admiralty.

ADM 51/964. Honorable Captain William Cornwallis–Swift. A journal of the proceedings of His Majesty's Sloop Swift the Honourable William Cornwallis Commander Between the 14th Day of October 1763 and the 23 day of November 1764.

Bastida, R., D. Elkin, M. Grosso, M. Trassens, and J. P. Martín. 2004. The sloop of war HMS *Swift* (1770): A case study on the effects of biodeterioration on the underwater cultural heritage of Patagonia. *Corrosion Review* 22(5–6):417–40.

Borrero, L. A. 1991. Experimentos y escalas arqueológicas. *Shincal* 3(1):142–45.

Dirección Nacional de Química. 1982. Informe sobre muestras de materiales hallados en la ría Deseado. Unpublished report, Instituto Nacional de Antropología, Buenos Aires.

Elkin, D., D. Vainstub, A. Argüeso, and V. Dellino. 2001. Proyecto arqueológico HMS *Swift*, Santa Cruz, Argentina. In *Memorias del Congreso Científico de Arqueología Subacuática ICOMOS*, P. Luna Erreguerena and R. Roffiel, coords., 143–62. Mexico City: Instituto Nacional de Antropología e Historia.

Elkin, D., D. Vainstub, A. Argüeso, and C. Murray. 2000. HMS *Swift*: Arqueología submarina en Puerto Deseado (Santa Cruz). In *Desde el País de los Gigantes. Perspectivas Arqueológicas en Patagonia*, vol. 2, pp. 659–71. Río Gallegos, Argentina: Universidad Nacional de la Patagonia Austral.

Gower, E. 1803. *An Account of the Loss of His Majesty's Sloop 'Swift', in Port Desire on the Coast of Patagonia, on the 13th* of March, 1770. London: Winchester and Son.

Hume, I. 1982. *A Guide to Artifacts of Colonial America*. New York: Alfred Knopf.

Hutchinson, G. 1995. Henry V's warship Grace Dieu. In *The Archaeology of Ships of War*, The International Maritime Archaeology Series, vol. 1, M. Bound, ed., 22–25. Oxford: University of Oxford Press.

Jones, O., and C. Sullivan. 1985. *Glass Glossary for the Description of Containers, Tableware, Flat Glass and Closures*. Ottawa: National Historic Parks and Site Branch, Parks Canada.

Laird Clowes, W. 1898. *The Royal Navy—A History from the Earliest Time to the Present*, vol. 3. London: Sampson Low, Marston & Co.

Little, B. 1994. People with history: An update on historical archaeology in the United States. *Journal of Archaeological Method and Theory* 1(1):5–40.

Moreno, P. 1997. *Botellas Cuadradas de Ginebra*. Buenos Aires: M. Moreno Editora.

Muñiz, M. E. 1999. Informe sobre el análisis químico de materiales del sitio arqueológico Swift. Unpublished report, MS on file, National Institute of Anthropology, Buenos Aires.

Muñiz, M. E. 2001. Informe sobre el análisis químico de materiales del sitio arqueológico Swift. Unpublished report, MS on file, National Institute of Anthropology, Buenos Aires.

Murray, C., coord. 1993. *Corbeta de Guerra* HMS *Swift —1763—Historia, Naufragio, Rescate y Conservación*. Buenos Aires: Comité Argentino del ICOMOS, Museo Regional Provincial Mario Brozoski y Municipalidad de Puerto Deseado.

Murray, C., D. Elkin, and D. Vainstub. 2003. The sloop-of-war HMS *Swift*. An archaeological approach. In *The Age of Sail*. The International Annual of the Historic Sailing Ship, vol. 1, N. Tracy, ed., 101–15. London: Conway Maritime Press.

Museo Argentino de Ciencias Naturales. 1983. Informe sobre muestras de materiales hallados en la ría Deseado. Unpublished report, Instituto Nacional de Antropología, Buenos Aires.

NMM Draughts, Box 52 nº 3606A ('sheer and profile' Swift & Vulture).

NMM Draughts, Box 52 nº 3642 ('Decks' Swift).

Orser, Jr., C. 1996. *A Historical Archaeology of the Modern World*. New York: Kluwer Academic/Plenum Press.

Rodger, N. A. M. 1986. *The Wooden World. An Anatomy of the Georgian Navy*. New York: W. W. Norton & Co.

Rodríguez, F. 2002. Material arqueobotánico del sitio Swift. Unpublished report, Instituto Nacional de Antropología, Buenos Aires.

Soncini, J. 2002. Informe final de beca—Comisión de Investigaciones Científicas. Unpublished report, MS on file, National Institute of Anthropology, Buenos Aires.

South, S. 1977. *Method and Theory in Historical Archaeology*. New York: Kluwer Academic/Plenum Press.

UDV Laboratory. 2001. Report on the content of bottles from the HMS *Swift* archaeological site. Unpublished report, MS on file, National Institute of Anthropology, Buenos Aires.

Zarankin, A., and X. Senatore. 1996. Reseña crítica sobre arqueología histórica colonial en la Argentina. *Páginas sobre Hispanoamérica Colonial. Sociedad y Cultura* 3:123–41.

CHAPTER 10

The Role of Benthic Communities and Environmental Agents in the Formation of Underwater Archaeological Sites

Ricardo Bastida, Mónica Grosso, and Dolores Elkin

INTRODUCTION

Neglected for decades, perhaps centuries, the importance of understanding the way in which nonhuman communities and ecosystems behave is now increasingly acknowledged by archaeologists. Especially important are taphonomic and other site formation studies that examine what happened to the material remains after they left the systemic context (*sensu* Schiffer 1987). A vast scientific literature on taphonomy has been published in recent years, but it is mainly focused on animal bone studies and land archaeology (see a review in Lyman 1994).

Perhaps partly because of its more recent development, marine archaeology has produced few general models concerning formation processes relevant to underwater sites. An important landmark in the mid-1970s was Keith Muckelroy's (1978) pioneer model based on shipwrecks in British waters, which has been the basis for a series of new studies. More recently, Ward, Larcombe, and Veth (1999) proposed a universal model of site formation with predictive ability, taking into account the action of physical, biological, and chemical processes in relation to the context of the depositional environment. This chapter reports an ongoing experimental study that uses ecological principles of succession as the basis for making predictive models about biodeterioration of archaeological materials in marine underwater sites.

Since 1997, the Argentinian research program called Investigación y Conservación del Patrimonio Cultural Subacuático Argentino (Investigation and Preservation of the Argentinean Underwater Cultural Heritage) of the Instituto Nacional de Antropología (National Institute of Anthropology) has conducted research at the wreck site of the HMS *Swift*, a British sloop of war that sank in 1770 in Puerto Deseado, now Province of Santa Cruz. From the beginning of the *Swift* archaeological project (Elkin 1997), one of our goals has been to understand the different natural and cultural processes that have played roles in the formation and transformation of the site. Some preliminary results have already been achieved (Bastida et al. 2004; Elkin 2000). In the long term, we expect to contribute to the development of predictive models applicable to other sites of similar archaeological and environmental contexts.

BIODETERIORATION AT MARINE UNDERWATER ARCHAEOLOGICAL SITES

Site formation processes that operate in an underwater site are very complex phenomena because they result from the permanent interaction of many agents acting in a combined manner, either simultaneously or sequentially. Understanding this interaction is crucial for an adequate contextual interpretation of the site and for research, survey, excavation, and conservation strategies and criteria (Bastida et al. 2004). We will therefore present the basic ecological principles of the fouling communities before moving on to our case study.

Although there is life in all environments of our planet, marine life provides good examples of the natural process of colonization. Any available patch of habitat (solid or liquid) in this environment is subject to colonization by organisms. There is always a supply of propagules from highly diversified species ready to colonize an unoccupied environment. Simplifying the process, we may say that the assemblage of organisms present in any environment is a composite of invasive opportunity and ability versus the propensity of the species already present to prevent further invasion (Valiela 1995). After colonizing, communities tend to establish and remain in a place for a certain period, although in any community there are always replacements of species over time.

Underwater archaeologists know about the harmful consequences of ecological succession, as most of the archaeological material and objects can be colonized by benthic communities known as biofouling. They are also aware that wood from wrecks can be attacked by different species of wood-boring invertebrates. In terms of biofouling, one point worth keeping in mind is that in natural environments there are few hard substrates that can be colonized, therefore shipwrecks in general tend to become immediately attractive for fouling communities. To better understand how these natural processes affect submerged marine sites, the experience obtained from experimental ecology of benthic communities can be a useful research tool for marine archaeology.

ECOLOGICAL MODELS

The study of biodeterioration requires an understanding of the ecological processes that take place in benthic environments. Odum's (1997) general system model of succession forms a functional general framework. Succession is based on the concept that the evolution of a system toward its climax stage is regulated by internal inputs that operate almost continuously together with external inputs that act periodically. Theoretically, internal autogenic inputs tend to move the ecosystem toward equilibrium, which is characterized by a balance between production (P) and respiration (R) and a stabilized species composition. In contrast, external allogenic inputs tend to break up the normal evolution of the ecosystem toward equilibrium, turning the succession back to younger stages, as happens in sea bottoms because of storms, mechanical actions, over sedimentation, water pollution, etc. On certain occasions, however, allogenic inputs can also accelerate the process toward a climax stage. Variations in succession are shown in Figure 10.1.

There are two modes of succession exhibited by plant and animal species: r-selection and k-selection (Colinvaux 1973; Margalef 1968; Odum 1997). For example, creation or exposure of open bottom spaces in any marine zone usually results in quick colonization by a series of opportunistic species (r-strategists), which tend to be rapid growing and have high reproductive rates. Most of these species are of small size and tend to be palatable as food for many consumer species because they are usually free of chemical or mechanical protections against predation.

As succession proceeds, most of the colonizing species in their adult stage tend to be larger, with slower growth, less reproductive potentials, more complex morphological and physiological systems, and highly specialized environmental requirements. There is also a shift toward k-strategists, which have a greater investment in the maintenance and survival of the adult. As time goes by, more species settle and community diversity increases. During succession and after some time, spatial heterogeneity of the community may also increase because more patches accumulate through time due to environmental disturbances and spontaneous detachment from the substrate. During the late stages of succession, the complexity of biological interaction increases, developing new regulatory mechanisms as chemical and mechanical inhibitions and symbiotic and interspecific relations in addition to predation and competition (Valiela 1995).The high degree of heterogeneity in the spatial distribution of species may form a mosaic of patches, each of which may

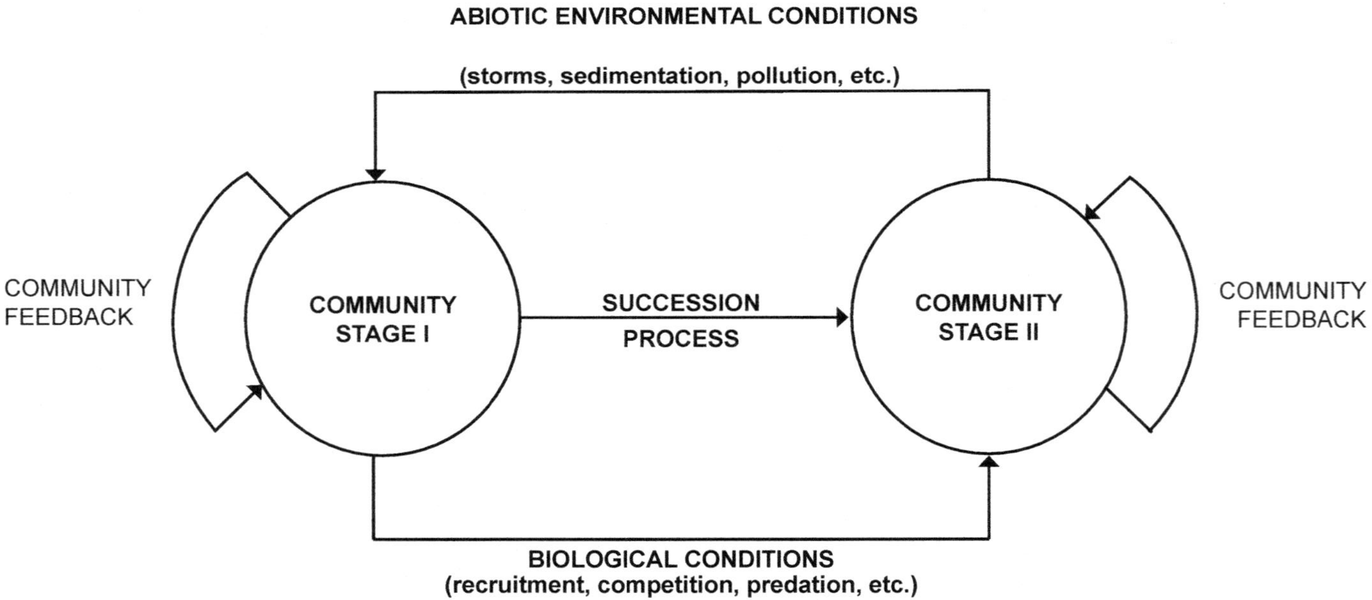

Figure 10.1 Ecological succession may bring a community from one condition to another, but other forces may cause sudden shifts in community states. Community feedback may preserve these changes.

be at a different stage of succession, either because of different age of the patch, or because of differential availability of recruitment species at the time when the substrate becomes exposed (Bastida 1971; Bastida, Capezzani, and Torti 1971; Levinton 1995; Sutherland and Karlson 1977; Valiela 1995).

Besides the main role of ecological succession in nature, we must remember that communities and ecosystems also require a continuous output of energy, storage capacity, and means to dissipate entropy (or the energy disorder of the system). In benthic communities or biofouling, energy flow is not a simple linear flow process but a complex network of energy flow which is called a food web (Bastida and L'Hoste 1976). Marine ecosystems are mainly detrital systems, as they only depend on less than 10% of fresh primary production of the sea, allowing the system to increase the energy storage. In the last decades, the study of food webs has become even more complex as part of the primary production is in a liquid form as dissolved organic matter (DOM), or dissolved organic carbon (DOC), over which microbial organisms find energy to develop what is known as DOM-microbial food chain, which is very important in the first successional stages of biofouling (Nybakken 2001; Valiela 1995).

In nature, it is possible to observe or define two kinds of succession: primary and secondary succession. *Primary succession* takes place in newly exposed natural substratum such as lava flow or different inert materials of cultural origin (e.g., archaeological artifacts). This kind of succession is generally very slow in terrestrial sites but very fast in marine environments. *Secondary succession* concerns community development in sites previously occupied by well-developed communities (old wrecks are normally under secondary succession processes). Ecological succession processes are strictly related to the availability of energy and its flow within the ecosystem. This can easily be observed through the high biomass concentration of tropical biofouling in contrast with temperate biofouling, which is characterized by energy fluctuation throughout the year leading to low biomass values during winter and higher values during spring and summer (Bastida 1971; Bastida et al. 1980; Brankevich, Bastida, and Lemmi 1988).

The ecological succession theory that we have summarized provides the stimulation for our experimental studies. The experimental technique has been adopted from the microcosm model based on studying ecosystems development at a microcosmic scale, based in small inert surfaces—such as glass—submerged in water under good light conditions, with a good balance of inorganic salts, and with the addition of sediments and propagules of plant and animal species from the natural habitat (Cooke 1967). This approach enables very

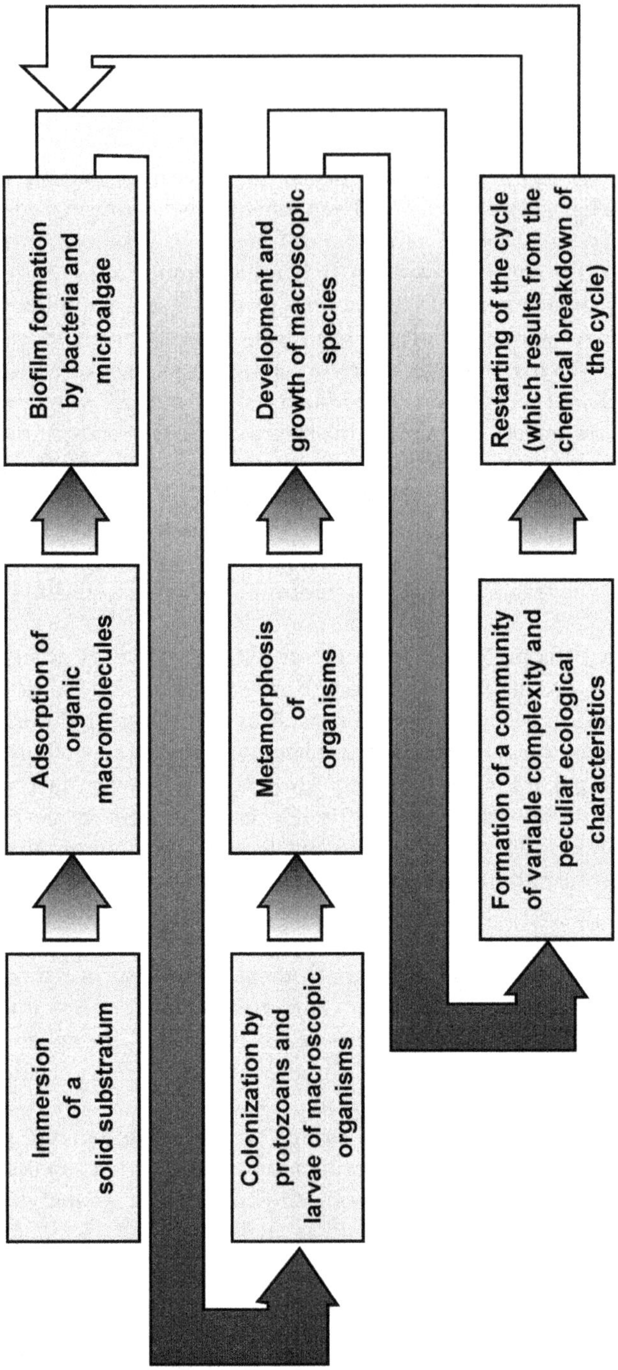

Figure 10.2 Main stages of biofouling development in coastal marine waters.

interesting observations on the main properties of ecosystems, such as photosynthesis (Ph), respiration (R), and biomass (B). The basic pattern of succession, which can be observed and quantified within a few weeks or months, is quite similar or parallel compared to development in a larger open system such as a terrestrial forest or a marine kelp forest. The main difference between them is time, but the basic stages are the same. Given these basic principles, experimental results taken from shipwreck sites such as the *Swift* can be used to understand the evolutionary processes that have led to the formation of the particular site, probably following theoretical models of benthic succession in coastal marine waters (Figure 10.2).

HMS *SWIFT* CASE STUDY

Environmental Setting

The sloop of war HMS *Swift* was built for the British Royal Navy in 1762. In 1770, while being commissioned in the British military base of Port Egmont in the Malvinas/Falkland islands, the ship sank close to the north shore of Deseado *ría*, in front of the current city of Puerto Deseado. The site lies at a depth ranging 10–18 m (33–59 ft), depending on the tidal variation and the topography of the sea bottom. It is partially buried in the seabed and it lists from bow to stern and from starboard to port (Elkin 2000; Elkin et al. 2000). Individual artifacts of various types (both organic and inorganic), as well as many structural components of the ship, are found in an extraordinary state of preservation. Because most of the site is still buried, we estimate that over 60% of the ship's original structure and contents remain intact (Elkin et al. 2000; Elkin et al. 2001; Murray, Elkin, and Vainstub 2003).

Currently, the ship is colonized by a great variety of fouling species that originated from hard natural bottoms of the area. In fact, it is precisely because many artifacts are covered by fouling that their *in situ* identification is not easy. Among the most conspicuous foulers are the solitary and colonial tunicate species, which are usually attached to large structural pieces of the ship such as the frames. Many invertebrate groups show preferences in colonizing different kind of substrates of the sites (molluscs, bryozoans, cirripeds, and polychaetes, among others). Algae are not an important group of the biofouling community, as the site is characterized by low light conditions. Giant kelp (*Macrocystis pyrifera*) can be sometimes found in the site. They are usually carried by the currents and become entangled with the timbers of the ship but are not really attached to it. The main environmental parameters of the *Swift* site are summarized in Table 10.1.

Table 10.1 Main environmental parameters of the *Swift* site.

PARAMETERS	VALUES
Water temperature	13^0 C (maximum) (summer) 4^0 C (minimum) (winter)
Salinity	33% (annual mean)
Currents	6 knots (in the central bed of the *ría*)
Tidal amplitude	6 m (spring tides)
Water oxygen content	High
Water Ph	7.8–8.2
Underwater visibility	0.30 m–2.00 m (regulated by hydro-meteorological conditions)
Sediments	Fine sand and mud with clay. High concentration of organic matter

The type of sediment in which the site is embedded has proven to be quite variable (Bastida, Trassens, and Martin 2000), although the prevailing fraction is very fine sand. There is also a considerable proportion of mud and clay. Larger grain fractions are represented, too, but in a lower proportion. The sediments also contain a high concentration of calcium carbonate particles derived almost exclusively from bioclasts of benthic invertebrates, mainly brachiopods, molluscs, and barnacles species. The concentration of organic matter, both of natural and cultural origin, is also high, with maximum values of up to 9% (Bastida et al. 2004). Finally, the negative values yielded by Redox potential analyses (ranging from −140 to −314), as well as the presence of hydrogen sulphide in many wooden artifacts that were completely buried in the sediment, indicate an anoxic environment in this site.

Research Goals and Methodology

The main goals of our study are to:

- identify the biofouling community at the *Swift* site and its relation with natural benthic communities of the area;
- gain an understanding of the colonizing cycles of main fouling species and successional strategies of the community; and

- evaluate the impact of biofouling on different archaeological materials of the site and substratum preferences of fouling species.

We have adopted a twofold methodology to achieve these goals. On the one hand, the archaeological material and the biotic communities associated with them are being observed and analyzed. In this case, we make systematic recordings of the biological coverage of artifacts and look for possible recurrences in the association between particular organisms and substrates, in relation to either the raw material, shape, or texture of the archaeological materials. This study is in its initial stages.

On the other hand, we have developed an experimental study based on the microcosm model discussed previously. This research aims to identify and monitor the biofouling processes occurring at the *Swift* site (Bastida et al. 2004). The microcosm model requires that the dimensions of the experimental surfaces used are consistent with the ecological concept of community minimum sampling area. This means that the experimental panel should be able to register at least one specimen of all the species that belong to the community (Margalef 1974).

The materials used for the experiments consist of acrylic micro-panels of 50 x 100 x 5 mm, which are screwed into a larger acrylic base panel coated with antifouling paint (Figure 10.3). Two of these base panels

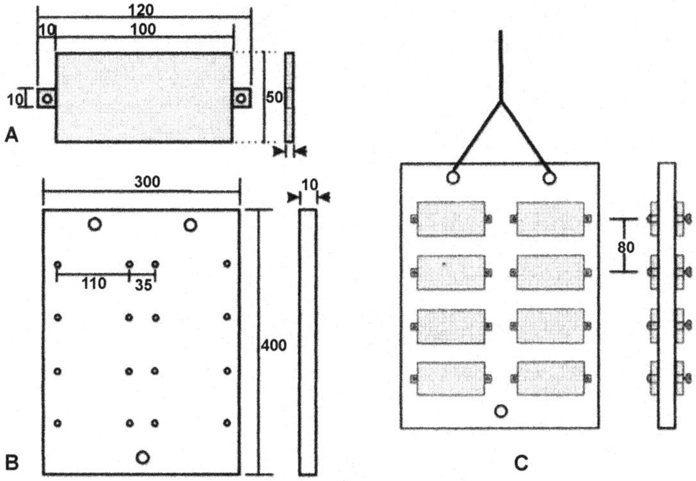

Figure 10.3 Experimental panels. A, acrylic micropanels; B, base frame; C, complete kit of base frame and micro-panels "sandwich" system (measurements are in millimeters).

containing a set of smaller ones were placed in the site, one in the bow area and the other in the stern area.

This experimental design was planned for two years maximum, the time span that is considered sufficient for a proper monitoring of the colonizing cycles of the main species and for community development (Bastida et al. 2004). During the twenty-four months of the study, the small acrylic panels were periodically removed and new micro-panels were installed. The use of multiple panels allowed us to amplify the number of fouling samples and to study changes in community evolution in relation to the time of the year the panels were placed in the water. It is worth pointing out that this experimental study, which optimizes space and materials, is an adaptation for our purposes of one that has been used successfully since the 1960s for fouling research in different harbors and coastal areas of Argentina (Bastida 1971, 1973, 1977; Bastida, Adabbo, and Rascio 1976; Bastida, Capezzani, and Torti 1971; Bastida and Lichtschein 1981, Bastida et al. 1980; Rascio, Bastida, and Bruzzoni 1973).

In conjunction with the biofouling research, we are also studying the action of marine wood borers. Although these benthic organisms are not included within the same ecological succession processes of biofouling communities, as they require different conditions for their development, they are worthy of study because they constitute a significant biodeterioration agent. In fact, holes made by marine borers have been identified in several wood elements at the *Swift* site (Bastida et al. 2004; Elkin 2000). For this reason, we have included pine wood micro-panels of the same size with the acrylic micro-panels used for the biofouling studies. The potential presence of wood borers in them will allow us to identify which species are present at the site as well as to characterize their biological and seasonal cycles.

FUTURE PERSPECTIVES

The experimental acrylic panels placed at the *Swift* site are currently in the last stage of sampling. As soon as this is finished, the last sets of micro-panels will be analyzed together with those extracted in previous periods. With all the results in hand, we will be able to identify and characterize the biofouling community structure, its main colonizing cycles, and the principal ecological succession stages. We can already conclude, however, that the experimental micro-panels system can make an important contribution to biofouling studies. We strongly recommend this approach for biological studies of underwater archaeological sites, both for understanding seasonal patterns of colonization as well as the evolution of the biofouling communities and the characterization of their successional stages. For Puerto Deseado waters, we suggest their use for immersion periods of six to nine months, depending on the time of the year the panels are placed in the water. Based on this first local experience, we believe that for longer periods it would be necessary to work with bigger panels to comply with the requirements of the concept of minimum area community sampling.

The wood micro-panels have not yet reached the two-year immersion period. To date, it has not been possible to observe the presence of wood-boring organisms with the naked eye. The presence or absence of these will only be confirmed when the micro-panels are sectioned under stereomicroscope, as a piece of wood can be completely attacked inside without showing any obvious external signs. Old remains of Teredinidae wood borer, *Bankia martensi*, have been found inside the tunnels analyzed in some of the archaeological wood; however, no wood borers have been found alive yet. The presence of these organisms inside the experimental panels will confirm their presence in the area and thus potentially in the site.

Another biological aspect of the biodeterioration of the *Swift* site is the presence of large kelp algae (*Macrocystis pyrifera*). As noted previously, they are normally quite abundant in the Puerto Deseado *ría* and are frequently observed entangled in the exposed structure of the ship. One aspect worth evaluating is their mechanical effects in combination with the strong currents of the site, particularly to the exposed frames that can, in turn, be structurally weakened in a differential manner (Bastida et al. 2004).

The future results of all these ongoing studies will allow us to asses the consequences of the activity of biofouling and wood borers in different materials and structures present at the site. In turn, such information can provide useful guidelines for aspects such as *in situ* conservation. For example, the confirmation of current activity of wood borers in the site would require some measures such as the physical protection of the wood remains.

All of the above, together with the information of physical and chemical processes of the water and bottom sediments, constitute the basis for developing predictive models that can allow us to achieve a better understanding of the processes that have taken place in the evolution of underwater archaeological sites in the south Atlantic and other similar environments.

ACKNOWLEDGMENTS

The authors wish to thank *Fundación Antorchas* for contributing funds to this research (Grant awarded to Dr. Dolores Elkin for Project Nr.

A-13740/1-7), to the HMS *Swift* project team, and to Dr. Juan Pablo Martin for his assistance with some of the graphics for this chapter.

REFERENCES

Bastida, R. 1971. Las incrustaciones biológicas en el puerto de Mar del Plata, Período 1966/1967. *Revista del Museo de Ciencias Naturales Bernardino Rivadavia, Hidrobiol* 3(2):203–85.

Bastida, R. 1973. Studies of the fouling communities along Argentine coasts. In *Proceedings 3rd International Congress on Marine Corrosion and Fouling*, R. F. Acker, B. F. Brown, J. R. DePalma, and W. P. Iverson, eds., 847–64. Evanston, IL: Northwestern University Press.

Bastida, R. 1977. Las incrustaciones biológicas ("fouling"). In *Protección de Superficies Metálicas*, Manuales Científicos 1, Series III, V. Rascio, W. Bruzzoni, R. Bastida, and E. Rozados, eds., 203–62. La Plata, Argentina: LEMIT.

Bastida, R., H. Adabbo, and V. Rascio. 1976. Toxic action of antifouling paints with different toxicant concentrations. *Corrosion Marine-Fouling* 76(1):5–17.

Bastida, R., D. Capezzani, and M. R. Torti. 1971. Fouling organisms in the port of Mar del Plata (Argentina). I. *Siphonaria lessoni* (Blainville 1824): Ecological and biometric aspects. *Marine Biology* 10(4):297–307.

Bastida, R., D. Elkin, M. Grosso, M. Trassens, and J. P. Martin. 2004. The sloop of war HMS Swift (1770): A case study on the effects of biodeterioration on the underwater cultural heritage of Patagonia. *Corrosion Review* 22(5–6):417–40.

Bastida, R., and S. L'Hoste. 1976. Relaciones tróficas de las comunidades incrustantes (fouling) del puerto de Mar del Plata. *CIDEPINT Anales* 76(3):159–203.

Bastida, R., and V. Lichtschein. 1981. Acción de las incrustaciones biológicas o fouling. In *Manual Ecomar de Corrosión y Protección*, 63–76. Buenos Aires: Servicio Naval de Investigación y Desarrollo (SENID).

Bastida, R., M. Trassens, and J. P. Martin. 2000. Informe preliminar sobre los sedimentos y bioclastos asociados con los restos de la corbeta HMS *Swift* (Puerto Deseado, Argentina). Unpublished interim report, Instituto Nacional de Antropología, Buenos Aires.

Bastida, R., M. Trivi, V. Lichtschein, and M. Stupak. 1980. Ecological aspects of marine fouling at the Port of Mar del Plata (Argentina). In *V Congreso Internacional de Corrosión Marina e Incrustaciones—Sección Biología Marina*, 299–320. Madrid: Garci.

Brankevich, G., R. Bastida, and C. Lemmi. 1988. A comparative study of biofouling settlements in different sections of Necochea Power Plant (Quequén Port, Argentina). *Biofouling* 1:113–35.

Colinvaux, P. 1973. *Introduction to Ecology*. Toronto: John Wiley & Sons.

Cooke, G. 1967. The pattern of autotrophic succession in laboratory microecosystems. *BioScience* 17:717–21.

Elkin, D. 1997. Proyecto arqueológico Swift. Unpublished archaeological project, Instituto Nacional de Antropología, Buenos Aires.

Elkin, D. 2000. Procesos de formación del registro arqueológico subacuático: Una propuesta metodológica para el sitio Swift (Puerto Deseado, Santa Cruz). In *Desde el País de los Gigantes. Perspectivas Arqueológicas en Patagonia*, vol. 1, 195–202. Río Gallegos, Argentina: Universidad Nacional de la Patagonia Austral.

Elkin, D., D. Vainstub, A. Argüeso, and V. Dellino. 2001. Proyecto arqueológico HMS *Swift*, Santa Cruz, Argentina. In *Memorias del Congreso Científico de Arqueología*

Subacuática ICOMOS, P. Luna Erreguerena and R. Roffiel, coords., 143–62. Mexico City: Instituto Nacional de Antropología e Historia.

Elkin, D., D. Vainstub, M. Argüeso, and C. Murray. 2000. HMS *Swift*: Arqueología submarina en Puerto Deseado (Santa Cruz). In *Desde el País de los Gigantes. Perspectivas Arqueológicas en Patagonia*, vol. 2, 659–71. Río Gallegos: Universidad Nacional de la Patagonia Austral.

Levinton, J. 1995. *Marine Biology: Function, Biodiversity, Ecology*. New York: Oxford University Press.

Lyman, R. L. 1994. *Vertebrate Taphonomy*. Cambridge: Cambridge University Press.

Margalef, R. 1968. *Perspectives in Ecological Theory*. Chicago: University of Chicago Press.

Margalef, R. 1974. *Ecología*. Barcelona: Ediciones Omega, S.A.

Muckelroy, K. 1978. *Maritime Archaeology*. Cambridge: Cambridge University Press.

Murray, C., D. Elkin, and D. Vainstub. 2003. The sloop-of-war HMS *Swift*. An archaeological approach. In *The Age of Sail*, N. Tracy, ed., 101–15. London: Conway Maritime Press.

Nybakken, J. 2001. *Marine Biology: An Ecological Approach*. New York: Benjamin Cummings–Addison Wesley Longman.

Odum, E. P. 1997. *Ecology: A Bridge between Science and Society*. Sunderland, MA: Sinauer Associates.

Rascio, V., R. Bastida, and W. Bruzzoni. 1973. Protección anticorrosiva y antiincrustante por medio de pinturas. In *Corrosión Metálica*, 253–319. Buenos Aires: Servicio Naval de Investigación y Desarrollo (SENID).

Schiffer, M. B. 1987. *Formation Processes of the Archaeological Record*. Albuquerque: University of New Mexico Press.

Sutherland, J., and R. Karlson. 1977. Development and stability of the fouling community at Beaufort, North Carolina. *Ecological Monographs* 47:425–46.

Valiela, I. 1995. *Marine Ecological Processes*. New York: Springer-Verlag.

Ward, I., P. Larcombe, and P. Veth. 1999. A new processes-based model for wreck site formation. *Journal of Archaeological Science* 26:561–70.

CHAPTER 11

Navigation in the Río de la Plata

Antonio Lezama

INTRODUCTION

As underwater archaeology in Uruguay develops as a discipline, it will play an important role in creating a new corpus of knowledge about Uruguayan history. A major focus will be the hazardous estuary of the Río de la Plata. Its strong winds and currents have caused an extraordinary number of shipwrecks in historic times, leading to an amazing archaeological treasure. From the beginning of the discovery era until lighthouses were built and even after, a large variety of ships have capsized in our waters in a wide variety of circumstances. These shipwrecks pay tribute to the difficulties of accessibility and navigation in the treacherous brown waters of the Río de la Plata. Cargo, equipment, and luggage have become material testimonies of particular moments and situations. These vestiges are particularly valuable because most of the time they are extraordinary well preserved. Turning this immense amount of potential information into concrete archaeological results is the challenge that Uruguayan underwater archaeology has accepted.

Underwater archaeology is part of naval history. Although many people think that the questions it has raised have already been answered by naval history, this is not so. Underwater archaeology produces qualitatively different information, based on real and tangible facts. These provide the last chapter in the history of a particular ship as no other reliable record can. These new data and the resulting interpretations will enrich history by raising new questions and creating fruitful contradictions that will cause archaeologists and historians to work together to create a deeper understanding of the characteristics of navigation along the Río de la Plata. This chapter is a first step in that direction, one that is being taken in other parts of the world and that will lead to a better integration between historical and archaeological approaches.

Navigation to and from the Río de la Plata is part of a broader picture: the history of navigation. The distinct historical periods—in which different nations were more powerful than others, the technical achievements, and the conflicts of war—are all reflected in our waters and are the framework for the interpretation of archaeological findings. Unfortunately, these elements—type of ships, navigation techniques, maritime routes, etc.—that are the bases of naval history have received very little attention in Uruguayan national history. We are a maritime country without a sea culture in the same way that we are an agricultural country that ignores the countryside. This brief survey of the history of shipping in the Río de la Plata illustrates the richness and value of the underwater cultural heritage in historical terms. It also demonstrates the need to strengthen underwater archaeological research as it is the only way to realize the latent value of the information it provides and ensures the preservation of this valuable historical resource.

PRE-COLUMBIAN NAVIGATION

When the first European expeditions arrived at the Río de la Plata, there were people already there who had been exploiting and sailing those waters for more than 4,000 years. Unfortunately, features of those ships have not yet been archaeologically established; archaeologists must make do with the descriptions made by the first explorers. Among these descriptions is one by Pero Lopes de Sousa in 1531 that refers to his encounter with indigenous people and their ships, near the county of San José. He met four monoxilous canoes, between 16 and 20 m 52.5 and 65.6 ft long, each with about forty men:

> I was two leagues away from the place I just left when four canoes or *almadías* with a lot of people inside came from land towards me; I dropped the canvas of the brigantine to wait for them: they were rowing so fast that it seemed as if they were flying ... their canoes were 10–12 fathoms long and half a fathom wide, made of very-well-worked cedar wood. They were rowing with very long oars which had at their end tufts and tassels made from feathers; in each of the canoes there were 40 people standing up and rowing. (Laguarda Trías 1957:126)

According to Schmidl (1938:57), the canoes of the Timbues were 8.4 m (27.5 ft) long and carried ten men. Laguarda Trías (1957) states that the cedar wood from which they were made was known as red cedar (*Cedra fissiles* or *C. brasiliensis*).

Other indirect testimony regarding the development of pre-Columbian navigation refers to the use of indigenous canoes on the coast of Brazil to reach Colonia del Sacramento in Uruguay at the beginning of the Portuguese occupation. These canoes, to which sails had been added, were big enough to sail from the Atlantic coast of Santa Catalina to the Río de la Plata. Presumably, sails were a technical incorporation sometime after the conquest. The data are based on information given by a group of Portuguese men captured in Uruguayan territory on May 28, 1680. They described "a big canoe with three sails" and "a big canoe which has trees" (Correa Luna 1931:181, 184). We believe that coastal navigation from the Atlantic to the Río de la Plata already existed in pre-Columbian times, as there were canoes big enough to sail that distance. However, this issue, like all others regarding pre-Columbian navigation, has no definite answers and must await new evidence from forthcoming archaeological investigations.

THE DISCOVERY JOURNEYS

The first stage of European navigation in the Río de la Plata, called the discovery period, was carried out by Spanish and Portuguese sailors. In 1516, during Juan Díaz de Solís's first trip, the first shipwreck occurred near Santa Catalina. From then on, expeditions by Fernando de Magallanes, Sebastián Gaboto, Diego García, Pero Lopes de Souza, Pedro de Mendoza, and others started to develop a local profile that can be archaeologically meaningful.

Shipwrecked mariners, deserters, punished criminals, and native people formed a half-breed population in Santa Catalina. Because of their knowledge of the area and of the native language, as well as the material support they could provide, they became a key factor in the reinforcement and supply of discovery and conquest expeditions. With the help of Enrique Montes, a shipwrecked sailor from the Solís expedition in Santa Catalina built a ship called a *galera* or brigantine between November 1526 and February 1527. Native people helped the Spaniards in constructing the deck or *tarazanal*. In 1531, the expedition of Lopes de Souza found this brigantine abandoned on the coast of Maldonado in perfect condition; the ship's provisions were native food, including pans of fish fat and fish meal, obtained by exchange and sometimes brought from as much as 200 km (124 miles) away. Another case is when Mendoza's expedition (1536) embarked with Hernando de Rivera, a resident of Santa Catalina who spoke Guarani.

We must not forget that the effective colonization of southern Brazil did not begin until 1530 with the expedition of Martín Alfonso de Sousa, head of the captaincy of San Vicente. This area remained open to diverse influences until 1567, when the French were completely expelled from the Guanabara Bay and Rio de Janeiro was founded. The presence of non-Portuguese ships on Brazilian coasts was constant during the 16th and 17th centuries. In 1591, Thomas Cavendish looted Santos, while other corsairs did the same in Recife and Pernambuco.

PORTUGUESE NAVIGATION

From the beginning, there was a strong Portuguese and Brazilian presence in the Río de la Plata, supported by local populations of Spanish, Portuguese, and indigenous people. We must remember that, between 1580 and 1640, the Portuguese and Castile realms were under the power of Castilian monarchs. Although separate Portuguese and Castilian colonial domains essentially from Lisbon still existed during that period, Spanish navigation bound to the Río de la Plata was carried out (Sánchez Barba 1992:197).

All known 16th-century maps are of Portuguese origin. The oldest one was made by Jácome de Paiva. He came with Mendoza, who, in 1573, took the caravel *San Cristóbal de la Buenaventura* back to Spain (Reitano 1996). This ship was built in Asunción del Paraguay, the first permanent establishment at the Cuenca del Plata, founded in 1537. In 1608, the guidebook *Hidrografia e Esame de Pilotos* was compiled by geographer Manuel de Figueredo and reprinted in 1625 in a corrected and augmented version. The book warns against sailing at night in the Río de la Plata (Medina 1887:254).

Argentinean historian Z. Moutoukias notes in relation to the Portuguese and Brazilian presence in the first half of the 17th century:

> The reality of the daily life was an intense inter-colony trade with Brazilian ports, carried out mainly by small ships of about 20 to 50 tons that went back and forth. It was common to try to reach the ports of Angola or Guinea from Buenos Aires. Sometimes, Portuguese ships coming directly from Africa or Portugal would appear, and also ships from the Netherlands (Moutoukias 1988:62).

According to E. Reitano (1996:85), in 1730 the Portuguese "lost nautical exclusivity in the region," and from that date on, Spanish, English, and French navigators began to create their own books of sailing routes. However, Portuguese *derroteiros* manuscripts continued to appear regarding navigation of the Río de la Plata, and Reitano links those to clandestine trade. Between 1718 and 1726, a series of navigation routes are known. In his *O Grande Rio da Prata na America Portuguesa* written in 1731, the Portuguese Jesuit Diogo Soares describes navigation in the

Río de la Plata based on both his personal observations and information from pilots and crew, some of whom had made more than thirty trips.

SPANISH NAVIGATION

From the very beginning, besides the Portuguese context (considering ships as well as their pilots), there was also a Spanish marine presence, which included repairing, careening, and even constructing ships mainly in the Asunción port. During the colonial period, there was a permanent shortage of *prácticos* or pilots; these were essential given the danger of the river. The map of Silvestre Ferreira de Silva, a Portuguese who worked for the Spanish, dates from 1748; in the map, he describes the south channel as "the hell of sailors."

During the second half of the 18th century, there was an ongoing attempt to improve cartographic knowledge of the river. Among the main maps are those by Becerra and González in 1771, the information from Alejandro Malaspina in 1789, and the so-called spherical maps by Oyarvide used in Argentina until 1875. These were the first maps that took into account the Earth's curvature, making it possible to calculate distances at different latitudes.

Spanish navigation increased with the *navíos de registro*, called thus because they were authorized (i.e., registered) to trade with America, outside the circuit of fleets and galleons. In 1621, the first of these ships arrived at Buenos Aires; by 1641 another ten ships had arrived; and between 1648 and 1660, another five ships came. This system developed further in the 17th century and became a general practice by 1740, when the system of fleets and galleons was abolished. To assure supply to the Pacific coasts, the route via Cabo de Hornos was opened for *navíos de registro* bound for the Pacific, making a stop in the Río de la Plata. De Bordejé y Morencos (1992:205) points out that Chile was largely isolated from Europe and that, "until decisive progress in navigation occurred at the end of the 17th century and beginnings of the 18th century, direct navigation through the Magallanes Strait first, and then through the Cape of Hornos could not be well designed."

Doubts about the true identity of the ships must be entertained, as many of the vessels considered Spanish had a different origin. These foreign ships were authorized as exceptions or well disguised in different ways. For example, the first trips to the Pacific registered by the Spanish were actually made by French ships. In 1767, a regular service of maritime mail was created. At the beginning, there were four ships per year. As a consequence of the expulsion of the English from the Malvinas (Falklands) in 1769, a small army was placed in Montevideo to control the islands.

THE DUTCH CONTRIBUTION

In addition to the Portuguese and the Spanish, there was a strong Dutch presence, mainly during the 17th century. Historian Z. Moutoukias states that between 1648 and 1702, around 150 illegal arrivals or *arribadas* were registered, of which 50% were Dutch, 24% Portuguese, 10% Spanish, 10% English, and 6% French. In the same period, only thirty-four legal ships arrived.

The term *arribada* was used for those ships specifically banned or without a permit, but which justified their arrival in port by special circumstances. This was also the case with *navíos de aviso*, or warning ships, whose mission was to warn of dangers but had arrived illegally without real notification of danger. These two kinds of vessels were the foundation for smuggling, because their goods, which were normally confiscated by the law, were put back into the trading circuit after a fake auction.

FRENCH AND ENGLISH PRESENCE

As a consequence of the War of the Spanish Succession (1702–1713), French trade developed with South America, particularly from the port of Saint Malo in Bretagne. In the Río de la Plata, the French maintained an important presence through the Guinea Company under which, beginning in 1706, they managed to introduce many ships of diverse origin and carrying all sorts of cargoes. The French presence was strongly related to the *navíos de registro* bound for the Pacific and making a stop at the Río de la Plata. Between 1701 and 1724, known as the "French period," there were 153 of these ships.

The "English period" was between 1715 and 1739, when sixty-one ships arrived carrying 18,400 black slaves and abundant cargoes. This presence increased as English hegemony over maritime trade became well established, although it fluctuated during the different wars. Their trading and warfare fleet that occupied the Río de la Plata during the English invasions in 1806 and 1807 was impressive, consisting of about 100 ships, seventy devoted to trade activities.

OTHER NATIONALITIES

As a consequence of the progressive development of the worldwide trade and Spain's political circumstances, ships from different nationalities became quite common in the Río de la Plata. In 1798, there were four Turkish ships and four Genoan ones in Montevideo; nine North American ships and two from Hamburg also arrived. Others from

Catalonia, Denmark, and Prussia started to arrive from the early years of the 19th century (Villalobos 1986:10–11). The presence of the United States in the last quarter of the 18th century increased mainly due to its participation in the jerky meat trade to Cuba from the beginning of the 19th century.

QUANTITY OF SHIPS

The statistical probability of finding archaeological remains of ships of various kinds and nationalities in the differing periods should be directly dependent on the number of ships that sailed the river in the first place. However, it is very difficult to determine the exact quantity because during colonial times and the period of national consolidation, river navigation was carried out in a very competitive context, both in commercial and military terms. Consequently, records are partial and incomplete (Lezama 1999; Moutoukias 1988).

The presence and, even more important, trading by foreign ships was banned during most of the time that the Spanish dominated. Trade with non-Spanish ships was illegal and obviously badly documented. During the years when the Customs Office in Buenos Aires registered almost no ships (Trelles n.d.), tradesmen in Lima were denouncing the presence of more than 100 ships in the area of Colonia (Villalobos 1986:20). According to our data, between 1586 and 1645, 457 ships arrived (an average of eight per year) and only 293 departed. This presence of illegal foreign ships is also reflected in the value of exports, which was approximately one-tenth of the value of imports (see Table 11.1).

Table 11.1 Ships to/from Buenos Aires 1580–1655.

Year	Number of ships	Observations
1580–1587	6	
1588–1602	85	Described as 30–40-ton-ships
1603–1609	68	
1610–1614	75	
1615–1618	37	
1619–1623	35	
1624–1655	132	

Between 1648 and 1702, only thirty-four ships arrived legally in the Río de la Plata. This number was increased by 158 *arribadas forzosas* (three per year), although Moutoukias (1988) believes that in that period more than 200 of this type of ship must have arrived. In Buenos Aires, this was the excuse used by ships to enter a port where trade was forbidden. This kind of ship practically disappeared from Buenos Aires records after the Portuguese founded Colonia del Sacramento in 1680.

During the 18th century, there was a considerable increase in ship numbers in the Río de la Plata, but it is still difficult to establish the exact number. The almost permanent presence of the Portuguese in Colonia del Sacramento created a goods traffic not registered by the Spanish authorities. Hostility with England, leading to the presence of unauthorized ships, made the situation worse. From 1706, the French had an important presence because of the permit established with the Guinea Company for slave trading, under which they managed to introduce ships of diverse origin loaded with various goods (Studer 1957). Between 1703 and 1715, thirty-four French ships arrived at Buenos Aires, only fifteen belonging to the Guinea Company. Between 1701 and 1724, between 153 and 210 French ships traveled to Spanish ports in the Pacific, making a stop in the Río de la Plata. Possibly some of these were among those ships mentioned above.

In the second quarter of the 18th century, there was an increase in the number of *navíos de registro* bound for Pacific ports as a consequence of the abolition of the fleet and galleons system and the establishment of navigation routes or *derroteros* of Cape Horn to supply those ports. The first Spanish records for Pacific ports are of French ships. By 1748, eighteen *navíos de registro* arrived at Callao; from 1748 to 1761, the number increased to fifty-six; and between 1761 and 1775, it decreased to forty-five. The number of these ships bound to Buenos Aires also increased, reaching twelve by 1752, among them the wrecked 217-ton *Nuestra Señora de la Luz*. There are occasional references to the real volume of traffic that existed in the Río de la Plata. For example, in 1762 when Colonia was captured, the Spanish caught twenty-seven ships "loaded with English products" (Villalobos 1986:21).

During the 18th century, there were some large fleets in the river. In 1777, Pedro de Cevallos, first viceroy of the Río de la Plata, had twenty warships and ninety-six transport ships. In 1781, after the war with England as a consequence of Spanish intervention supporting North American independence (1777–1783), a fleet of twenty-four ships left from the Río de la Plata carrying mainly leather. In 1805, under the command of Commodore Sir Home Popham, the Royal Navy conquered the Cape of Good Hope and then occupied the Río de la Plata, an episode known as the "English invasions." These invasions, which resulted in the occupation of Montevideo in 1807, permitted the arrival of ships in massive numbers; seventy arrived, warships included, loaded with goods. Then, between February 4 and July 4, 1807, 133 ships arrived in Montevideo and 138 sailed.

Between 1779 and 1783, the local commercial circuit was basically only with Brazil. According to Levene (1940:296), from 1792 to 1796, an average of about sixty ships a year moved into Buenos Aires. From 1799, foreign ships that were admitted as neutral, in particular those from the United States, started taking part in trading activities. Certain types of commercial activity, such as the slave trade, were better documented and provide us with an idea of the actual volume of shipping. In 1804, sixteen ships carrying slaves from Africa and nineteen ships from Brazil arrived, whereas in 1805, there were twenty ships from Africa and thirty-nine from Brazil.

River navigation, mainly between Montevideo and Buenos Aires, was carried out in small ships described generally as *sumacas* or *balandras* (schooners and sloops). An average of 500 trips per year is recorded between 1793 and 1798. In 1802, 188 ships (151 Spanish and thirty-seven non-Spanish) entered Montevideo; 169 left and eighty-two stayed in port. At the same time, 648 ships involved in coastal traffic came to port and 640 left (Araujo 1908:499–500).

Considering all these figures, we can estimate that during the 17th century there were approximately 1,000 registered trips including both arrivals and departures, 2,000 for the 18th century, and this number was easily duplicated in the 19th century.

TYPES OF SHIPS

From the perspective of underwater archaeology, it is important to know what kind of ships sailed the river at different times. Structural characteristics and nomenclature that identify them are quite varied. In general, the existence of a vast number of terms used to describe different types of ships does not reflect large structural differences between the hulls. Rather, they refer to the number of masts and the placement of the canvas (i.e., mainly different types of rigging). The character of variation is problematic for archaeological research because normally the masts and spars are lost during a shipwreck.

The depth of the Río de la Plata (4–6 m; 13–19.5 ft) imposes a limitation on the size of ships. This is why most would be relatively small, up to around 250 tons, mainly known as brigantines, *sumacas*, sloops, ketches, luggers, *polacras*, and boats. One of the commonest types, *sumacas*, are described by Malaspina (1938:141) as "a sort of schooner with a deck and is very good for the navigation of the river."

Small ships have been characteristic since the first expeditions. Diego García's fleet in 1526 was formed by a 60-gauge-ton caravel (www.ceha-madeira.net/canarias/hia4.html), a 25-ton *patache*, and a smaller *fusta*, probably a rowing boat. The eighty-five ships that arrived at Buenos Aires between 1588 and 1602 are described as boats or *barcas*, of about 30 to 40 tons. Even when talking in military terms, the vessels referred to are smaller ships (e.g., frigates, *fragatillas*, corvettes, schooners, and *pingues*). Ships larger than 400 tons appeared in the Río de la Plata until the end of the 17th century. Therefore, because small ships, mainly brigantines and *sumacas* up to about 200 tons, continued to be used during the 18th and 19th centuries, we can only establish a direct relation between ships' dimensions and their age for ships that were bigger.

Malaspina was in charge of the expedition of the corvettes *Descubierta* and *Atrevida*, which left Spain in 1789 to correct the available cartography of the American coasts and investigate the political state of the colony. On September 20, 1789, when Malaspina's expedition arrived, there were ten frigates, one corvette, two brigantines, and twenty-two two masted ships in Montevideo. Most were from European trade, others from the army, and one from the Lima trade circuit.

In 1770, Montevideo consolidated itself as a *plaza naviera* or "naval place" and was the base of a medium weight fleet that was at its peak between 1799 and 1806. Francisco de Medina, who owned up to seven ships, was one of the first to make interoceanic trips, when he bought the English frigate *El Vértiz* in 1779. Other tradesmen bought ships of up to 700 tons in Spain and brought them to Montevideo. Between 1801 and 1806, the biggest ships arriving in Montevideo were between 400 and 800 tons. The largest, at 800 tons, was the frigate *Spick*, a Portuguese ship built in India "to last forever" (Bentancur 1997). Many of these ships had been captured by corsairs and were sold at auction. Because of the war with England in 1801, the Buenos Aires consulate created the first Corsair Navy of the Plata, which acted mainly against the Portuguese and was the precursor of the navy of 1815.

In 1801, Oyarvide made his "spherical map of the Uruguay River" based on a survey from a sloop. For the same task in the Río de la Plata, he used a frigate, a schooner, and a *falucho* or small boat with oars and one lateen sail. In 1805, Oyarvide died on board a *mistico* (coasting vessel) while on duty protecting the entrance to the Río de la Plata from the English. Araujo (1908:499–500) describes the naval force and identifies the ships from Montevideo: one frigate, two corvettes, twenty-one *lanchas cañoneras* or gunboats, four *lanchas obuseras* (a lighter provided with howitzers), four brigantines, two feluccas, and three *misticos*, described as being in charge of the correspondence between

Colonia and Buenos Aires. He also specifies the use of *sumacas* in the coastal traffic.

An official note dated September 3, 1812, describes the number and type of ships existing at Montevideo: one brigantine, one schooner, three *sumacas*, twenty-three sloops, two *lanchas* or small boats, one big boat, three *chalupas* or shallop, one *garendumba*, two *botes* (another kind of small boat), eight *lanchones de tráfico de puerto* or port traffic lighter, and thirty *guadaños*, a small boat with an awning used in the traffic of the port of Havana. There were also eighty-four smaller ships. To these should be added twenty-five frigates to sail in high seas and forty-one brigantines and other vessels, as well as thirty-four vessels for coastal trade (Capillas 1962:118).

Another important factor for identifying the ships wrecked in the Río de la Plata is the early presence of small dockyards in every coastal city. In 1780 in Buenos Aires, there were 162 "river carpenters." Records from 1799 mention the building of three frigates and a "portion" of brigantines and big boats. Félix de Azara, Spanish official and cartographer, mentions the construction in Buenos Aires of "seven big ships" and the existence of 170 schooners and boats for local navigation (Azara 1943:23). Around 1801, more than twenty ships were built in Paraguay, and another five in Corrientes. It is also known that by 1805, the frigate *Nuestra Señora de los Dolores* was built in Asunción and that almost at the same time a brigantine was built in Montevideo (Villalobos 1986:104). To these we should add the ships built locally, as those in Chile, where nineteen brigantines and frigates were built in the last thirty years of colonial domination.

CARGOES

Cargoes are perhaps the main element to identify a ship. Because the Río de la Plata served as a frontier for several nations like Spain, Portugal, England, Holland, and France, smuggling, particularly of precious metals, was an important problem. At the same time, inland trade routes made it possible to export exotic products, such as cocoa from Guayaquil, first through Buenos Aires and later through Montevideo.

Difficulties in identifying a ship through its cargo do not end here. Sometimes records were faked, even within legal trade. This is the case with the *navíos de registro*, which, although authorized by the register, were of unknown nationality. There was no real interest in recording it, as it was inferred from the nationality of the pilot and crew. In the same way, the actual content of cargoes, including weight and volume, was unknown; cargoes were counted by bunches and boxes, which varied in weight, measure, and content.

An example is the Portuguese ship *Nuestra Señora de la Luz*, bought as "old," with its hull repaired in 1748. The crew was mostly Portuguese, apart from the captain and most important officers. Its real cargo was mostly gold and silver coins, as evidenced by the result of past and recent diving activities. In this case, partners in the business signed a private contract to pay 178,000 pesos to buy the cargo, but their public claims for the same cargo amounted top 839,000 pesos. As some of the partners did not have enough money to pay their share, they asked for loans at a rate known as "sea risk," with interest of between 50% and 60%. This gives an idea of the expected profit (Apolant 1992).

The same difficulties apply to the slave traffic, because often concessionaires used this privilege to introduce or take out goods illegally. There were also corsair activities, through which different kind of goods were gathered. However, there are some patterns in the cargoes that can be identified and could indicate the ship's probable origin. For example, leather and, from the end of the 18th century, the big cargoes of jerky meat were bound to Brazil and Cuba. Some of these ships continued to Spain and then back to Montevideo; others came straight back to Montevideo loaded with sugar and liquor.

Finally, the permanent and clandestine extraction of silver from the Potosí, which was the original Castilian name for the Paraná Guazú (the "big big river," the aboriginal name for the Río de la Plata), was the main reason for colonization of the region and consequently for the navigation of the Río de la Plata (Camargo 1996; Lezama 1999). The first silver smuggling took place as early as 1587, with the shipwreck of the *San Antonio* in the zone known as "the other band," referring to Buenos Aires, near Colonia del Sacramento. The same happened in 1728 with the shipwreck of the *Sea Horse*, a ship authorized for slave trade, and with *Nuestra Señora de la Luz* in 1752. In 1804, a fleet of four frigates sailed from Montevideo, loaded with "five million *duros* that belong to the king and particulars" (Guillén 1960:75).

CLOSING COMMENTS

I have reviewed the basic knowledge necessary for understanding the maritime history of the Río de la Plata: actors, ship types, and cargoes. These constitute a critical knowledge base that underwater archaeology can build on. The history of shipping in the Río de la Plata is but a part of the history of shipping in general. Dominance of the seas by different nations, technical advances, wars, and so on casts its reflection on our waters and provides the framework for our archaeological interpretations.

The sea has always been a road kept open for economic reasons, quite beyond the reach of purely political desires. Over the open seas, both the wanted and the unwanted arrive and have always arrived: prosperity and poverty, stability and turmoil. But the sea is not a foreign agent. The sea is an extension of what we do on dry land. It is on land that ships are built; where crews are recruited; where ports are built; and where passengers and goods are loaded and unloaded. The sea is therefore inseparable from the shore in the same way that the shore is inseparable from its hinterland.

I have presented the maritime history of the Río de la Plata from the point of view of underwater archaeology, an auxiliary of maritime history, capable of delivering unique answers to the general questions of the history of shipping. However, archaeology provides information that is qualitatively different because it is based on tangible findings that narrate the last chapter of vessels. Here is the very place where the ship was wrecked. Was it on its expected position or was it far away from it? Was it there willingly or unwillingly? Here are the remains of the ship. What did she look like and what were her structural strengths and weaknesses? Here is the cargo, legal or illegal. Here lived the passengers and the crew, in real surroundings, real people with public and private lives and leaving behind information hidden in material remains, most of the time extraordinarily well preserved in the seabed. Answers to these questions and more data will open new fields of vision and enrich the sources for the study of the maritime history of the Río the La Plata region, raising questions and baring contradictions that will advance the work of both historians and archaeologists.

The purpose of this chapter is to contribute to the development of a theoretical model, in the sense described by Muckelroy (1978). The first task, attempted here, was to provide the historical setting for shipping in the Río de la Plata: Who sailed along those waters, why, and in what type of vessel? To complete this theoretical framework, we should follow up with other chapters dealing with the physical geography of the Plata estuary, to help explain the circumstances of the diverse naval events and their influence on the configuration and conservation of the remains. From this chapter, however, future archaeologists can gain an understanding of the dimension and complexity of the problem. The chapter is a call to pay the utmost attention to detail and correct recording and to design methodology with a view to exactness and precision as the best way to ensure that we can differentiate between events and thus arrive at sound interpretations of history.

ACKNOWLEDGMENTS

My recognition and gratitude for Sofia Buschiazzo for translating this chapter from Spanish into English, to Miguel Peirano for editing the

English version, and to Pilar Luna Erreguerena and Margaret Leshikar-Denton for their sustained efforts to make this publication a reality.

REFERENCES

Apolant, J. A. 1992. *El Naufragio del Navio Nuestra Señora de la Luz (Montevideo 1752).* Montevideo: Instituto Uruguayo de Numismática.

Araujo, J. J. 1908. *Guía de Forasteros del Virreinato de Buenos Aires para el Año 1803.* Buenos Aires: Junta de Historia y Numismática, Colección de Libros Raros e Inéditos sobre la Región del Río de la Plata.

Azara, F. de. 1943. *Memoria sobre el Estado Rural del Río de la Plata y Otros Informes,* Biblioteca Histórica Colonial dirigida por Julio César González, vol. 1. Buenos Aires: Ed. Bajel.

Bentancur, A. 1997. *El Puerto Colonial de Montevideo.* Vol. 1, *Guerras y Apertura Comercial: Tres Lustros de Crecimiento Económico 1791–1806.* Montevideo: FHCE.

Camargo, F. 1996. *Britânicos no Prata, Caminhos da Hegemonia.* Passo Fundo, Uruguay: Ed. Universitária.

Capillas de Castellanos, A. 1962. Historia del consulado de comercio de Montevideo. Primera parte (1795–1815). Montevideo: Revista Histórica, vol. 32.

Correa Luna, C. 1931. *Campaña del Brasil, Antecedentes Coloniales,* vol. 1. Montevideo.

De Bordejé y Morencos, F. 1992. *Tráfico de Indias y Política Oceánica.* Madrid: MAPFRE 1492.

Guillén, J. F. 1960. *La Independencia del Plata en los papeles del Archivo de Marina.* Madrid: Instituto Histórico de Marina.

Laguarda Trías, R. A. 1957. Viaje del portugués Pero Lopes de Sousa al Río de la Plata en 1531. *Revista de la Sociedad Amigos de la Arqueología* vol. 15:101–70.

Levene, R., dir. 1940. *Historia de la Nación Argentina,* vol. 4. Buenos Aires: Academia Nacional de Historia.

Lezama, A. 1999. Raíces coloniales del puente Colonia-Buenos Aires. In *Cuadernos del CLAEH,* CLAEH, ed., 7–28. Historia & Historiografías, vols. 83–84. Montevideo: Centro Latinoamericano de Economía Humana.

Malaspina, A. 1938. *Viaje al Río de la Plata en el Siglo XVIII.* Buenos Aires: La Facultad.

Medina, J. T. 1887. *Historia del Tribunal del Santo Oficio de la Inquisición de Lima (1569–1820),* vol. 1. Santiago de Chile, Chile: Imprenta Gutemberg.

Moutoukias, Z. 1988. *Contrabando y Control Colonial en el Siglo XVII.* Buenos Aires: Centro Editor de América Latina.

Reitano, E. 1996. Navegantes, cartas y derroteros en el Río de la Plata Colonial. *Revista de Historia Naval* 14(55):81–96.

Sánchez Barba, M. H. 1992. *El Mar en la Historia de América.* Madrid: MAPFRE 1492.

Schmidl, U. 1938. *Derrotero y Viaje a España y las Indias.* Santa Fe, Argentina.

Studer, E. F. S. de. 1957. *La Trata de Negros en el Río de la Plata durante el Siglo XVIII.* Buenos Aires: Universidad de Buenos Aires.

Trelles, M. R. n.d. *Registro Estadístico de Buenos Aires, Buenos Aires, 1859–1867.* Buenos Aires.

Villalobos, S. 1986. *Comercio y Contrabando en el Río de la Plata.* Buenos Aires: Ed. Eudeba. Available online at www.ceha-madeira.net/canarias/hia4.html (accessed May 15, 2008).

CHAPTER 12

Bermuda's Shipwreck Heritage

Edward Cecil Harris

BACKGROUND

The islands of Bermuda lie at 32° north latitude and 64° west longitude, some 3,000 miles from Europe and about 650 miles from the coast of North Carolina, the nearest land on the North America continent. Considered by mariners of old as the "second remotest place known," the Bermudas are one of the most isolated islands in the oceanic domain. Nonetheless, the presence of the northward-flowing Gulf Stream and easterly blowing trade winds brought shipping from the Caribbean into the vicinity of the island on voyages bound for Europe. Used as a navigational beacon in the days of sail before the invention of the Harrison chronometer, Bermuda often became the death trap of ships, rather than a venue of safe passage. Over 300 shipwrecks are thought to lie on its reefs.

Replete with human material culture, these vessels were of international import, not only for the range of their voyages, but in the nature of their cargoes (Smith and Harris 2002). Thus, a wealth of heritage came to rest in Bermuda waters over the five centuries since European shipping began to transit the Atlantic Ocean, to and from the Americas. This heritage remained largely hidden until the wider use of the scuba tank in the 1950s and the discovery of gold on one such site at that time. That finding led to the passage of the Wreck and Salvage Act (1959), intended to protect the historic shipwreck heritage found at Bermuda, but belonging to all peoples. As it was part of the existing law on salvage in the island, the 1959 act was essentially flawed. It allowed for compensation to be paid to the finder, should the government wish to possess the artifacts recovered. This led to unscientific destruction of shipwrecks to find objects of intrinsic value in terms of monetary compensation. Coupled with the fact that former governments had no interest in parting with tax dollars in exchange for cultural heritage objects, there was a loss of most of the material taken from shipwrecks into the 1990s. Conservation of artifacts was not considered at all in the 1959 legislation, therefore much of what was discovered over the ensuing thirty-year period was lost because it was not scientifically treated in a conservation laboratory.

EARLY RESEARCH

The promise of early work by Dr. Mendel Peterson (1965) of the Smithsonian Institution, in cooperation with salvage divers at Bermuda, did not result in a conversion of the divers into archaeologists, as now professionally defined, though some claim such a status. The close relationships of government officials and treasure hunters remained a salient feature of the decades following the passage of the 1959 act and that alone perhaps ensured that no significant progress was made in improving the shipwreck heritage law for Bermuda. Consequently, Peterson's book comprised much of the only surviving evidence of several decades of intensive working of the shipwrecks at Bermuda before the 1980s.

ESTABLISHMENT OF THE MUSEUM

In 1974, the Bermuda Maritime Museum was established in a six-acre fort at the old Royal Naval Dockyard at the western end of the island. From that time, the advocacy for preservation of shipwreck heritage as an archaeological resource may be said to have begun in earnest. From 1975, the first chairman of the Board of Trustees, the late Dr. John Carstairs Arnell, pressed the governments of the day for changes to the law. Dr. Arnell was a chemist and spent much of his career in the Arctic regions of Canada looking for signs of nuclear testing by the Russians. Nonetheless, he had acquired a fine sense of museums and archaeology and a deep understanding of related ethics and methods.

A retrospective paper about his early advocacy of control of Bermuda's historic shipwrecks makes interesting reading (Arnell 1992). Arnell discusses how, in 1975, he and other members of the museum thought "that the Museum should take a strong lead in furthering underwater archaeology" and as part of a proposed project on the wreck of the *Sea Venture* (1609), a "restoration laboratory" should be created. Four years later, Arnell was writing to the government to warn again about the disregard for the law and the continued destruction of shipwreck heritage without proper record. The response from a customs official at the time was that the "department had never asked the police to act in investigating diving activities over the reefs, and in consequence they took no interest." Arnell replied with a memo on the subject that included the prescient suggestion that a "National Marine Archaeological Collection" be established, with the museum designated as its custodian (Arnell 1992).

Bureaucratic inertia prevented results, and the government advisory committee responsible for underwater heritage coalesced into a somewhat pro–treasure hunting body. Private individuals were considered more trustworthy than institutions such as museums, thus ensuring that into the 1990s treasure hunters and salvors were given most of the shipwreck permits.

ADVOCACY FOR CHANGE

In 1980, Dr. Edward Harris, a Bermudian and professional archaeologist, assumed the new post of executive director of the museum; several years later, he was placed on the government shipwreck committee, but to little effect. Because Drs. Arnell and Harris continued to press for changes in the law and in attitudes toward underwater cultural heritage, a bill for a new law was brought forward near the end of 1989. This bill, however, was flawed as it still allowed for the disbursement of artifacts into private hands, although on a more restricted fashion than the original 1959 law.

Politics, ever present, intervened, as there was a general election late in 1989. Under the new administration, the shipwreck bill was shelved. Later, the government attempted to introduce another shipwreck bill, but its pro–treasure hunting provisions resulted in its withdrawal, such was the change of attitude in the House of Assembly, Bermuda's Parliament. The shelving of that retrograde bill was made possible as some government members made it clear that they would vote with the opposition ranks against it.

Looking back over this somewhat unsavory period, two ranks of protagonists for shipwreck preservation emerged in the 1980s and 1990s. On the one hand, the then opposition Progressive Labour Party developed a keen interest in all matters of heritage preservation and asked for briefings on the subject of shipwrecks on several occasions. On the other hand, the evolution of the Bermuda Maritime Museum into a professional institution adhering to international ethics on archaeology was predestined to promote the preservation of shipwreck heritage and its examination by archaeological means.

CHANGE BY LEADERSHIP

From 1980 onward, the Bermuda Maritime Museum has taken a leadership role in attempting to change attitudes toward underwater heritage by conducting professional archaeological research programs. Such projects have been undertaken mostly with the assistance of overseas educational institutions, and many field schools have been held since the early 1980s. From 1989, with Richard and Susan Butterfield of Bermuda as benefactors, the museum has published the annual *Bermuda Journal of Archaeology and Maritime History* (*BJAMH*) as a means to record the results of that research.

The first volume contained a paper by Richard Gould (1989) on the wreck of HMS *Vixen*. Professor Gould, with his team from Brown University, has remained a stalwart in underwater research at Bermuda. Beginning in the early 1990s, Dr. Gordon Watts and teams from East Carolina University, Greenville, North Carolina, have conducted an outstanding series of underwater archaeology projects, most of which have been published in the *BJAMH* (Watts 1993, 2003), and they are preparing a major book on Bermuda shipwrecks. Many more archaeologists, conservators, and others have also helped advance professional underwater archaeology at Bermuda.

With a population of some 45,000, Bermuda does not have that much to draw on for archaeological expertise, so the assistance of overseas institutions has been vital to the development of both underwater and land archaeology on the island. We acknowledge a considerable debt to all those institutions and individuals who have given freely of their time and resources, as most work as volunteers to preserve Bermuda's underwater heritage and to promote changes in attitude by leading and doing professional archaeological work.

NEW LAW FOR SHIPWRECKS

The Progressive Labour Party (PLP), which had won government for the first time in November 1998, produced a new shipwreck bill. That government has since proved very receptive to many aspects of material cultural heritage. The bill was suggested in part by a committee of the Bermuda National Trust and the Bermuda Maritime Museum, which responded to the lack of progress from prior government circles. However, its final form, as passed into law, is credited to the PLP government.

Coupled with changing international standards and protocols, including the *ICOMOS International Charter on the Protection and Management of Underwater Cultural Heritage* (1996), which culminated in the adoption of the new *UNESCO Convention on the Protection of the Underwater Cultural Heritage* (2001) in November 2001, the coalescence of the opposition PLP and the Bermuda Maritime Museum, along with the Bermuda National Trust, eventually brought about the necessary change in the shipwreck law, resulting in the Historic Wrecks

Act (2001). The final form of the 2001 bill on Bermuda's historic shipwrecks closely mirrored the important UNESCO guidelines. All reference to the dispersal of artifacts into the hands of individuals and the tit-for-tat compensation of money-for-artifacts was removed, and the bill passed successfully through the House of Assembly and the Bermuda Senate, becoming law.

After half of a century of destruction, Bermuda finally had a law worthy of the name and equal to the task of protecting what still exists of a once-extraordinary underwater cultural heritage. That the law came into being at all seems to owe much to the diligence and determination of the cabinet of the PLP government and its then leader and then premier of Bermuda, the Hon. Jennifer M. Smith, a long-serving politician who shared with her party a keen interest in preserving human heritage and the natural environment.

This new act closely followed the new guidelines set out by UNESCO in November 2001 and provides for the protection of Bermuda's underwater heritage as archaeological monuments. No reference to compensation by government exists in this act, except that the minister of the day may, at his or her discretion, give an honorarium to a finder. All objects found belong to the nation, and arrangements for conservation must be made before any work can be carried out. Licenses will only be granted on consideration of proposals that are scientifically based on archaeological standards. The act allows for the position of a custodian of wrecks, a government agent responsible for overseeing of the terms of the act.

ARCHAEOLOGICAL ETHICS

The changes to the Bermuda shipwreck laws, which exceeded the UNESCO guidelines, were not wrought without considerable difficulty. The PLP, the Bermuda Maritime Museum, and the Bermuda National Trust were vilified by treasure hunters and their fellow travelers, which included, one must say with dismay, some archaeologists. One prominent archaeologist claimed in the Bermuda press that it was part of the "golden allure" of Bermuda that sightseeing divers should be allowed to take artifacts from shipwreck sites for display on their mantelpieces back at home. It is also fair to say that some of the leading maritime museums in the United States undermined heritage efforts at Bermuda. As has been seen in other areas of archaeological looting and artifact acquisition, many museums still need to improve their ethical standards (Harris 2006).

In any country of the Caribbean, one need not too loudly remind the people and their governments of the tremendous, indeed incalculable, heritage losses that have occurred in our waters since the 1950s because of the depredations of treasure hunters. The economic losses to our small countries are large as well, for the destruction of this heritage deprives us of materials for our museums that, as interesting and often unique, would attract discerning visitors. It is hoped that in Bermuda we have seen the end of the degradation of our historic shipwrecks and that the example of the new Historic Wrecks Act (2001) will be of assistance to the islands in the West Indies, which have suffered as much at the hand of treasure hunters.

It is time to reverse the trend whereby those countries that can least afford these heritage losses are being exploited by citizens of those lands that are already wealthy. The new law from Bermuda shows a way forward that is entirely in keeping with the new principles on underwater archaeology and its preservation now espoused by UNESCO. It may, in fact, be the strongest such national legislation in existence. Although some may speak of the implementation of the UNESCO guidelines, the government in Bermuda has instead taken action. We hope that the future of the underwater heritage that remains after the wastage and destruction of former decades is now assured.

The Bermuda government has spoken in terms that are of international importance: Shipwreck heritage is no longer up for grabs in our waters, and with UNESCO, we say it should not be so in any other jurisdiction. Archaeology and treasure hunting are often presented as two sides of a coin, as two valid points of view, but this has never been the case. As people everywhere try to hold or reclaim their identities and heritage in a global world often at war with such individual cultural identities, it will be increasingly obvious that the only way to claim shipwreck heritage and to hold it for future generations is by the archaeological method. One would hope that many professionals, who take high-minded views in other areas of archaeology, will throw their weight into the international scene to promote the preservation of underwater heritage.

REFERENCES

Arnell, J. C. 1992. Underwater archaeology at the Bermuda Maritime Museum 1975–1983. Unpublished paper, Bermuda Maritime Museum.

Gould, R. A. 1989. HMS Vixen: An early ironclad ram at Bermuda. *Bermuda Journal of Archaeology and Maritime History* 1:43–80.

Harris, E. C. 2006. Archaeology and the ethics of scientific destruction. In *Between Dirt and Discussion: Methods, Methodology, and Interpretation in Historical Archaeology*, S. N. Archer and K. M. Bartoy, eds., 141–50. New York: Springer-Verlag.

Historic Wrecks Act. 2001. Bermuda: Bermuda Government.

ICOMOS International Charter on the Protection and Management of Underwater Cultural Heritage. 1996. Paris: ICOMOS.

Peterson, M. 1965. *History under the Sea*. Washington, DC: Smithsonian Institution.

Smith, Jr., C. E., and E. C. Harris. 2002. Underwater cultural heritage in Bermuda. In *International Handbook of Underwater Archaeology*, C. Ruppe and J. Barstad, eds., 299–312. New York: Kluwer Academic/Plenum Press.

UNESCO Convention on the Protection of the Underwater Cultural Heritage. 2001. Paris: UNESCO.

Watts, Jr., G. P. 1993. A decade of shipwreck research at Bermuda. *Bermuda Journal of Archaeology and Maritime History* 5:12–57.

Watts, Jr., G. P. 2003. A second decade of shipwreck research at Bermuda. *Bermuda Journal of Archaeology and Maritime History* 14:61–147.

Wreck and Salvage Act. 1959. Bermuda: Bermuda Government.

CHAPTER 13

The Sinking of the Slave Ship *Trouvadore*: Linking the Past to the Present

Nigel Sadler

INTRODUCTION

Archaeological projects on historical sites are undertaken in two ways. One way is to discover a site and then work out what it is from the artifacts and archival research. The other is to discover the story in the archives and then look for the site. Historically, the first approach is usually taken, often in the face of development. However, when a project starts off with archival research, it can lead to a more focused study by the archaeologists and can be more rewarding in terms of information recovered.

The *Trouvadore* project is a classic example of this second approach (see www.slaveshiptrouvadore.com). It started with the Turks and Caicos National Museum's interest in a shipwreck and soon grew into trying to uncover the full potential of the *Trouvadore* story. The project is an example of a collaborative process, mixing not only professionals and amateurs but also a wide range of disciplines. It has involved researchers in eight countries, family historians, cultural historians, university lecturers, scientists, archaeologists, documentary filmmakers, and publishers. This approach has allowed the data to be analyzed in many ways: from an academic perspective to a more popular one, and from a broad subject down to individual family connections. This variety of interpretations has opened debates on how the material should be researched and presented.

The primary focus of the project in the early days was to understand the *Trouvadore* in national terms. This is a powerful aspect of the study, wherein the identification, preservation, interpretation, and management of the *Trouvadore* site have compelling links to living people in the Turks and Caicos Islands. But there is more: It became apparent that the project would also provide important insight into what was happening in this transitional period from slavery to emancipation in the Americas. As European and American countries underwent degrees of emancipation at different times, the British Navy tried to prevent the trans-Atlantic slave trade, seizing 1,600 ships and freeing 150,000 Africans between 1807 and 1867.

THE START OF THE TRAIL

Prior to the opening of the Turks and Caicos National Museum in 1991, there was no collecting agency for the Turks and Caicos Islands, so many important items left the country. In the mid-1990s, museum founder Grethe Seim, along with Dr. Donald Keith, Ships of Discovery, tried to locate some of these items and came across letters referring to items donated to the American Museum of Natural History in New York by George Gibbs, a 19th-century resident of Grand Turk. Seim and Keith visited the American Museum of Natural History to see these items.

Their main interest was the precolonial Lucayan material but they also viewed two idols mentioned by Gibbs in a letter to the Smithsonian secretary:

> Two African idols, found on board the last Spanish slaver, of wood with glass eyes [schr Esperanza'] wrecked in the year 1841 at Breezy Point on the Caicos Islands. The slaves from this vessel were taken possession of by the Government and brought to the Grand Turk Island. The captain of the slaver, escaped the penalty (by being a Spaniard), of being hung according to the British laws. The slaves were apprenticed for the space of one year and they and their descendants form at the present time, viz the year 1878 the pith of our present labouring population. (Gibbs 1878)

The Smithsonian had identified the idols (on display in the Pacific Gallery at the Museum of Natural History) as being from Easter Island, sparking an interest in Grethe Seim and Dr. Donald Keith that would start to shed light on a story long forgotten.

Researchers were commissioned by the museum to find references to this sunken slaver at the Public Record Office in London, and soon the story emerged. Unfortunately, the data are confusing because of inaccuracies that appear in history books written in the last forty years. Nonetheless, each account has sufficient information to establish that it refers to the same wreck. Are the accounts just the combination of two or more stories? If so, would it be simple to untangle these stories?

STORY OF THE *TROUVADORE*

Wrecking and Rescue

Researchers soon identified that the ship that sank in 1841 was the *Trouvadore*, not the *Esperanza*. Gibbs was confusing two slavers that wrecked off the Caicos Bank. Recent research has identified the *Esperanza* as a Portuguese slaver wrecked in 1837. Along with the crew, 220 Africans came ashore but eighteen died before all the survivors were taken to Nassau. It is possible some were returned, as 189 liberated Africans were sent from Nassau to the Turks and Caicos Islands between 1833 and 1840.

The *Trouvadore* was a brigantine sailing under Spanish papers from Santiago, Cuba. The crew were Spanish, but during the crossing to Africa some died and were replaced by Portuguese sailors picked up on São Tomē. We have yet to confirm where the enslaved Africans were loaded, or how many there were. As the ship docked at São Tomē, they would have been collected there or nearby on the west coast of Africa; the ship would not have remained there, risking capture by the British Navy. Fortunately for the Africans, after a month at sea en route to Cuba, the

Figure 13.1 Breezy Point, East Caicos 2001. This is the location where the records say the Africans came ashore (photograph by Turks and Caicos National Museum).

ship wrecked on the Caicos Bank (Figure 13.1), saving them from a life of slavery.

The ship was carrying twenty crew and 193 slaves when it sank, but soon after landing one African was shot dead. The captain offered Mr. Stevenson, one of the rescuers from Middle Caicos, $3,000 USD to obtain a vessel to take the crew and slaves on to Cuba. This may seem excessive, but a slave could obtain a profit of $185 and a captain might make around $12,600 for a voyage. Mr. Stevenson delayed the captain long enough so that the authorities in Grand Turk could dispatch two ships and a detachment of seventeen soldiers to pick up the survivors.

Distribution of the Liberated Africans

Once collected, the survivors were taken to Grand Turk, where the ship's crew were imprisoned in the upper room of the old court house, while the Africans were placed inside the crowded prison. A better long-term solution was needed. Should they be returned to Africa, sent to Nassau for the Bahamas government to deal with, or released into the local community?

The last option was preferred, but the authorities needed to recover their costs for rescuing the Africans. They also needed the support of the salt proprietors, so a compromise was reached. Of the 192 Africans, 168 were distributed among salt pond owners on Salt Cay and Grand Turk on a one-year contract. The eighty-nine men, twenty-six women, thirty-nine boys, eleven girls, and three infants were given clothing, food, accommodation, and medical care in return for their labor (Figure 13.2). The established church was to teach them to speak English and Christian ways, including being christened and attending services.

Twenty-four Africans—twenty men and four women—could not be absorbed into the local community and were taken to Nassau along with the slaver's crew. At Nassau, the crew of the *Trouvadore* were released into the custody of the Spanish consul who took them to Cuba for trial, but the fate of the twenty-four liberated Africans is not known.

In the Turks Islands, the only work was salt production. Raking was carried out by the men, whereas both sexes worked together moving the salt to the dock. Women bagged the salt (Figure 13.3). Working conditions had improved since emancipation, but it was still a hard, unrewarding job. For this reason, the salt proprietors were eager to take in the liberated Africans as cheap labor.

Figure 13.2 Salt rakers in *ca.* 1900. This is the work into which the Africans were apprenticed. This photo may show some of the descendants of the *Trouvadore* survivors (courtesy of Turks and Caicos National Museum).

Figure 13.3 Women bagging salt in the 1930s. This is the type of work into which the female survivors of the *Trouvadore* would have been apprenticed (courtesy of Turks and Caicos National Museum).

1842 AND ONWARD—A MOVE TO THE CAICOS BANK?

Did the Africans find compassion, or were the local population just frustrated at having new unwelcome guests and wanted to get rid of them? This question may be resolved when research identifies their final destination after 1842.

The head right system in the Turks Islands gave all British citizens an equal share of the salt ponds. It worked well for the proprietors when a slave's shares went to their owners, but now the freed slaves were on equal footing. Wealthier whites, concerned their privileged way of life was threatened, lobbied to replace head right with a leasehold system. It was during this period that the *Trouvadore* wrecked. The influx of Africans would have weakened the former slave owners' rights even further. They would have accepted them as cheap labor, but at the end of that year the Africans would have been entitled to a share in the salt ponds. This would be unacceptable to the white population, which would have seen sending them to the less-populated Caicos Islands as the best solution. Also, as the black population increased and gained positions in the community, the social order of pre-1834 was threatened.

The British government did have certain ideas about how to treat recaptives. It was aware of the issues surrounding the arrival of so many first-generation Africans into small communities and that's why it tried to keep them together. In the Bahamas, the government set up separate settlements where their own communities could develop, but there are no records of any of these for the Turks and Caicos Islands.

Most of the population produced salt in the Turks Islands, which are low lying with little rainfall, limiting the amount of freshwater and food that could be produced. Living there was difficult, even in the best of times. On the other hand, the Caicos bank was greener and more fertile; it was able to sustain a population that was willing to lead a subsistence way of life. If the liberated Africans went to the Caicos Islands, where would they have settled? There are only two possibilities: Middle Caicos and South Caicos.

Middle Caicos

Local historian H. E. Sadler (1997:91) recorded that Bambarra, Middle Caicos, was settled in 1842 by survivors from the wrecked slaver *Gambia*. However, a report by Stipendiary Magistrate Mr. Eve in 1842 records that only 168 liberated Africans had settled in the Turks and Caicos Islands in the previous three years, this being the number from the *Trouvadore*. There is no evidence of liberated Africans from another ship landing here in this period, nor any records for a ship called *Gambia* being captured by the British Navy or wrecked in the Bahamian Archipelago for the years 1807 to 1860. Is this just a case of confusing the ship's name and the origins of the Africans?

Bambarra is the only settlement in the Turks and Caicos Islands with an African name, suggesting strong links with first-generation Africans, and making a good case for a link to the liberated Africans from the *Trouvadore.* This circumstantial evidence makes a good argument, but it's still not proof. Local folklore gives Bambarra two origins. The first is that slaves owned by William Forbes settled here, accounting for why the surname Forbes is common. The second explanation is that they are descendants of Africans from a wrecked slaver. It is likely that both stories have some basis in truth.

South Caicos

In 1842, salt production began in earnest on South Caicos. This development occurred at the right time to provide employment to the liberated Africans from the *Trouvadore.* Further expansion occurred after 1848, and it is likely that as salt production developed on South Caicos, it attracted workers not only from the Turks Islands but also from the Caicos Islands. This development would have suited the liberated Africans from the *Trouvadore*; they had experience working in the salt ponds, so they would have been some of the earliest people to seek work in the newly developed ponds. If they had been moved to Middle Caicos, it might have only been temporary.

The Population of the Turks and Caicos Islands

In 1843, the Bahamas government recorded the Turks and Caicos population as 2,495. If all 168 liberated Africans from the *Trouvadore* had survived until 1843, they would have made up 6.7% of the population. The Turks Islands had equal numbers of men and women, whereas the Caicos Islands had a large difference between them. Was this because single men went to the Caicos Islands in search of work, or was it because the liberated Africans from the *Trouvadore* had been moved there, taking their unequal numbers with them?

ENTERING THE COMMUNITY

Folklore and the Remnants of African Society—The Cultural Links

What evidence is there to tie the liberated Africans from the *Trouvadore* to today's population? It is not clear how documentary research can show cultural identity that is the result of, or influenced by, the influx of so many first-generation Africans. These Africans entered a community divided between those who had been slave owners and those who had been slaves. The former slaves were also divided between those brought to the islands by the Loyalists, the salt rakers, and those born on the Islands. One must also remember that the former slaves would have had their origins in a variety of regions in Africa.

This creates a web of cultural influences. It is this rich tapestry that forms the basis of modern-day customs of the "Belongers," the name adopted by the local islanders. Anthropologists may be able to help unravel some of this web, but what about the local community. What can it tell us?

Storytelling allows history to be passed orally from generation to generation, especially in an illiterate society. It is through oral history that one might tie families and individuals to their ancestors, who could have come from the *Trouvadore*. The museum has been working closely with David Bowen, director of the Culture and Arts Commission, who is trying to instill national pride in the Turks and Caicos Islands' culture through music, dress, language, songs, and storytelling. He also has a personal interest in the story, as one of his distant relatives allegedly came from a wrecked slave ship, and had lived at Bambarra.

Local crafts and arts are used as indicators of people's cultural background. Maybe it is just a coincidence, but today the remaining straw workers are based in Middle and North Caicos. It is likely that as there has not been excessive development on these islands, local skills and crafts with their origins in African society have survived. Perhaps, too, they have survived because modern Caicos Island residents are more closely related to first-generation Africans than are those on Turks Island. We must remember that straw work was carried out from the earliest days of slavery because the workers needed hats to protect their heads and baskets for storage. What needs further study is how the baskets are made. Perhaps different styles could be linked back to Africa and even to particular regions. Have the basketmakers developed their own identity and style? This may seem to be overreaching, but in 1891 Stark observed that liberated Africans in the Bahamas had brought with them the secret of making African thatch for roofing houses and, as they did not share their knowledge, this thatch only appeared in areas settled by liberated Africans.

Another important aspect of any culture is music and means of celebration. Ripsaw, the local style of music, has a beat that is clearly African influenced. A typical celebration is Junkanoo, and like the music, evolved during the days of slavery, but did the Africans from the *Trouvadore* add anything to them?

THE FIELDWORK

After many years of seeking out the information in the archives, it was time the team got their feet wet. One question raised was what is left of *Trouvadore*? Research indicates that extensive salvage was undertaken in 1841, hardly surprising as the locals had grown up as "wreckers." The salvaged items—including sails, rigging, and chain cables—were sold for £71.3.5, suggesting that much of the ship may have been recovered.

In 2003, the Turks and Caicos National Museum was given access to a helicopter to fly over East Caicos. This aerial reconnaissance had three objectives: to locate shipwrecks that were visible from the air and get clues to their wrecking processes; to look for suitable boat-mooring locations for a field season; and to take photographs for use in grant applications. Two metal-hulled shipwrecks were identified from the air and recorded.

In 2004, the project team led by Dr. Donald Keith of Ships of Discovery carried out a short survey off East Caicos. Half of the funds to finance this phase of the fieldwork came from hotels and tourist organizations in the country that wanted to provide their staff with more information about the cultural background of the local people. A week of field time was lost because of Hurricane Frances but, even so, the goals of the project were fulfilled. The survey area was covered by tow-boarders, pulled behind a boat to visually survey the seabed; several isolated finds were recorded, and two historic wrecks—one wooden-hulled and one metal-hulled—were located. As the project was operating under a survey license, it could only look and not touch. However, it was noted that at the wooden wreck site there had been some recent disturbances, probably by treasure hunters.

The 2004 season proved that wooden shipwrecks could survive in the area, but no diagnostic material was found, so a further season was required. The lack of historic wrecks in the survey area was also of concern, bringing up the question of the effectiveness of tow-boarding. Therefore, in preparation for the 2006 field season, a test excavation license was obtained to carry out limited-intrusive work on the site of the wooden-hulled wreck while the survey area was extended. Visual survey work continued with tow-boarders, but this time a magnetometer was also used to cover the whole area surveyed during the 2004 and 2006 seasons.

The results from the 2006 season were mixed. It was shown that the tow-boarders had been effective in finding everything human-made lying on the surface of the seabed. In addition, the magnetometer identified several buried magnetic anomalies not visible on the surface. In fact, the largest anomaly was around 100 m away from the wooden shipwreck and is believed to be associated with that wreck by the similarity of nails and fasteners, though only a small area of the anomaly was excavated.

Unfortunately, the test excavations at the sites of the wooden wreck and the associated magnetic anomaly were inconclusive. The work had shown that the ballast mound was very limited, suggesting that the ship was carrying a cargo when it wrecked, but lack of physical remains of any cargo leaves questions. Had the cargo dissolved, like a shipment of salt? Had it been salvaged and carried to shore? A possibility remains that the cargo may have been human beings, who were rescued from the *Trouvadore*. The work also showed that the ship was well built and was at least 36.58 m (120 ft) long, which differed from our preliminary findings in 2004 that suggested a smaller ship of 18.29–24.38 m (60–80 ft) in length. Even though large timbers, including a cathead, were located as well as metal fittings, diagnostic materials to help date the wreck have not been found.

THE NEXT STEP

The museum will continue its archival research. However, some of this will be directed toward finding information about other shipwrecks located off East Caicos to exclude them as possibilities for the wooden wreck.

Research on *Trouvadore* will continue, as there are loose ends that need to be tidied up and new information is still coming to light. An important element of this story continues to be tying the local culture to its African roots, and this will require extensive work not only in studying oral traditions and local crafts but also in using modern scientific aids such as DNA sampling. *Trouvadore* is a prime example of the monumental effect that a shipwreck can have on a local population. It is hoped that further archaeological work will facilitate telling the *Trouvadore* story in a museum display, planned to become the pivotal exhibition in a new museum. Such tangible remains can also be used in a traveling exhibition to go to all the countries that have assisted the research process or are linked to the *Trouvadore*.

The *Trouvadore* project is also going to be used to promote good practices in the exploration and recovery of material from shipwrecks. Like the seas surrounding many countries in the region, treasure hunters look on these waters as containing untapped resources. Their primary goal is to remove anything that they can sell, a practice that does not benefit the local population in understanding their history. With a high-profile project like *Trouvadore*, the museum has the opportunity to illustrate how a properly managed archaeological research program can benefit the local population.

The museum, along with maritime archaeologists will be using the *Trouvadore* project as an example of why the Turks and Caicos Islands must protect its shipwrecks from unscrupulous treasure hunters. Licenses should be issued with the proviso that the goal is the retrieval of information rather than the financial rewards of selling the finds. Laws are in place, but it is the interpretation of the regulations, the monitoring of licenses, and the understanding that the benefit to the country is above that of the individuals involved that need to be clarified. Without such policies, wrecks like the *Trouvadore* are open to plundering before the full importance of the ship and its story can be uncovered. The country can only win from this approach, as there will be a greater understanding of the history of the country, and maybe the origins of its people, and the life of past generations.

CONCLUSIONS

The project will provide information to the local population, most of whom are tied by blood or marriage to the survivors from the *Trouvadore*. We may not be able to identify any cultural activity directly linked to the survivors, but the museum and Culture and Arts Commission are raising awareness that the islands' culture is heavily influenced by its African roots, whether the people came here as slaves or from shipwrecks. These strong cultural roots should be celebrated, not ignored or replaced by a homogenized Caribbean and/or American culture. The museum, along with other agencies in the Turks and Caicos Islands, has a role to research, interpret, and protect not only the material objects and buildings, but also the dynamic culture. Locally, the museum will portray these cultural ties to a wide audience. The *Trouvadore* project also has captured the attention of international media, and it is likely that a TV documentary and book will follow, increasing the availability of the research to a much wider audience.

ACKNOWLEDGMENTS

The fieldwork was only possible through the financial support in 2004 of Hartling Group (Developers of Sands at Grace Bay and the Palms), Turks and Caicos Tourist Board, Royal West Indies Resort, Turks and Caicos Hotel and Tourism Association, Ocean Club Resort, Sumner Gerard, San Francisco Foundation, Brooke Fox, Dayton Foundation, Teddy Foundation, and Friends of the Turks and Caicos National Museum and in 2006 of NOAA Ocean Exploration Program, Turks and Caicos Islands Conservation Fund, Teddy Foundation, Dayton Foundation, Turks and Caicos Islands Tourist Board, San Francisco Foundation, Frey Family Fund, and Friends of the Turks and Caicos National Museum.

REFERENCES

Gibbs, G. 1878. Letters. Unpublished letters, American Museum of Natural History, New York.

Sadler, H. E. 1997. *Turks Island Landfall.* Jamaica: Marjorie Sadler Publisher.

Stark, J. H. 1891. *Stark's History of and Guide to the Bahamas.* Boston: JH Stark and Plimpton Press.

Trouvadore Project. 2006. Available online at www.slaveshiptrouvadore.com (accessed May 20, 2008).

Special note: This chapter also benefits from unpublished material held in the CO23 and CUST34 files at the National Archives, Kew, London.

CHAPTER 14

The Cayman Islands' Experience: Yesterday, Today, and Tomorrow

Margaret E. Leshikar-Denton and Della A. Scott-Ireton

A FRUITFUL PARTNERSHIP

The Cayman Islands Maritime Heritage Trail initiatives interpret the islands' unique history for residents and tourists with the goal of fostering stewardship and encouraging preservation. Based on the premise that knowledge inspires appreciation among the public for cultural heritage sites and results in enlistment of allies in the guardianship of these irreplaceable resources, the Cayman Islands National Museum, National Trust, National Archive, and Department of Environment (DoE), collectively the Maritime Heritage Trail Partners, initiated a three-tiered approach to protect, manage, and interpret the islands' maritime heritage sites.

The first and most fruitful result of the partnership so far has been the land-based Cayman Islands Maritime Heritage Trail, launched in 2003, which widely promotes the islands' maritime legacy through public interpretation of Cayman's historical maritime landscape. Encompassing thirty-six sites located throughout the three Cayman Islands, the interactive trail combines heritage, education, and recreational tourism. Florida's established and successful Maritime Heritage Trail program served as a model (see http://dhr.dos.state.fl.us/archaeology/underwater/maritime/) for the Cayman Islands Trail. Accessible to all, it is an innovative and exciting addition to the islands' attractions for residents and visitors. It is the first maritime trail of its kind in the Caribbean.

A second initiative is underway to create the Cayman Islands' first Shipwreck Preserve at the site of the *Glamis*. Certain robust sites, such as *Glamis*, are suitable for interpretation for snorkelers and divers, where appropriate access is beneficial for the resource and the adventurous public. Here, people may visit shipwrecks that are not fragile and that have a management plan in place. The activity is fun, interactive, and educational and makes people feel a part of the dramatic wreck experience.

We believe that once people interact with history through the Maritime Heritage Trail and shipwreck preserves, they will better appreciate and understand that some sites are sensitive and fragile and might include information not available elsewhere in the world. These rare sites deserve special protection and study, forming the third tier of the management approach. Research can result in publications, museum exhibitions, and filmed documentaries whereby people are invited to share knowledge extracted from these special sites by professional archaeologists. Presently, no shipwrecks are under archaeological excavation in the Cayman Islands. There are, however, significant early heritage sites located in the islands that deserve archaeological attention. The first step in fostering value for all cultural sites is to educate Cayman's citizens and visitors about the islands' rich heritage. This is accomplished by encouraging visits to maritime sites and providing information and interpretation that explain the sites' importance and the need for continuing protection.

If the Cayman Islands succeed in developing this creative and interactive three-tiered scheme for protecting, managing, and interpreting the islands' maritime historical sites, the heritage resources, general public, tourism, and government will all be winners. Furthermore, this example might serve as a model for other countries with tourism-driven economies that are struggling with preserving and managing their cultural heritage. In this chapter, we describe development of the foundations of maritime heritage management in the Cayman Islands, current strategies for preservation and interpretation, and aspirations for the future.

LEGAL PROTECTION FOR SHIPWRECKS

As early as 1966, in an attempt to regulate the recovery of objects from historical shipwrecks in the Cayman Islands, the government enacted the Abandoned Wreck Law 5 (1966 [1997]). All historical shipwrecks located on the seabed of the islands' territorial waters (12 nautical miles) for more than fifty years are claimed under the Abandoned Wreck Law, with ownership of artifacts "vested in Her Majesty in right of Her Government of the Islands." This clause has been used to protect historical shipwrecks, but the law has two primary deficiencies: (1) it does not recognize shipwrecks as cultural property; and (2) it was enacted to ensure that the government receives a percentage of the value of articles recovered from shipwrecks. Consequently, once the government enters into an agreement with a prospector, it is obliged to return to the prospector at least one-half of the value of the wreck.

Although the government can retain salvaged artifacts, if it does so, it must pay the prospector a percentage of their appraised value. In effect, the government gives up rights to more than 50% of a shipwreck and then pays the prospector to buy it back.

Fortunately, in the 1990s, the Cayman Islands denied all applications from treasure hunters and determined that the Abandoned Wreck Law is inadequate to protect and manage Cayman's underwater cultural heritage. A Marine Archaeology Committee was established by the Ministry of Culture with a view to achieving new legislation. This legislation, yet to be enacted, can take into account two new international documents that provide guidance regarding the protection and management of underwater cultural heritage. These include the *ICOMOS International Charter on the Protection and Management of Underwater Cultural Heritage* (1996), which outlines best professional practice, and the *UNESCO Convention on the Protection of the Underwater Cultural Heritage* (2001), a legal document. As Cayman's historical shipwrecks are managed *in situ*, interpreted as shipwreck preserves, or archaeologically investigated for research purposes, they will require specific physical and legal protection suitable to their needs. Thus, these issues need to be considered in relation to the proposed new law and implementing regulations. The new maritime initiatives should encourage action on legislation development.

HISTORY OF UNDERWATER ARCHAEOLOGY IN THE CAYMAN ISLANDS

To provide context for the current heritage management initiatives, it is helpful to look back to the foundations of professional underwater archaeology in the Cayman Islands, which began when a team from the Institute of Nautical Archaeology (INA), under the direction of Roger Smith, surveyed the islands' waters in 1979–1980 and recorded seventy-seven sites (Leshikar-Denton 1997, 2002; Smith 1981, 2000). A 1979 law created the National Museum, which opened its doors to the public in 1990. In the early 1990s, Leshikar-Denton investigated the "Wreck of the Ten Sail," the loss of the frigate HMS *Convert* and nine ships and brigs of her fifty-eight-ship merchant convoy (Leshikar 1993; Leshikar-Denton In press). In 1994, research results were featured in a 200th-anniversary exhibition at the National Museum, a publication with the National Archive (Leshikar-Denton and Pedley 1994), a special stamp issued by the Postal Service, and a commemorative coin minted by the Currency Board.

In the early 1990s, the museum facilitated surveys for prehistoric sites on all three islands by University College London and the Florida

Museum of Natural History, Gainesville, although negative results suggest that Cayman was not occupied prehistorically by indigenous peoples. Assisted by volunteers, museum archaeologist Leshikar-Denton also continued to build the islands' shipwreck inventory, which today numbers over 140 physical sites representing five centuries and at least fifteen nationalities. Museum collaboration with the DoE, the agency in charge of marine resources and parks, facilitated this offshore research. A more formal relationship is planned, whereby the DoE will provide support for a systematic program to identify, document, protect, and manage Caymans' shipwreck sites.

Although cooperation among the museum, archive, trust, and the DoE had been ongoing for more than a decade, in 2002, the Maritime Heritage Trail Partnership was created formally. This resulted in the Maritime Heritage Trail in 2003 and plans to create shipwreck preserves, using the Florida model as related by Scott-Ireton (2005). Over the years, rare sites have been protected through the Crown's claim of ownership, but limited human and financial resources have not enabled adequate investigation, although it is hoped that this will be addressed in the future. Finally, there has been discussion of proposing nomination to the World Heritage Site list of Little Cayman and its offshore reefs and sounds, which have centuries of shipwrecks embedded in them.

During the past twenty-eight years, the foundations of maritime heritage management have been laid in the Cayman Islands through this chronology of steps. At the time of this writing, a dedicated Cayman Islands Maritime Archaeology Programme (CIMAP, pronounced "Sea-Map") is being developed, with the objective of bringing together, expanding, and advancing all aspects of maritime archaeology practiced in the Cayman Islands during the last three decades. CIMAP's mission will be to protect and promote the maritime cultural heritage of the Cayman Islands for the multifaceted benefit of present and future generations.

OVER FIVE CENTURIES OF MARITIME HERITAGE

With an understanding of the status of legal and archaeological maritime heritage initiatives in the Cayman Islands, a review of the Cayman Islands' complex maritime history will help explain the need for education and protection. Centuries of activity have produced archaeological sites, both on land and underwater, that are related in their maritime focus. Intense commercial development and lack of knowledge about the sites combine to threaten the physical remains of the islands' heritage, a situation the Maritime Heritage Trail can help rectify.

The history of the Cayman Islands is tied to the sea (Craton 2003; Leshikar 1993; Smith 2000). Because evidence of prehistoric occupation has not been found, it appears that an untouched natural environment existed before European arrival in the 1500s. The earliest European mariners considered the islands to be navigational landmarks and hazards, but easily recognized the abundant sea turtles as a fine source of provisions to feed their hungry crews. Christopher Columbus sighted Cayman Brac and Little Cayman on May 10, 1503, during his fourth voyage, and called them Las Tortugas. English navigator Sir Francis Drake came ashore in Grand Cayman in April 1586, and although the expedition's crew found no water, they captured 100 turtles and described a variety of plants and animals, including crocodiles, or caimans, for which the islands became known as Las Caymanas. For centuries, the islands were frequented for food by seafarers from Spain, Holland, France, and England.

After the English occupied Jamaica in 1655, they began sparse settlement in the Cayman Islands, notably in a semipermanent turtle fishing village on Little Cayman. Spain disputed England's rights to these territories until the 1670 Treaty of Madrid. In the late 1600s and early 1700s, pirates and privateers came ashore to find water or refuge and at times to trouble the earliest occupants. Spanish privateer Manuel Rivero Pardal raided the turtling camp in Little Cayman in 1669 and burned turtling vessels at anchor there, and Englishman Neal Walker salvaged the wreck of the Spanish ship *San Miguel*, lost on the island's reefs in 1730.

In the 1700s, the most powerful European countries vying for control of Caribbean islands were Great Britain and France, whose warships patrolled the Caribbean Sea. Surveyor George Gauld drafted the first British Admiralty Chart of Grand Cayman in 1773. HMS *Convert*, formerly the captured French *l'Inconstante*, and nine vessels of her convoy wrecked on the East End reefs of Grand Cayman in 1794. Of the two forts built in the late 1700s, the one at George Town was rebuilt after destruction by Spaniards from Cuba. Caymanian settlers began building their own ships and boats at this time, a tradition that continued for the next two centuries.

According to official census-taker Edward Corbet (Pedley 1992), in 1802 the population of Grand Cayman had reached 933 people, about half of whom were enslaved. The Cayman turtle fishing industry, shipbuilding, and merchant trade continued to evolve. News of emancipation arrived via ship from Jamaica in 1835, and soon there were newly free citizens who undertook maritime activities to build their own lives. In the 19th century, numerous ships were wrecked in the Cayman Islands, among them ships trading internationally as well as locally built schooners lost in major hurricanes in 1838, 1846, and 1876 (National Shipwreck Inventory n.d.).

Although a series of lighthouses were built throughout the Cayman Islands in the early 1900s, the islands remained a hazard to international shipping, claiming many vessels in fair weather and foul. In 1913, the Norwegian-owned barque *Glamis* was lost on Grand Cayman and salvaged by Caymanians. The highest loss of local vessels continued to be associated with hurricanes, particularly those occurring in 1903, 1910, and 1932. Local shipbuilders sometimes employed their distinctive methods on civic building projects, resulting in unique Caymanian vernacular architecture. World War II brought heightened awareness of and participation in international affairs to the isolated country, and Caymanian seamen plied the world's oceans on bulk carriers in the merchant marine. Meanwhile, turtling and shipbuilding continued to thrive in the first half of the 20th century, being replaced in modern times by tourism-associated maritime activities, including fishing, boating, water sports, and cruise ship arrivals.

WIDE RANGE OF MARITIME SITES

Given the long and varied history described above, it is not surprising that the Cayman Islands have a rich maritime heritage legacy and that maritime traditions link the past with the present. Prominent among this wide range of maritime heritage sites are hundreds of shipwrecks embedded in the reefs and sounds of the islands. Additional wrecks probably lie nearby in deep water off the Cayman Wall. The Cayman Islands National Museum currently maintains the National Shipwreck Inventory, which today contains over 140 registered sites, although the true number is higher. Lost over the course of five centuries, ships from Great Britain (England, Scotland, Wales, and Ireland), Spain, France, the Netherlands, Norway, Sweden, Germany, Jamaica, the Bahamas, Honduras, Nicaragua, Colombia, the United States, Canada, and the Cayman Islands wrecked here.

Evidence also remains of salvage and survivor campsites and other land-based maritime sites. Ships and boats still drop their anchors in long-established anchorages, especially off Hog Sty Bay and in North Sound and South Sound in Grand Cayman as well as in the Sister Islands of Cayman Brac and Little Cayman. In days gone by, careening activities were undertaken at well-known locations suitable to hauling vessels over to clean their hulls; today these careening places hold significant chronologically intact artifact records of Cayman's maritime past.

Remains of Fort George and a marker at the former Prospect Fort remind us of a time when Caymanians formed militias to protect their homeland from invaders. Lighthouses, both historical and active, stand in prominent places to aid shipping around the islands. Large cuts in the coastal ironshore formations mark places where ships were launched in days gone by, calling to mind the majestic schooners, catboats, and other vessels that were built nearby and employed in turtling and trading. Caves, especially on Cayman Brac, continue to provide shelter to Caymanians in times of tempest and hurricane. Buildings such as Elmslie Memorial Church and the George Town Post Office are perhaps the best places to see the skills of Cayman's shipbuilders, especially on their ceilings, which look like the inverted hulls of ships. The busy port in George Town and smaller docks in Little Cayman and Cayman Brac attest to continued thriving maritime industries throughout the Cayman Islands.

MARITIME HERITAGE TRAILS AND PRESERVES

With such a diverse array of maritime sites on the Islands, the maritime heritage trail Partners sought a method for educating the local and visiting public about the sites while promoting preservation. A maritime heritage trail linking the sites in a thematic and entertaining manner seemed the perfect solution. Existing maritime trails in other locations could be used as models, although the Cayman Trail would reflect the islands' unique environment, history, and culture. With the belief that increased knowledge leads to a sense of ownership and therefore protection, sites selected for inclusion were carefully researched and their histories prepared for interpretive literature. In addition, the trail was envisioned as something that would encourage visitation around the islands, leading to heritage tourism at locations otherwise seldom seen by tourists.

The concept of presenting maritime heritage sites as opportunities for visitation has increased in popularity over the last decade (Scott-Ireton 2003, 2005). As heritage tourism in general continues to be one of the fastest-growing segments of the travel industry, cultural resource managers recognize the possibilities of utilizing maritime sites to attract tourists and tourism revenues and for capitalizing on the public interest in such sites to increase appreciation for the preservation of these nonrenewable resources. Maritime heritage trails, in the form of multiple maritime-related locations thematically interpreted for the public, offer an enjoyable interactive activity through which visitors and local people can learn about the seafaring heritage of a location or culture. The interpreted sites benefit by being actively managed and by being increasingly appreciated through effective public education.

Underwater archaeological preserves and shipwreck parks offer a similar opportunity for diving and snorkeling visitors. In areas where diving and other water sports already draw tourists, such as the Cayman Islands and Florida, presenting historic shipwrecks as both recreational and educational tourism attractions adds another layer to the visitor's experience. Shipwrecks benefit by being presented as historically significant sites deserving of conservation and as ecologically important locations for natural resources such as coral, fish, and other marine life. Because some shipwrecks may be too fragile or sensitive to support the increased visitation resulting from interpretation and promotion, decisions about appropriate access must be made by the resource managers. Many wrecks, however, have become stable in the marine environment and are capable of sustaining large numbers of visitors. Some wrecks have been visited for many years by divers who have no idea of the ships' history. Interpretation through brochures, underwater plaques, on-shore markers, web sites, and other means can help educate visitors about a dramatic seafaring episode and foster a sense of appreciation for the wreck as part of the maritime heritage.

The Cayman Islands Maritime Heritage Trail is based on the model of the Florida Maritime Heritage Trail (see http://dhr.dos.state.fl.us/archaeology/underwater/maritime/). In 1997, the State of Florida's Division of Historical Resources embarked on a project to promote heritage tourism through highlighting the state's maritime history. Because Florida is so large, a virtual "information trail" was conceived that would present the state's maritime heritage in a manner that could be explored through a comprehensive web site as well as a series of colorful poster/brochures with information on one side and images on the other. The poster/brochures were designed to feature six themes: historic shipwrecks, lighthouses, coastal communities, ports, coastal forts, and coastal environments. The poster/brochures indicate sites around the state that can be visited, including time and admission information, but also present information on sites that may no longer exist or that are not available for visitation. The Florida Maritime Heritage Trail has been extremely popular, with thousands of poster/brochures distributed and tens of thousands of hits on the web site leading to increased heritage tourism and education.

The model of the Florida Trail was presented to the Cayman Islands Maritime Heritage Trail Partners. The partners liked the Florida model, in particular the poster/brochure idea, but envisioned changes that would make the Cayman Islands Trail more suitable for an area that can easily be circumnavigated in a day or two.

CAYMAN ISLANDS MARITIME HERITAGE TRAIL

In 2002–2003, the Cayman Islands Maritime Heritage Trail partnership provided the funding, support, and personnel to establish the land-based

Maritime Heritage Trail, with the assistance of Scott-Ireton who provided expertise based on experience with the Florida Maritime Heritage Trail. In addition to the Maritime Heritage Trail, the partners are playing an integral role in determining the feasibility of establishing a shipwreck preserve trail for the Cayman Islands and in implementing a program to achieve it. The ministries and government departments that deal with culture, education, tourism, and environment, the private-sector Cayman Islands Tourism Association, and the general public must also participate for the long-term success of these initiatives.

The Maritime Heritage Trail Partners believe that there are sound reasons to develop and maintain maritime heritage attractions in the Cayman Islands. The interactive trail and shipwreck preserve initiative will provide enjoyment and education for residents and visitors, thereby increasing appreciation and fostering stewardship for the Cayman Islands' maritime heritage sites. Importantly for the local economy, it will enhance and diversify the islands' tourism possibilities.

During development of the Cayman Islands Maritime Heritage Trail, three important keys to success became evident. First, building relationships with experts, governmental agencies, and the public is vital. Second, established, successful trail and preserve programs like those in Florida, Australia, and several of the U.S. national marine sanctuaries can be used as models to avoid "reinventing the wheel" (see these web sites, all accessible as of May 2008: http://www.environment.sa.gov.au/heritage/shipwreck_trails.html#Kangaroo_Island; http://www.fknms.nos.noaa.gov/sanctuary_resources/shipwreck_trail/welcome.html; http://thunderbay.noaa.gov/). Third, recognizing the need for flexibility in all areas is imperative.

THE LAND-BASED TRAIL

In considering sites to be included in the land-based Maritime Heritage Trail, a set of criteria was developed. The partners agreed that the trail should encompass sites on all three Cayman Islands and cover a range of maritime themes. To be considered, the site had to have historical significance and interesting visual features. The viewing area had to be safe and accessible to the public. Finally, interpretation must not impact sensitive sites. By using these criteria in site selection, the partners were able to choose sites that are appropriate for, and robust enough to sustain, tourism.

Once the partners had substantially developed a format for the Maritime Heritage Trail, they held public "focus group" meetings on all three islands. The intention was to publicize the project, to promote a feeling of public ownership of the trail, to encourage community involvement, and to ask advice about the proposed sites. These meetings proved valuable in achieving these objectives.

In the summer of 2003, the Cayman Islands Maritime Heritage Trail was launched in conjunction with the Cayman Islands Quincentennial, a year-long celebration of the 500th anniversary of the sighting of the

Figure 14.1 The Grand Cayman Maritime Heritage Trail poster/brochure (courtesy Cayman Islands Maritime Heritage Trail Partners).

Figure 14.2 Maritime Heritage Trail sign (photograph by Margaret Leshikar-Denton).

Cayman Islands by Christopher Columbus. The trail is a land-based driving tour that interprets historically significant maritime sites around all three islands through two colorful poster/brochures. There is one for both the Sister Islands and Grand Cayman (Figure 14.1), together with a series of signs that mark locations of public access on land (Figure 14.2) (Cayman Islands Maritime Heritage Trail Partners 2003).

The trail leads visitors to a wide range of maritime-themed sites. At each stop, explorers can learn in an entertaining and interactive way about a particular aspect of Cayman Islands history and heritage. Stops include information about early explorers, origins of maritime place names, historic anchorages, shipwrecks, wrecking practices, lighthouses, seaside forts, shipbuilding, turtle-fishing, and hurricanes. The following narrative presents information about the interpreted sites as a kind of "virtual tour" of the Cayman Islands Maritime Heritage Trail. Readers are invited to journey along the trail and investigate Cayman's history.

The Sister Islands Maritime Heritage Trail

On May 30, 2003, the first route of the Maritime Heritage Trail was launched on the two Sister Islands. There are eight trail stops on

Cayman Brac. The first is the "1932 Storm Mass Grave," the burial site of nineteen people who perished together when catastrophic winds and a tidal wave destroyed the newest house on the northwest coast during a tragic hurricane. The second and third stops interpret "Shipbuilding & Launching Sites," and "Invention of the Caymanian Catboat," for many Cayman Brac families maintained shipyards, producing distinctive schooners and small sailing craft, called catboats, that were used to pursue sea turtles as far away as Cuba and Central America. "Peter's & Rebecca's Caves," stops 4 and 8 on the trail, are known as hurricane caves. They and other caves have long provided refuge for island residents during violent hurricanes. Rebecca's Cave, notable for a grave inside, is named for an infant girl who died of exposure after her family managed to reach shelter.

The fifth stop is at the Cayman Brac Lighthouse, perched at the highest point in the Cayman Islands, 42.67 m (140 ft) above the Caribbean Sea, atop a high limestone bluff at the East End of Cayman Brac. "Columbus Sights the Sister Islands" is commemorated at the sixth trail stop. On May 10, 1503, during Christopher Columbus's fourth and final voyage to the New World, his fourteen-year-old son Ferdinand wrote of two small and low islands with abundant turtles in the sea around them; from the location and description of these islands that he called Las Tortugas, the two must have been Cayman Brac and Little Cayman. At trail stop 7, one can look out to sea to view the location where the Norwegian-registered merchant vessel *Prince Frederick* wrecked on the southern reefs of Cayman Brac in 1897. Visitors are reminded that all shipwrecks are protected under Caymanian law as part of our irreplaceable maritime heritage.

Moving to Little Cayman, there are also eight trail stops. Trail site 9 draws attention to the tragic wreck of the island transport vessel *Soto Trader*, which sits upright in 18.28 m (60 ft) of water, just offshore the southwest coast of Little Cayman. The wreck, sunk with her cargo of cement mixers and trucks as the result of a fiery explosion, is a popular dive site today and a candidate for a future Shipwreck Preserve. Trail stop 10 reveals that in 1669, "Privateer Manuel Rivero Pardal" attacked a small English turtling village at Little Cayman, where the Jamaican ship *Hopewell*, along with several other turtling vessels, was anchored. His reprisal commission had been granted by Spain against English holdings in the Caribbean, in retaliation for Henry Morgan's sacking of Porto Bello in 1668.

The origin of "Maritime Place Names" is highlighted at site 11, using the example of Owen Island and Blossom Village being named in honor of British Navy Surveyor Richard Owen, aboard HMS *Blossom*, who conducted the first official hydrographical survey of the Sister Islands in 1831. Interpreted at trail stop 12, the Spanish brigantine *San Miguel* ploughed into the reefs of Little Cayman in October 1730, with the loss of all but four of her crew. English pirate Neal Walker salvaged part of the vessel's cargo of fruit, brandy, and wine. The guide reinforces the point that *San Miguel* is protected under law as part of our maritime heritage. Trail site 13 illuminates a maritime mystery: Is a wreck off the south coast of Little Cayman the remains of the Norwegian bark *Rosita*, built in 1875 and lost in 1897, or the Irish-built ship called *Rosetta* that wrecked in 1867? Further historical and archaeological research will help solve the mystery. Trail stop 14 on Little Cayman also commemorates "Columbus Sights the Sister Islands," as in trail stop 6, above. A "Historic Anchorage" located off the north coast of Little Cayman near Bloody Bay and Jackson's Point is highlighted at site 15; here, at least twelve anchors are embedded in the sea bottom, ranging from colonial wooden-stocked anchors to British Admiralty issue to iron-stocked schooner tackle. Trail stop 16 draws attention to the Baltimore schooner *Maggie E. Gray*, built in 1867 and engaged in phosphate shipping in Little Cayman when she wrecked in 1892. The vessel's anchor and rigging still are visible among the coral heads of the reef; remains of mule pens and the small tramway that was used to move phosphate are visible on shore.

The Grand Cayman Maritime Heritage Trail

The third island, Grand Cayman, has twenty stops in its maritime heritage trail. On the northwestern side of the island, site 1 commemorates Sir Francis Drake, who on his 1585–1586 voyage stopped at Grand Cayman with a fleet of twenty-three ships. Drake's crew found no water, but plenty of food in the form of turtles and other beasts. Trail stop 2, "Old West Bay Historic Anchorage & Town Centre," was an important sheltered bay and commercial seaside town on Grand Cayman. Schooners anchored offshore, and goods for the community were landed by catboat at the government wharf. *E.L. Banks*, a Caymanian schooner that wrecked at anchor in the bay with casks of lard aboard, is under consideration for a shipwreck preserve. Trail stop 3 is at Boatswain's Bay, where a lighthouse marks the north end of Grand Cayman, warning approaching mariners of danger. This area, associated with the late 19th-century phosphate industry, was also included in one of the island's earliest land grants in 1741. Site 4, "Barkers Shipwrecks," highlights the fact that offshore from the Cayman Islands' first national park lie the wreckage of HMS *Jamaica*, run aground in 1715, *Augustus Caesar*, wrecked in 1765, *Emily* and *Sarah Phelan*, a pair of Caymanian schooners lost in the 1876 hurricane, and *Lydia E. Wilson*, a schooner built in 1931and burned in a fire in 1968. The brochure emphasizes that all of these wrecks are protected under Caymanian law and that their integrity must be respected. Trail stop

5, "Historic Turtle Crawls," interprets the essential role that sea turtles have played in Cayman's 500 years of recorded history. Generations of islanders fished for turtles around the Cayman Islands, Cuba, and Central America; captured turtles were confined in "crawls," often built of vertical stakes set in the shallow waters or sounds, until they could be sold or slaughtered.

Trail stop 6, "George Town Harbour Shipwrecks," highlights the island's main historic anchorage and vessels lost nearby. The Jamaican freighter *Balboa* foundered in the 1932 hurricane, whereas the "rice wreck" *Cali*, a four-masted barkentine, wrecked in 1948; today, both are accessible to snorkelers, divers, and glass-bottom boats. The freighter *Kirk Pride*, sunk in 243.84 m (800 ft) of water in a nor'wester in 1976, can be approached by the public in a deep-water submarine. The freighter *Gamma*, run aground on a reef in 1980 and later washed to the shoreline, is still visible on the beach. Trail site 7, "Fort George," was built around 1780 in response to war between European nations that also embroiled their New World colonies, and was manned by a volunteer militia.

In World War II, a submarine lookout, manned by the Home Guard, was perched in a silk cotton tree at Fort George. "Maritime Architecture" is celebrated at stop 8 near Elmslie Memorial Church, as generations of experienced shipwrights who built schooners, catboats, and other vessels also applied their skills to civic architecture. Visitors can see the shipwright's craft in the unique and beautiful ceilings. Site 9, "Historic Hog Sty Bay," is still the site of a bustling port and an anchorage for local vessels and visiting merchant, navy, and cruise ships. Trail stops 10 and 19 feature "Shipbuilding," for family shipyards were dotted around all the coasts of Grand Cayman. Most families launched their home-built craft from slipways and coves, called barcaderes, carved by nature or man into the ironshore.

On the southwest coast, "*Pallas* & Pull-and-be-Damned Point" is featured at site 11. Trail explorers can see iron wreckage protruding above the sea, a clue that here lies the Norwegian barque *Pallas*, built in Scotland in 1875, and swept up on the reef in the hurricane of 1910. Pull-and-be-Damned Point earned its colorful name from the futile efforts by a rower to fight the rush of water exiting South Sound. Trail stop 12, "Early Prospect," illuminates facts about the area: Scotsman Thomas Thompson started a settlement here after 1760; a monument today marks the site of an 18th-century fort; and offshore some of the islands' schooners were lost in hurricanes in 1846 and 1876.

Site 13, the historic home called Pedro St. James, built in 1780, is the oldest remaining building on Grand Cayman. Located on a high bluff, it commands a clear view of shipping. From the steps of Pedro St. James, an official proclamation freeing all slaves in the British Empire, including the Cayman Islands, was read in 1835. "Duck Pond Careenage," trail stop 14, illuminates a nautical process called careening, whereby wooden craft were run into shallow water and hauled over on each side so the bottom could be examined and repaired. This careenage is marked on the first Admiralty Chart of the island, created by British Navy surveyor George Gauld in 1773.

The concept of "wrecking" is introduced at trail stop 15, in the tale of the barque *Iphigenia* of Cardiff, Wales. Stranded on the Bodden Town reefs in 1874 through reckless navigation, *Iphigenia* was overrun by local salvagers before Captain Joseph Boase gave her up. This incident gave rise to an 1875 law entitled "Instructions to Receivers of Wreck Concerning Their Duties in Respect of Wreck, Casualties and Salvage"; these rules for wrecking formalized the salvage system. At site 16 on the southeast coast, one can look into the crashing waves offshore to see an anchor-fluke of the wrecked Norwegian-flagged *Inga* (or *Juga*), lost in 1888. East End wreckers were aboard the ship minutes after she foundered; they helped the crew and quickly negotiated salvage rights with the captain.

The East End Lighthouse, trail stop 17, marks a beacon used to guide ships away from the hazardous reefs of Grand Cayman. The first proper lighthouse at the site was constructed in the early 1900s, whereas the latest is a modern, solar-powered light. "The Wreck of the Ten Sail," the 1794 loss of HMS *Convert*, and nine of her fifty-eight merchant ship convoy, is featured at trail stop 18. The treacherous East End reefs are the site not only of *William & Elizabeth*, *Moorhall*, *Ludlow*, *Britannia*, *Richard*, *Nancy*, *Eagle*, *Sally*, and *Fortune*, wrecked along with *Convert* in 1794, but also of the *Cumberland* (1767), *Weymouth* (1845), *Dene* (1846), *Glamis* (1913), *Ridgefield* (1962), and *Rimandi Mibaju* (1964). The guide reinforces the fact that all ships wrecked in the Cayman Islands are protected under law as part of our maritime heritage.

Site 20, "Rum Point," was first noted on George Gauld's 1773 British Admiralty Chart of Grand Cayman, although no explanation was given for the name. The Caymanian schooner *Seagrim* wrecked in 1919 at Rum Point, and archaeological remains suggest that turtle butchering, probably by passing mariners, took place along the north coast as early as the 1700s. Islander oral histories tell of courting voyages made by suitors going to see their sweethearts along aquatic trails between Rum Point and other points around the North Sound.

Value for the Cayman Islands

The multiple values of the Cayman Islands Maritime Heritage Trail are instructive for heritage planners elsewhere. It is a land-based attraction, accessible to all, that uniquely interprets the Caymanian maritime landscape. It encourages travel around the coastlines of all three islands, while enhancing the patronizing of local businesses along the route. It is a management tool that uses and interprets existing heritage resources, promoting history, national pride, and historic preservation through education. The trail is a sustainable tourism model that encourages stay-over visitors to enhance the local economy. Finally, it is the first of its kind in the Caribbean region, setting a precedent for the interpretation and protection of maritime cultural resources in other Caribbean nations.

THE OFFSHORE TRAIL

The Maritime Heritage Trail Partners always intended that the Cayman Islands Maritime Heritage Trail would represent Phase I in a multiphase program for maritime cultural resource preservation and promotion. A second phase is intended to introduce a series of shipwreck preserves in the Cayman Islands. Inspired by models seen in Florida, Australia, and national marine sanctuaries in the United States, the shipwreck preserves are envisioned to become a shipwreck preserve trail around all three islands. It will consist of a variety of shipwreck sites accessible to the public that are managed, preserved, interpreted, and legally protected by Cayman Islands law for the benefit of present and future generations.

Models of underwater archaeological preserves and shipwreck parks developed in other areas of the world provide valuable insight that will be drawn on in developing the Cayman Islands Shipwreck Preserve Trail. For example, experience in establishing historic shipwrecks as heritage tourism attractions indicates that community support and stewardship are key components in ongoing management and site protection. Interpretive materials used successfully in many shipwreck park programs include brochures, underwater site guides, site markers and plaques, and web sites. These strategies will be implemented for the Cayman Islands, as will other methods appropriate for specific sites and desired by visitors.

Shipwreck Preserve Criteria and Methodology

Just as selection criteria were developed to guide the partners in choosing sites for the Maritime Heritage Trail, a historic shipwreck must meet certain criteria to become a shipwreck preserve. The following criteria have been proposed, although refinement is expected as the preserve project progresses. First, a site must be located in Cayman territorial seas (to 12 miles) or in the contiguous zone (to 24 miles). The shipwreck must be historically significant, have a reasonably verifiable identity and history, and have recognizable features. The marine area in which the

Table 14.1 Steps for the establishment of Cayman Islands Shipwreck Preserves.

1. A shipwreck is nominated to become a preserve by the Maritime Heritage Trail Partners in consultation with other government agencies, the Cayman Islands Tourism Association (CITA), the Cayman National Watersports Association, other interested organizations, and the general public.
2. The wreck site is inspected by the archaeologist to determine if it meets the necessary criteria for preserve status.
3. The archaeologist advises the Maritime Heritage Trail Partners about the suitability of the shipwreck to become a preserve based on the criteria, and a final determination is made. This determination is forwarded to the nominating group. If the shipwreck is suitable, it is announced to the public as a preserve candidate.
4. The archaeologist, with the assistance of local and overseas professional archaeologists, DoE staff, qualified academic institutions, local volunteer divers, and water sports operators surveys and records the shipwreck to prepare an accurate archaeological site plan. In addition, the ship's history is researched and verified. An assessment and inventory of the site's biological diversity is conducted by DoE personnel.
5. An official site report is prepared containing all information about the preserve, the site plan, and a description of the educational, cultural, and economic benefits of the preserve, and is distributed to the Maritime Heritage Trail Partners.
6. Interpretive materials are created (possible products include: brochure, booklet, site guide, poster, web site, underwater monument, etc.).
7. A grand opening celebration is held to dedicate the Shipwreck Preserve and to introduce and distribute promotional and interpretive materials.
8. Cooperative arrangements are developed for ongoing management and promotion (e.g., permanent mooring maintenance and environmental monitoring by DoE, site monitoring by Archaeology Programme personnel, plaque cleaning and site policing by adoptive dive operator(s), literature reprints by the Maritime Heritage Trail Partners, promotional liaison with the Department of Tourism and local and overseas media groups, etc.).

site lies must be environmentally healthy and stable as determined by the DoE. The site must be robust enough to withstand sustained visitation without compromising archaeological integrity. Finally, the site must be accessible to the public and have safe visitation conditions.

A formalized method for developing shipwreck preserves is needed to ensure that all shipwrecks proposed for the trail receive consistent consideration, research, recording, interpretation, and management. Steps proposed to guide establishment of Cayman Islands shipwreck preserves are presented in Table 14.1 and can be modified as needed to fit any specific conditions, whether environmental, archaeological, or political.

Glamis as a Shipwreck Preserve

As an example of the processes used to select shipwreck preserves, it is useful to examine the case study of the *Glamis* shipwreck. The Cayman Islands Shipwreck Inventory site numbered GC 013 is believed to be the wreck of the iron-hulled barque *Glamis*, built in Dundee, Scotland, in 1876 and lost under the Norwegian flag in 1913 (Leshikar-Denton and Ho 2004). The site is characterized by large sections of iron hull components, anchors, and multiple sailing-ship deck features, located in a shallow reef environment in clear water off the East End of Grand Cayman (Figure 14.3). Frequently

Figure 14.3 Panoramic underwater view of the wreck of the *Glamis* off Grand Cayman's East End (photograph by Steve Broadbelt).

visited by divers from several East End watersports resorts and plagued by misidentification and lack of interpretation about the wreck's role in Caymanian history, the *Glamis* site is a perfect candidate to become the Cayman Islands' first shipwreck preserve. Wrecks like *Glamis* that are structurally stable and located in a healthy environment are appropriate for *in situ* interpretation and reasonable access by the public. The best way to manage these sites for the present and future is to establish them as dynamic underwater museums and shipwreck preserves.

The *Glamis* site represents tangible evidence of the ship's iron construction techniques and its rich history as a sailing barque in the closing days of the Age of Sail (Ho 2004; Leshikar-Denton and Ho 2004). *Glamis* had a celebrated career with the Dundee Clipper line, carrying not only jute, timber, and other cargo but also immigrants across the great oceans of the world at the end of the 19th century. *Glamis* survived to have a second successful career as a Norwegian-owned bulk cargo shipper in the first years of the 20th century. She is testimony to the fact that the oceans are avenues of communication and commerce. Although it may seem that ships are isolated communities at sea, in fact, they are transporters of ideas, cargoes, and human populations. Together they tie countries together, rather than separate them.

When *Glamis* wrecked in the Cayman Islands, she gained a third role as part of the important wrecking industry that existed in the Islands. Wreckers from shore quickly reached the stranded vessel, helping to save the crew and salvaging much of her cargo. After wrecking and salvage, *Glamis* was taken over by the sea, where she became a home for tropical fish and corals. Marine life on the *Glamis* site is abundant, with many varieties of corals and fish present. Brain coral, soft coral (gorgonians), large branches of Elkhorn coral, and swaying sea fans are represented in the surrounding reef area and cover portions of the wreckage. Fire coral is also present. Schools of sergeant majors and grunts congregate around the high relief portions of the site, as do banded butterfly fish, yellowtail snapper, blue tangs, and black durgons. Queen and stoplight parrotfish, angelfish, and Nassau grouper also frequent the site, and the careful viewer can discern small trumpet fish and spiny lobster taking shelter under hull plating and structure on the site. Rare copper sweepers also live beneath a section of the hull. Barracuda, nurse sharks, moray eels, and sea turtles are attracted to the area. The DoE is scheduled to complete a survey and more detailed interpretation of marine life on the *Glamis* site.

Today, *Glamis* has the potential to tell her story in a wonderful new way by becoming the first underwater shipwreck preserve in the Cayman Islands. Although there is no gold in her story, *Glamis* is a Cayman Islands historical shipwreck treasure.

Accessibility and Dive-Operator Assessment

We asked Steve Broadbelt of Ocean Frontiers Dive Resort, located near the *Glamis* wreck site at East End, to compile a dive-operator

Table 14.2 Broadbelt assessment of proposed shipwreck preserve site.

Advantages of the *Glamis* wreck	Disadvantages of the *Glamis* wreck
Close to major resort areas in the district	Access can be restricted subject to weather at certain times of the year (November–February). The site should be usable 200–250 days per year
Close to public and private docks for boat access	Area over the wreck can be a little choppy and cause seasickness to passengers on dive/snorkeling vessels
Suitable for snorkelers as well as divers because of the shallow depth	Wreckage has some sharp edges
Within close range of other existing dive and snorkel sites and moorings	
Actual wreck site large enough and with sufficient points of interest to make it a feature site for visitors	
Abundant quantity and variety of fish and other marine life	
Mooring pin at the site for safe mooring and direct positioning of the site	
Reliably good visibility throughout the year	
Away from navigational channels and hazards	
Very safe because no areas permit penetration inside the wreck by divers	

site assessment for *Glamis*. Mr. Broadbelt's assessment is intended to provide a commercial dive operator's evaluation of the feasibility of establishing a shipwreck preserve at the *Glamis* site. Because commercial dive operators are expected to be the primary means for visitors to experience the *Glamis* Preserve, Mr. Broadbelt's opinions offer valuable insights and recommendations for a successful preserve. Table 14.2 presents his lists of advantages and disadvantages of the *Glamis* Preserve.

Recommendations

Based on information presented, the *Glamis* site is appropriate to become Cayman's first shipwreck preserve. Interpretation can include any or all of the following: brochures or pamphlets, laminated site guide for use on a self-guided tour of the shipwreck, on-site marker or plaque, shore-based signage, museum exhibit, poster, web site, publications/articles about the ship's history in magazines and newspapers, and patches and stickers.

Before the proposed *Glamis* Shipwreck Preserve is opened to the public, the issues of management, methods of interpretation, and legal protection of *Glamis* for the benefit of present and future generations must be considered. Maritime Heritage Trail Partner discussions will take place in consultation with the relevant ministries and government departments including the Department of Tourism, the Cayman Islands Tourism Association, and the general public to help answer these concerns.

If successful, the *Glamis* Shipwreck Preserve model will facilitate the creation of other historical shipwreck preserves in the Cayman Islands. Together, the preserves eventually will form the Cayman Islands Shipwreck Preserve Trail around all three islands.

SENSITIVE ARCHAEOLOGICAL SITES

Other sites in Cayman waters, particularly the earliest shipwrecks, are more fragile and not appropriate to become shipwreck preserves. Instead, they should be protected and managed so that the knowledge they contain can be researched, archaeologically investigated, and featured in National Museum exhibitions and in publications.

Among such candidates in Grand Cayman are HMS *Jamaica*, lost in 1715, a possible 16th- or 17th-century wreck of undetermined nationality, a mid-18th-century Spanish wreck, and the Duck Pond careenage, to name a few. In the Sister Islands, Jamaica sloops and other turtling vessels lost in the 1670 battle with privateer Manuel Rivero Pardal, a late-17th-century site of undetermined nationality, and *San Miguel*, wrecked in 1730, are among the candidates.

Although *in situ* preservation should be considered as a first option for all shipwrecks, if excavation for the purpose of research or mitigation becomes an option at any of these rare sites, responsibilities for funding, professional expertise, documentation, conservation, site stabilization, collections management and curation, and dissemination of information to the public come into play.

CONCLUSIONS

The Cayman Islands Maritime Heritage Trail and shipwreck preserves are the result of a concerted effort to preserve, protect, and promote the maritime history of a small Caribbean nation. Many of the Cayman Islands' archaeological sites, both on land and underwater, are endangered by construction projects and other results of unprecedented economic growth. Most Cayman residents and visitors, however, feel the islands' heritage sites are deserving of protection. In recent years, historic preservation initiatives such as the restoration of the Pedro St. James site (number 13 on the Maritime Heritage Trail) and the creation of historical themed walking tours in George Town and West Bay highlighted the islands' land-based history. The trail and shipwreck preserves are efforts to focus attention on Caymanian maritime history.

One of the most important results of the trail project is the formation of the Maritime Heritage Trail Partners. Each of the partnering agencies offers expertise and authority in separate but complementary areas, resulting in a dynamic organization capable of bringing about change, influencing policy, and creating new products. The continued work of the partners will, it is hoped, make the legal protection of submerged cultural resources in the Cayman Islands a reality and result in the formal creation of CIMAP, the Cayman Islands Maritime Archaeology Programme.

The land-based Maritime Heritage Trail and the offshore Shipwreck Preserve Trail will be the first comprehensive maritime heritage and ecotourism initiatives of their kind in the Caribbean and will enhance the local economy by diversifying Cayman's tourism product. The trails are expected to provide enjoyable, interactive cultural experiences for visitors that increase knowledge and appreciation for the past while instilling a sense of stewardship for maritime heritage resources. The ultimate goal for the trails, however, is to protect and preserve the maritime heritage of the Cayman Islands.

REFERENCES

Abandoned Wreck Law 5. 1966. Revised 1997. Cayman Islands: Cayman Islands Government.

Cayman Islands Maritime Heritage Trail Partners. 2003. *The Cayman Islands Maritime Heritage Trail, Grand Cayman and Sister Islands* (poster/brochures). Cayman Islands: Maritime Heritage Trail Partners.

Craton, M. 2003. *Founded Upon the Seas: A History of the Cayman Islands and Their People*. Kingston, Jamaica: Ian Randle Publishers.

Florida Keys National Marine Sanctuary. 2006. Shipwreck Trail. Available online at http://www.fknms.nos.noaa.gov/sanctuary_resources/shipwreck_trail/welcome.html (accessed May 21, 2008).

Government of South Australia, Department for Environment and Heritage. 2006. Shipwreck Trails. Available online at http://www.environment.sa.gov.au/heritage/shipwreck_trails.html#Kangaroo_Island (accessed May 21, 2008).

Ho, B. 2004. An archaeological study of *Glamis*: The role of a 19th century iron barque. Unpublished MA thesis, Florida State University, Tallahassee.

ICOMOS International Charter on the Protection and Management of Underwater Cultural Heritage. 1996. Paris: ICOMOS.

Leshikar, M. E. 1993. *The 1794 Wreck of the Ten Sail: A historical study and archaeological survey*. Ph.D. thesis, Texas A&M University, College Station; University Microfi lms, Ann Arbor, Michigan.

Leshikar-Denton, M. E. 1997. Underwater cultural resource management: A new concept in the Cayman Islands. In *Underwater Archaeology*, D. C. Lakey, eds., 33–37. Corpus Christi, TX: Society for Historical Archaeology.

Leshikar-Denton, M. E. 2002. Problems and progress in the Caribbean. In *International Handbook of Underwater Archaeology*, C. Ruppe and J. Barstad, eds., 279–98. New York: Kluwer Academic/Plenum Press.

Leshikar-Denton, M. E. In press. *The Wreck of the Ten Sail*. Gainesville: University Press of Florida.

Leshikar-Denton, M. E., and B. Ho (with contributions by D. Scott-Ireton, A. Evans, and W. Anderson). 2004. *The Probable "Glamis" Site: Archaeological Mapping and Potential for a Shipwreck Preserve, Grand Cayman, Cayman Islands*. Cayman Islands National Museum Shipwreck Preserve Series 1. Cayman Islands: CINM.

Leshikar-Denton, M. E., and P. E. Pedley, eds. 1994. *The Wreck of the Ten Sails*. Our Islands' Past 2. Grand Cayman: Cayman Islands National Archive and Cayman Free Press.

National Shipwreck Inventory. n.d. Unpublished files, Cayman Islands Government.

Pedley, P. E. ed. 1992. *Edward Corbet's Report and Census of 1802 on the Cayman Islands*. Our Islands' Past 1. Grand Cayman: Cayman Islands National Archive and Cayman Free Press.

Scott-Ireton, D. A. 2003. Florida's underwater archaeological preserves. In *Submerged Cultural Resource Management: Preserving and Interpreting Our Sunken Maritime Heritage*, J. D. Spirek and D. A. Scott-Ireton, eds., 95–105. New York: Kluwer Academic/Plenum Press.

Scott-Ireton, D. A. 2005. Preserves, parks, and trails: Strategy and response in maritime cultural resource management. Unpublished Ph.D. thesis, Florida State University, Tallahassee.

Smith, R. C. 1981. The maritime heritage of the Cayman Islands. Unpublished MA thesis, Texas A&M University, College Station.

Smith, R. C. 2000. *The Maritime Heritage of the Cayman Islands.* Gainesville: University Press of Florida.

State of Florida, Department of State. 2006. Florida Maritime Heritage Trail. Available online at http://dhr.dos.state.fl.us/archaeology/underwater/maritime/ (accessed May 21, 2008).

Thunder Bay National Marine Sanctuary. 2006. Maritime Heritage and Shipwrecks. Available online at http://thunderbay.noaa.gov/ (accessed May 21, 2008).

UNESCO Convention on the Protection of the Underwater Cultural Heritage. 2001. Paris: UNESCO.

CHAPTER 15

The Jamaican Version: Public Archaeology and the Protection of Underwater Cultural Heritage

Dorrick E. Gray

INTRODUCTION

The territorial waters of Jamaica (Figure 15.1), like those of our Caribbean neighbors, are littered with the material culture of the various people who, from prehistoric times to the present, occupied and utilized these sea-lanes for their subsistence, transport, commerce, and "discoveries." Jamaica stands in a unique position, however, with underwater sites that contain important aspects of our terrestrial history, culture, and heritage. In particular, our own Port Royal contains not only shipwrecks similar to those found in the waters of other countries, but also remains of entire buildings and their contents submerged following a tragic earthquake in 1692. Archaeological research has placed this seemingly small and quiet town of ours into the category of one of the most important 17th-century underwater "catastrophic" archaeological sites in the world (Hamilton and Woodward 1984). Port Royal studies can be considered alongside other worldwide "disaster archaeology" literature (see, e.g., Grattan and Torrence 2002).

Our underwater cultural heritage includes not only world-renowned sites like Port Royal, but in the broadest sense of the word "all traces of human existence in Jamaica that are found partially or completely submerged underwater and are 100 years or older" (UNESCO 2001:2). These include the sea-going vessels of the first Jamaicans (the Tainos), Spanish and English shipwrecks on the offshore Cays of Jamaica (e.g., Pedro Banks and Morant Cays), and the old ports of Falmouth and Saint Ann's Bay in the north and Savanna-la-mar and Black River in the south.

Figure 15.1 Archaeologist conducting a survey with a metal detector on the Pedro Banks (photograph courtesy JNHT Sites and Monuments Record).

These rich sites must also be added to all the simple finger wharfs of the 18th and 19th centuries that dotted the bays and coves in and around Jamaica, to mention but a few sites in the maritime cultural heritage landscape of Jamaica.

This chapter traces the history of heritage studies of the underwater cultural heritage of Jamaica from its origin and shows how Jamaican heritage organizations changed gears from antiquarianism to scientific investigation. I will also discuss the attempts of treasure-hunting interests in recent times to salvage important shipwrecks in the archipelagic waters of Jamaica. Public archaeologists have been faced with the daunting task of ensuring that the licenses and agreements granted by the government were adhered to and reflected the requirements of the international community in the research and preservation of Jamaica's underwater cultural heritage. Insights into the history of management of Jamaica's underwater cultural heritage have also been presented in Gray (1997) and Leshikar-Denton (2002:287–90).

PORT ROYAL

The earliest recorded interest in the underwater cultural heritage of Jamaica is related to the material remains left in the aftermath of the

1692 earthquake at Port Royal, as discussed in detail in Chapter 16. Looters and various organized expeditions began salvage operations on the dry and underwater sections of the town immediately after the catastrophic earthquake (Mayes 1972; Pawson and Buisseret 1975:44–45). More recently, the *Falmouth Post* (1859) newspaper carried an article by British Navy diver Jeremiah D. Murphy who found sections of a fort in the underwater sections of the town.

By the 20th century, a flurry of interest developed about what could be found and recovered from the city affected by the 1692 earthquake. In 1954, Mr. and Mrs. Alexi Dupont (Americans) were alleged to have found an arched doorway and a flight of ten stairs with quantities of bottles, bricks, and roof tiles (Mayes 1972). However, the first organized 20th-century exploration of the underwater city was conducted by Edwin Link (an engineer by profession) in 1959 under the joint sponsorship of the National Geographic Society, the Smithsonian Institution, and the Institute of Jamaica. The areas of Fort James and the Kings warehouse, all underwater, were explored. Link's team produced the first accurate map of the 5.26 ha (13 acres) of land that comprise the underwater portion of the old city (Link 1960).

During the 1960s, the government employed Norman Scott and Robert Marx to examine the underwater city in advance of plans to construct a cruise ship pier in the area (Marx 1968). At that time, underwater archaeology worldwide was still in its infancy. Not surprisingly, many who were involved in activities directed at the underwater cultural heritage of Jamaica were more antiquarian in their approach than scientific. However, these early explorers were able to confirm that the sunken city of Port Royal still existed and showed that there was an important need for preservation and scientific research. Consequently, a political shift in policy toward preservation and scientific investigation was the hallmark of the 1970s–1990s.

PROTECTION OF UNDERWATER CULTURAL HERITAGE

The Jamaican government established the Institute of Jamaica in 1879 and enacted the Jamaica National Trust Commission Act in 1958 and the Jamaica National Heritage Trust Act in 1985. Beginning in the 1970s, it became the consistent policy of the government and its heritage agencies, the Institute of Jamaica and the Jamaica National Heritage Trust (JNHT), to only give permission for archaeological research in our terrestrial and marine environment to qualified archaeologists.

In 1981, the Institute of Jamaica entered into a collaborative agreement with Texas A&M University (College Station), and the Institute of Nautical Archaeology (College Station, Texas), to carry out research on the underwater city of Port Royal in advance of government implementation of a proposal to build a cruise ship pier. This project, described in Chapter 16, was headed by Professor Donny Hamilton between 1981 and 1990 and became the most scientific and comprehensive research ever carried out on Jamaica's underwater cultural heritage. Not only were important archaeological features identified and thousands of artifacts recovered with their context from ten years of research, but the information gleaned has enabled researchers to reconstruct what happened on that fateful day of June 7, 1692—when a devastating earthquake and tsunami hit the 17th-century city of Port Royal—and to reconstruct its aftermath.

Although analysis and conservation is ongoing (e.g., innovative glass-conservation described by Smith in Chapter 17), a variety of studies including published works, unpublished manuscripts, and students' theses have already been produced (see Clifford 1991; Hamilton 1985, 1988, 1990, 1991, 1992, 1996, 1997, 2000, 2004, 2006). This research provided crucial information for policymakers charged with designating specific marine areas of Port Royal off limits to any development that might negatively impact this important underwater cultural heritage of the Americas.

Also significant for this project was the multifaceted training of Jamaicans and marine archaeology students in techniques of archaeology and conservation. The methodology learned in the field laid a solid foundation for future marine archaeology practitioners and managers in Jamaica and the Caribbean.

The Jamaican government, faced with an increase in illegal poaching and applications for treasure-hunting activities, decided in 1990 to approve a policy of allowing only professional archaeological excavations in the territorial waters of Jamaica. Treasure hunting and commercial salvage of historic shipwrecks were prohibited. This bold and principled stand by the government, supported by its related heritage agencies, encouraged a flurry of archaeological research both on land and underwater at Seville (Armstrong 1990; Parrent 1992; Smith 1987, 1988), Port Royal (Mayes 1972; Priddy 1975), and the Pedro Banks (Hoyt 1983; Parrent 1989).

Positive spin-offs from these activities included international publicity that portrayed Jamaica as having a matured and positive attitude and concern for protecting archaeological sites containing vital information about the history and development of both the Old and New Worlds. In a fitting historical backdrop, Jamaica was also asked to host the Society for Historical Archaeology annual conference in 1992, the largest grouping of archaeologists and cultural resource managers ever assembled in the English-speaking Caribbean. This event also encouraged and helped develop a small core of Jamaican archaeologists who received the necessary training and experience and resulted in the formation of a cadre of local cultural resource managers.

COMMERCIAL EXPLOITATION

In the late 1990s, the Jamaican government was again faced with increased unauthorized activities on its offshore sites and received more applications for treasure hunting licenses. Consequently, it reviewed and amended its policy of 1990 by seeking to protect these vital underwater resources through an agreement with a private company that would recover and conserve underwater remains for the benefit of the people of Jamaica. But this was truly a nonbeneficial agreement for Jamaica, and it was signed prior to the adoption of the international UNESCO Convention on the Protection of the Underwater Cultural Heritage by eighty-seven countries, in 2001, including Jamaica. This agreement was carried out in the context of the presumed renewed interest worldwide in treasure hunting and advances in technology to access underwater cultural heritage sites; as perceived by the government, this advanced technology had allowed for increased and easier access to underwater sites and important shipwrecks without government authorization. The then minister of education pointed out that,

> with Jamaica's limited resources to monitor unauthorized activities and being aware of the ever present danger of undetected operations in our territorial waters resulting in damage or loss of important cultural artefacts a decision was taken to review the existing policy. (Minister of Education and Culture 2002)

Against this background, the decision was made

> in the best interest of Jamaica to recover and conserve for the benefit of Jamaica the artefacts and their information from the underwater cultural heritage. It was noted that a bar to such recovery and conservation has always been and continues to be the high cost required to carry out such operations. (Government of Jamaica 2000)

After careful consideration, but with less than unanimous support among heritage professionals, the policy was amended in 2000 to include commercial exploitation of the underwater cultural heritage within certain specific guidelines. Foremost in the new policy is the use of advanced technology that would enable users to "identify and discriminate the specific nature of objects as to minimize the necessity for excavations causing minimal damage to the underwater cultural heritage and other living and non-living marine resources" (Government of Jamaica 2000). In other words, companies could pinpoint precious metals that could be extracted without seriously damaging the archaeological site and marine environment.

The new policy also included a requirement for the presence of observers from the Jamaica National Heritage Trust, the Jamaica Defence Force, the National Environment Protection Authority, and the Fisheries Division to ensure that the work is carried out in accordance with the requirements of these government organizations. The policy called for licenses to be granted for a designated area for a period of not more than three years in the first instance, with the licensees bonded as to preservation and conservation, proper conduct of the operations, and proper performance of such contracts as may be entered into in respect of recompense and/or entitlements.

ROLES OF PUBLIC ARCHAEOLOGISTS

Public archaeologists at the Jamaica National Heritage Trust were asked to monitor and ensure that the Government of Jamaica's (GoJ) signed agreements and licenses would include the research, preservation, and recovery of material culture to "*internationally accepted marine archaeological standards*" (Government of Jamaica License 99/001; emphasis added). As public archaeologists, the question was: How could we ensure that our archaeological ethics were not compromised and at the same time comply with this agreement that was signed by the GoJ on behalf of the people of Jamaica?

We were cognizant of other shipwrecks that had been "examined" by commercial outfits like these and knew what the consequences were. In the case of the early 17th-century galleon *Atocha*, shares were sold by the salvage company to investors who were promised a good return on their investment. The investors either lost their money or were given artifacts that were worth less than their initial investment. The treasure salvage of the *Wydah*, *DeBraak*, and *El Nuevo Constante* was inadequate in terms of careful artifact collection, provenience control, and amount of time given for artifact analysis. The project on *El Nuevo Constante* did not even have an archaeologist on site to supervise the excavations (Carrell 1990).

Johnston (1992:52–53) noted that at many professional gatherings a subject frequently discussed was the minimum conditions a conscientious archaeologist might impose on a treasure-hunting outfit if the two were to work together on a work site. Johnston wrote that several hypothetical suggestions arose from these discussions, which included the following:

1. The archaeologist must retain complete authority and control over the proper field recording and recovery of artifacts.
2. The budget must be adequate to conserve all the recovered material.

3. Funding must be dedicated to the proper research and publication of the site.
4. The artifact assemblage must be preserved intact and endowed with sufficient funding to ensure its long-term survival and it must be made available to the public and professional audiences.

Delgado (2000:12–13) also summed up what was at stake. He argued that the great dividing line comes when we find ourselves engaged in a more complex challenge, as we grapple with the Pandora's box that has been opened in the deep ocean to new technology and as we face the increasing sophistication of treasure hunters who now talk our talk with greater regularity. This is not just to complain about treasure hunting, he assured us, but we must ethically and professionally oppose and not participate in looting, nonscientific recovery of material from archaeological sites, and marketing of antiquities. This statement was and remains of utmost significance to us; as cultural resource managers, we had an obligation to the government and people of Jamaica to ensure that what was entrusted to us to monitor is carried out according to the best interest of the cultural heritage and Jamaica, given the very challenging circumstances. What was at stake because of the GoJ system of licensing?

The Pedro Cays

The Pedro Cays are a large submerged plateau-like formation located on the south coast of Jamaica and cover some 7,247 km^2 in the archipelagic waters of Jamaica. Depths over most of the plateau average 18–35 m, but shallow reefs and cay formations on the southern perimeter of the plateau create extremely dangerous obstacles to ships (Zans 1958). The archaeological significance of the Pedro Cays results from its proximity to the major shipping lanes in the Caribbean. In historic times, navigators of sailing ships departing from Cartegena, Colombia, and other countries in South America often chose to follow the Leeward Passage, a route around the Yucatan peninsula and into Havana, to avoid contrary winds on the return trip to Europe. This route took them between the Pedro Cays where many vessels were lost (Hoyt 1983).

The earliest recorded European vessel wrecked in the Pedro Cays was a Spanish caravel on its way to Hispaniola in 1511. This is still the third-oldest European ship known to be in Jamaican waters, the earliest being the *Capitana* and the *Santiago de Palos*, two ships beached by Columbus in 1503 somewhere on the north coast of Jamaica. In the ensuing years, numerous Spanish ships suffered the same fate (e.g., those lost in 1579,

1605, 1691, 1730, and 1755). Many wrecked vessels remained unrecorded. One of the last-recorded vessels that met its fate on the Pedro Cays was the *Estella*, a Cuban slave ship laden with 299 enslaved Africans that ran aground and sank in 1838. It is recorded that no attempt was made to rescue its cargo. This vessel remains the only recorded "slaver," complete with its human cargo, that has been lost in Jamaican waters.

Given the number of important wrecks dating back to the early 16th century, which makes the Pedro Cays a natural graveyard for ships and the final resting place for many ancestors of the Caribbean people, public archaeologists in Jamaica had to ensure that any activities directed at this underwater cultural heritage be carried out in a manner that respects and adheres to international marine archaeology standards. Uppermost in our minds was the need to ensure that a detailed project design was prepared under our guidelines and that qualified persons with the necessary experience were included in the project.

In the project proposal, we requested that this be done under the supervision of public archaeologists at the Jamaica National Heritage Trust. This proposal includes an outline of the specific goals and activities of the project, background archival research, the manner of carrying out field surveys and excavations, and how the data will be recovered, recorded, conserved, and analyzed. Equally important were the restrictions that prohibited explosives and prop wash deflector equipment. Airlifts, water dredges, and pressurized air, other than for breathing, could only be used with the written approval of the Jamaica National Heritage Trust. It was also required that the licensee generate and maintain a record of the site, the activities, and the artifacts to be delivered to designated persons on request. These guidelines have created the framework in which public archaeologists would be able to monitor the operations.

Further, we requested that the principal investigator be an archaeologist with a minimum of five years' experience and hold postgraduate degrees in maritime history, marine archaeology, or historical archaeology. In addition, the principal investigator was to be a member of recognized professional archaeological organizations. Conservators working on the project were also required to be qualified with postgraduate degrees in conservation and a minimum of five years of experience and be members of recognized professional organizations. All other personnel were to be trained in the field related to their specific assignments, with a minimum of two years of full-time professional experience in the relevant discipline. If these standards were not met, the project would be a non-starter. At the same time, efforts were made to discuss the various challenges faced with the international community and to support the work of UNESCO in creating an international instrument that would protect the underwater cultural heritage. This was our strictly monitored program, one that looked difficult to some but was the basic requirement; it was comparable to requirements that all professional marine archaeologists are accustomed to in their normal day-to-day research.

JAMAICA AT PARIS UNESCO MEETINGS

Jamaica was actively involved at the various UNESCO meetings of governmental experts in the discussions leading to the adoption of the Convention on the Protection of the Underwater Cultural Heritage in 2001. The government has recognized the need for an international instrument to protect underwater cultural resources. It has noted that developing countries like itself lack the necessary financial and technical resources to ensure the complete monitoring and management of this unique heritage. Hence, adequate provisions and assistance are needed to cope. Jamaica's position at the meetings of governmental experts to discuss the draft convention was as follows:

1. States were encouraged by Jamaica to use their best efforts to arrive at a consensus text that recognized the sovereignty and jurisdiction of coastal and archipelagic states established by international law and in the United Nations Convention on the Law of the Sea.
2. In lieu of the convention's prohibition of commercial exploitation and preference for *in situ* preservation as the best method of protecting the underwater cultural heritage, it was felt that some mechanism was needed to provide developing states with financial and technical resources, as well as expertise, to ensure the preservation of the underwater cultural heritage.
3. Jamaica also recognized that the existing agreement with private enterprise concerning underwater cultural heritage might not be fully compatible with the provisions of the convention. Thus, Jamaica was aware that the convention should include a provision to recognize such agreements and allow a time frame for state parties to the convention to bring previous agreements, laws, and regulations into compliance with it.
4. Jamaica also attached great importance to the preservation of the marine environment and proposed that it was essential that the convention include a provision that comprehensively covers the protection and preservation of the marine environment. It should include the precautionary principle in cases where the underwater cultural heritage has to be removed to guarantee its preservation.

5. Jamaica supported those articles of the convention that facilitated the transfer of technology and promoted international cooperation.

Given these positions, Jamaica supported the contents of the final draft on underwater cultural heritage at the meetings of governmental experts and reiterated its support for the final document accepted by the UNESCO General Conference in November 2001.

UNESCO MEETING OF THE AMERICAS

It was an honor for Jamaica to host the first UNESCO regional Americas meeting in Kingston on the UNESCO Convention on the Protection of the Underwater Cultural Heritage in 2002. Delegates from over forty-four countries from North, Central, and South America, Europe, and the Caribbean discussed and sought clarification on implications for the adoption and ratification of this important international instrument.

Delegates, including Jamaica, discussed a wide range of issues unique to our region and agreed on some of the main issues. It was clear from the discussions held at the meeting of the Americas that many of the Caribbean states still believe that they will require changes in their legislation first before the convention can be ratified. Conversely, representatives from other Caribbean countries felt that they could ratify the convention and then work toward developing compliant national legislation.

CURRENT GOALS FOR JAMAICA

The UNESCO Convention has created the national and international framework within which Jamaica must now actively begin to identify, research, and preserve these underwater sites. To achieve our goals we must begin to consistently and systematically initiate the following activities:

1. encourage Jamaica and countries in the Caribbean region to ratify the UNESCO Convention on the Protection of the Underwater Cultural Heritage;
2. ensure that all permits for research on underwater cultural heritage sites in Jamaica are carried out within the context of the convention and the annex;
3. initiate a national inventory of underwater sites in our territorial waters;

4. actively explore for more opportunities to train professional archaeologists in the field of underwater archaeology;
5. seek the assistance of local divers, fishermen, volunteers, and the general public in providing information on underwater cultural heritage that they may encounter; and
6. provide information to the general public as to what should be done when these underwater sites are found.

Despite all the efforts, satisfactory protection of Jamaica's underwater sites cannot be achieved without new national legislation that, on one hand, recognizes the UNESCO Convention on the Protection of the Underwater Cultural Heritage, and, on the other hand, provides for stronger protection than what now exists, both for the sites and their associated artifacts. But the single most important activity is public education of the people who will become our eyes and ears on the "grounds of preservation." As stated by the minister of education and culture (2000):

> In light of this convention, and in the context of new experience and evolving new structures and arrangements in the international community, the Government of Jamaica will keep its policy on marine exploration under ongoing review. We wish to ensure that the best is done to enlighten the minds, and stir the imagination and strengthen the psyche of present and future generations.

Public archaeologists and cultural resource managers must now recognize that it is possible to protect this heritage if, through various battles, we consistently and systematically demonstrate the importance of researching and preserving our underwater cultural heritage by upholding our ethics and archaeological principles. After all, this underwater heritage belongs to all citizens of the state of Jamaica but, even more importantly, it belongs to all humanity.

REFERENCES

Armstrong, D. 1990. *The Old Village and the Great House: An Archaeological and Historical Examination of Drax Hall Plantation, St. Ann's Bay*. Urbana: University of Illinois Press.

Carrell, T. L. 1990. Ethics versus commercial exploitation: What's it worth to the future? In *Predicaments, Pragmatics, and Professionalism: Ethical Conduct in Archaeology*, J. N. Woodall, ed., 61–72. Special Publication No. 1. Society of Professional Archaeologists, Baltimore, Maryland.

Clifford, S. A. 1991. A preliminary report on a possible 17th-century shipwreck at Port Royal, Jamaica. In *Underwater Archaeology Proceedings from the Society for Historical*

Archaeology Conference, J. D. Broadwater, ed., 80–83. Richmond: Society for Historical Archaeology.

Delgado, J. 2000. Underwater archaeology at the dawn of the 21st century. *Journal of the Society for Historical Archaeology* 34(4):9–13.

Falmouth Post. 1859. October 7.

Government of Jamaica. 2000. Policy on Marine Archaeological Exploration by Commercial Enterprises or Interest. January. Sites & Monument Record, Jamaica National Heritage Trust, Kingston.

Grattan, J., and R. Torrence, eds. 2002. *Natural Disasters, Catastrophism and Cultural Change*. London: Routledge.

Gray, D. E. 1997. Managing underwater archaeological resources: The Jamaican experience. Unpublished paper presented at the Society for Historical Archaeology Conference, January 8–12, 1997, Corpus Christi, Texas.

Hamilton, D. L. 1985. The city under the sea. In *Science Year, 1986, The World Book Science Annual*, R. O. Zeleny, ed., 92–109. Chicago: World Book.

Hamilton, D. L. 1988. Underwater excavations of 17th-century buildings at the intersection of Lime and Queen Streets. In *Underwater Archaeology Proceedings from the Society of Historical Archaeology Conference*, J. P. Delgado, ed., 9–12. Reno, NV: Society for Historical Archaeology.

Hamilton, D. L. 1990. A decade of underwater research at Port Royal. *Institute of Nautical Archaeology Newsletter* 17(2):4–7.

Hamilton, D. L. 1991. A decade of excavations at Port Royal, Jamaica. In *Underwater Archaeology Proceedings from the Society for Historical Archaeology Conference*, J. D. Broadwater, ed., 90–94. Richmond: Society for Historical Archaeology.

Hamilton, D. L. 1992. Simon Benning, pewterer of Port Royal. In *Text-Aided Archaeology*, B. J. Little, ed., 39–53. Boca Raton, FL: CRC Press.

Hamilton, D. L. 1996. Historical archaeology on British sites in the seventeenth-century Caribbean. In *The Archaeology of Sixteenth and Seventeenth Century British Colonization in the Caribbean, United States and Canada*, H. D. Miller, D. L. Hamilton, N. Honerkamp, S. R. Pendery, P. E. Pope, and J. A. Tuck, eds., 3–12. Ann Arbor, MI: Society for Historical Archaeology.

Hamilton, D. L. 1997. Port Royal. In *Encyclopaedia of Underwater and Maritime Archaeology*, J. P. Delgado, ed., 316–18. London: British Museum Press.

Hamilton, D. L. 2000. Port Royal Project. Available online at http://nautarch.tamu.edu/portroyal/ (accessed May 20, 2008).

Hamilton, D. L. 2004. Port Royal: A buried treasure. In *Patrimonio Cultural Subacuatico/Underwater Cultural Heritage*, V. Marín, ed., 34–35 and 102–03, English and Spanish versions. Havana: UNESCO.

Hamilton, D. L. 2006. Port Royal, Jamaica: Archaeological past and development potential. In *Underwater Cultural Heritage at Risk: Managing Natural and Human Impacts*, R. Grenier, D. Nutley, and I. Cochran, eds., 49–51. Paris: ICOMOS.

Hamilton, D. L., and R. Woodward. 1984. A sunken 17th-century city: Port Royal, Jamaica. *Archaeology* 37(1):38–45.

Hoyt, S. 1983. Pedro Banks survey: The 1981 and 1982 seasons. Unpublished report to the Government of Jamaica, Jamaica National Heritage Trust Sites and Monuments Record.

Johnston, P. 1992. Treasure salvage, archaeological ethics and maritime museums. *International Journal of Nautical Archaeology and Underwater Exploration* 21(1): 39–53.

Leshikar-Denton, M. E. 2002. Problems and progress in the Caribbean. In *International Handbook of Underwater Archaeology*, C. Ruppe and J. Barstad, eds., 279–98. New York: Kluwer Academic/Plenum Press.

Link, M. C. 1960. Exploring the drowned City of Port Royal. *National Geographic* 117(2):151–82.

Marx, R. 1968. Excavating the sunken city of Port Royal. *Jamaica Journal* 2(2):12–18.

Mayes, P. 1972. *Port Royal, Jamaica: Excavations 1969–70*. Kingston: National Heritage Trust.

Minister of Education and Culture, Jamaica. 2002. Opening remarks at the UNESCO Conference of the Americas, Kingston, June, provided as a press release.

Parrent, J. 1989. Report on archaeological investigation on the Pedro Banks in context of cultural heritage resource management. Unpublished report to the Government of Jamaica, Jamaica National Heritage Trust Site and Monuments Record.

Parrent, J. 1992. The Columbus Caravel Archaeological Project (CCAP). Unpublished report to the Government of Jamaica, Jamaica National Heritage Trust Sites and Monuments Record.

Pawson, M., and D. Buisseret. 1975. *Port Royal, Jamaica*. London: Oxford University Press.

Priddy, A. 1975. The 17th and 18th-century settlement pattern of Port Royal. *Jamaica Journal* 9(2 & 3):8–10.

Smith, R. C. 1987. The search for the lost caravels. *American Archaeology* 6:109–13.

Smith, R. C. 1988. The voyages of Columbus: The search for his ships. In *Ships and Shipwrecks of the Americas*, G. F. Bass, ed., 33–44. London: Thames and Hudson.

UNESCO. 2001. *UNESCO Convention on the Protection of the Underwater Cultural Heritage*. Paris: UNESCO.

Zans, V. A. 1958. The Pedro Cays and Pedro Bank. Report on the survey of the cays, 1955–57. *Jamaica Geologic Survey Department Bulletin* 3.

CHAPTER 16

Port Royal, Jamaica: Archaeological Past, Present, and Future

Donny L. Hamilton

Today, Port Royal, Jamaica, is a small isolated fishing village with little influence in Caribbean affairs, but beneath the earth and the adjacent waters of Kingston Harbour lies the only sunken city in the New World, a city that played a pivotal role in Caribbean politics and economics for centuries. Port Royal is one of the premier English historic sites of the Americas. Founded in 1655 soon after the English invasion and conquest of the Spanish island of Jamaica, it went through a spectacular rise involving rich merchants, notorious pirates, government-sanctioned privateers, and affluent planters.

In 1692, Port Royal was arguably the largest and most affluent English town in the New World and had far-reaching influence. Its unrivaled success ended dramatically on June 7, 1692, when much of the town sank during a disastrous earthquake. Port Royal's significance as perhaps the best-preserved 17th-century English site in the world brings with it a great responsibility to all who undertake excavations of the site in terms of proper excavation, careful recording, conservation of the recovered material, and publishing the results. Equally important is the responsibility of the government of Jamaica to protect the different areas of the town, properly house the recovered material, conserve the artifacts, display and interpret the recovered material, and carefully develop the site for present and future generations.

In this chapter, I discuss the range of archaeological research that is possible at Port Royal, the potential dangers because of modern development, and plans to develop Port Royal into a tourist center. I also consider the Jamaican government's responsibilities to protect the incomparable archaeological record of this historic town and explore opportunities to interpret this irreplaceable cultural resource to local and international audiences.

17TH-CENTURY PORT ROYAL

Anyone visiting Port Royal just prior to the 1692 earthquake would have been impressed with its multistoried brick buildings, high population density, and general appearance of wealth as compared to other English colonial towns of the period in the New World. Many claim that Port Royal, with an estimated population of 7,000–8,000, was the largest and most affluent English town in the Americas at this time, rivaled in size and economic importance only by Boston with 6,000 or so citizens (Black 1983:49; Hamilton 1992:40; Pawson and Buisseret 2000:136). Port Royal had all the amenities and vices of any 17th-century port town and because of its loose-living citizenry, it was widely referred to as "the wickedest city in the world." During its heyday, Port Royal, laid out with broad unpaved streets named after familiar streets in London, each lined with buildings one to four stories in height with brick sidewalks along the front of many, covered some 21.04 ha (52 acres) of land.

In 1692, the density of structures in the city were comparable to London and the rent was as high as that paid in London's high-rent district of Cheapside (Taylor 1688:252). Following the earthquake in 1692, when 13.36 ha (33 acres) of the town sank into the harbor, only 8.09 ha (20 acres) survived as an island at the end of the long, narrow sand spit separating Kingston Harbour from the Caribbean Sea.

Fort Charles, the church, and a few other buildings, only remotely resembling 17th-century Port Royal, remain today. Visitors now see a small fishing town with just over 2,000 citizens along with an abandoned 19th-century British naval base and the headquarters of the Jamaican Coast Guard. Very little exists above the ground or the water to indicate the past glory of Port Royal during its pinnacle in the 17th century, or during its prosperous days in the 18th–19th centuries when it served as a British naval base. Exceptions include the old naval hospital built in 1814 as the first prefabricated iron structure in the Caribbean and various buildings inside the old naval base. When the naval base closed in 1905, Port Royal's prominent role in the economy of Jamaica ended. Fortunately, this circumstance has resulted in the preservation of much of Port Royal's archaeological deposits, both terrestrial and underwater.

PORT ROYAL DISASTERS

Port Royal belongs to one of a select group of archaeological sites which includes Pompeii and Herculaneum in Italy and Ozette in the state of Washington. Sites such as these are unique "catastrophic" sites—sites created by some disaster that preserves the cultural

> features and material and the all-important archaeological context. At this type of undisturbed site, the archaeologist is not dealing with a situation where—over a long span of time—houses, shops, warehouses, churches, and other buildings were constructed, added onto, fell into disrepair, were abandoned, eventually collapsed, were razed and then possibly built over. Port Royal is strikingly different: after only 37 years of existence this bustling city literally sank into the harbor in only a matter of minutes during a severe earthquake. (Hamilton and Woodward 1984:38–39)

The 1692 earthquake that both destroyed and preserved Port Royal, as referred to by Hamilton and Woodward, is only one of an unusually high number of catastrophes that have struck Port Royal. Port Royal experienced earthquakes in 1692, 1722, 1770, 1812, 1824, 1858, 1867, 1907, 1914, and 1956. Hurricanes impacted it in 1670, 1680, 1683, 1686, 1689, 1712, 1722, 1726, 1744, 1751, 1782, 1786, 1787, 1805, 1818, 1830, 1884, 1886, 1903, 1951, 1988, and 2004. The most significant disasters of these include: the 1692 earthquake, the 1703 fire that burned the town to the ground, the 1722 and 1744 hurricanes, the 1770 earthquake that largely destroyed the hospital, the 1815 fire that extensively burned the town, the 1907 earthquake, and the 1951 hurricane that left only four buildings standing in the business/residential center of town. All of these catastrophic elements and events played a major role in creating the different archaeological components represented in the archaeological record of the town today. Thus, archaeological research into Port Royal fits within an emerging body of "disaster archaeology" literature (Grattan and Torrence 2002). Taken as a whole, there are few sites that rival the potential at Port Royal to conduct research on domestic, business, and military structures dating between the 17th and 20th centuries.

PORT ROYAL ARCHAEOLOGICAL EXCAVATIONS

Over the past half-century, the submerged parts of the 17th-century town of Port Royal have received the most attention, but there are incomparable terrestrial opportunities as well. Three major underwater archaeological excavations have been conducted in the areas of the old town submerged in Kingston Harbour (Figure 16.1).

Edwin Link, in cooperation with the National Geographic Society and the Smithsonian Institution, undertook the first excavation (Link 1960); the 1959 Link excavations concentrated around Fort James, Littleton's Tavern, and the King's Warehouse. In 1965–1967, Robert Marx (1973), in association with the Institute of Jamaican Culture, conducted the second and largest excavation along Fisher's Row. The

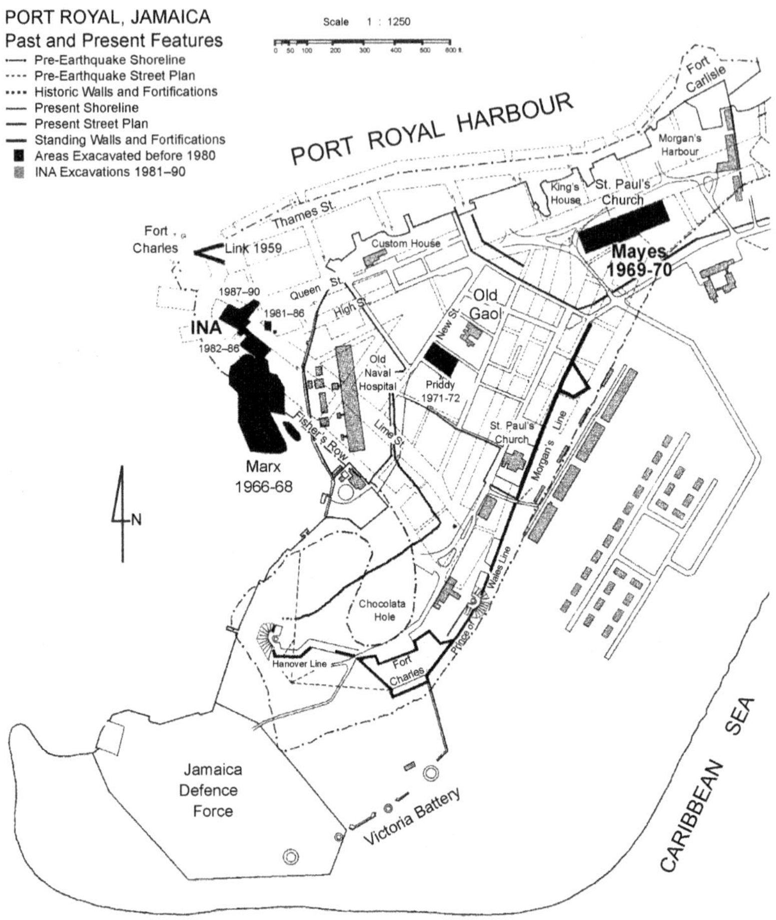

Figure 16.1 Port Royal town plan with major excavations.

third and longest running excavation (1981–1990) was directed by Donny Hamilton (1991, 1992, 2000; Hamilton and Woodward 1984) in conjunction with the Institute of Nautical Archaeology (INA), Texas A&M University, and the Jamaican National Heritage Trust. Hamilton's excavations focused along Lime Street at the intersection of High and Queen Street and resulted in the recording of the best-preserved structures and *in situ* artifacts thus far discovered at Port Royal (Figure 16.2).

The underwater archaeological excavations revealed the unexpected affluence of the old town, as evidenced by the prevalence of brick

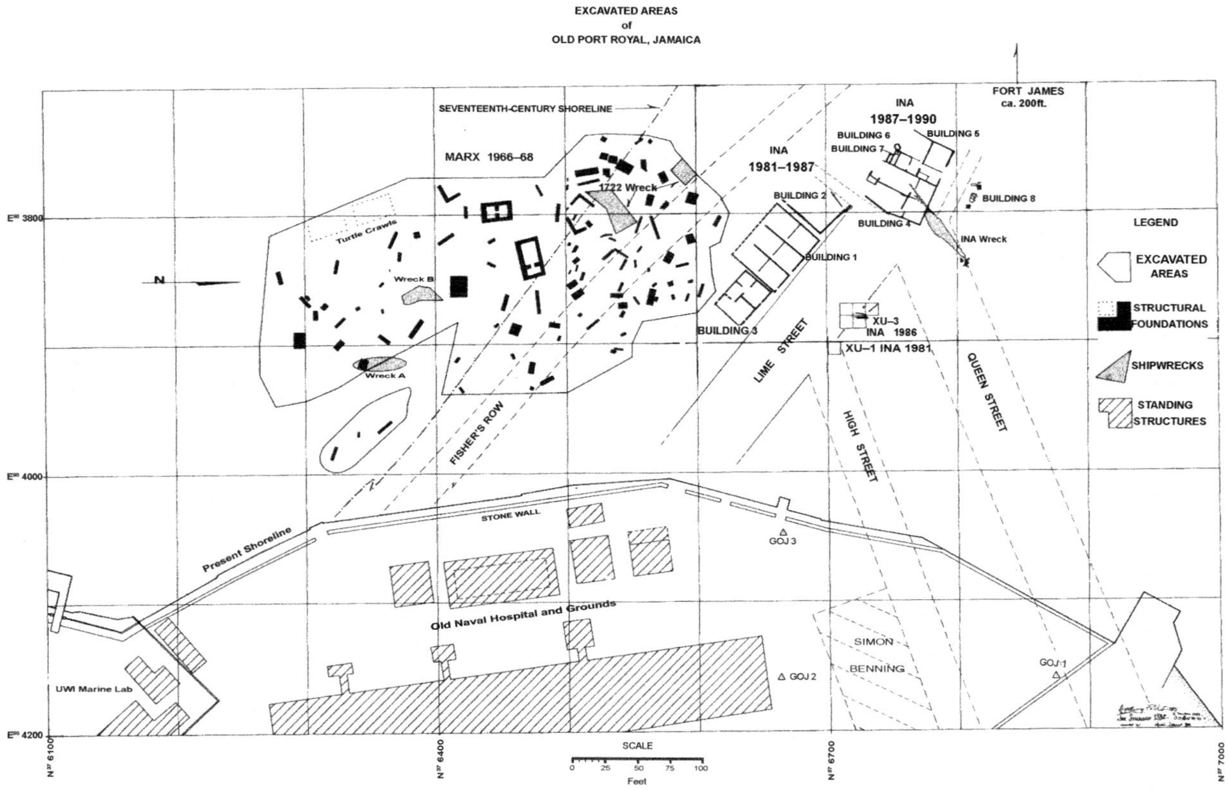

Figure 16.2 Underwater excavations conducted by the Institute of Nautical Archaeology and Robert Marx.

buildings, the density of construction, and the vast array of material culture in the latest styles of the period (Figures 16.3, 16.4, and 16.5).

In addition to the major underwater excavations, there have been two major and numerous small land excavations. Most of the small land excavations (conducted usually in reaction to some form of construction or development) remain unpublished. In some instances, readily available historical and archaeological information

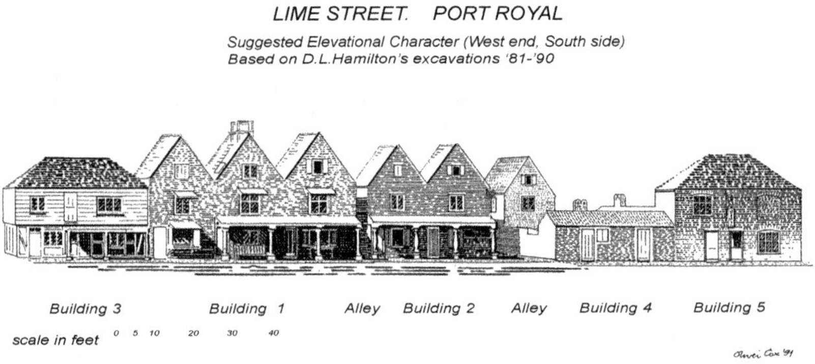

Figure 16.3 Architect's conception of five buildings excavated by the Institute of Nautical Archaeology.

Figure 16.4 Archaeologist investigating remnants of a stair well and brick floor of Building 1, sunk in the earthquake.

Figure 16.5 Array of artifacts from the underwater excavations.

was not utilized when various utility and building projects were undertaken. Historic documentation, old maps, and data contributed by archaeologists were sometimes overlooked. The 1988 water line installed to the Coast Guard Station at the south end of town is an example. Workmen dug the pipeline trench across a present-day soccer field that overlies the land end of historical Lime Street. The trench crossed the middle of the building blocks along the south side of Lime Street but could have run down the middle of the street, thus missing all the buildings. Were it not for the presence of the INA archaeologists, the trench would have gone unrecorded; instead they salvaged archaeological data from loss. Over the years, it has been the developments and improvements in the town that have done the most damage to the archaeological record.

The archaeological richness of this area of town and the well-preserved nature of the terrestrial deposits is further validated by the small test excavation conducted by the Museum of London (MoL) (Schofield 1988) along the south side of Lime Street near its eastern intersection with Church Street. Results of both the trench and the MoL excavations demonstrate the richness and well-preserved nature of the deposits located beneath the present-day soccer field; the deposits lie under a protective layer of fill brought in to raise the ground level by the British Navy after it acquired the unused and burned out area in the mid-19th century.

Philip Mayes (1972) conducted the largest land excavation at Port Royal located in the center of the 19th-century naval base. His work is known primarily for the partial excavation of St. Paul's Church, which sank beneath the surface during the 1692 earthquake through the phenomenon known as liquefaction, which is commonly associated with earthquakes. Finally, Antony Priddy (1975) excavated a densely packed building block facing onto New Street, containing buildings dating from the 1660s up to the fire of 1815 and perhaps a while later (Brown 1996).

There are known shipwrecks dating from the 17th and 18th centuries lying close to the seawall along the harbor side of Port Royal. In fact, the only archaeological evidence that can be unequivocally equated to piracy and privateering is found in shipwrecks. Marx's excavation (1965–1967) located and tentatively identified three shipwrecks, labeled A, B, and 1722 Wreck on the excavation plan (Figure 16.2). Along the southeast side of the excavation area, Wreck A is identified as HMS *Swan*. Just west of this ship is Wreck B, identified as the "French Prize," and at the north end of the excavated area are two sections of a ship that Marx identified as the 1722 Wreck on the basis of a 1721 French coin (Marx 1973:202).

Historic accounts describe how the sea overwhelmed Port Royal, whereas twenty-six merchant vessels were lost along with 400 persons who perished in the harbor during the disastrous August 28, 1722 hurricane (Millás 1968:178). According to another observer, only four man-of-wars and two merchant ships survived the storm out of fifty sailing ships in the harbor (Millás 1968:178). One ship lost in this 1722 hurricane crashed through and demolished much of the town; it destroyed once and for all Port Royal's chance to revive its former prominence. The ship had been sailed by the notorious 18th-century pirate, Bartholomew Roberts.

After establishing the 1692 boundary of the harbor side of Port Royal (Figure 16.1), it is clear that the shipwreck Marx identified as HMS *Swan* lies in the old harbor, not the town. As the ship lies outside the town boundary, it cannot be HMS *Swan*, which was being careened at the time of the earthquake and subsequently washed into town, landing on top of the house of Lord Pike (Oldmixon 1969:324). A more likely candidate for HMS *Swan*, a 5th-rate warship, is the shipwreck that rammed through the front wall of Building 4 and lies at the ends of Lime and Queen Streets in the INA/TAMU excavation (Clifford 1991:82) (Figure 16.6).

It is impossible to conclusively state that this wreck is the *Swan*, but it does fit the description of the ship: There is no ballast on the shipwreck site, which suggests it was being careened; the ship's remains lie on top of a building; and the keel compares to the same 22.55 m (74 ft) length as described for the *Swan* (Clifford 1991). This example is the first archaeological evidence documenting a ship that literally rammed through the front door of an occupied house during the earthquake. That in itself is an exciting discovery and one that illustrated to my nautical archaeology colleagues that I was finally doing shipwreck archaeology, not just excavating buildings underwater.

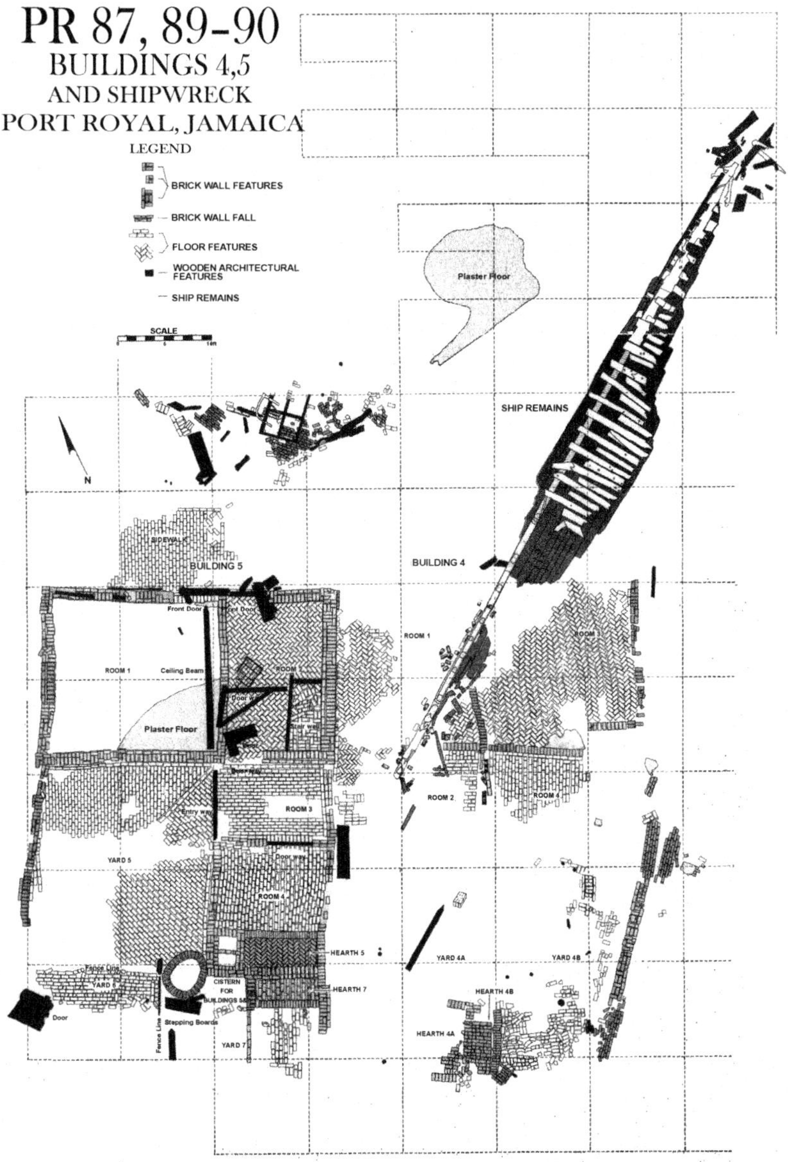

Figure 16.6 Excavation plan of Building 4/5, with remains of ship that crashed through the front wall of Building 4.

TOURISM DEVELOPMENT PLANS

Throughout Port Royal's history, up to the closing of the naval base in 1905, Port Royal was one of the most heavily fortified towns in the New World. Enemies never attacked the city because of its formidable defenses. During the 17th century, it boasted four forts (Charles, James, Carlisle, and Rupert) and three armed lines (Morgan, White, and Hanover). The 1692 earthquake destroyed Forts James, Carlisle, and Rupert. These were replaced during the 18th century by the Polygon Battery, at the east end of the town, and in 1888 by the Victoria Battery, at the south end of town just behind Fort Charles. The 1907 earthquake shifted the gun pits and the interconnecting tunnels, putting both of these batteries out of commission. Still, from an archaeological perspective, they are in good condition with numerous associated features. Even the painted signs remain visible on the walls.

Over the past two decades, a number of plans have been put forward to develop Port Royal into a major tourism center. To date, none of these proposals have gone beyond the discussion and planning stages, largely because of their scale and magnitude, coupled with a lack of funding to carry them out. The latest plan, submitted by the Port Royal Development Co. Ltd. (1998), includes proposals for major development in the land section of Lime Street, the Old Naval Yard, the Chocolata Hole anchorage, the harbor area, Fort Charles, the center of historical Port Royal, and more. This development plan has the potential to significantly impact, and to some degree destroy, parts of the archaeological record in the affected areas.

Jamaica, like most Caribbean countries, often faces conflicting interests between politicians, developers, tourism officials, and heritage concerns but it has a long history of interest in its cultural heritage, having established laws and institutions for their protection, management, and interpretation. As such, the government of Jamaica has accepted responsibility for seeing that the archaeological damage is mitigated as much as possible and to make sure that an experienced archaeologist, well versed in the history and archaeology of Port Royal, participates from the outset, in the planning stages of any development project.

Further archaeological research must be conducted in conjunction with any large-scale development of the town of Port Royal, a site that is worthy of international heritage attention and protection. In fact, the terrestrial and underwater components of Port Royal, if appropriately managed, could well be proposed for World Heritage Site status. There is great tourism development potential in Port Royal; the economy of the depressed town needs to be rejuvenated; and the whole country could benefit from well-considered initiatives. Development need not compromise the surviving historical structures, however, or the incomparable archaeological record that still lies untouched beneath the earth and the adjacent harbor of Port Royal.

REFERENCES

Black, C. V. 1983. *History of Jamaica.* Kingston: Longman Caribbean.

Brown, M. J. 1996. An archaeological study of social class as reflected in a British colonial tavern site in Port Royal, Jamaica. Unpublished MA thesis, The University of Texas at San Antonio.

Clifford, S. A. 1991. A preliminary report on a possible 17th-century shipwreck at Port Royal, Jamaica. In *Underwater Archaeology Proceedings from the Society for Historical Archaeology Conference*, J. D. Broadwater, ed., 80–83. Richmond: The Society for Historical Archaeology.

Grattan, J., and R. Torrence, eds. 2002. *Natural Disasters, Catastrophism and Cultural Change.* London: Routledge.

Hamilton, D. L. 1991. A decade of excavations at Port Royal, Jamaica. In *Underwater Archaeology Proceedings from the Society for Historical Archaeology Conference*, J. D. Broadwater, ed., 90–94. Richmond: The Society for Historical Archaeology.

Hamilton, D. L. 1992. Simon Benning, pewterer of Port Royal. In *Text-Aided Archaeology*, B. J. Little, ed., 39–53. Bacon Raton, FL: CRC Press.

Hamilton, D. L. 2000. Port Royal Project. Available online at http://nautarch.tamu.edu/portroyal/ (accessed May 21, 2008).

Hamilton, D. L., and R. Woodward. 1984. A sunken 17th-century city: Port Royal, Jamaica. *Archaeology* 37(1):38–45.

Link, M. C. 1960. Exploring the drowned City of Port Royal. *National Geographic* 117(2):151–82.

Marx, R. F. 1973. *Port Royal Rediscovered.* New York: Doubleday.

Mayes, P. 1972. *Port Royal, Jamaica: Excavations 1969–70.* Kingston: National Heritage Trust.

Millás, J. C. 1968. *Hurricanes of the Caribbean and Adjacent Regions, 1492–1800.* Miami: Academy of the Arts and Sciences of the Americas.

Oldmixon, J. 1969. *The British Empire in America.* New York: Augustus M. Kelley-Publishers.

Pawson, M., and D. Buisseret. 2000. *Port Royal, Jamaica.* Kingston: The University of the West Indies Press.

Port Royal Development Co. Ltd. 1998. Port Royal Development Concept. Available online at www.portroyal-jamaica.com (accessed June 27, 2004).

Priddy, A. 1975. The 17th and 18th century settlement pattern of Port Royal. *Jamaica Journal* 9(2 & 3):8–10.

Schofield, J. 1988. Port Royal Archaeological Project, Third Report, 1988. Archaeological report submitted to the Jamaica National Heritage Trust, Kingston.

Taylor, J. 1688. Unpublished 1688 manuscript held by the National Library of Jamaica, Kingston.

CHAPTER 17

Preservation of Waterlogged Archaeological Glass Using Polymers

C. Wayne Smith

CHALLENGES FOR CONSERVATION

Mandates for the displaying and curating organic material culture and advances in archaeologically based material science studies are placing new demands on the preservation of organic artifacts. In response, organic polymer preservation techniques have been developed and implemented to meet the changing needs of museums and educational institutions. This chapter primarily addresses the preservation of artifacts from nautical excavations of the 17th-century site of Port Royal, Jamaica, but the results have important implications for maritime archaeology in other areas of the world.

Glass bottles from England and other European countries, the Tupperware of their day, were plentiful in 17th-century Port Royal, Jamaica. Generally, these green glass vessels were quite bulbous or globular in body style. Archaeological evidence suggests that they were used for storing water, wine, lamp oils, and many other liquids. Typically, most of the bottles recovered from underwater excavations at Port Royal are fragmented because of advanced deterioration and depositional disturbances. Usually, neck fragments are recovered as whole pieces, whereas the more fragile, thin-walled bodies of these vessels do not survive intact. Because this poor-quality glass tends to deteriorate leaving flaky, layered dead glass (which spalls or exfoliates, much like the layers of an onion when air dried), these bottles are often called onion bottles.

Long-term stabilization of waterlogged glass from Port Royal, Jamaica has been a problem. Because of the lack of controlled-environmental curation, many of the bottles preserved using conventional polyvinyl acetate (PVAC) treatments have been irreparably damaged because of the ever-increasing chemical instability of the glass over time, resulting in exfoliation of surface layers of glass. Experimentation aimed at developing conservation strategies to preserve this important assemblage of 17th-century material culture from the Caribbean has generated new conservation strategies that are now being applied to the preservation of waterlogged glass from other significant sites around the world. This research has also generated new questions regarding chemical reactivity and the potential of polymers for the preservation of archaeological materials. Because of the absence of controlled-environmental storage, we know that using PVAC polymer processes to treat glass and other materials is ineffective for the long-term stabilization of the Port Royal glass assemblage. As always, necessity is a prime motivator for change.

Although PVAC is considered to be a stable consolidant that is resistant to yellowing, it has a low glass transition temperature (T_g, 28^0C) and is prone to cold flow, a dimensional change of the material over time from continuous load or pressure (Bettembourg 1976). Additionally, dust and dirt tend to accumulate on the surfaces and deep crevices of glass treated with PVAC (Errett, Flynn, and Brill 1984). Both of these factors appear to affect the Port Royal glass assemblage. Over time, bottles exposed to ranges in temperature, humidity, and exposure to ultraviolet light have developed thick layers of oxidation on their surfaces. The joints between fragments become weak and often disintegrate. In other cases, outer surfaces of the bottles have exfoliated, resulting in the loss of diagnostic attributes.

One interesting avenue of research has been the use of aminopropyltrimethoxysilane, a common silane coupling agent, which has been used to facilitate bonding of two pieces of glass (when epoxy systems are used as adhesives to repair broken artifacts). Coupling agents improve the adhesion of polymers to glass (Geuskens, Borsu, and David 1972; Horie 1987; Newton and Davison 1989). Because of its ability to retain strong silicon-carbon (Si-C) bonds, we have included methyltrimethoxysilane (MTMS) along with other polymers in an experiment to determine which viscosities (centistokes) of polymers best preserve archaeological glass. MTMS is a trifunctional monomer that is resistant to solvents and photo-oxidation (Torraca 1968). When used as a pretreatment to the edges of glass fragments being repaired with an adhesive, silane groups in the monomers act to reduce absorption of water into the adhesive joint, resulting in a longer lasting bond with better adhesion qualities. This means that the junction of the repaired pieces of glass is less prone to absorption of atmospheric moisture than the glass surrounding the site of repair. It is the ability of silane to form strong Si-C bonds that reduce moisture absorption that makes it potentially beneficial for the stabilization of archaeological glass.

PREVIOUS RESEARCH

Since 1997, several experiments have been conducted at the Texas A&M University Archaeological Preservation Research Laboratory, College Station, to evaluate the ability of selected short-chain, silanol-ended polydimethyl siloxane polymers to conserve similarly sized shards of devitrified glass (Smith 2003:103–08). Acetone/polymer displacement was the mechanism used to introduce polymers into the glass shards. This is a commonly applied process using the rate of evaporation of acetone, at either a reduced or ambient pressure, to displace acetone with a polymer solution. Catalyzation of the polymer-impregnated glass was accomplished using vapor deposition of a tin-based catalyst. Treated samples were then subjected to accelerated weathering tests to determine each polymer's ability to protect the glass from environmental damage.

Prior to treatment, scanning electron microscopic (SEM) analysis and neutron activation analysis were conducted on a small fragment of a nearly complete onion bottle. Microscopy revealed that, in the case of our onion bottle, there is a distinct outer layer or crust. This layer consists of heavily oxidized "dead glass." The inner surface of the weathered crust, closely associated with the solid surface of the bottle, contained low proportions of calcium and high readings of magnesium and silica. The inner core of glass contained higher proportions of calcium. This variability is the result of absorption of magnesium from seabed sediments and the consequent leaching of calcium from the core of the glass outward to the surface of the vessel. The greatest area of chemical exchange appears to be between the inner edge of the weathering crust and the outer surface of the inner glass core. Silica content in the crust is higher than the silica content detected in the core glass (Table 17.1).

Energy dispersive spectroscopy, conducted during SEM analysis of the surface of the Port Royal glass specimens, indicates that the surfaces consist of a thick crust of oxidized glass, soluble and insoluble salts, and concreted materials. This crust is hydrophilic and contains amorphous silica compounds. The core of the glass is highly hydrated, resulting in a complex matrix that is difficult to stabilize.

The general instability of the Port Royal onion bottles conserved in the past may, in part, be attributed to the viscosity of PVAC V25 and its inability to bond effectively with glass. Inspection of several bottles indicates that the consolidant may have only partially penetrated the outer surface of the glass. Because the consolidant did not form an effective barrier on the surface of the core glass, it did not act as an

Table 17.1 Sample locations and elements in parts per million (ppm).

ppm-Element	Na	Mg	Al	Si	K	Ca	Fe	Cl
Sample Location								
Crust								
Outer Edge	.46	3.12	4.32	68.98	5.44	9.45	2.91	2.17
Inner Edge	.48	4.77	1.91	72.53	4.07	6.17	7.33	1.27
Glass Core								
Outer Core	.62	1.41	.90	53.10	7.73	30.69	3.64	.76
Inner Core	.49	1.19	.70	51.88	8.21	31.67	3.12	.89

effective adhesive between layers of flaking glass. Vinyl polymers, like PVAC, have a refractive index similar to glass and remain generally stable. Accordingly, many conservators prefer to use vinyl polymers for conserving waterlogged glass. Although lower molecular weight solutions of PVAC are resistant to yellowing, they are prone to cold flow.

CONSERVATION OF PORT ROYAL GLASS

Chemical analysis of the Port Royal assemblage indicates that the surfaces of the glass samples generally have a thick exterior crust consisting of oxidized glass, soluble and insoluble salts, and concretion from close association with other artifacts. The surface crust of the glass is hydrophilic, consisting of amorphous silica compounds, whereas the core of the glass is highly hydrated. The resulting complex matrix is difficult to stabilize. Viscous materials, such as PVAC V25, do not penetrate easily into the solid core of glass, resulting in a superficial skin that is prone to spalling (Figure 17.1). Lower viscosity consolidants may penetrate throughout the matrix of the glass, but fail to act as an adhesive between the crust and core, resulting in poor consolidation.

To successfully conserve waterlogged glass with silicone oils, water within its matrix must be displaced using a series of alcohol-acetone baths. Acetone is then replaced by a hydroxyl-ended, functional polymer mixed with a cross linking agent. To facilitate displacement of acetone with polymer, each sample was placed into a vacuum chamber. At reduced pressure, the boiling point of acetone is lowered; the acetone is rapidly vaporized and driven from the glass. Rapid solvent vaporization allows the polymer/cross linker solution to permeate the matrix of the glass more easily.

Figure 17.1 Exfoliating surface layers on a Port Royal onion bottle preserved with PVAC V25 (photograph by Wayne Smith).

Through experience, we have found that PR-10, a low viscosity, hydroxyl-ended polymer, measuring less than 30 centistokes, is an ideal bulking agent for waterlogged Port Royal glass. To a sufficient volume of PR-10 (into which a complete onion bottle can be immersed), a 5% addition of MTMS was added (by weight). MTMS or CR-20 cross linker is a hydrolysable, multifunctional alkoxysilane, capable of tying two or more polymer chains together. DBTDA catalyst, also known as dibutyltin diacetate (DBTDA), was then applied to the artifact using vapor deposition.

EXPERIMENTATION

Prior to treatment, artifact PR87 244-5 onion bottle was stored in fresh water. Before treatment, the bottle was rinsed additionally in a series of ten baths of deionized water to remove any remaining soluble salts. Each bath was exchanged for fresh deionized water after twenty-four hours. The artifact was then placed into 1 l of fresh, industrial-grade acetone. Immersed in the solvent, the artifact was placed into a vacuum chamber and a reduced pressure of 5333.33 Pa (40 Torr) was applied for six hours at room temperature. Cessation of rapid bubbling from the artifact was used as a visual indicator that free-flowing water and air had been displaced by acetone during dehydration of all the shards. After dehydration, the bottle was then immersed in a solution of PR-10 with 5% MTMS added by weight, and a vacuum of 40 Torr was applied again for six hours. After bulking in a reduced pressure environment, the bottle was left in the solution at ambient pressure for an additional twenty-four hours.

Following the acetone/silicone oil displacement step, the bottle was removed from the polymer solution and placed on an aluminium screen to allow any free-flowing solution to drain from its surfaces for approximately three hours. With the surface nearly dry to touch, all that remained before the catalyzation step was to gently remove polymer observed to be pooling on the surfaces of the glass by using gauze wetted with a few drops of MTMS. An important issue to be emphasized at this point is that after acetone/polymer solution displacement is completed, the artifact should be quite stable. Accordingly, there is no need to rush to the catalyzation stage. It is better to surface clean the glass, making it aesthetically correct, before applying a catalyst.

For the purpose of vapor deposition, a plastic 1-pint container with tight-fitting lid was ideal. The lid and body of the container were placed in an inverted position so that the lid formed the flat base of a containment chamber. A 40 g capacity aluminium dish was placed in the center of the base of the unit. Fifteen grams of DBTDA catalyst were placed in this dish. A section of aluminium mesh was placed over the dish to form a platform on which a shard of glass could be placed during catalyzation. Several thicknesses of paper towel were placed on the screen to absorb any free-flowing silicone oils. With the bottle positioned on the screen and paper towel, the body of the container was placed over the lid and, with firm pressure, snapped into place. A small hole was made in the upper surface of each chamber to prevent pressurization during the catalyzation process (Figure 17.2). The containment chamber was placed into a vented warming oven and exposed to a constant temperature of 71°C for eighteen hours. Applying heat during catalyzation accelerates vaporization of the DBTDA catalyst. After catalyzation, the bottle was removed from the warming oven and allowed to slowly cool to room temperature inside the containment chamber. The final step in the preservation process is the simplest: Place the artifact on lint-free cloth and allow it to sit in fresh air in a fume hood.

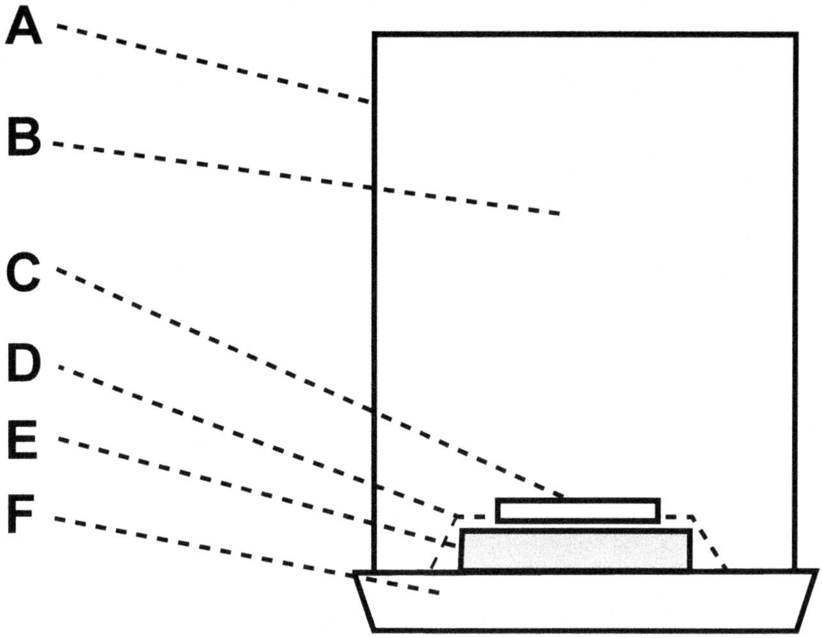

Figure 17.2 Containment chamber configuration: (A) body of chamber, (B) warmed catalyst vapor in close proximity to artifact, (C) glass artifact, (D) aluminium screen and paper towel, (E) 15 g of DBTDA catalyst in aluminium dish, and (F) lid acting as the base of the unit.

An Alternative Method of Catalyzation

Using a small aquarium pump, catalyst vapors can be directed to ensure thorough catalyzation. In the case of long-necked and small-mouthed bottles, use of a directed flow catalyzation is more effective. Figure 17.3 illustrates a directed flow catalyzation configuration that our laboratory has used successfully to treat these types of bottles. Note that although only 2 or 3 g of DBTDA are needed for this process, the catalyst is warmed and therefore more volatile. A temperature-controlled warming glove is ideal for warming DBTDA to an effective temperature of 22°C.

Small Artifacts Treatment Strategy

An alternative method for polymer processing of small objects is total immersion. This technique has been used to successfully preserve glass and faience beads, seeds, and other small artifacts. After dehydration, small artifacts can be placed into a silicone oil/cross linker solution,

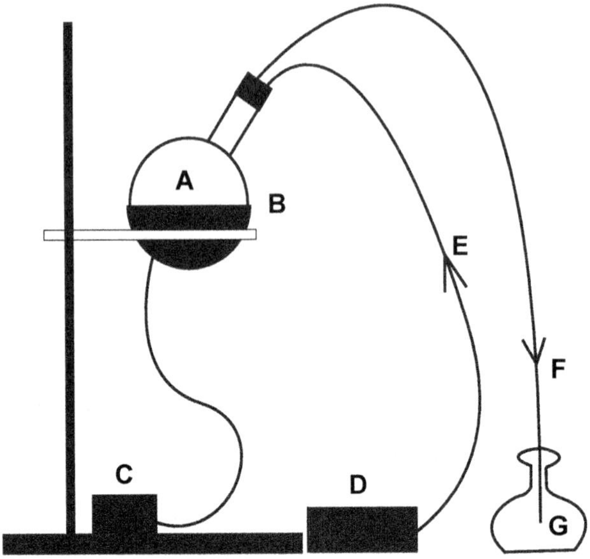

Figure 17.3 A vapor deposition configuration consisting of (A) a beaker containing a few grams of DBTDA, (B) a warming glove heat source, (C) transformer for warming glove, (D) a small aquarium pump, (E) air flow to beaker, (F) forced air with DBTDA catalyst vapors to interior of bottle, and (G) bottle.

consisting of a 5% (by weight) addition of MTMS added to silicone oil. Generally, short-chain polymers ranging from 10 to 100 centistokes are best for the preservation of fragile, badly deteriorated glass. A reduced pressure of no more than 40 Torr is then applied to the beads in solution until the cessation of slow bubbling is noted. In the case of small glass beads, bubbling may continue for several minutes.

Precision tweezers should then be used to remove the artifact from the solution, placing it directly onto a lint-free cloth. After allowing the free-flowing polymer solution to drain from the surfaces of the artifact for one or two minutes, the artifact should then be fully immersed into a second beaker containing DBTDA catalyst. Once immersed, the artifacts should be closely monitored, as chemical reactivity between the DBTDA and the polymer solution will be immediate. After thirty seconds, the artifact should be removed from the DBTDA beaker and placed onto a lint-free cloth. After gently dobbing the surfaces of the artifact with lint-free cloth, reimmerse the artifact in the polymer solution beaker for thirty seconds. The process of alternately immersing the artifact in the polymer solution followed by immersion in the catalyst solution can be repeated several times. However, after the initial stage of reduced pressure treatment to dehydrate the artifact, no further vacuum processing is needed.

To effectively treat a single glass bead or even several beads at one time, the set-up procedure is the same. To prepare beads for treatment with silicone oil, they should be first dehydrated in three baths of acetone. Initial dehydration is conducted at ambient pressure for two days; the second dehydration bath is for two hours. The beads are then transferred into a fresh beaker of acetone and a vacuum (40 Torr) is applied. The third dehydration bath is the same time duration as the second. All of the glass beads are allowed to sit for a period of time in this solution. A short-chain polymer, ranging from 10 to 100 centistokes and mixed with a 5% MTMS cross linker (by weight of silicone oil) was added to create a reactive polymer solution. In a separate beaker, a sufficient volume of DBTDA is poured so that the glass beads can be completely immersed. Wire baskets constructed of aluminium window screen are ideal for batch processing of small artifacts.

Once the acetone/polymer exchange is complete, most artifacts will be stable enough to allow additional cleaning. Excess polymer solution should be allowed to drain from the artifact and, until catalyzation is initiated, additional cleaning and adjustment of the artifact can now be accomplished. For small artifacts, vapor deposition catalyzation is an ideal process for finishing the treatment. Small Ziploc bags are ideal low-cost containment chambers. Simply place the artifact into a Ziploc bag along with a small aluminium dish containing a few grams of DBTDA. At room temperature, it may be necessary to continue the catalyzation process for two or three days, as after approximately eighteen to twenty-four hours the catalyst in the tray oxidizes and becomes inactive. Accordingly, it is necessary to replace the catalyst daily until the catalyzation process is complete. Caution must always be taken to ensure that the catalyst does not come into direct contact with the artifact. Areas of an artifact that have come into direct contact with DBTDA may require surface cleaning since they may have a thicker area of polymer deposition. Lint-free soft cloths worked around Q-tips dipped in MTMS are useful for posttreatment cleaning of pooled polymers from the surfaces of an artifact.

During the catalyzation process, it is common to note small, white specks on the surfaces of the artifact. During the catalyzation process, small amounts of catalyst vapors may concentrate in areas that have not been adequately surface cleaned. As polymerization occurs, these areas will appear white because of the heavier concentration of polymer in that area. A small amount of MTMS applied using a Q-tip or soft cotton swab will gently remove the excess polymer from the surface of the artifact.

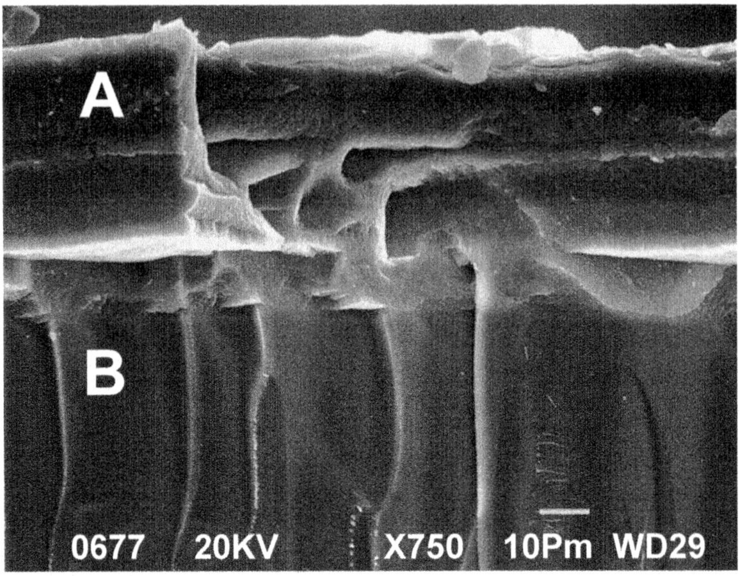

Figure 17.4 Cross-section microscopic view of conserved onion bottle glass, showing complex surface layers: (A) surface layer (barrier) of silicone oil and (B) surface layer of bottle (photograph by Wayne Smith).

SEM analysis of samples of Port Royal glass conserved using the same polymer solution clearly show that a complex barrier coat had been formed on the surfaces and within the matrix of the glass. This complex barrier is visible in Figure 17.4. Posttreatment chemical analysis of the glass indicates that the PR-10/MTMS polymer solution has permeated deeply into the voids of the glass, forming an effective barrier that is chemically bonded to the glass.

Accelerated Weathering Tests

Accelerated weathering testing has been conducted on Port Royal glass using a Q-Panel, Q-U-V Accelerated Weathering Tester. Weathering cycles consisting of alternating six hour cycles of high humidity (95%) and high temperature (45°C) with a UVA light, followed by six hours at lower humidity (60%) and a lower temperature (20°C) with no light exposure were used to "age" the artifacts.

CONCLUSIONS

Independent testing and computer modeling of the accelerated weathering process concluded that glass treated with a short-chain, hydroxyl-ended polymer/methyltrimethoxysilane solution followed by immersion catalyzation appears to be stabilized for a predicted period of 250 years (minimum). Based on this small sample group, it is impossible to predict accurately how long polymer-treated glass will remain stable. However, after ten years of curation in the noncontrolled environment of a classroom, the treated glass bottles and beads have not altered in appearance, weight, or physical size.

From past experimentation, a direct correlation between polymer chain length, penetration into voids, and the ability to create a protective barrier against oxidation and environmental exposure has been noted. Glass onion bottles recovered from the Port Royal site, still prone to exfoliation even after treatment with traditionally used PVAC solutions, have been successfully treated and conserved using polymer stabilization. Additionally, for small glass beads, the total immersion process appears to work well. Ancient beads from the Bronze Age Uluburun shipwreck and small colored glass beads from La Salle's 17th-century vessel, *La Belle*, have all been successfully treated using total immersion processing. To date, thousands of polymer-treated glass beads from the *La Belle* assemblage are on display in the Bob Bullock Texas State History Museum in Austin, Texas. These, and hundreds of other artifacts conserved using polymer processes, have remained stable in the museum environment six years after treatment.

Numerous artifacts excavated from terrestrial sites have also been preserved using polymer processes. Indeed, treatment of these artifacts is often easily accomplished as stages of dehydration are not needed before treatment. In many cases, artifacts need only be surface cleaned before a topical application of PR-10 polymer with 3% (by weight) CR-20 cross linker is applied. A catalyst can then be applied topically or as a vapor in a closed environment.

Polymer treatments are also beneficial for stabilizing fragile, friable material culture. In the study entitled "Preservation of a Composite Artifact Containing Basketry and Iron Shot" (Smith 2003:74–80), polymers used to consolidate fragile basketry also coated numerous iron shot. After being excavated from the basket, the polymer-coated shots were subsequently treated using electrolytic reduction. Pretreatment using polymers affected the treatment time in electrolytic reduction, but after treatment the surfaces of the iron shot were less pitted and aesthetically pleasing than shot that had not been topically treated with polymers.

Conservators might benefit from the use of polymers in conjunction with more traditional conservation strategies. Conservators at the Conservation Research Laboratory at Texas A&M University routinely combine conservation technologies to address the needs of each artifact. This is an important aspect of research at the university.

ACKNOWLEDGMENTS

Funding from the National Center for Preservation Technology and Training, 645 University Parkway, Matchitoches, LA 71457, made this research possible. I also thank Dow Corning Corporation for assistance in conducting accelerated weathering experiments and for their support of research at the Archaeological Preservation Research Laboratory, Texas A&M University.

REFERENCES

Bettembourg, J. M. 1976. Protection des verres de vitraux contre les agents atmosphériques. Etudes des films de résines synthétiques. *Verres et Réfract* 30(6):87-91.

Errett, R., M. Flynn, and R. Brill. 1984. The use of silanes on glass, adhesives and consolidants. Proceedings of the 10th International Institute for Conservation of Historic and Artistic Works Congress, Paris. Paris: ICOM.

Geuskens, G., M. Borsu, and C. David. 1972. Photolysis and radiolysis of polyvinylacetate-III: Effects of temperature on the photolysis. *European Polymer Journal* 8(22):1347-53.

Horie, C. V. 1987. *Materials for Conservation: Organic Consolidants, Adhesives and Coatings*. Boston: Butterworths.

Newton, R., and S. Davison. 1989. *Conservation of Glass*. London: Butterworths.

Smith, C. W. 2003. *Archaeological Conservation Using Polymers*. Anthropology Series. College Station: Texas A&M University Press.

Torraca, G. 1968. *Synthetic Materials Used in the Conservation of Cultural Property*. Paris: UNESCO.

CHAPTER 18

Development of Maritime Archaeological Tourism Using the Wreck of the English SS *Mediator* in Curaçao

Wil Nagelkerken, Theo van der Giessen,
Raymond Hayes, and Dennis Knepper

INTRODUCTION

During the last decade, more and more countries have begun to express concern about the need to preserve, protect, and conserve their underwater cultural heritage in their coastal seas, rivers, and inland lakes. Conservation projects applying *in situ* preservation of submerged resources is not always possible because of demands for harbor development, attempts at salvage by professional groups or individuals, traffic from oil tankers, assorted types of cargo ships and cruise ships, or hazards of navigating narrow and confined spaces in poor weather conditions. Nonetheless, such historical remains are in peril and, if not protected, are rapidly damaged and eventually disappear without public awareness.

Other options to *in situ* preservation are excavation, raising the remains, and land-based conservation. This has been the choice for the *Vasa* (Sweden), the *Mary Rose* (England), the *De Braak* (Delaware, the United States), the *La Belle* (Texas, the United States), the *Hunley* (South Carolina, the United States), and, in part, the *Monitor* (Virginia, the United States). In each of these cases, the intent has been to prepare the ship for long-term display as part of a maritime museum or as a dedicated exposition.

In some instances, it is impractical or technically impossible to remove a historical wreckage from its original location. When left *in situ*, slow disintegration still results from the addition or removal of sediment, as described from the HMS *Pandora* wreck site on the Great Barrier Reef (Ward, Larcombe, and Veth 1998; Ward et al. 1999). Also, electrolytic degradation of metals occurs, as documented for the SS *Xantho* off Western Australia (McCarthy 2000). Faced with these realities, a submerged wreck should be protected from additional stresses and efforts should be made to retard the full impact of disintegrative processes, when feasible.The emergence of heritage tourism as an endpoint for underwater archaeological stewardship has enabled an *in situ* preserved submerged shipwreck to become an opportunity for public education and understanding about maritime history, in particular, and underwater archaeology, in general. Both visitors and local residents, especially the young, can then learn about the past through preserved sites and the associated events of the past.

Through visitation of submerged sites, trained divers can also become a part of this experience resulting in a rich and meaningful cultural heritage exposure. This option has been developed in Palau in relation to the ships and aircraft left behind after World War II. An underwater park containing these military vessels has become a popular dive destination for tourist divers visiting the area who become acquainted with the natural and cultural resources of these Pacific islands.

In the Netherlands Antilles, a significant effort toward heritage tourism has been initiated by the STIMANA (Stichting Mariene Archeologie Nederlandse Antillen), which is protecting the submerged remains of a ship that sank in the harbor entrance of Willemstad, Curaçao, in 1884. The English steamship *Mediator*, of the Harrison Line from Liverpool, sank after collision with a German ship. She exceeds 91.44 m (300 ft) in length and now lies 18.29 m (60 ft) below the surface. Because the *Mediator* was beyond any conceivable likelihood of being raised, either in part or in its entirety, the decision by the island territory of Curaçao was to preserve her *in situ* and at the same time to stimulate the local economy. This decision has provided a unique wreck site in the harbor, which can be used for diving, combined with a museum display of artifacts. The *Mediator* represents an addition to the history of trans-Atlantic maritime trading on the island and is an example of how maritime archaeology can be applied in a small island nation of the Caribbean region.

HISTORICAL BACKGROUND

From 1634–1791, the West Indies Company operated as a commercial enterprise, conducting trade in America and Africa with rights from the Dutch State to govern and defend occupied bases in the New World. During that period, Willemstad developed as a major trading center. The Handelskade was the entryway into the natural deep water harbor of Willemstad and the principal mooring site for ships visiting that harbor. Buildings were erected around the harbor entrance. The walled Fort Amsterdam, containing government offices and public servant residences, was built on one bank of the harbor entrance, and a fortress was constructed on the other side. Outside the walled fort were the dwellings and warehouses of those residents engaging in trade. A protected bay, the Schottegat, extending from the Handelskade, provided a natural safe haven from hostility and storms (Figure 18.1).

For centuries, the harbor has been a source of prosperity for Curaçao. Because of its geographical location, the island provides an excellent transfer site, or entrepôt, for goods from Europe, Africa, and North America destined for distribution to the Caribbean, Central America, and South America. Trading through Curaçao meant that ships were constantly arriving and leaving the harbor. Off-loaded goods were transported daily by small vessels to shallow harbors at other islands or on the northern coast of South America.

With the advent of the ocean-going steamships in the 19th century, offices and warehouses were established along the shore of the Handelskade for commercial enterprises. The Koninklijke West Indische Mail Dienst (KWIM) was formed in 1882 to provide a steamship connection

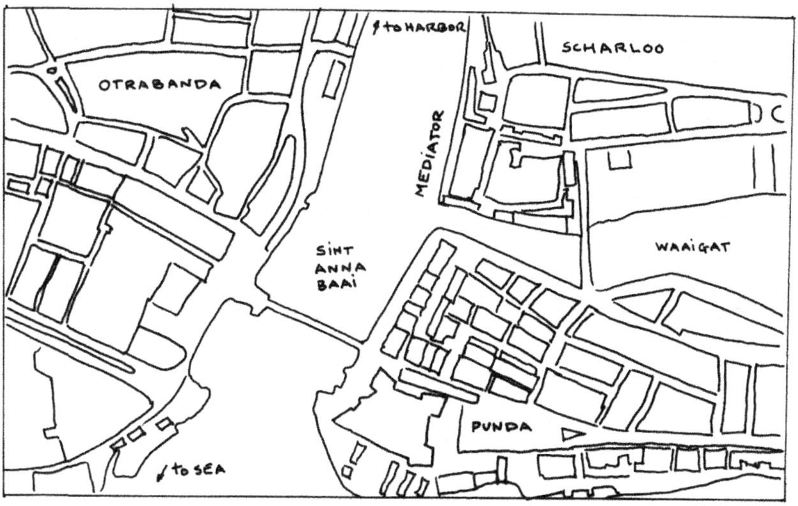

Figure 18.1 The modern entry channel to Willemstad harbor. The SS *Mediator* site lies parallel to the small wharf quay in Scharloo along St. Anna Bay. The Waaigat channel extends to the right from the main harbor entry.

between Curaçao and the Netherlands. The first ship of the KWIM, the *Orange Nassau*, arrived in Curaçao on April 23, 1884.

Steamships arriving at the harbor usually docked at the Handelskade, the site of the warehouses for transfer of goods. However, according to an official communication in 1885, there was room for only one steamship at a time at that site. Therefore, when a steamer arrived, it had to be unloaded quickly, not only to assure prompt delivery, but also to make room for other incoming vessels. If docking space was not available when a ship arrived, anchorage was provided at the Kleine Werf (small wharf). From there, off-loaded cargo was transferred to small wooden boats or "ponchis" that tied up directly to the ships. The ponchis carried the cargo to the Handelskade warehouses or to other vessels.

In 1884, several shipping lines made regular stops at the Kleine Werf. They were the Nederlandse KWIM Dienst, the American Red D Line, the German Hamburg America Line, the Dutch Holland America Line, Ltd., and the English Harrison Line. The J & R Harrison Line, Ltd. was a major commercial trader in this trans-Atlantic traffic (Hyde 1967). Harrison Line ships sailed from its home port of Liverpool, England, to the southeastern Caribbean. One of the ships of that line was the steamship, *Mediator*, built in 1872 by R & J Evans of Liverpool (Figure 18.2). All ships in the Harrison fleet were named after vocations. They included *Author, Architect, Chancellor, Commander, Discoverer, Engineer, Editor, Governor, Historian, Inventor, Legislator, Mariner, Merchant, Orator, Professor, Statesman,* and *Warrior.*

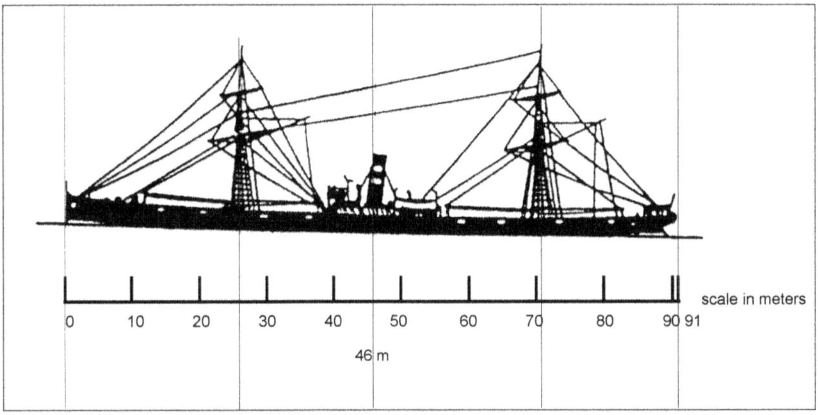

Figure 18.2 The only known representation of the SS *Mediator*. This silhouette profile is displayed over a metric scale to localize the excavation points at 26, 46, and 70 m (courtesy of the T & J Harrison Line, Ltd., of Liverpool, England).

The *Mediator* departed Liverpool for her trans-Atlantic crossing under Captain R. Ellis on June 14, 1884. She stopped in Barbados on June 30 and in Trinidad on July 1. She made two stops in Venezuela at Porto Guaira and Porto Cabella. During these three stops, she off-loaded 333 tons of cargo from her original load of 1,158 tons. She arrived at the Handelskade early in the morning of July 5, 1884 and moored at the Kleine Werf. Soon thereafter, before off-loading was complete, another steamship, the *Thuringa* of the Holland America Line, entered the harbor, was swept off course, and collided with the *Mediator*. A gash in the starboard hull of the *Mediator* opened up below the water line, and she began to take on water rapidly. According to eyewitness reports in the local newspaper, there was only time for those on board the *Mediator* to abandon ship during those crucial few minutes. She sank with a residual cargo of more than 750 tons of "fine goods" still aboard. Although some parcels floated off and minimal salvage efforts were attempted by hearty swimmers, the cargo holds of the steamship were unreachable.

For over a century, the *Mediator* lay undisturbed and unrecognized because of the accumulation of coral sand, old tires, and assorted harbor debris. The remains of the *Mediator* were discovered in 1986, lying upright at a depth of 20 m. Since then, plans have been underway to map the site, to clear it of overburden, to protect it from unnecessary damage due to ship traffic in the harbor entrance, and to develop an *in situ* preservation and utilization plan for the site (Nagelkerken, Hayes, and Knepper 2003).

It is now evident that the *Mediator* site represents an excellent potential model for public education about maritime history and underwater archaeology. *In situ* preservation was chosen as an effective and economical way to capture the educational and historical value of this steel-hulled, steam-powered ship. The *Mediator* has now stabilized in its submerged location, does not appear to be threatened by rapid degradation, and is not an obstacle to navigation.

ARCHIVAL RESEARCH

The local newspaper for the region, the *Curaçaosche Courant* is a major source for information about the wreck site of the *Mediator*. Old issues are available on microfilm in the National Archives of the Netherlands Antilles in Willemstad. In the issue published on July 6, 1884, a first-hand account of the collision between the *Mediator* and the German freighter *Thuringa* of the Holland America Line and the subsequent sinking of the *Mediator* is provided. This report was filed by Curaçaoan witnesses in the harbor when the event occurred.

UNDERWATER ARCHAEOLOGY

During multiple visits between 1997 and 2003, teams of trained and experienced underwater archaeological volunteers from the Maritime Archaeological and Historical Society (MAHS) participated in an archaeological project at the *Mediator* site. The senior underwater archaeologist from the Archaeological and Anthropological Institute of the Netherlands Antilles, Dr. Wil Nagelkerken, invited MAHS to assist with surveying and mapping the site. This activity has led to several reports with results of trilateration, photo documentation, and sketching

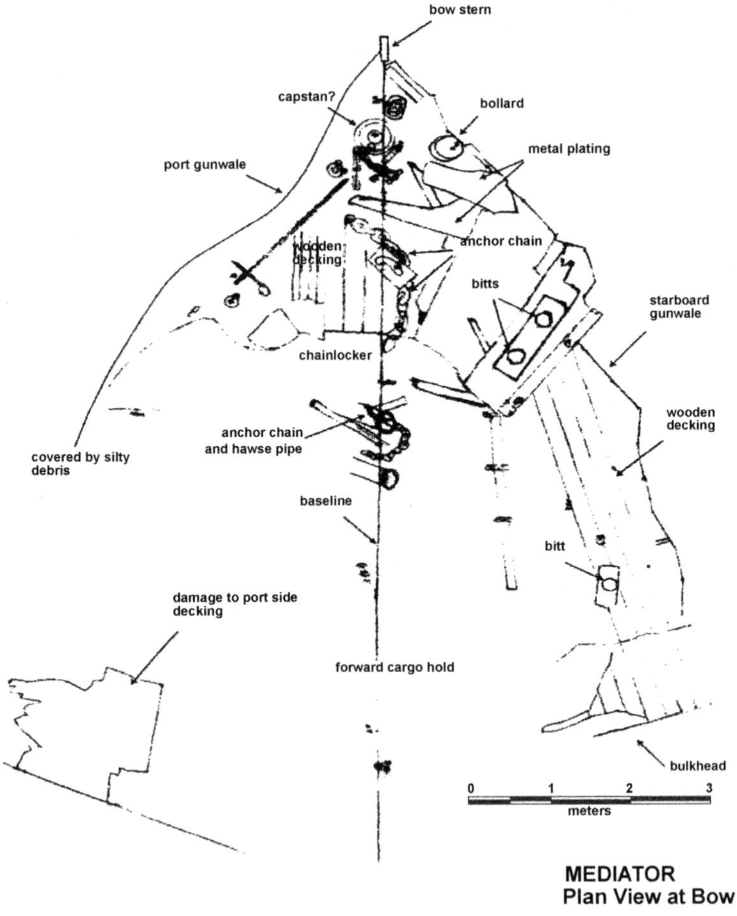

Figure 18.3 Scaled survey map of the forward deck of the SS *Mediator* generated from trilateration data supplied by volunteers from the Maritime Archaeological and Historical Society (MAHS).

surveys made on the vessel (Figure 18.3). These efforts were conducted while excavations were underway to remove considerable overburden on the vessel using a compressor-driven airlift.

MUSEUM DISPLAY AND SITE VISITS

Plans have been assembled and presented to the government to fund the first of several two-year project proposals to develop the *Mediator* as a heritage tourism site. Eventually, this submerged site, the adjacent shore, and the museum will become a maritime quarter. The proposal includes the creation of historical information and case displays about the *Mediator* in the Curaçao Maritime Museum. The proposal also includes the development of a facility to support diving on the underwater site as archaeological efforts are in progress. The museum is within walking distance from the point of entry to the underwater site.

Information about the *Mediator* will include videotaped views of the wreck, maps locating the site, and an explanation of the archaeological efforts applied to preserve the site. A limited display of artifacts found at the *Mediator* site has already been organized and formally inaugurated in the museum exhibition area. Included in that display are coal, glass and ceramic bottles, dinnerware, brass fittings, and ships' fasteners dating from the late 19th century that were found within the hull and beneath the decking of the ship. These artifacts provide clues to shipboard life and the ship's construction, operation, and cargo.

Local and tourist divers will be offered access to the underwater site and will be guided to and around the wreck by trained personnel. Submersible site maps will be provided to indicate features and to orient the divers to the parts of the ship. A quayside dive facility will be constructed to facilitate access to the archaeological site. Because the site, the dive facility, and the museum are near each other, a tour package that transitions from orientation and education at the museum display, to outfitting, dressing and water entry, to a guided dive on the submerged site is easily accomplished (Figure 18.4). This entire experience may be completed in a morning or afternoon excursion from a hotel or residence in Willemstad. Parking and refreshments will be available in the plaza. Other attractions will be added to the area, such as a floating sailing ship replica, the *Negrita*. The overall plan is to provide the visitor a truly comprehensive maritime experience while visiting this section of town.

The SS *Mediator* site lies adjacent to the main shipping channel for the harbor entrance and it is therefore off-limits to divers, fishermen, and salvors. Access to the quay is controlled by the Curaçao Port Authority (CPA) that supervises activities in the harbor area. Exclusive permission to access the site for archaeological purposes has been granted to

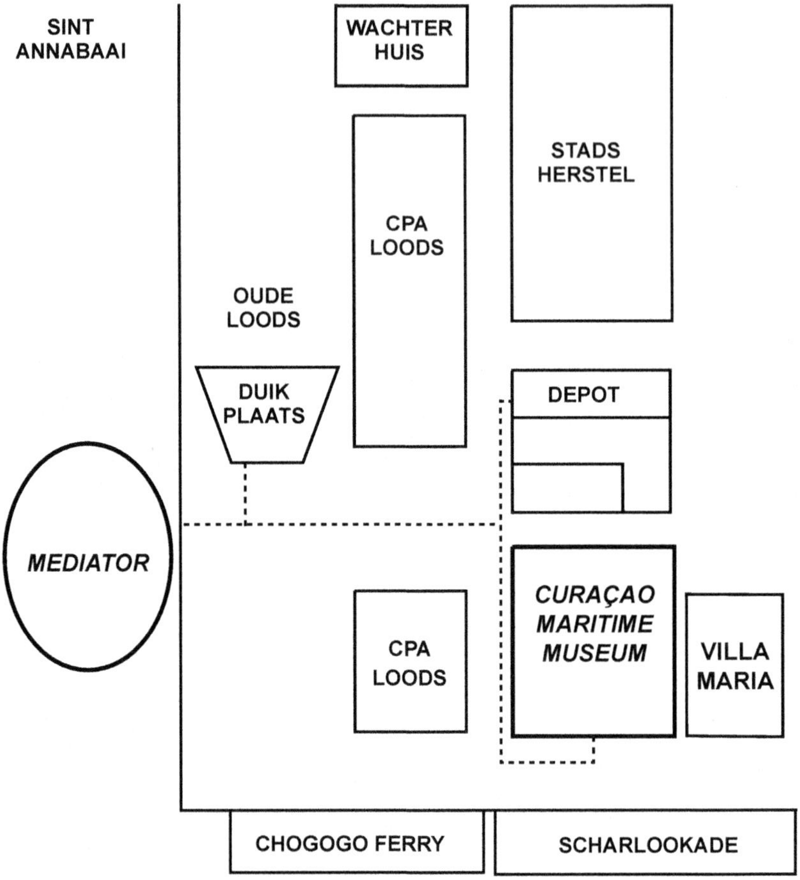

Figure 18.4 The plan for maritime archaeological tourism along the Kleine Werf in Scharloo. The Curaçao Maritime Museum is to the lower right, and the SS *Mediator* site is to the far left. A quayside Dive Pavilion (*duik plaats*) will be for outfitting and orienting divers and controlling site entry and exit. Other attractions being considered for addition to the maritime quarter are a restaurant (Villa Maria), warehouses (CPA *loods*), an office building (*Stads Herstel*), and an open plaza (*oude loods*). A ferry boat that offers harbor tours docks at the entrance to the Waaigat (Chogogo Ferry).

STIMANA. Twenty-four-hour security is assured by the presence of a gated and guarded dockside entry maintained by CPA. These controls have prevented destruction of the site. Preservation will be sustained through regulation of access and the use of guides during exposure of the site to others.

Previous studies of iron steamships have provided important contributions to our understanding of the maritime technology of the period of transition from sail to steam (Souza 1998). The degradation and stabilization of iron wrecks, as well as the detailed examination of the steam engines used to power these ships, are also issues of great importance (McCarthy 2000). The *Mediator* offers the appeal of contributing significantly to our historical understanding and to our marine technological understanding of the late 19th century. Furthermore, the *Mediator* holds in its as yet unexamined cargo a revelation of trading preferences for goods transferred from Europe to the Americas. The archaeological efforts underway at this site will eventually reveal, through controlled scientific analysis, a time capsule of that mercantile activity.

The general focus of the SS *Mediator* site project is undoubtedly to be public education. Maritime history, mercantile trade, Antillean cultural heritage, and underwater archaeology will be presented in the tour. That exposure will include a discussion of the importance of preserving submerged cultural resources on a global scale for the common good and a review of the long-term historical significance of the natural harbor of Curaçao. For those qualified and interested SCUBA divers, the MAHS video course, "Diving into History: An Introductory Course in Underwater Archaeology," will be available for administration through Uniek Curaçao. Archaeological training for local divers is expected to generate dive guides and volunteers for assistance on the *Mediator* project and on other projects in the Netherlands Antilles that are supervised by STIMANA. In the rear of the museum, along with STIMANA offices, there will be an archaeological conservation laboratory for public visualization of work in progress.

CONCLUSIONS

As a contribution to archaeological tourism, the SS *Mediator* symbolizes a very important phase in development of trans-Atlantic maritime trade from England into the Caribbean and American regions during the late 19th century. As such, it is not only worthy of preservation, but also a significant attraction for tourism and an influential adjunct to conservation activities and displays at the Curaçao Maritime Museum. *In situ* preservation is considered the most effective way to capture the educational and historical value of this steamship. The development of the *Mediator* site is expected to promote an interest in Caribbean maritime history and underwater archaeology for visitors and residents of Curaçao, Netherlands Antilles.

ACKNOWLEDGMENTS

The authors gratefully acknowledge the Curaçao Port Authority for technical and supply support of research activities and American Airlines as the sole travel sponsor for volunteers from the MAHS.

REFERENCES

Hyde, F. E. 1967. *Shipping Enterprise and Management, 1830–1939: Harrison's of London.* London: Liverpool University Press.

McCarthy, M. 2000. *Iron and Steamship Archaeology: Success and Failure on the* SS Xantho. New York: Kluwer Academic/Plenum Press.

Nagelkerken, W., R. Hayes, and D. Knepper. 2003. The 19th century trans-Atlantic shipping trade into the Caribbean as represented through maritime archaeology of the English Steamship *Mediator* in Curaçao, Netherlands Antilles. Proceedings of the Society for Historical Archaeology (abstract of conference program proceedings for the 36th Annual SHA Conference on Historical and Underwater Archaeology), January 14–19, Providence, Rhode Island.

Souza, D. 1998. *The Persistence of Sail in the Age of Steam, Underwater Archaeological Evidence from the Dry Tortugas.* New York: Kluwer Academic/Plenum Press.

Ward, I., P. Larcombe, R. Brinkman, and C. Carter. 1999. Sedimentary processes and the *Pandora* wreck, Great Barrier Reef, Australia. *Journal Field Archaeology* 26(1):41–53.

Ward, I., P. Larcombe, and P. Veth. 1998. Towards new process-oriented models for describing wreck disintegration: An example using the *Pandora* wreck. *Bulletin Australian Institute Maritime Archaeology* 22:109–14.

CHAPTER 19

The Historical Anchorage of Kralendijk, Bonaire, Netherlands Antilles

Wil Nagelkerken and Raymond Hayes

INTRODUCTION

Historical ship anchorages in natural harbors such as Kingston, Jamaica, and Charlotte Amalie, St. Thomas, U.S. Virgin Islands, offer a wealth of information about local customs and popular utilization of trade goods because of the submerged cultural artifacts they contain. In recent years, we have completed surveys of historical anchorages for Orange Bay, St. Eustatius (Nagelkerken 1985) and Roseau, Dominica (Nagelkerken, Knepper, and Hayes 2004). Based on three surveys conducted in 1987, 1998, and 2000 along the western coast of Bonaire, Netherlands Antilles, the historic anchorages for Kralendijk and Fort Orange have been discovered and described. At the northernmost extreme of this latter historic anchorage, we discovered archaeological evidence of the wreck site for ZM *Sirene*, a Dutch brigantine that was identified on the basis of the location of ballast stones and verified by archival records from the National Archives of the Netherlands. The *Sirene* sank in 1831 during an intense and unexpected hurricane.

Bonaire is one of five islands in the Netherlands Antilles. It is located in the Caribbean Sea just north of Venezuela at approximately 68° W longitude and 12° N latitude. The island is about 288 km^2 of inland area. Bonaire was originally settled by Caiquetio Indians of the Arawak tribe from Venezuela. In 1496, Amerigo Vespucci, the Spanish explorer, claimed the island and Spain held it for the next 140 years. The Spanish imported goats, sheep, and pigs to the island. During that period, most of the Indians were either killed or returned to South America. Since 1634, a succession of European nations has claimed Bonaire. However, the Dutch West Indies Company established headquarters there in 1636 and built Fort Orange at Kralendijk in 1796 (Figure 19.1). Since 1816, the island of Bonaire has been controlled exclusively by the Dutch.

During the 17th and 18th centuries, boats arrived regularly in Bonaire to unload slaves and to pick up salt, dyewood, hardwood, fish, and meat. As a plantation outpost of Curaçao and part of the Netherlands Antilles, Bonaire was valued by the Dutch for the production of animal skins and meat, for the collection of dyewood such as from the Brazil tree, *Haematoxylin brasillete*, and for hardwoods such as *Lignum vitae* and *Guaicum officinale* that were used in ship construction (Hartog 1978).

Anchorage sites for ships in Bonaire were concentrated along the southwestern coast of the island that is protected from prevailing winds. Sailing ships came from Europe, South America, and neighboring islands, especially Curaçao. These ships would anchor offshore and load cargo onto small boats. These small boats were used to transport goods to and

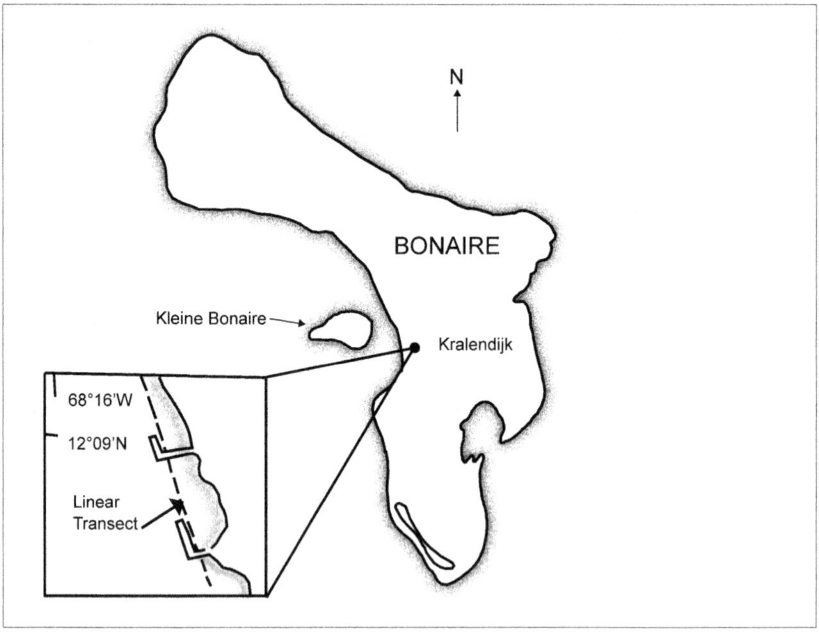

Figure 19.1 A map of Bonaire, Netherlands Antilles. The historical anchorage studied in this project was at Kralendijk, the site of Fort Orange, built by the Dutch in 1796. The insert shows the location of our extended 750 m linear transect that was set parallel to shore for recording the distribution of surface artifacts identified by research divers.

from piers or the beach. The log of William Dampier, an English pirate, describes the major anchorage site of Bonaire in 1681 as follows:

> The harbour is on the southwest side, close to the middle of the island from where it becomes a rather deep bay. The ships, which arrive from the east side, sail close to the east side and lower their anchor at sixty fathoms [140 m] and at half the length of a cable [90–100 m] from shore. But at the same time, they have to be ready to take a rope to shore with a boat and to fasten this on the beach, for otherwise the boat would float out to sea again as soon as at night the wind turns and becomes a land wind, for the ground slopes so sharply toward the sea that no anchor will hold once it starts to slide. (Gray 1927:51)

METHODS

Three successive surveys have been made along the coast of Kralendijk to delimit the extent of the historical anchorage and to identify, as well as determine the frequency of, submerged artifacts at that site. In 1987 and from 1998 to 2000, groups of archaeological divers from the Archaeological and Anthropological Institute of the Netherlands Antilles, the precursor to the foundation Stichting Mariene Archeologie Nederlandse Antillen surveyed this anchorage (Nagelkerken and Hayes 2002). Trained volunteers from the American-based Maritime Archaeological and Historical Society (MAHS) also assisted in this effort (Hayes and Nagelkerken 2002). In this chapter, we summarize our findings from these archaeological surveys.

A running linear baseline was established parallel to the coastline at an approximate depth of 10–15 m. GPS coordinates were recorded for the zero datum point along each 50 m segment of the baseline. A 50 m tape used as the baseline was shifted following each dive so as to stretch continuously as a linear transect for nearly 1,000 m across the site of Fort Orange. The baseline began 600 m to the north of Fort Orange and extended another 300 m to the south. Over 600 exposed artifacts were collected for identification, categorization, and assembly into our database.

ARTIFACT DATABASE

Collected artifacts were classified according to type, vintage, and country of origin. Consumer objects found included glass, stoneware, creamware, pearlware, and whiteware. Wine bottles, gin bottles, and mineral water jugs were all recovered. Delft or tin-glazed ceramics from Holland were also found. Ranked according to their frequency, countries of origin were Holland, England, Germany, France, and Spain, although there may well

Figure 19.2 Bottles from the Bonaire site. To the left is a Dutch wine bottle (onion type), 1725–1750. Height is 19.4 cm and base is 14.1 cm with a deep kickup, a glass pontil, and an overlapping string rim. In the middle is a brown/green Dutch case bottle, 1790–1860. Height is 27.1 cm and base is 6.6 x 6.7 cm, with blunt corners, a deep kickup, wooden mold, iron rod pontil, tapered collar, and irregular shoulder. On the right are two stoneware jugs with enlarged inserts. The top one is a brown French mineral water jug with the inscription "Boissin Fils, Brasserie a Marseille." It is 25.2 cm high with a base of 7.9 cm. The bottom one is a gray Dutch gin jug, made in Germany, with the letters "P, G and Weesp." It is 27.6 cm high and the base is 9.8 cm.

be a difference between the country of production and the country of distribution of these artifacts.

Shifts in consumer demands over time are indicated by the different types of bottles represented in the twelve periods that were identified. Wine bottles reached a peak around 1800, but square bottles peaked at 1825. Mineral water jugs peaked at 1850, beer bottles around 1875, and gin bottles at 1900 (Figure 19.2).

Several clay amphoras from the early Spanish occupation of Bonaire were found (Figure 19.3). Other earthenware predominated in the 18th century. But English ceramics, including creamware, pearlware, and whiteware/ironware, appeared successively with time. In the 19th century, Germany produced stoneware jugs for the Dutch gin factories. Although Germany was the country of origin of these jugs, Holland was the country of distribution to Bonaire.

The Dutch West Indies Company had settled Bonaire as early as 1636, but the earliest Dutch artifacts found date from the first part of the 18th century. These were onion-shaped wine bottles, one from the period 1725–1750 (see Figure 19.2) and the others from the period 1750–1775.

Figure 19.3 Ceramics from the Bonaire site. On the left is an unglazed pot, probably made by local Afro-Caribbean people and of unknown date. It is 11.3 cm high with a base of 6.3 cm and greatest width of 13 cm. In the middle is a Spanish unglazed jar, 1580–1800. It is 30 cm high, 24 cm wide, and the mouth opening is 4 cm. To the right is a Dutch pearlware chamber pot showing a Chinese landscape print inside. On the 14.8 cm base is a maker's mark reading "P(etrus) Regout, 1836, Maastricht" within the ovals and "Miller" outside the ovals.

Most of the 18th-century bottles found were from the first half and last quarter of the century.

The majority of the bottles from the 18th century were for wine. English wine bottles exceeded those from Holland and France. However, this does not necessarily reflect the frequency of anchorage of vessels from these countries because Holland imported English wine and this was carried to Bonaire on Dutch ships. French wine bottles predominated during the first half of the 19th century. Beer bottles were mostly Dutch and English, but 35% were from Venezuela. Square bottles from Holland comprise 14.3% of the total number of artifacts (see Figure 19.2). Seventy-one percent of these were 19th-century products and the remainder were from the 18th century. These square bottles contained gin, the preferred drink for the health of the crew of sailing ships. These bottles were also used for brandy.

Stoneware jugs were used for mineral water and gin. These bottles came to Bonaire from Holland, although the bottles were made in Germany (see Figure 19.2). The mineral water jugs date from 1775 to 1850, and the gin jugs from 1875 to 1950. Most of the gin jugs found in Bonaire were made for the Dutch gin firm of Blankenheym & Nolet.

Tin-glazed ceramic dinnerware dating from the first half of the 18th century and known as "Dutch delft" was found in Bonaire. The delftware probably originated from Holland and England and reached Bonaire via ships from both nations. The use of this earthenware began to decrease around 1760 because of the increasing popularity of English creamware. Pearlware appeared in 1810 (Figure 19.3). The latter was more plentiful in Bonaire: 7% of artifacts were pearlware, compared to 4% that were creamware. After 1820, whiteware and semiporcelain ceramics predominated. Six percent of the artifacts were of these latter types. Also, a few shards of expensive Chinese porcelain that was only used by prosperous individuals were found in Bonaire. Nineteenth-century pharmaceutical and perfume bottles were also found in Bonaire. These were probably produced in Holland, France, and England. Several of these were identifiable because the name of the firm was imprinted in the glass.

WRECK SITE OF ZM *SIRENE*

During the underwater survey of the historical anchorage of Kralendijk, Bonaire, ship remnants believed to be from the Dutch brigantine ZM *Sirene* were discovered (Hayes and Nagelkerken 2002). This ship was lost during the Trinidad-Yucatan hurricane of June 24, 1831. A historical account published in the *Curaçaosche Courant* (July 2, 1831) indicates that around 9:00 A.M., strong winds shifted from NW to SW, causing the ship to capsize and wreck on the shallow reef. In our site survey, ballast stones, one cannon, copper sheathing, scattered copper nails, and ships' fasteners were identified. A segment of wooden hull planking covered by a tar-impregnated, burlap-quality fabric, and nailed copper sheathing was also found. This hull covering characterizes early 19th-century Dutch, English, and French warship construction.

The use of copper sheathing began as a protection against anti-fouling below the waterline of ships and against the action of boring organisms such as the shipworm, *Teredo navalis*, the wood-boring pelecypod mollusc. The ship's carpenters of the Dutch East India Company (VOC) used several methods to protect the hull against boring of worms and algae growth. Doubling of the planking, application of a layer of lead-containing paint and tar, use of a cover with iron nails with flat heads that formed a hard rust layer, or covering with lead sheathing were all attempts to protect ships from penetration by marine growth.

Before it was launched, the hull planking of the wooden ship was allowed to swell as the dry wood slowly soaked up seawater. Gaps between planking were filled with a soft, sticky caulking material containing animal hairs or vegetable fibers mixed with tar pitch. The planking was covered with a tar layer that was heated so it would flow into the porous wood and between wood planks, thus providing a firm adhesion between the wood and the copper sheathing nailed over the fiber-filled tar base. Doubling of the planking of VOC ships required the application of an extra layer of thin fir planking. Between the outer and inner planking was a mixture of tar and horsehair or fiber as protection against shipworms. The idea of covering the hull below the waterline with copper sheathing emerged during the 18th century (Bingeman et al. 2000), but the high cost of copper restricted its application mostly to warships.

Descriptions of the sinking and wreckage of the *Sirene* in Captain van der Hart's official report in The Hague (Hart 1831) and a series of articles published in the *Curaçaosche Courant* (July 2, 16, and 21, 1831) are remarkably concordant. They independently depict in meteorological and nautical detail the force of the storm winds and rain as well as the efforts of the officers and crew to save the ship. The accuracy of the account for the timing of events that began in the dead of night and continued throughout the morning hours is remarkable. The description of the disassembly of the ship is also described in graphic detail in the account. The captain's version lists the names and roles assumed by each of the officers. The *Courant* version offers a more detailed description of the storm itself, which includes its full impact on the island as a whole.

Archival records recovered from The Hague revealed activities of the *Sirene* just before the storm struck and how it was anchored at Fort Orange. The response of the ship's officers and crew were also detailed in these documents. The time course and sequence of events during the wrecking of the brigantine are well described in these papers. Furthermore, we learn the fate of the crew and the coordination of the rescue and salvage efforts on June 25–26, 1831. Finally, we have learned from these papers the fate of the captain, who was issued an honorable discharge from duty based on his commendable service in his attempt to save the ship. The *Courant* articles corroborated the accuracy of the official records in The Hague about the loss of the ship. The newspaper articles also demonstrate that the captain's report was complete and objective in coverage. In addition, the first *Courant* article describes in great detail the progress of the storm and its impact on the island community in general.

As noted by Schomburgk (1847), on June 23, 1831, an awful gale struck the island of Trinidad, causing great injury and property damage. As it swept across the southeastern Caribbean, the impacts of the storm were severe in both Tobago and Grenada. It eventually made landfall on the coast of Mexico along the Yucatan peninsula. From descriptions of the wind velocity and direction, the eye of the storm must have passed directly over the small island of Bonaire, causing extensive damage to structures on land as well as boats at sea. The distance between Trinidad and Bonaire is about 750 km. There is no land intervening between these two islands, as Bonaire is the easternmost of the southern Netherlands

Antilles. The storm must have gathered strength to hurricane levels as it passed over open water and moved parallel to the northern coast of South America.

The storm that struck Bonaire on June 24 was one of two that hit the southern Caribbean in 1831. The other was the "Great Barbados Hurricane" of August 10–11, 1831 (Schomburgk 1847). The latter tracked slightly north of the June storm and missed Bonaire. The June storm would be best described as the "Trinidad-Yucatan Hurricane," named for its extreme points of landfall. The eyewitness account of that storm described in the *Courant* presents weather conditions before the storm, the appearance of the skies, the intensity of the rain, the cyclonic movement of the winds, and the impact of the storm on the landscape and the surrounding seas. From these data, it is possible to identify this storm clearly as a hurricane and to understand the damages within and around the island of Bonaire.

The bulk of the wreckage of the *Sirene* was sold to local buyers. Contents as well as parts of the ship were salvaged, cataloged, and transported to Curaçao. However, based on our analysis of the pile of ballast stones, a small number of wooden ship parts, and the archival data, we believe that we have discovered the wreck site of the Dutch warship, the brigantine ZM *Sirene*. That vessel was the only naval loss reported from Bonaire during hurricanes and tropical storms between 1784 and 1897. The site lies within the historical anchorage that was the original object of our archaeological survey. We have attempted to document this finding and to relate it to the artifacts identified within this historical anchorage for Fort Orange and the town of Kralendijk. Our survey results have been written into a final report (Nagelkerken and Hayes 2002) that was formally presented to the government of Bonaire along with all conserved artifacts and a computerized database. These data represent significant additions to the maritime and cultural history of the island of Bonaire.

CONCLUSIONS

This underwater archaeological survey of the historical anchorage of Kralendijk, Bonaire, provides significant information about the maritime cultural landscape that reflects the utilization of the harbor by ships, residents, and visitors to the island over several centuries. Data from this survey document a traditional zone of transport geography (transport zone) as conceptualized by Westerdahl (1992) and Parker (2001). The survey also identifies the site of an historic shipwreck. Included within the anchorage site are components from the probable wreck of a Dutch naval brigantine that was lost in a storm in 1831. That this site represents remains of ZM *Sirene* is supported by archival records, consisting of newspaper articles that were published at the time the ship was lost. The information derived from this study provides a basis for development of a maritime museum in Bonaire and contributes to local awareness about the maritime cultural heritage of the island.

ACKNOWLEDGMENTS

The authors gratefully acknowledge Freewinds for photographic services and for base support provided to archaeological divers, the Prince Bernhard Foundation for technical and supply funding of research activities, and American Airlines, the sole travel sponsor for MAHS.

REFERENCES

Bingeman, J. M., J. P. Bethell, P. Goodwin, and A. T. Mack. 2000. Copper and other sheathing in the Royal Navy. *International Journal of Nautical Archaeology* 29(2): 218–29.

Curaçaosche Courant. 1831. De Storm. Issues of July 2, 16, and 21.

Gray, A. 1927. *A New Voyage Round the World by William Dampier*. London: The Hakluyt Society, Argonaut Press.

Hart, C. van der. 1831. Report to Department of the Dutch Navy, June 26, 1831. On file in the Algemeen Rijks Archief (ARA), The Hague.

Hartog, J. 1978. *A Short History of Bonaire*. Aruba: De Wit Publishers.

Hayes, R., and W. Nagelkerken. 2002. The historical anchorage of Kralendijk, Bonaire, the site of wreckage from the Dutch warship *Sirene*. Proceedings of the Society for Historical Archaeology (abstract of conference program proceedings for the 35th Annual SHA Conference on Historical and Underwater Archaeology, January 8–12, Mobile, Alabama.

Nagelkerken, W. P. 1985. *Preliminary Report on the Determination of the Historical Anchorage at Orange Bay, St. Eustatius*. Netherlands Antilles Historical Archaeology, Special Publication Series Number 4. Willemstad, Curaçao.

Nagelkerken, W., and R. Hayes. 2002. The historical anchorage of Kralendijk, Bonaire, Netherlands Antilles, including the wreckage of the Dutch Brigantine "*Sirene*" (1831). STIMANA *Marine Archaeological Series* 2:1–105.

Nagelkerken, W., D. Knepper, and R. Hayes. 2004. Preliminary report from a survey of the historical anchorage in the harbour at Roseau, Dominica. Foundation for Marine Archaeology of the Netherlands Antilles (STIMANA), January.

Parker, A. 2001. Maritime landscapes. *Landscapes* 2(1):22–41.

Schomburgk, R. K. 1847 (reprinted 1971). *The History of Barbados*. London: Cass.

Westerdahl, C. 1992. The maritime cultural landscape. *International Journal of Nautical Archaeology* 21(1):5–14.

INDEX

A

B

C

D

E

F

G

H

I

J

K

L

M

N

O

P

Q

R

S

T

V

W

Y

Z

About the Authors

About the Editors

Archaeologist **Margaret E. Leshikar-Denton** (Ph.D.) served with the Cayman Islands National Museum for sixteen years, conducting research, creating exhibitions, enlarging a shipwreck register, launching a maritime trail, identifying shipwrecks to become preserves, and advocating legislation. She is working for establishment of a dedicated Cayman Islands maritime archaeology program. Before moving to the Caribbean, she served with the Texas Historical Commission. She has worked in the Caribbean, Mexico, the United States, Spain, and Turkey. Chair of the SHA UNESCO Committee, and a research associate with INA, she also serves on the ICOMOS ICUCH and the ACUA. She is a member of the Register of Professional Archaeologists.

Archaeologist **Pilar Luna Erreguerena** (M.S.), head of the underwater archaeology area of the National Institute of Anthropology and History (INAH) since 1980, is the pioneer of Mexican underwater archaeology. She has directed several projects in Mexican marine and continental waters and has worked in the Bahamas, the Cayman Islands, Jamaica, Panama, and Turkey. She is an Emeritus member of the ACUA and a member of the SHA UNESCO Committee, the ICOMOS ICUCH, the Ships of Discovery Board, the Waitt Institute for Discovery's Advisory Committee, and chair of the Underwater Archaeology Scientific Committee for ICOMOS México. She is one of the four international advisors for the National Geographic Society.

About the Contributors

Eugenio Acevez Núñez is a professional open water and cave diving instructor, specializing in underwater video and photography. He has participated in several underwater archaeology and exploration projects with Mexican INAH's Underwater Archaeology Vice-Directorate. He has also participated in several government training programs for natural protected areas.

Santiago Analco Ramírez (†) was one of the first Mexican archaeologists dedicated to underwater archaeology projects at the National Institute of Anthropology and History (INAH). He participated in almost every project since 1980 and was a key person, especially during the field seasons, because of his efficiency, kindness, and good sense of humor. He passed away in December 2005.

Naturalist **Jerónimo Avilés** is a professional scuba diving specialist in cave exploration and mapping. He is also an underwater photographer and videographer and has participated in several underwater archaeology projects with Mexican INAH's Underwater Archaeology Vice-Directorate. He got his cave diving training from NACD and his open water instructor certificates from PADI and NAUI.

Marine biologist **Ricardo Bastida** (Ph.D.) is the pioneer of scientific diving in Argentina. He works for the National Research Council (CONICET) as senior researcher and is professor of marine ecology at the National University of Mar del Plata. He is a specialist in marine biodeterioration processes and a member of the Underwater Archaeology Program of the National Institute of Anthropology and Latin American Thought (INAPL).

Martha Elena Benavente Sanvicente is an undergraduate student of physical anthropology and a member of the Area of Prehistory and Evolution of the Institute of Anthropological Investigations at the National Autonomous University of Mexico.

Architect **Octavio del Río Lara** graduated in 1994 from the first Underwater Archaeology Masters-level course given at the National School of Anthropology and History in Mexico. Since then, he has collaborated on several projects of INAH's Underwater Archaeology Vice-Directorate at the Yucatan Peninsula. He is also a full cave and technical diving instructor and has been exploring underwater caves in Mexico for over ten years.

Archaeologist **Dolores Elkin** (Ph.D.) is a researcher at the National Research Council (CONICET), Argentina, and is the head of the Underwater Archaeology Program of the National Institute of Anthropology and Latin American Thought (INAPL) since 1995. She is the director of the HMS *Swift* and the Península Valdés projects and she is developing a national shipwreck register. She serves as a member of the SHA UNESCO Committee and the ACUA.

Archaeologist **Roberto E. Galindo Domínguez** works as a researcher at the Underwater Archaeology Vice-Directorate of the National Institute of Anthropology and History (INAH) of Mexico. He is the main person responsible for the remote sensing system called ESPADAS (Equipment and Systems for the Acquisition Platform of Submerged Archaeological Data) applied to the Research Project on the 1630–1631 New Spain fleet and the Inventory and diagnosis of submerged cultural resources in the Gulf of Mexico.

Biologist **Arturo González González**, undergraduate student in archaeology, is the director at the Desert Museum in Saltillo, Coahuila, Mexico. He formerly co-directed the project on the archaeological atlas for the recording, study, and protection of cenotes in the Yucatan Peninsula that the Underwater Archaeology Vice-Directorate of the National Institute of Anthropology and History (INAH) has been carrying out since 2000.

Archaeologist **Dorrick Gray** is presently acting technical director of archaeology at the Jamaica National Heritage Trust. He has been actively involved in the research, management, and protection of Jamaica's terrestrial and marine resources for over twenty years. He is a member of the SHA UNESCO Committee, the ICOMOS ICUCH, and the Culture Advisory Committee of the Jamaica National Commission for UNESCO.

Mónica Grosso works as a research assistant for the Archaeology Program of the National Institute of Anthropology and Latin American Thought (INAPL), Argentina. She has been a team member on the HMS *Swift* Project since 1997 and she is working on biodeterioration processes at the *Swift* site for her undergraduate thesis.

Archaeologist **Donny L. Hamilton** (Ph.D.) is a professor in the Nautical Archaeology Program at Texas A&M University, College Station, and is the president of the Institute of Nautical Archaeology. He specializes in the conservation of artifacts and is best known for his excavations on the 17th-century town of Port Royal, Jamaica.

Archaeologist **Edward Harris** (Ph.D.) has been the director of the Bermuda Maritime Museum since 1980. In that position, he has coordinated underwater research by the museum and has been an advocate for new legislation on Bermuda's submerged cultural resources.

Raymond Hayes (Ph.D.) is past vice-president of the Maritime Archaeological and Historical Society (MAHS) and a member of the Board of Directors for both STIMANA (Curaçao) and the Institute of

Maritime History (IMH) in Washington, DC. He is Professor Emeritus and a biomedical scientist at Howard University (Washington, DC). He has served as an associate member of the ACUA.

Curator **Patricia Meehan Hermanson** works as a researcher at the National Coordination for the Restoration of the Cultural Patrimony and the Underwater Archaeology Vice-Directorate, both dependencies of the National Institute of Anthropology and History (INAH) of Mexico. She did the main archival investigation in Spain for the project on the 1630–1631 New Spain fleet.

Archaeologist **Paul F. Johnston** is curator of maritime history at the Smithsonian Institution's National Museum of American History in Washington, DC. He has worked on shipwrecks in the Mediterranean, Caribbean, and Baltic Seas; the Atlantic, Pacific, and Indian Oceans; and the Great Lakes and some smaller lakes, rivers, and harbors. He is an Emeritus member of the ACUA. He served as a co-discussant for the LAC symposium at WAC-5.

Archaeologist **Donald H. Keith** (Ph.D.) is a maritime archaeologist and president of Ships of Discovery, a publicly supported scientific research and educational organization based at the Corpus Christi Museum of Science and History, Corpus Christi, Texas. A trustee of the Turks and Caicos National Museum, he has conducted numerous research projects there as well as in other locations in the circum-Caribbean area. His interests include discovery-period shipwrecks, shipwreck excavation, artifact analysis and conservation, and museum display design. He served as a co-discussant for the LAC symposium at WAC-5.

Archaeologist **Dennis Knepper** works in terrestrial archaeology for Versar, Inc. of Springfield, Virginia. He is a member of the Board of Directors for STIMANA in Curaçao, Netherlands Antilles, and vice-president of the Maritime Archaeological and Historical Society (MAHS) in Washington, DC.

Antonio Lezama (Ph.D.) is the director of the Underwater Archaeology Program in the Department of Archaeology at the University of the Republic in Montevideo, Uruguay. He has created an underwater field school, Sitio Escuela de Arqueología Subacuática, to train graduated archaeologists. He is currently directing a research project in search of the flagship of the Portuguese expedition of Martim Affonso de Souza, sunk off the Uruguayan coast in 1531.

Archaeologist **Vera Moya Sordo** works as a researcher at the Underwater Archaeology Vice-Directorate of the National Institute of Anthropology and History (INAH) of Mexico. She is responsible for the development of a Geographical Information System (GIS) for the Research Project on the 1630–1631 New Spain fleet and the Inventory and diagnosis of submerged cultural resources in the Gulf of Mexico.

Wil Nagelkerken (Ph.D.) is founder, president Emeritus, and a member of the Board of Directors for Stichting Mariene Archeologie Nederlandse Antillen (STIMANA) in Curaçao, Netherlands Antilles. He is a retired marine biologist and a member of the Order of Orange Nassau in the Netherlands.

Archaeologist **Carmen Rojas Sandoval** formerly co-directed the Underwater Archaeological Atlas for recording, studying and protecting cenotes in the Yucatan Peninsula that the Underwater Archaeology Vice-Directorate of the Mexican National Institute of Anthropology and History (INAH) has been carrying out since 2000.

Archaeologist **Nigel Sadler** (M.A.) is founder of Sands of Time Consultancy and former director of the Turks and Caicos Islands National Museum. Nigel spent four years as a field archaeologist then retrained in museum work, spending nine years working in museums in Britain before moving to the Caribbean. Nigel's main interest is slave history, especially the illegal African slave trade post-1808. He has led research on the *Trouvadore* project.

Archaeologist **Della A. Scott-Ireton** (Ph.D.) is the northwest regional director of the Florida Public Archaeology Network, an organization dedicated to public outreach and education in archaeology. She previously served with the Florida Bureau of Archaeological Research where she was responsible for the Underwater Archaeological Preserve Program and she has assisted the Cayman Islands with development of a maritime heritage trail. She is an officer and elected board member of the ACUA and a member of the Register of Professional Archaeologists.

Conservator **Wayne Smith** (Ph.D.) is an associate professor in the Nautical Archaeology Program, Department of Anthropology, Texas A&M University, College Station. He is director of the Archaeological Preservation Research Laboratory and the Wilder 3-Dimensional Imaging Laboratory at the university. He and colleague Dr. Donny L. Hamilton hold four patents for the development of conservation methodologies for organic material culture.

Wolfgang Stinnesbeck is a professor of geology and paleontology at the University of Heidelberg in Germany.

Alejandro Terrazas Mata is a candidate for the Ph.D. and coordinator of the Area of Prehistory and Evolution of the Institute of Anthropological Investigations at the National Autonomous University of Mexico.

Ethnohistorian **Flor Trejo Rivera** works as a researcher at the Underwater Archaeology Vice-Directorate of the National Institute of Anthropology and History (INAH) of Mexico. She is the coordinator of the historical investigation of the Research Project on the 1630–1631 New Spain fleet. In 2005, she won a three-month scholarship from the Carolina Foundation to do research at the main archives in Madrid and Seville, Spain.

Theo van der Giessen is the executive director of Uniek Curaçao and a member of the Board of Directors for Stichting Mariene Archeologie Nederlandse Antillen (STIMANA).

Since 1994, archaeologist **Adriana Velázquez Morlet** has been the director of the National Institute of Anthropology and History Centre in the state of Quintana Roo, southeast Mexico. She directs a program related to the classification and management of the important Zone of Archaeological Monuments in Tulum-Tancah. She collaborates on INAH's underwater archaeology projects in Quintana Roo.